SPRINGBOARD
TO VICTORY

**To the memory of
my brother Jim
1940-2016**

SPRINGBOARD TO VICTORY

Great Yarmouth and the Royal Navy's dominance in
the North Sea and the Baltic during the French Wars
1793-1815

David Higgins

PHOENIX PUBLICATIONS

Published in 2020 by Phoenix Publications
email: phoenix.p20@outlook.com

Origination and printing by
DSD Printers, King's Lynn, Norfolk Tel: 01553 661166.

British Library Cataloguing in Publication Data
A catalogue record for this book is available from the British Library

ISBN 978-0-9540684-7-9

Contents

Acknowledgements / Picture Credits   vi

Preface   vii

Introduction   ix

Prologue: No Stranger to Conflict   1

Part One: Naval and Military Operations

1. The North Sea Naval Command 1793-1797   9

2. Mutiny and Camperdown 1797   21

3. The Helder, Copenhagen and Peace 1798-1802   31

4. The North Sea and Baltic Commands 1803-1814   45

Part Two: The Support Services

5. Victualling   59

6. Naval Stores   83

7. Ordnance Stores   95

8. The Roads Anchorage   101

9. Raising Seamen   109

10. The Sick and the Wounded   119

11. Prisoners of War   143

12. Communication   155

13. Defence   171

Part Three: Victory and its Aftermath

14. Peace and Closure   189

Epilogue   195

Notes and References   201

Sources   227

Index   231

Acknowledgements

I am grateful for the assistance given to me by the staff of the various repositories where the source material is held, namely the National Archives, the National Maritime Museum (Caird Library), the Norfolk Record Office, the Time and Tide Museum at Yarmouth and the relevant libraries of the Norfolk Library Service. I must thank Bob Malster and Colin Tooke for their advice and for supplying photographs, I am indebted to Roger Knight, who kindly read the first draft of this book and made many valuable comments on both its structure and content. It goes without saying, however, that the final format and any remaining errors are entirely my responsibility. He also made available to me a transcript of the Pitt/Lewes letter book (PLLB), produced by his wife, Jane. To her I am also grateful. Thanks are also due to Dale Thorne at DSD Printers for his skill and patience in preparing this book for publication. Last, but by no means least, I must thank my wife Sheila for her unstinting support. Not only did she type the first draft, but she accompanied me on numerous trips to the National Archives and to the Caird Library, digital camera in hand. It is fair to say that without her involvement this book would never have been written.

Picture Credits

Preface

Great Yarmouth is best known for being a seaside resort and for its former status as the country's leading herring fishing port, but what has largely been forgotten is that during the French Revolutionary War (1793-1802) and the two Napoleonic Wars (1803-1815) it was the main support base for naval and military operations in the North Sea and the Baltic. It was not until I researched a book called *The Beachmen* that I became aware of this dramatic period in the history of the town and the nation and I was surprised to find that nothing substantial had been written on the subject. Of course, a great many books had been produced on the navy's involvement in these wars, but most concentrated on the high drama of the six major fleet actions and the exploits of Horatio Nelson rather than the equally important, but more mundane, means by which the navy's warships were kept at sea.

This situation began to be redressed in 1989 when Brian Lavery produced *Nelson's Navy. The Ships, Men and Organisation, 1793-1815*. While the focus of this work is the Royal Navy's activities afloat, it does make reference to its shore based support facilities. Shortly afterwards, at the local level, John Fone wrote two monographs on thematic aspects of the topic; *The Naval Yard at Yarmouth in the Napoleonic Wars* (1992) and *Signalling from Norwich to the Coast in the Napoleonic Period* (1996). These were followed by John Barney's, *The Defence of Norfolk 1793-1815* (2000), which provides something of the local military context for Yarmouth during the period in question. In 2013 Jonathan Coad's *Support for the Fleet. Architecture and Engineering of the Royal Navy's Bases 1700-1914* was published. The basis for this well produced-book is an extensive survey of the facilities created, but mention of Yarmouth is limited to the two major construction projects, the Royal Naval Hospital and the Royal Arsenal. The same year Robert Malster produced the second part of his *Maritime Norfolk*, a volume wholly devoted to Yarmouth. Three years later Julian Foynes wrote *East Anglia against the Tricolour 1789-1815*. Both these books acknowledge Yarmouth's involvement in these wars, but understandably do not pull the strands together into one cohesive narrative. By then Roger Knight and Martin Wilcox had produced *Sustaining the Fleet, 1793-1815. War, the British Navy and the Contractor State* (2010), an authoritative study of the victualling process, which includes a chapter on the provision of this service at Yarmouth during the French Revolutionary War. Roger Knight followed this in 2013 with *Britain Against Napoleon. The Organisation of Victory 1793-1815*. Described as 'a gripping story of how an entire nation was mobilized to triumph against the odds' it draws on a comprehensive appraisal of the existing literature and, in making numerous references to Yarmouth, highlights the town's significance as a naval anchorage and support base. With this review providing the platform for the detailed research necessary to flesh out the story I decided the time was right to produce this study, a project I had long been contemplating. I should add that in 2010 I acquired an apartment in the residential complex that had been the Royal Naval Hospital and relaxing in the former mess-room, where convalescing seamen had once taken their meals, has given me a tangible connection with the men who fought in those now distant wars.

David Higgins
South Wootton
June 2020

Introduction

Throughout what has collectively been called the 'First Great War' the Royal Navy ruled the waves. By largely preventing the warships of France and her allies leaving port, and defeating them in battle on the rare occasions they did so, the navy thwarted all serious attempts to invade the British Isles and obstructed a number of undertakings aimed at threatening British interests overseas. For much of this time, however, the French held sway over mainland Europe and the British army had little success with Continental ventures until well into the Napoleonic period. This force of arms stalemate led each side to pursue policies designed to ruin the other's economy. The main strand of the French strategy was to try to prevent British merchants trading with their overseas counterparts, and vice-versa, through control of the ports of their allies and satellites, while at the same time encouraging privateers to take British merchantmen. Britain's approach was the reverse of the same coin with its blockading fleets and squadrons preventing merchantmen of any colour freely entering enemy ports and its cruisers taking large numbers of such vessels as prizes long before they reached their destinations. In addition these nautical workhorses protected British merchantmen going about their business via the convoy system and in turn captured many enemy privateers.

To maintain the navy's grip on maritime affairs the Admiralty expanded its network of naval stations, those designated areas of sea within which fleets or squadrons operated under the orders of a commander-in-chief, usually an admiral or vice-admiral. Each station contained one or more anchorage with associated shore based support facilities. Together they provided what was necessary to keep warships in a state of readiness, namely unconstrained moorings, dockyards, victualling supplies, naval stores, ordnance stores, replacement seamen, medical care and places to confine prisoners of war.

The most active naval station was that which covered the Mediterranean Sea and the southern coast of Spain. Fleets stationed there won the Battles of Cape St. Vincent, the Nile and Trafalgar, three of the six major naval actions of the wars. But the most important station was that covering the English Channel. The Channel Fleet was the mainstay of the navy's defence of the British Isles, distinguishing itself in particular at the battle known as 'The Glorious First of June.' Within this station's operational area lay the anchorages of Spithead, St. Helens, Plymouth Sound, Cawsand Bay and Torbay, and the major naval bases at Portsmouth and Plymouth. Resourced in this way this Fleet would have been more than adequate to keep the enemy out of home waters had not the Dutch been coerced into changing sides, thereby providing the French with a ready-made navy that was well situated to menace the east coast of Britain. In response to this threat a naval station with a squadron was created to cover the North Sea, with the Yarmouth Roads being designated as its anchorage and the town as its main support base. Service hubs on a smaller scale were also established at Harwich, Hull, North Shields and Leith. From Yarmouth the North Sea Squadron set sail to win a hard fought battle off Camperdown and a fleet was sent to defeat the Danes at Copenhagen, the other two major naval actions of these wars. This book tells the story of this crucial partnership.

The Admiralty had good strategic reasons for stationing the North Sea Squadron at Yarmouth for unlike the anchorages of the Nore (off the mouth of the Thames) and the Downs (off the East Kent coast), where it was initially based, the Roads anchorage was directly opposite the Texel where the main Dutch Fleet lay at anchor. In addition the town was situated on a relatively sheltered river and had sufficient land and buildings to accommodate most of the navy's service requirements, although the support base never became fully self-sufficient as it had to rely on the naval dockyard at Sheerness for major ship repairs and the Deptford yards for the replenishment of victualling supplies and naval stores.

As with all naval stations the control and management of the North Sea warships, anchorages and support services, was subject to the complex multi-agency system that characterised the navy at that time. Below Cabinet level the overall responsibility for the navy was vested in the Admiralty Board under the leadership of the First Lord of the Admiralty. It appointed all naval officers and gave those afloat their orders in relation to the deployment of fleets, squadrons and individual warships. Answering to the Admiralty Board were a number of subordinate Boards the principal ones being the Navy Board, the Victualling Board, the Sick & Hurt Board and the Transport Board. The Navy Board was responsible for the design and construction of warships and for keeping them in good order through arranging repairs. It also provided naval stores and managed the navy's use of anchorages. The Victualling Board provided the seamen with food and drink. The Sick & Hurt Board supplied medical care and dealt with prisoners of war before these duties were transferred to the more efficient Transport Board, which was originally created to move men and materials. Separate from the navy structure was the Ordnance Board, responsible to the Master-General of the Ordnance. This organisation supplied weapons and ammunition to both the navy and the army and maintained the country's fixed defences. It had both a civilian and a military branch. In addition all matters to do with garrisons and troop movements were the purlieu of the Commander-in-Chief of the army. Each of these organisations had its own agent in the town and significantly these men were not directly answerable to the station's commander-in-chief or, later in the wars, the shore based port-admiral.

To understand how this worked in practice it is worth considering what the crew of a North Sea cruiser had to deal with on anchoring in the Yarmouth Roads after a successful patrol in search of enemy merchantmen and privateers. The captain would immediately report to the senior officer in charge of the station from whom he would, like as not, receive fresh orders. Meanwhile his officers and men would be preparing the vessel to put to sea again. Sick and wounded seamen would be landed and taken to the surgeon at the naval hospital and prisoners of war would be marched to the prison and handed over to the turnkey there. As far as stores were concerned the storekeepers at the naval yard and the ordnance store would be presented with written 'demands' for the items required and the vessel's purser would visit the various victualling contractors, or their agents, to make good any deficiency in supplies of food and drink. In addition, if the vessel's complement of seamen was under strength, men might be procured from the local receiving ship or pressed from merchant ships. There was no 'one stop shop' for processing these requirements and much depended on the personal and

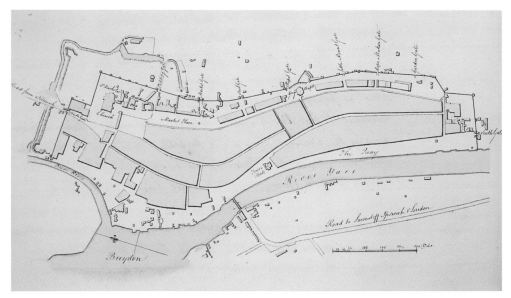

1. A plan of Yarmouth prepared by Major Thomas Reynolds in 1797 as part of his assessment of the defensive state of 'the Principal Part of the Eastern District.'

professional skills of all those concerned for the support base to function efficiently and effectively.

***

At the outset in writing a work of history an author has to reconcile the chronology of the subject with its thematic content. Where the latter is homogenous it is easy to adopt a straightforward timeline based structure, but in this book, where the themes can stand alone as narratives in their own right, it has been deemed more appropriate to adopt a hybrid arrangement. After a prologue highlighting Yarmouth's long association with sea-borne conflict there are four chapters which, taken together, chronicle the naval and combined operations which took place in the North Sea and the Baltic during these wars and the involvement of the town, its anchorage and support base in these events. These are followed by nine chapters which detail the nature and development of each service, divided into the two main periods of warfare. The book concludes with a chapter describing the ultimate victory and its aftermath and an epilogue which continues the story to the present day. As Napoleon's brief return to power, in 1815, did not unduly affect Yarmouth what did occur is included in this final chapter.

The service sectors of the support base can be classified as either 'ins' or 'outs' with the former comprising large numbers of sick/wounded seamen and prisoners of war and the latter replacement victualling, naval and ordnance stores. Extensive documentation exists for these functions, but for day to day operational activity record survival is somewhat mixed. For the 'ins' comprehensive registers exist for the men received into care and custody, but for the 'outs' there are no ledgers of stores issued. To help fill this gap there is a series of account ledgers of payments made to private victualling contractors and these can be used, to some extent, to deduce the ebb and flow of demand, not only for food and drink, but also for naval and ordnance stores. Nevertheless this deficiency has to borne in mind when reading the chapters on these three service areas.

There is also a problem with knowing what to call Yarmouth as a naval facility. Strictly speaking a naval base was a place where there was a major dockyard for building and refitting warships. At smaller ports, such as Yarmouth, where this was not the case, there was no specific collective term for what amounted to an assemblage of independent services. For the narrative to flow, however, a description is necessary and for this purpose I have adopted the term 'naval support base.'

A further problem concerns the name of the town. It has included the prefix 'Great' since early medieval times in order to differentiate it from Little Yarmouth (Southtown), which lay on the opposite side of the river. Throughout these wars, however, the official records consistently refer to it as North Yarmouth to distinguish it from Yarmouth, Isle of Wight, which had a small naval presence at the time. In the interests of clarity I have chosen to use the unqualified term Yarmouth throughout the text.

One final point, as this account is largely drawn from primary source material I have been able to adopt a 'warts and all' approach, which has allowed the participants, wherever possible, to speak for themselves. In order to make this a seamless exercise for the reader I have broken with convention and inserted their words into the text rather than treating them as separate indented quotations, although the fact that they are quotations has been acknowledged in the usual way.

Prologue: No Stranger to Conflict

Yarmouth's support for naval operations in the North Sea and the Baltic during the twenty year period of these wars was the climax of many centuries of service to the Crown in this respect. With its proximity to mainland Europe, its significance as an anchorage and its dominance of the herring fishery the town was always a major player in the North Sea and as such was no stranger to conflict. Its townsmen were involved in wars against the Scots, French, Spanish, Dutch, Danes, Swedes, Russians and Germans, but their earliest confrontation was with fellow Englishmen, the Portsmen of the Cinque Ports. In the early medieval period, when Yarmouth was still in its infancy, the Portsmen were the most powerful seafarers in the country and with there being no standing navy at the time, successive monarchs relied on these men to provide ships for their Continental ventures, issuing them with commissions to inflict 'all such harm as lay within their power' on the King's enemies.[1] In return they were granted substantial rights at the Yarmouth Herring Fair. As Yarmouth grew to become a major maritime power in its own right, so its burgesses increasingly resented the authority the Portsmen exercised in the town. The arrival of their officials was always accompanied by a degree of ceremony sufficiently provocative for there to be disruptive incidents.[2] But it was at sea that the feud was, 'as bitter and violent as the circumstances of the age permitted.'[3] Throughout the 13th century the ships of Yarmouth and the Cinque Ports frequently attacked one another, especially when they were brought together in the service of the King. In 1297 Edward I set sail from Winchelsea with a large force carried in ships provided by Yarmouth and the Cinque Ports and landed safely at Sluys, in Flanders. No sooner had he done so, however, than the Portsmen set about their rivals, with such vigour that they almost destroyed the Yarmouth squadron.[4] This was the nadir of the feud and as the power and wealth of the Ports faded so the arrival of the officials became little more than social occasions. They last came to the town in 1663.[5]

It was in the first half of the fourteenth century, during wars with the Scots and the French, that the town first became significant as a naval support base, a status it was to hold in one form or another until relatively recent times. Two major naval fleets assembled at Yarmouth in that period, one bound for Scotland, in 1327, the other for the Continent, in 1338. The seamen of both had access to the victuals that were regularly warehoused in the town because of the need to feed large numbers of people during the Herring Fair.[6] At the time the Yarmouth merchant fleet consisted of 60 to 100 vessels of at least 100 tons and these were frequently being 'arrested' for use on naval service, with the town often being the largest contributor of such ships north of the Thames and sometimes the whole country.[7] When fleets were assembled for service in the North Sea command would be given to an officer termed 'the Admiral of the King's Fleet North of the Thames'. Some of these were Yarmouth men and prominent amongst them was merchant and ship-owner John Perbroun, whose role in this

2. The Battle of Sluys, 1340. Yarmouth ships formed the backbone of England's naval forces at this time.

respect was much the same as that performed by Admiral Duncan some 500 years later. He held the commission on and off from 1322 and was involved in the English victory at Sluys in 1340 where, he 'did there greate service, and the shippes of the towne of Greate Yarmouthe were comended for their service, above all the English navye at that time.' Yarmouth ships were also prominent at the siege of Calais in 1347 and to mark this exceptional service a grateful monarch gave the town permission to replace the herring heads on its coat of arms with those of his own royal lions, thereby creating the arms borne by the town today.[8]

In Tudor times the development of a 'royal navy', (i.e. a collection of ships built and owned by the monarch specifically for the purpose of warfare), affected Yarmouth's naval role. By the time Henry VII died, in 1509, there were five royal warships and when Henry VIII followed him to the grave, in 1547, there were 40. The transition from one system to the other was a slow process for of the 197 ships employed against the Spanish Armada in 1588, only 34 were owned by the Crown, but from having once been a supplier of a significant part of the monarch's navy, Yarmouth now performed the far less glamorous role of providing the range of services needed by warships anchoring in the Roads.[9]

The reign of James I was largely a peaceful one, but shortly after his accession, in 1625, Charles I declared war on France and the town's merchants began to suffer from the depredations of the Dunkirk privateers. Fearing that they might land and sack the town, representations were made to the government, an inspection of the defences was carried out, and a schedule of expensive improvements was produced. These were not all implemented, but 12 demi-culverins were sent from the government's ordnance store and an artillery yard

2

was created where the townsmen were taught gunnery skills.[10] At the start of the Civil War, in 1642, Yarmouth declared for Parliament. With the King's navy largely doing the same there was little danger of an attack from the sea, so the focus at Yarmouth was on a possible landward assault. To counter this threat a line of bastioned earthworks was established in front of the medieval town wall, at its northern end, and those that already existed to the south were repaired. In all nine new batteries were constructed.[11]

With the Civil War over Yarmouth's attention returned to the need to protect the town and the roadstead from attack from the sea, especially by a new enemy, the Dutch. Throughout the first half of the century mercantile competition between the English and the Dutch East India Companies had been quite aggressive and there were also clashes over control of the North Sea herring fishery. This rivalry prompted three Anglo-Dutch wars which had serious implications for the East Coast, although Yarmouth's involvement was not as much as could have been expected.[12] Initially the threat came from royalist refugees who had established themselves in Holland, determined to carry on their struggle via activity at sea. To counter this, in 1648, the town agreed to erect a fort at the harbour's mouth, but did not start building it until the outbreak of the First Anglo-Dutch war, in 1651. It took two years to complete.[13] Naval ships anchored in the Roads during this conflict and local merchant and ship-owner, Major William Burton, was appointed governor of the town, with instructions to assist them. In 1653-4 he was carrying out the roles that would later be performed by a trio of officers in relation to victualling, naval stores and contact with the Admiralty.[14]

Yarmouth was not a major naval support base in the Second Anglo-Dutch War (1665-1667) nor the Third (1672-74), which J. D. Davies suggests was due to the town's support for the Commonwealth.[15] In the early part of these wars, however, there was a naval presence in the town in the shape of Surveyor of Victualling, Richard Gibson, who served in that capacity before becoming advisor to Samuel Pepys and chief clerk at the Admiralty. On the face of it he did not have much to do, for while in 1664 the Yarmouth allocation of supplies for naval seamen was set at a sufficiency for 1,000 men, he only issued what was required by 11. This was explained by Pepys himself, who noted that, 'the smallness of the last year's issue arose from the plague.' Of those East Coast ports with an allocation Harwich, at 4,000 men, was the most significant.[16]

Yarmouth was also involved with the navy in other ways at this time. With the rapid expansion of warship numbers after 1649, the pressure on the Royal Dockyards was such that private yards, including those at Yarmouth, were employed, not for the last time, to make up the shortfall. In addition there was the ever present need for seamen and places like Yarmouth were issued with quotas to fill, such as that for 150 men in 1664. Never a popular duty to perform, on 14 June 1666 Prince Rupert, from his cabin on the *Albemarle*, wrote to the bailiffs of the town, complaining of their tardiness in this respect and telling them that, 'what seamen there are within your Liberty, or which may be imprested by you for ye Kings Service in ye present expedition, you forthwith apply yourselves with all diligence to take them up & send ym, on Board such of his Mats. Friggotts as are in your Road for that purpose.' In addition, during the Third Anglo-Dutch War the Fort was used as a prison for those captured at the Battle of Sole Bay. Several Dutch captains escaped from there, despite having given their parole.[17]

Over the next century Yarmouth remained an anchorage of convenience for single warships, the captains of which could expect to source a range of services from local agents. The exception to this was during periods of actual warfare, when naval personnel and ships were sent to the town. Soon after the 'Glorious Revolution' of 1688 England fought a nine year war with France. While the major battles took place elsewhere enemy privateers once more roamed the North Sea and naval cruisers patrolled to 'protect trade.' Closely associated with the town at this time was Gabriel Millison. Promoted captain in 1688 he served in the North Sea in the *Katherine* yacht and the *Portsmouth*. In 1693 he was gifted the Freedom of the Borough, 'for services to the Corporation,' and after his discharge he retired to the town where he died in 1709. During the War of the Austrian Succession (1740-1748), his son, also called Gabriel, is variously described as the 'Naval officer at Yarmouth' or 'our Officer at Yarmouth.'[18]

As the century wore on so some of the officers we shall meet later begin to appear in the records in relation to the provision of naval stores, food and drink, and medical care. In the 1760's David Urquhart was the officer responsible for naval stores. When he died in 1774 he was succeeded by his one time office junior and late associate, Robert Warmington.[19] Urquhart was also involved in victualling, referring to himself as 'Agent Victualler for the Navy' in the subscribers list to Swinden's history of the town.[20] Palmer records that John Mash was 'surgeon to the sick and wounded' and was succeeded in that role by Benjamin Fielding from at least January 1775 when he carried out a 'survey' of the crew of the sloop *Alderney*, finding three men unserviceable.[21] This vessel was closely associated with Yarmouth, her captain having from September 1770 to January 1771, been required to raise men there, taking those not needed to complete his own complement to the Nore. At the same time Captain Anthony Hunt, assisted by two lieutenants, was on impress duty in the town, although a slow start was made, for according to John Ives Junior, 'We have got a regulating captain come down but he has not yet begun to press, as the merchants endeavour to keep it off till the fishing is entirely finished.'[22]

It was the American Revolutionary War (1773-1783), or more specifically the Fourth Anglo-Dutch War component of that conflict that once more brought Yarmouth into sharp focus as a naval support base. In the early years of that war Dutch merchants provided the American rebels with arms and ammunition and after the French declared war, in 1778, the merchants of Amsterdam became heavily involved in supplying England's old enemy with naval stores, thereby weakening the impact of the British naval blockade of the French coast. By the terms of earlier treaties, the Dutch were perfectly entitled to do so, but it was a loophole the British government moved swiftly to close. Declaring naval stores to be contraband, the embargo was enforced by stopping and searching Dutch (and other neutral) vessels. This resulted in strong protests from the Dutch merchants and prompted their government to seek armed support from other neutral powers. To forestall this, in December 1780, Britain declared war on the United Provinces (Holland).[23]

Within weeks of the commencement of hostilities, more than 200 Dutch merchant ships, carrying cargo to the value of 15 million guilders, had been captured by British warships and privateers and 300 more were stranded in foreign ports.[24] To reinforce this success in May 1781 command of a newly created North Sea Squadron was given to Vice-Admiral Sir Hyde Parker (whose son of the same name we will meet later). He was directed to protect British trade and at the same time 'annoy the Cruizers & Trade of His Majesty's Enemies & His

Rebellious North American Subjects.' In August that year he encountered a strong Dutch squadron under Admiral Johan Zoutman and fought what was to be called the Battle of Dogger Bank, an inconclusive affair, which proved to be the only fleet action in the North Sea during that war.[25] Feeling he was not adequately resourced to take the fight to the Dutch Parker resigned. He was quickly replaced by Rear-Admiral Sir John Lockhart Ross who was tasked with, in addition to protecting trade, keeping the Dutch blockaded in the Texel. His squadron was based in the Downs, but when at sea, if it needed to run into port for shelter or to take on water, provisions or stores, it was to make for the Humber or Leith Roads.[26] Ross, however, became ill and in June 1782 struck his flag. As an interim measure his ships were placed under the command of Vice-Admiral Drake, the commander-in-chief at the Downs, who was ordered to send frigates to cruise along the Dutch coast, especially off the Texel, in order to monitor the movements of the Dutch men-of-war. The remainder of the squadron's ships and vessels were to be sent to Spithead. He stayed in charge of activities in the North Sea until the cessation of hostilities.[27]

Although Yarmouth was not designated to sustain the squadron it *was* set up to service those naval vessels pursuing the war on trade.[28] The civilian agents retained to provide naval stores, medical care and victualling responded to the increased demand, with in September 1781 the victualler being called upon to provide live cattle and, 'a proportion of Onions, Cabbages, Carrots, Turnips and Potatoes', to Commodore Keith Stewart's small squadron operating off the east coast of Scotland.[29] But wartime required additional facilities such as a prison for prisoners of war and a rendezvous for the impress service. Acting on instructions from the Sick and Hurt Board, in early 1781, Benjamin Fielding identified premises to accommodate prisoners for an annual rent of £40, with a fitting out cost of £135. In February

3. The Yarmouth Roads, 1778. The frigate Surprize lies at anchor ready to take on supplies. In the foreground stands the Jetty and the iconic public lookout.

the Admiralty directed the Board to hire the building for 'one year certain, & for such further time afterwards as the Service may require.'[30] By May there were 'eighty or more' French, American and Dutch prisoners being detained there.[31] As far as raising men was concerned as early as August 1775 Lieutenant James Watson was directed to set up a rendezvous in the town and he was succeeded in 1777 by Captain Francis Richards, the former commander of the Yarmouth based sloop *Alderney*.[32]

With a naval squadron and a number of cruisers active in the North Sea the Admiralty felt satisfied with its response to the threat posed by the United Provinces, but, given the town's proximity to the enemy coast, its lack of up to date defences and the fact that most Dutch seamen were familiar with its anchorage, the townsmen of Yarmouth feared that their former friends may 'attempt to take or Destroy the Shipping in the Harbour & Roads.'[33] As a result in early 1781 the Corporation wrote to Lord Townshend complaining about the town's defenceless state and asking for batteries to be built along the seashore. Following a survey by military engineers, Colonel Bramham recommended the construction of four batteries armed with eighteen 24 pounders and left plans with the Mayor for their construction. The Corporation began building one of these in the centre of the beach, but soon ran out of money. Stepping in the government completed it and built two more to command the anchorage. A small battery, was also constructed on the cliffs at Gorleston.[34] To further bolster the defences the Corporation wanted a 50 gun ship stationed in the Roads, under the command of a flag officer, to act as a guard-ship and a receiving-ship, but despite approaches to the Admiralty, in March 1781, and again a year later, nothing was forthcoming, leaving the town to rely for protection on the *Kitty* tender and the warships that regularly frequented the Roads. Chief amongst these were the *Fly* and *Alderney* sloops, the former until August 1781 commanded by Billy Douglas, who decades later was to become Yarmouth's port-admiral. The merchants of the town were sufficiently pleased with the performance of these vessels to cause a subscription to be raised to provide inscribed silverware for their captains.[35]

Overriding any concerns about a speculative attack was the fear of a full blown invasion and with Yarmouth being considered to be one of the likely landing places troops were stationed in or near the town. Major-General Tryon, the recently retired governor of New York, was given command of the area, fixing his headquarters at Somerleyton Hall. The Huntingdon Militia and the East Essex Militia were stationed at Hopton Camp and were later augmented by the Cambridgeshire Militia and the 10th Foot. In winter these soldiers were quartered in the town, where it was reckoned that at least 50 of them were necessary to guard the prisoners of war. In 1780 a company of volunteer infantry, called the Armed Association, was raised from among the townsmen and others were trained in the use of the guns at the batteries.[36]

The war came to an end in February 1783 and the support base was reduced to its peacetime level. While its naval services had not been called upon to sustain the capital ships of the North Sea Squadron, it had played a part in facilitating the war on trade and the creation of the infrastructure for this purpose had provided useful experience for what was to come when British warships once more exchanged broadsides with those of France and her allies.

Part One
Naval and Military Operations

1.
The North Sea Naval Command 1793-1797

Revolutionary France declared war on Britain and the United Provinces in February 1793. It was not unexpected for in the previous 'peaceful' decade the French and the British had maintained their traditional suspicion of one another and between 1787 and 1791 there had been a number of international incidents which suggested that there would soon be a resumption of hostilities.[1] With Britain having maintained her naval supremacy throughout this period, it was a simple matter to confine the French men-of-war to port, with Brest, Lorient and Rochefort being subjected to an open blockade by Admiral Lord Howe's Channel Fleet and Toulon being watched by Vice-Admiral Lord Hood's Mediterranean Squadron. Ships-of-the-line were also stationed elsewhere to help protect and expand British interests in the West Indies and to combat French activities in the Indian Ocean. In the North Sea, however, there was no perceived need to deploy such warships for although the Dutch and the Danes had sizeable navies they were considered to be friendly nations posing no threat to their British neighbours.[2] But this important seaway facilitated considerable trade between the Baltic states and both Britain *and* France and it also supported the flow of local goods along the East Coast of Britain, especially coal. These circumstances immediately made the North Sea the stage for a war on trade, an economic conflict that was pursued with much vigour throughout these wars, with Yarmouth at the very heart of it.

The ships and vessels employed in both the offensive and defensive aspects of this war were largely frigates, brig-sloops and ship-sloops and before the creation of the North Sea command, their captains received their orders directly from the Admiralty or from the commanders-in-chief at the Downs or the Nore. Largely operating on their own these cruisers could call in at Harwich, Hull, Newcastle, Leith, and Yarmouth for supplies, there being civilian agents in all these places to service naval vessels. At Yarmouth there were agents in place for victualling, naval stores, ordnance supplies and medical care. A regulatory captain had a rendezvous in the town and as he was the only resident naval officer he was the Admiralty's point of contact. In addition a building had been acquired to house prisoners-of-war, the shoreline batteries had been re-commissioned and militiamen had marched in to provide some measure of protection, although civil unrest was thought to be more likely than an enemy attack. From the beginning of 1793 until the arrival of the North Sea Squadron in mid-1796 nearly 70 naval ships and vessels took advantage of these services, many of them on more than one occasion. Closely associated with Yarmouth throughout this early period were the frigates *Lizard* and *Greyhound*, the ship-sloop *Thorn* and the brig-sloops *Otter, Chilvers, Weazle, Curlew,* and *L'Espiegle*, a vessel which was to have a distinguished career in the North Sea until the end of the war.[3]

While the British preferred to use naval ships and vessels to fight the war on trade, the French relied on privateers to try to capture British and allied merchantmen because these vessels were financed by private enterprise and as such were not a drain on government resources. Most of those operating in the North Sea hailed from Dunkirk and were relentlessly pursued by the British cruisers when intelligence was received that they were on the coast.[4] The British government, however, was not against the use of privateers in principle and large numbers of privately owned armed vessels were issued with 'letters of marque', the means by which their activities were legalised, although it has to be said that very few prizes were sent into Yarmouth by privateer captains. The port's revenue and excise cutters, however, acted in a similar capacity, their captains obtaining letters of marque in February 1793. These government vessels were to account for a significant number of captures, while continuing to apprehend smugglers.[5]

The enemy privateers would often use a *ruse de guerre* to fool their prey. In April 1793 four merchantmen, including the *Triton* of Yarmouth, were sailing four leagues off the Humber when a 22 gun French privateer approached under English colours. Suddenly raising the tricolour she took one of the vessels, a large coal laden brig, then proceeded to chase another. The other vessels escaped to tell the tale.[6] By then, however, the British cruisers had brought into the Roads a number of privateers and merchant vessels, the first of which was the *Le Custine*, a Dunkirk lugsail privateer, armed with six swivel guns, taken in a spirited fashion by Captain Fraser of the ship-sloop *Savage* off Orford Ness and brought in on 27 February. On 7 March the frigate *Lizard* arrived with two more Dunkirk privateers, *Le Sans Culotte*, sporting eight carriage guns, which had been out five days without making any captures and *Le Vaillant Custine* of 16 guns. She had been at sea for ten days, but had only taken a Danish dogger bound for Amsterdam.[7] Other frigates were just as successful. In March the *Cleopatra* sent in a Danish galliot, with wheat, bound for Brest or Bordeaux and in May 1794 the *Aurora*

4. The frigate Cleopatra, one of many naval vessels that brought captured prizes into Yarmouth Roads. She is shown here in three different positions.

brought in four Scandinavian vessels suspected of being destined for France. In April 1795 a dis-masted privateer of eight guns was towed in, having been captured by the *Vestal* and in May and June that year the *Greyhound* sent in a brigantine laden with wheat, deals and fruit, together with the *Goede Verwagtig*, with wheat and sundry goods.[8] In March 1793 the revenue and excise cutters brought in their first prizes. The *Hunter*, under Captain Thomas Riches, had secured an English brig, carrying Spanish wine to Ostend and a few days later, together with the *Lively*, under Captain Matthew Gunthorpe, had captured the *Isabella*, a French fishing vessel belonging to Dunkirk, carrying 300 cod and other fish. In April the *Hunter* sent in the *St. Peter*, a fishing boat from Nieuport and another from Dunkirk, *Le Fruit de la Mere*. In April the following year Riches sent in an American brig, *Mary*, with wheat, barley and beans, which had sailed from Bremen, and a Swedish hoy, *St. Peter*, with wheat from Wismar.[9]

In order to encourage a vigorous approach to the taking of enemy merchantmen and privateers a system of 'prize money' had long been established, whereby the officers and crew of a prize-taking vessel would receive the whole of the value of the vessel and its cargo, divided amongst the crew according to a fixed scale. The calculation of each share could be complex, depending on whether there were other naval ships in the vicinity or whether the prize-taker was under the direction of a flag officer, which was usually the case. Nevertheless successful commerce raiding captains became wealthy men and those lower down the pecking order could enjoy useful windfalls when the prize money was eventually paid out. With the vessel seized a prize crew would be sent on board to sail it to a British port, to be processed at an admiralty court. Although Yarmouth had its own Vice-Admiralty jurisdiction its court dealt almost exclusively with salvage work. Most of the prizes arriving in the Roads were sent on to London for adjudication in the High Court of Admiralty, but some small vessels and large amounts of cargo, especially perishable goods, were auctioned locally, usually by Messrs T. and A. H. Steward, who were the prize agents at the port. Much of it was purchased by local merchants at knock down prices. It was quite commonplace for those frequenting the public lookout by the Jetty to witness the arrival of prizes and during the Revolutionary War the local newspapers recorded close on 800 such vessels as having been sent into Yarmouth by the North Sea cruisers. No doubt there were others that went unrecorded.[10]

The defensive backbone of the war on trade was the convoy system. Merchantmen grouped together under the watchful eye of a naval vessel were far less likely to be taken than a merchant ship sailing alone, but it was not a system popular with the merchants as it could slow down their vessels and also bring them to the attention of the press gangs. To prevent merchantmen being tempted to take the risk of sailing without 'benefit of convoy' the system was enforced by Act of Parliament, although some ships, known as 'runners', were allowed to sail alone, if they were fast enough and well-armed.[11] A route was established along the East Coast for standing convoys (later called coastwise convoys). There was a regular return service from the Downs and the Nore via Yarmouth, Hull and Leith and on into the Baltic. Merchant ships would assemble at the ports on the route and join the convoys as they sailed by.[12] Entries such as the one that appeared in the Yarmouth column of the *Norwich Mercury* in July 1797 were not uncommon; 'On the 17th inst passed by the Outward bound Baltic Fleet, under convoy of the *Garland* and *Martin*, and 7 vessels from the port joined the fleet.'[13] This system was not fool-proof however. In late February 1793 the *Industry*, bound for

Hamburg, with packs, left Yarmouth harbour to await a convoy, but with it not materialising she returned to the safety of the haven. A month later she tried again, together with the *Fanny*, only to suffer more disappointment.[14] Later, when there was an admiral based in the Roads, he would regularly arrange for one of his vessels to escort groups of merchantmen that had congregated in the haven to await this service.

While Yarmouth merchants benefited from the convoy system they also needed naval vessels to provide fishery protection. In April 1793 the town Mayor, on behalf of those merchants involved in the fishery, wrote to the Admiralty seeking the appointment of a patrol vessel for the spring mackerel season. Lieutenant Columbine of the cutter *Resolution* was given the task, being required to use his, 'best endeavours to secure them (the fishing boats) from any attempts of the Enemy's Privateers or other Cruizers...' Similar arrangements were made for both the mackerel and the herring fisheries throughout the wars.[15] Regarding the autumn herring fishery the Dutch had traditionally been involved and were a popular visitor attraction in the town. They came over as usual in 1793 and again in 1794, but this was before the Dutch, as the Batavian Republic, became Britain's enemy.[16] In October 1796 some 26 Dutch fishing schuyts arrived in the Roads. They flew Prussian colours, but were never-the-less detained until the Admiralty ordered their release. It was subsequently decided that the Dutch could fish provided the catch was only used to feed their civilian population.[17]

***

The sequence of events that led to a naval station being established in the North Sea, with Yarmouth as its headquarters, had its origins in the early days of the war. In mid-February

5. Dutch fishing vessels on Yarmouth beach. The arrival of these popular visitors was suspended while Britain was at war with the Batavian Republic.

1793 the French *Armée de Hollande* invaded the United Provinces and as a result the British government decided to send military assistance to its Dutch counterpart. On 1 March a brigade of guards, under the command of the Duke of York, landed at Hellevoetsluis.[18] Three weeks later reinforcements aboard five transports assembled in Yarmouth Roads, before, on the 30th, setting sail for that Dutch port, under the watchful eye of the ship-sloop *Martin*.[19] In November the townsfolk of Yarmouth opened a subscription 'for the laudable purpose of supplying the brave troops under the Duke of York with additional warm Cloathing,'[20] and in May 1794 it was reported that, 'The news of the glorious successes obtained on the Continent was received at Yarmouth on Thursday with the greatest demonstrations of joy. The bells were immediately rung and a general display of colors took place on the Town–hall, Shipping, etc. and yesterday *a feu-de-joie* was fired by the Leicestershire Militia, which was answered by his Majesty's ships in the roads.'[21] The joy was short-lived, however, for despite some early success the campaign ended in a retreat to Bremen where, on 14 April 1795, the army was re-embarked for England. Arriving in Yarmouth Roads on 4 May several units were landed to be temporarily quartered in the town and in Norwich before the remainder sailed for Harwich and Portsmouth. In the words of fortescue, 'Thus disgracefully ended the first expedition of Pitt and Dundas to the Low Countries.'[22]

Left without allies and with his own people threatening to hand him over to the French, the Dutch head of state, Willem V, Prince of Orange, grew concerned about his safety and that of his family and decided that they should all flee to England. Sending his family ahead, 'the Princess, with her daughter-in-law, her little grand-daughter, the child's nurse and two gentlemen of her household, embarked on board a fishing-boat, open to the weather, into the hold of which they were let down (there being no steps) by being held under the arms. Here they all lay, covered with sails, as a defence against the inclemency of the elements, which were terrifically boisterous. The passage proved to be both difficult and dangerous; but at length on the 19th January, 1795, they were landed in safety at Yarmouth.'[23] There they were treated with kindness by the townsfolk who, as was the custom when receiving dignitaries, removed the horses from their carriage and drew the refugees twice round the market place, before conveying them to the Mayor's house.[24] The Prince of Orange soon followed, embarking with his sons on a coal barge at Scheveningen and landing at Harwich. Quickly making his way to Yarmouth he was reunited with his family in the middle of the night and the following day they all set out for London. As they did so they missed the Duke of York who had travelled to Yarmouth via a different route to welcome them. Finding them gone he stayed for a few hours before returning to the capital, but not before he too became acquainted with the town's horseless carriage tradition.[25]

Back in the United Provinces the French army pushed north, in what was a particularly severe winter, and found a significant part of the Dutch fleet icebound in the Texel, near Den Helder. General de Brigade Johann Willem De Winter was sent with a regiment of hussars to secure the warships, which he did on 23 January.[26] Whether the Dutch fleet would have set sail to escape capture if not icebound is open to question, but what is certain is that with it effectively in the hands of the French it posed a threat to British naval supremacy in the North Sea and raised the spectre of invasion.[27] As a precautionary measure, on 17 January, the government placed an embargo on all Dutch warships and merchant vessels and directed the admirals in charge at Portsmouth, Plymouth, Sheerness, Spithead and the Downs to detain

6. The departure of Wilhelmina, Princess of Orange, and her family from Scheveningen for England in a fishing boat. They arrived at Yarmouth on 19 January 1795.

any ship of that description anchored 'within the limits of their commands.' Three weeks later all operational naval captains were instructed to apprehend and bring into port any Dutch ship or vessel they came across.[28]

With these stop gap arrangements in place the decision was taken to create a naval station in the North Sea with Vice-Admiral Adam Duncan as its commander-in-chief. According to his eldest daughter his appointment was a matter of chance for, 'in going over the list of Admirals with Mr. Henry Dundas Lord Spencer said 'What can be the reason "Keppel's Duncan" has never been brought forward? Upon this Mr. Dundas said that he thought he would like employment and added that he had married his niece. The same night he was appointed commander-in-chief in the North Sea.'[29] Duncan was officially appointed on 11 March 1795, 'to be commander-in-chief of His Majesty's Ships and Vessels employed and to be employed in the North Sea and on the Coasts of England and Scotland from Harwich to the Islands of Orkney & Shetland.' The same day he was ordered to hoist his flag on the 74-gun *Venerable*, when she arrived at the Nore.[30] On 17 April he was given more specific instructions including, 'You are constantly to keep, during the Summer months as many Ships and Vessels of your Squadron cruizing off the Texel, and between that place and the Coasts of Denmark and Norway as in your opinion will be sufficient to afford effectual Protection and assistance to the British Convoys passing to and fro' between the Baltic and Archangel, Hambro' and the Northern Coasts of this Kingdom…'[31] In essence he was to blockade the Dutch warships moored in the Texel and be responsible for protecting British merchant ships in Northern waters. By then Rear-Admiral Thomas Pringle had been appointed his second-in-command.[32] Geographically and from a navigational point of view Yarmouth Roads was

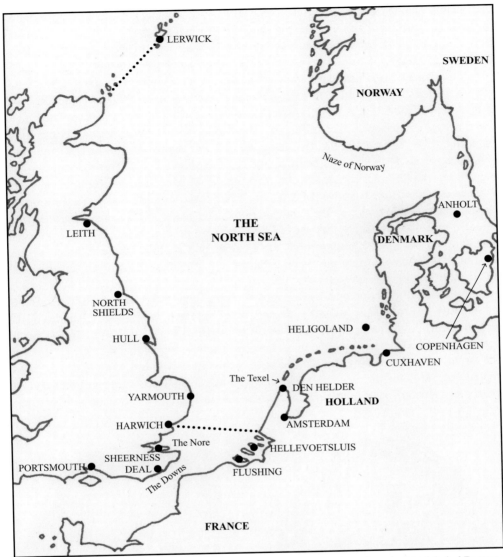

7. The operational area of the North Sea naval command as defined in the orders given to Admiral Duncan in March and April 1795.

the obvious place to station the new squadron, but initially this location was overlooked in favour of the more well-established Downs anchorage, supported as it was by the naval facilities at Deal, a base well outside the area of Duncan's command. It was also decided to place Pringle in the north, at Leith. By early 1796 Duncan was a little closer to the North Sea, being based at the Nore.

The North Sea Naval Squadron assembled in 1795 was a makeshift affair for the established naval stations had the pick of the best ships. The core formed on 24 March comprised four ships-of-the-line, four frigates and two cutters.[33] Expansion was rapid, but the additional warships allocated to Duncan were largely old, ex-French prizes or hastily converted merchantmen and these were constantly being taken away for other duties, thereby preventing the admiral creating an identity for his squadron. To make matters worse a poor quality Russian squadron was placed under his command. In February a treaty of mutual assistance had been drawn up between Catherine the Great's Russia and the British government and as part of this the Empress agreed to supply her new ally with a number of warships. As a result she dispatched Vice-Admiral Hanikoff, together with Rear-Admirals Makaroff and Tate, with twelve ships of the line and eight frigates to work with the North Sea Squadron. The first of these arrived in the Downs in early August, escorting a convoy of British merchantmen from the Baltic.[34] On the face of it the Russians were welcome reinforcements and the Admiralty was keen to satisfy their needs because of the psychological advantage the support of a significant naval power represented, but to Duncan and his subordinate admirals they were more trouble than they were worth. Although aware that they were under Duncan's orders the Russians tended to act on their own initiative, constantly challenging what they were directed to do. What's more they were a drain on resources, as Eunice Turner observed, 'Drawing on the English authorities for provisions and medical supplies, ordnance and repairs, without obvious return, it is perhaps not surprising that the Russian squadron was felt to be a liability, at least by those at sea;...'[35]

For much of 1795 Duncan operated an open blockade of the Texel whereby a small number of warships kept a close eye on the 'Frenchified Dutchmen,' while the remainder of the squadron carried out other duties or remained in the Downs.[36] Duncan himself only put to sea in August and November when the Admiralty had intelligence that the Dutch Fleet was out or was about to come out. In October, while Rear-Admiral Pringle's ships were replenishing at Leith, the crew of the *Defiance* (74) mutinied. It was left to Captain William Bligh, himself no stranger to such an occurrence, to resolve the dispute with Pringle's

8. Admiral Adam Duncan, Commander-in-chief of the North Sea Naval Station, 1795-1800.

9. Rear-Admiral Thomas Pringle, Duncan's second-in-command, 1795-96.

indecisive involvement doing little to enhance his reputation. In January 1796 he hoisted his flag on the frigate *Ambuscade*, the only naval ship available to him at Leith, and in late February he was ordered to take charge of the squadron Duncan was assembling off the Texel. Arriving there on 23rd he transferred his flag to the *Asia* (74) and sent the brig-sloop *Seagull* to check on the Dutch warships. On the 24th the *Seagull* returned, seemingly being pursued by an enemy squadron, estimated by Pringle to be in the order of 18 ships and vessels, 11 of them large.[37] The two forces were fairly evenly matched, but Pringle did not offer battle and the following day took his squadron into Yarmouth Roads. Pringle remained there nearly three weeks, in which time his ships and vessels were re-provisioned and provided with ships' stores. This was the first time in the war a squadron of naval warships had been serviced at Yarmouth. The Admiralty, however, was unimpressed by the Rear-Admiral's lack of vigour and when he prevaricated over leaving the Roads Duncan was sent to collect his subordinate's ships and patrol off the Naze of Norway in search of the Dutch Squadron. This he did on 14 March.[38]

Duncan was to remain at sea a punishing two months off the Naze and later off the Texel. An idea of the conditions he faced can be gained from a letter he wrote to Evan Nepean, secretary to the Admiralty Board, on 30 March. In it he states, 'since my last Letter of the 18th Instant, by the *Phoenix* Cutter, it has been almost a constant Gale of Wind from the NE, attended with Snow and Hail, which drove the Squadron far to the Southward, but that I am now nearly on my Rendezvous again.'[39] Pringle was with him, but not for much longer, for the Admiralty had decided a change was needed and on 12 April 1796 he was ordered to shift his flag to the *Tremendous* (74) and proceed to the Cape of Good Hope, to be second-in-command of the squadron there.[40] It seems his replacement had already been chosen for in writing to Duncan on 15 April Lord Spencer informed him that, 'Admiral Pringle's services having been required in another quarter of the world, we have taken him from you, and intend that Vice-Admiral Macbride should hoist his flag under your command in the North Sea, who I hope, from his knowledge of that sea and his well-known activity, will prove a useful second to you.'[41]

On 21 April Duncan wrote to the Admiralty from off the Naze of Norway with intelligence from the British consul at Christiansand that the Dutch squadron he was seeking was not in the vicinity and in view of this he intended to return to the Downs. The consul had also said that the Dutch force at the Texel was greater than his own.[42] Alarmed by this the Admiralty ordered Duncan to remain at sea and to proceed to the Texel where he would be reinforced by Admiral Tate's Russian ships.[43] The previous day the Admiralty had instructed Macbride to proceed to the Nore and place himself under Duncan's orders. He was to hoist his flag on the *Ramillies*, *Robust* or *Russell* (all 74's) and, 'hasten by every means in your power the re-equipment for sea, of the Ships above-named, as well as any others belonging to the Squadron under the Command of the said Admiral, as may be arrived at Sheerness or the Nore.'[44] Not grasping the urgency of his appointment, Macbride, who was 'on the beach' at Cowes at the time, replied that he had problems with the transportation of his baggage and that, 'In a few days I shall Set out for Sheerness taking London in my way and will call at the Office for any commands their Lordships may have for me.'[45] By return he was told, 'your Services are immediately necessary at the Nore where you will probably find orders for proceeding to sea, & that Adm Sir P. Parker has been directed to send Another vessel to Cowes for the purpose of removing your Baggage & Stores to the Nore.'[46] Suitably chastened Macbride proceeded to the Nore, raised his flag on the *Russell* and was given orders to proceed to the Texel.

Duncan arrived off the Texel on 8 May. Eight days later he reported the capture of the Dutch frigate, *Argo*, together with three armed brigs, but also that his stock of water and bread was so depleted that he did not think it safe to continue at sea.[47] On 18 May he brought the *Venerable* to anchor at the Nore in company with the *Repulse* (64), *Glatton* (56) and the frigates *Phoenix* and *Proserpine*, together with the four Dutch prizes.[48] Needing to restore his health he applied to the Admiralty for leave to attend to private matters and with Macbride in place he was granted the customary rolling fortnight. In the event he stayed in London until the middle of September, issuing orders from his town-house there.[49] Duncan and Macbride had a few days together at the Nore before on 22 May the vice-admiral set sail for

10. Vice-Admiral John Macbride, Duncan's second-in-command, 1796.

11. Vice-Admiral Richard Onslow, Duncan's second-in-command, 1796-98.

the Texel. After the *Russell* had run aground on the edge of the Middle Sand, which Macbride blamed on poor pilotage, and having experienced difficulties with the 'rotting' Russian ships attached to his squadron, he arrived off the Dutch coast on 29 May.[50]

Associated with Macbride's appointment was the Admiralty's decision to concentrate the servicing needs of the North Sea Squadron at Yarmouth. It had taken the Lords Commissioners over a year to come to the conclusion that the Roads anchorage was more convenient for the ships blockading the Texel than either Leith Roads or the Nore and despite some teething problems Pringle had shown that it could be done. Accordingly in May the Victualling Board made arrangements to establish a depot in the town, 'It being expected that a considerable number of His Majesty's Ships will occasionally rendezvous off Yarmouth in Norfolk...'[51] On 18 June 1796 Macbride received the Admiralty's order, issued by Duncan as protocol demanded, 'to return to Yarmouth Road to refit and victual,' his squadron.[52]

Leaving the frigate *Reunion*, with the cutters *Active* and *Nancy*, to watch the Texel he anchored in Yarmouth Roads on 25 June as commander of the first naval squadron to be ordered to be serviced at Yarmouth.[53] It comprised the ships-of-the-line *Russell* (his flagship), *Robust*, *Director* (64), and *Lion* (64), the frigates *L'Imperieuse* and *Phoenix*, the ship-sloops *Nautilus* and *Ranger*, together with Tate's Russians, the 66 gun-ships *Europa*, *Graf Orlov*, and *Retvizan*, the frigate *Venus* and the brig-sloop *Dispatch*.[54] These warships lay at anchor in the Roads for the best part of a month, taking on provisions, beer and water, as well as boatswain's and gunner's stores. On 22 July they returned to the Dutch coast, but were back in the Roads again in early August. After a five day stay they resumed their surveillance of the Texel.

Macbride, however, was not a well man. On 3 September he informed Duncan that, 'I have for some time been affected with violent pains in the head, which occasions a dizziness that has of late become more frequent and is very unpleasant. Mr Stephenson, Surgeon of this Ship (*Russell*) thinks a relaxation from business, for a short time, absolutely necessary.'[55] He was granted 14-days leave, but he was never to return to his command, being officially ordered to strike his flag on 14 January 1797.[56] The timing of Macbride's incapacitation could not have been more inconvenient for hearing that the Dutch were discontented with their new leaders the British government decided to take possession of the Helder and Texel Island and to destroy the Dutch fleet that lay there using fireships.[57] Ordered to resume command of the North Sea Squadron Duncan arrived at Yarmouth on 17 September and took control of the ships which had returned to the Roads earlier that month

Despite repeatedly being instructed to put to sea Duncan did not do so until 29 October,

12. Two of the allied Russian men-of-war at anchor off Sheerness in 1796.

citing the problems that the victualling boats had in getting out to the warships because of a persistent easterly wind. It was the first occasion he had spent any length of time at Yarmouth and it gave him the opportunity to evaluate the suitability of the roadstead for sustaining the squadron. That he expressed doubts to Spencer is suggested by a letter written to him on 2 November by the Earl in which he states, 'we continue to think Yarmouth the best place for you to return to.'[58] It was a view the Admiralty were to hold for the remainder of the wars.

The same adverse weather conditions that had delayed his departure made a landing on enemy soil impossible, but Duncan remained off the Dutch coast until 27 November. Returning with his ships to the Nore he was once more granted leave and after spending some days in London, set off for Edinburgh.[59] He was able to do so for, uncertain whether Macbride would be able to return to duty, on 19 November, the Admiralty had appointed Vice-Admiral Sir Richard Onslow to replace him.[60] He arrived at Yarmouth on 4 December and hoisted his flag on the *Nassau(I)* (64).[61]

With Duncan on leave Onslow was in command of the North Sea Squadron throughout the remaining winter months, carrying out 'port duties' from his flagship in the Yarmouth Roads. These involved managing the strategic and day to day business of the ships and vessels under his command, as directed by the Admiralty or, in the absence of such direction, on his own initiative. Until then these duties were carried out by whoever happened to be the most senior naval officer in the Roads, but with Onslow in port for a full three months Yarmouth had, in effect, its first 'port-admiral.' The almost daily correspondence between Onslow and the Admiralty's secretary, Evan Nepean, gives a good indication of what he had to deal with. At the operational level he maintained the blockade of the Texel, at a much reduced winter deployment and appointed vessels for convoy work. He also sent others to search for privateers in specified areas of the North Sea, such as when he received intelligence in February from a Mr Basset of Margate that 16 privateers from Dunkirk and 8 from Ostend had sailed, 'for the annoyance of the Coal trade.'[62] He also made frequent returns on the state and condition of his ships and vessels and dealt with a variety of matters to do with his sailors, including appointments, court-martials and desertions. In addition he oversaw victualling, the issuing of other stores and decided when ships needed to be sent to the Nore for repair. To work effectively he needed a good relationship with the town authorities, but this seems not to have been the case, for in late January the following year, the Mayor made a complaint to the Admiralty about the vice-admiral's inactivity to which Onslow haughtily replied, 'I feel my situation too high to be affected by such a sort of letter not founded in either strict truth or justice.'[63]

2.
Mutiny and Camperdown 1797

On 3 March 1797 Lord Spencer, the First Lord of the Admiralty, informed Duncan that eight Dutch ships-of-the-line had sailed from the Texel and four from Hellevoet and he was to intercept them. Swiftly returning to active service, on the 8th he arrived in the Yarmouth Roads from the Nore in his flagship *Venerable* with three other ships-of-the-line. By then, however, he knew that the Dutch fleet was no longer at large, nevertheless eight days later he sailed for the Texel with 21 ships and vessels and remained there until returning to the Roads on 24 April, little knowing that he was about to become embroiled in a major naval mutiny.[1]

Dissatisfaction with pay and conditions had long been a justifiable grievance among the navy's seamen. Pay had fallen well behind that of the soldiers and sometimes could take over a year to be disbursed. The warning signs that matters were coming to a head were plain to see, but the Admiralty failed to heed them and on 16 April 1797 cheering from the rigging of Admiral Gardner's Channel Fleet ships signalled the start of a mutiny at Spithead. Although by the letter of the law it was a mutiny, in many respects it resembled a modern day industrial action with the sailors maintaining order and submitting their demands in writing and with the Admiralty responding with concessions, especially in relation to pay, which were embodied in an Act of Parliament. With a general pardon being granted the Spithead mutiny ended on 13 May.

By then though 'mutinous intent' had spread to the ships in the Yarmouth Roads and those at the Nore. On 1 May Duncan reported to the Admiralty that on the previous day he had been surprised to hear unauthorised cheering on board the *Venerable*. Demanding to know the cause he had questioned five men who told him that, 'as their Friends at Spithead had done so, they thought no harm and they wished to know when their increased Pay and Provisions was to commence.'[2] He went on to say that 'having satisfied them on that head, I pointed out the enormity of the crime of Mutiny and pardoned the Offenders; good order was again established,…'[3] It may not have been as straight-forward as he suggested, however, if credence is given to the anecdote that he was only prevented from plunging his sword into one of the seamen by the intervention of the ship's chaplain.[4] If, as was the case at Spithead, the cheering was a signal to set in motion a full scale mutiny in the North Sea Squadron, it did not succeed for only the sailors of the *Nassau(I)* followed suit and Vice-Admiral Onslow quickly diffused the situation on board what was his flagship. Through force of character Duncan had quelled this first attempt at mutiny in the Yarmouth Roads, but the underlying feeling of grievance remained strong and over the next three weeks he and his officers had to deal with further outbreaks of disorder.

On 5 May sailors on the *Standard* (64) placed themselves behind a barricade and directed four guns aft. They remained there until their captain managed to persuade them to return to duty.[5] More serious was the rising on the *Adamant* (50) on the 13th. Acting swiftly Duncan hoisted his flag on that ship, mustered her crew and proceeded to address them. After declaring he would rather acquire their love than their fear he told them, 'I will with my own hand put to death the first man who shall display the slightest signs of rebellious conduct.' He then asked if anyone disputed his authority or that of his officers to which a man replied, 'I do'. Seizing the man by the collar Duncan thrust him over the side of the ship where he held him suspended by an arm before saying, 'My Lads, look at this fellow, he who dares to deprive me of the command of the fleet.' With yet another display of strength order was restored.[6] Four days later he reported to the Admiralty that, 'the Crew of His Majesty's Sloop the *Albatross* were very riotous and disorderly last Evening, but by the determined and officerlike Conduct of Captain Scott, who presented a pistol at the first man that appear[ed] and of Lieutenant Lambert, who cut down another with his hanger, the business was soon settled.'[7]

13. 'Seizing the man by the collar Duncan thrust him over the side of the ship where he held him suspended by the arm'. A depiction of Duncan quelling the rising on the Adamant, 13 May 1797.

While such firefighting was keeping things in check, Duncan was busy trying to remove a primary cause of the mutinous behaviour, the problem with pay. In relation to the demand for greater remuneration, on 11 May, he distributed to the squadron printed copies of the Act of Parliament that increased the seamen's pay and provisions, won for the whole navy by the men of the Channel Fleet.[8] Prior to that he had sent to the Admiralty a list of eight ships with the dates their crews were supposed to have been paid. Other than the *Nassau(I)* (6 months) and the *Director* (4 months) they were all less than two months in arrears. Nevertheless the Admiralty replied that as soon as the service would allow the *Standard* and the other ships would be ordered to the Nore for that purpose.[9] This was the case on 19 May when the Admiralty directed Duncan, 'to send the *Nassau* and any one of the other two decked Ships, to the Crew of which the Pay shall have been longest due, to proceed to the Nore, provided the Wind should not be favourable for the Sailing of the Dutch fleet from the Texel.' But events at the Nore were soon to render this course of action unwise.[10]

A week earlier Admiral Buckner's flagship *Sandwich* (98) had been seized by her crew, thereby starting the mutiny at the Nore. But these mutineers were a very different breed to their brethren at Spithead. Although they organised themselves on much the same lines, they lacked restraint and swayed by the oratory of their leader, Richard Parker, a former warrant officer who styled himself 'Admiral of the Floating Republic', they let their new found power go to their heads. Regularly landing at Sheerness to hold meetings, 'They then parade the streets and ramparts of the garrison with a degree of triumphant insolence, and hold up the bloody flag of defiance as a mark of scorn to the military.'[11] It was not until 20 May that Buckner, having met their delegates relayed the mutineer's demands to the Admiralty. By then, however, the Channel Fleet had returned to duty and with Duncan repeatedly reporting that the North Sea Squadron was obedient to his orders, the Lords Commissioners decided to take a stand, as they did not want mutiny to become an acceptable method of airing grievances. Accordingly on the 21st Buckner was instructed to inform the mutineers that, 'since all that could reasonably be expected by the seamen and marines has been already granted them, their lordships cannot accede to any such further requests,' but as an inducement to return to their duties they were offered a pardon, 'not withstanding all they have done.'[12]

Rejecting the Admiralty's response, on 22 May, 'Parker's Fleet' moved from Sheerness to the Nore and both sides turned to the North Sea Squadron for support. Commandeering the cutter *Cygnet* the mutineers sent delegates to Yarmouth to try to persuade the sailors there to join them. Being advised of this by the Admiralty, Duncan ordered the frigate *Vestal* to patrol off the buoy of the Gunfleet and the *Hope* lugger and *Rose* cutter to cruise between Lowestoft and Orford Ness, 'to prevent all communication from the Nore with the Ships in this Road.'[13] On the evening of the 26th the *Rose* cutter came across the *Cygnet* and captured all those on board, but by then three of the delegates had landed and set off for Yarmouth. Having successfully made contact with Duncan's sailors they returned and gave to Lieutenant Reddy of the *Hope*, who by then was holding the other delegates, a letter from the men of the North Sea Squadron. This stated that they were perfectly satisfied, were going to put to sea and that the Nore delegates were on their way back to their anchorage in order to persuade the crews of the ships there to return to duty. Naively Reddy allowed them to continue on their way.[14]

Meanwhile, on 21 May, the Admiralty, anticipating that the mutineers would react negatively to the rejection of their demands, despatched a messenger to Duncan to direct him not to send any ships to the Nore to be paid. The following day Nepean wrote to him to enquire if the ships of his squadron could be relied upon if they were ordered to the Nore to bring the mutineers 'to reason'.[15] Duncan did not like the idea, but replied that, he would not 'shrink from the business if it could not be resolved in any other way.'[16] Still uncertain about the loyalty of the North Sea Squadron, on 26 May, Lord Spencer decided to send Captain Bligh to assess the situation for, 'till we know what we can look to from your squadron it will be very difficult for us to know how to act,' he told Duncan.[17] At the same time Nepean informed Duncan that the Admiralty Board intended to go to Sheerness to offer the mutineers a pardon, but if this did not lead to the restoration of order he would be directed 'to act against them.'[18]

If this was not bad enough, information had been received from the captain of the frigate *Minerva* that there were lying in the Texel, ready for sea, 18 ships of the line, 22 frigates, sloops and brigs, from 10 to 44 guns, and 42 large transports being fitted out for troops. There seemed little doubt that invasion was contemplated.[19] As a result, on 24 May, Duncan had been directed to proceed with his squadron to his station off the Texel, if the wind should turn easterly. This was the day William Youell wrote in his diary, 'For somtime past the Sailors on board of Admiral Duncans Ships in the Roads have been in a state of Mutiny. They come on shore every day & behave very violently, breaking windows &c.'[20]

14. 'For sometime past the Sailors on board Admiral Duncan's Ships in the Roads have been in a state of Mutiny. They come on shore every day & behave very violently, breaking windows etc'. William Youell 24 May 1797.

Not knowing where events would lead him and with his crews all too accessible to external subversion, on 26 May, Duncan told the Admiralty that, 'altho the Wind may be westerly in the Morning I shall put to Sea with the whole of the Squadron except the *Nassau*, and I believe the *Standard*, whose Companies appear determined not to weigh their anchors until they are paid the Wages due to them. I have therefore ordered Vice-Admiral Onslow to hoist his Flag on board the *Adamant* for the present.'[21] The following morning (27th) he set sail with the *Venerable*, *Adamant*, *Agamemnon* (64), *Belliqueux* (64), *Lion* (64), *Glatton*, *Standard*, *Leopard* (50), *Monmouth* (64), *Ardent* (64), *Isis* (50), and *Repulse*, but with the wind still westerly he decided to remain at the back of the sands. It was this action that finally brought about the full scale mutiny of the sailors of the North Sea Squadron.[22] The *Montagu* (74) and *Nassau(I)* had refused to weigh anchor and had remained in the Roads when the squadron had sailed. Early on the 29th Duncan found that the *Standard* and the *Lion* had deserted him in the night and later he spotted them in the Roads with the *Nassau(I)*, the

Montagu having already departed for the Nore. All were flying red flags and shortly afterwards the *Belliqueux* joined them.[23] On the 30th, with the wind northerly, Duncan decided to set sail for the Texel. He was joined by the frigate *Garland*, but the *Repulse* and *Monmouth* soon deserted him. The next day, one by one, the *Isis*, *Leopard*, *Ardent*, *Agamemnon*, and *Glatton* followed suit. By the time Duncan looked into the Texel his squadron comprised two ships-of-the-line, (*Venerable* and *Adamant*), together with the frigate *Garland* and the ship-sloop *Stork*. The frigate *Trent* joined them later that day.[24]

Watching the warships return to the Roads, with the red flags of mutiny flying at their mastheads, the townsfolk of Yarmouth must have feared the worst, given the sailor's recent bad behaviour in the town, but in the event their fears proved groundless for it was the mutineers intention to join their brethren at the Nore, not establish a separate mutiny in the Yarmouth Roads. As at Spithead and the Nore delegates were appointed and one of them was sent ashore to assure the Mayor that no harm would come to the town and that they intended to fire a salute in honour of the day (the restoration of Charles II), which they did, lowering their flags as they did so. On the following day they set sail for the Nore, to be joined there, on 6 June, by the other ships that had deserted Duncan.[25]

Left with such a small force at his disposal, Duncan had to decide how best to fulfil his orders. Onslow suggested a retreat to Leith Roads as security against a Dutch attack or the return of the rebel ships from the Nore, but Duncan would not hear of it. Ever a man of action he decided that the *Venerable* and *Adamant* would block the narrow entrance to the Texel and, if necessary, fight until they sank and that should he survive he would sail to the Nore 'to reduce "those misguided men" to obedience.'[26] But with the wind blowing largely from the west and gambling on the fact that the Dutch might not know how weak he really was he considered a little subterfuge might serve to even the odds, thereby creating one of the most memorable incidents of the Revolutionary War. For three days he cruised off the enemy coast, each morning looking into the Texel. On the first day his two ships passed in front of the Dutch fleet, one flying the flag of a rear-admiral of the red on the mizzen mast. Next day they appeared again with captains pendants only, suggesting there were two squadrons. After being joined by the *Russell* and *Sans Pareil* (80) a 'third squadron' appeared off the Texel wearing Duncan's proper colours as an admiral of the blue. On all these occasions signals were being made to imaginary warships beyond the horizon. That the deception worked was confirmed by the master of the American brig *Eliza*, who at the time was in the Texel and was subsequently captured by Lieutenant Brodie in the *Rose* cutter. He asserted that the Dutch thought the four British ships were decoys for a much larger force in the offing.[27] On 10 June, with the Dutch still at anchor, Duncan was joined by Rear-Admiral Sir Roger Curtis, with six ships of the line, and on the 13th a small Russian squadron of three men-of-war and a frigate arrived, under Rear-Admiral Mackaroff.[28] The following day the Nore Mutiny was brought to a close when Parker's 'flagship' *Sandwich* surrendered to the Sheerness port-admiral, following a counter rebellion on several of the other ships, once it became clear to their mutineers that the Admiralty was going to starve them out.[29] In all 12 ships had deserted the North Sea Squadron for the Nore, doubling the number of mutinous ships at that transit anchorage and it was the crew of one of these, the *Leopard*, that initiated the mutiny's collapse. The crisis had ended without Duncan having to use force against the mutineers, nor let the Dutch out of the Texel.

***

Duncan and the North Sea Squadron were to spend the remainder of the summer months off the Texel. For the sake of discipline after the naval mutinies it was felt important to keep the ships at sea, but the main reason for such a long period off the Dutch anchorage was to prevent the sailing of the substantial invasion force that had been assembled there. In June Captain Boorder of the brig-sloop *L'Espeigle* reported that 11,000 French troops had been embarked on transports in the Texel and 25,000 more in the Pampus (a nearby anchorage).[30] Their intended destination was Ireland, but this was not known to the British at the time.[31] On 23 June the Russian Squadron set sail for home following orders from the unstable Tsar Paul, who had succeeded his mother, Catherine, in November 1796. As protocol demanded Duncan wrote to thank Rear-Admiral Makaroff for his assistance and in return received a reply which included the sentiment, 'Your thanks for my poor services done in the service of His Britannic Majesty will remain indelibly stamped on my mind.'[32] The Russian 'services' had indeed been poor and Duncan was relieved to see the warships go, especially as the size of his squadron had increased with the return of several of the mutinous ships from the Nore, enabling Onslow to shift his flag from the *Ardent* to the *Monarch*(74).[33] Impressed by the loyalty shown by the sailors of the *Venerable* and the *Adamant* during the recent mutiny in the Yarmouth Roads, and their subsequent part in fooling the Dutch, the town raised £54 to provide them with porter and vegetables. On 23 July Duncan was asked by the sailors of the *Venerable* to, 'communicate to the Gentlemen, Merchants and Traders of the Town of Yarmouth our most grateful thanks for their liberal present of porter which has (under your own direction) afforded us seasonable refreshment for ten days.'[34]

For some time Duncan had been concerned that he was not allowed to stop all the vessels entering and leaving the Texel, especially those 'trading under false pretences,' but in early August he was given permission to tighten his grip by declaring a formal blockade of the anchorage, which he did on the 8th.[35] By then, however, the squadron was in need of re-provisioning. This was usually achieved by sending ships into port, but such was the concern about the enemy's invasion plans that the decision was taken to send victuallers out to them. Lord Spencer explained the reasoning for this to Duncan in the following terms, 'We have sent you out wine, fresh meat, and water, and will continue to supply you with these necessary refreshments at every opportunity, as it would be wrong to quit your station at present while so excellent an effect is produced not only here but all over Europe by your remaining there.'[36] Throughout August victuallers did their best to supply the squadron, but in the first two weeks of September it was struck by a series of gales and hurricanes which caused havoc amongst the vulnerable warships, so much so that several of them had to be sent to Yarmouth or the Nore for repairs.[37] Alive to the squadron's plight and hearing that the enemy's plans to invade Ireland had been postponed, on 18 September the Admiralty ordered Duncan to take his ships to Yarmouth to be refitted and provisioned, but it was to be done as quickly as possible and he was to be ready to return to the Texel if the wind changed to the eastward.[38] In the event the *Speculator* lugger did not deliver the order to Duncan until the 29th, but as soon as he received it he sent a cutter to Yarmouth to prevent any more victuallers setting sail and the following day made the signal for the squadron to proceed to the Yarmouth Roads, leaving behind the frigate *Circe*, together with the *Active* cutter and *Speculator* lugger to watch the

Dutch ships in the Texel. On 3 October the *Venerable* anchored in the Roads with 15 ships-of-the-line and the race was on to get them to sea again.

Regardless of the fact that the invasion force had been disembarked, the absence of Duncan's blockading squadron presented the Dutch government with a face-saving opportunity it could not resist. On 5 October Admiral De Winter was ordered to sail from the Texel and engage the North Sea Squadron, in whole or in part, if there was a reasonable chance of success. Against his better judgement he put to sea on the 7th.[39] On discovering that the Dutch fleet was preparing to sail Captain Halkett of the frigate *Circe* had immediately sent the *Speculator* lugger to inform Duncan of the fact.[40] On the morning of the 9th the admiral spotted the lugger at the back of Yarmouth Sands, signalling that the Dutch fleet was either out or preparing to be so. A bustle of activity followed and, in the haste to get to sea, some officers were left on shore, unable to regain their ships. At 11 o'clock on the 10th Duncan unmoored the squadron and soon after departed the Roads in the *Venerable*, accompanied by the *Monarch*, *Belliqueux*, *Montagu*, *Bedford* (74), *Director*, *Veteran* (64), *Lancaster* (64), *Triumph* (74), *Ardent* (64), and *Monmouth*. The *Agincourt*, which was taking on powder, was to follow and on the way to the Texel he was joined by the *Isis* and the *Powerful* (74). By then the Dutch fleet was being shadowed by a small squadron under Captain Trollope of the *Russell*. With him were the *Adamant* and two frigates. Early on 11 October the North Sea Squadron joined this observation force and, with the enemy strung out in a line, Duncan gave the order to prepare for battle. Eager to engage the Dutch ships before they reached the safety of the shoal water Duncan changed course and directed his ships to bear down on the enemy, following this with a signal to engage them on arrival. With no time to form a line the British squadron broke into two groups. Leading one of them, in his flagship *Venerable*, Duncan

15. The Battle of Camperdown, 11 October 1797. Duncan's flagship Venerable is depicted defeating the Dutch flagship Vrieheid.

drove into the Dutch van, while Onslow in the *Monarch* led the other group in an assault on the outnumbered enemy rear. The fighting was fierce, but the British sailors' superior seamanship and skill in heavy weather gunnery soon began to tell and eventually the Dutch were forced to capitulate.

 The Battle of Camperdown, as the action became known, was an outstanding British victory, there never having been one like it where the opposing forces were more or less equal. More by luck than judgement it seems Duncan had won the day by ignoring convention and breaking through the enemy line. It was a lesson not lost on the recently promoted Rear-Admiral Nelson, who was to employ the same tactic at Trafalgar eight years later.[41] Once

16. The surrender of Admiral de Winter to Admiral Duncan on board the Venerable after Camperdown. The figure standing behind Duncan's right arm is George Patterson, the flagship's master, who a year later became the Master Attendant at Yarmouth.

Admiral De Winter had surrendered his sword Duncan wrote to the Admiralty informing their Lordships of his triumph, entrusting the delivery of the letter to Lieutenant Brodie of the *Rose* cutter.[42] The news of this morale boosting success sparked an outbreak of national rejoicing, but back off the Dutch coast there was little time for celebration. For two and a half hours the opposing forces had battered each other, inflicting a devastating toll on both men and materials. At least 750 British and Dutch seamen had been killed and 1,250 wounded out of a total of 15,400 combatants. As far as the ships were concerned the Dutch, as was their custom, had concentrated their fire on the British hulls, filling them full of holes, whereas their opponents had focused on their enemy's masts and rigging, dismasting many in the process.[43] It was on this chaotic scene that Duncan had to impose a measure of order if he was to get his ships and their prizes safely back to England.

 After closing round the admiral's flagship, it was not until late morning the following day that the squadron and its prizes set sail, after a frenetic period of great exertion by all concerned. Musters had been taken, the dead consigned to the deep and the wounded attended to by overworked surgeons and their mates with, on some ships, special gun room platforms being constructed by the carpenters for that purpose. Prize crews had been placed on board the nine captured enemy warships and many Dutch prisoners had been transferred to their British counterparts. Several of these prizes were taking in so much water that their crews were constantly at the pumps, while carpenters made all manner of repairs to the splintered woodwork including, where necessary, the erection of jury masts. Sails had been replaced and the seamen were employed knotting and splicing the shattered rigging.[44] The *Ardent*, which had lost her captain, Richard Rundell Burgess, just 10 minutes into the action, had sustained more casualties and damage than any other ship and had to be taken in tow by the *Bedford*. The dismasted Dutch prizes were also under tow.

Throughout the day of the 13th the crippled combined fleet limped westward in breezy conditions, but after anchoring in the early evening the weather took a sharp turn for the worse and gale force winds started battering the vulnerable warships. On the 14th the squadron was in desperate straits, with masts being carried away and frantic pumping taking place as water surged on board the leaky ships. Such was the *Bedford's* distress that seven of her upper deck guns had to be jettisoned, but the main casualty was the Dutch prize *Delft*, being towed by the *Veteran*.[45] Filling with water she sank with the loss of some 200 of her crew.[46] The gale scattered the ships and when Duncan anchored near Orford Ness that evening, only Onslow's *Monarch*, the *Powerful*, *Lancaster* and the frigate *Beaulieu* were in sight. The following morning, with no other ships having arrived, he took on board the prisoners from the *Beaulieu* before sending her with the *Lancaster* to seek out and, if possible, assist the remainder of the squadron.[47] With this done at 10.30 he set sail for the Nore accompanied by the *Monarch* and *Powerful*. The three ships anchored there on the 20th, but the previous day Duncan had temporarily struck his flag and proceeded in a cutter to Margate, leaving Onslow in charge.[48]

It was not until the evening of the 15th that one by one most of the remaining ships of the squadron reached the Suffolk coast, anchoring in the vicinity of Sole Bay. In view of the disabled nature of the warships and their prizes, it had been Duncan's intention to take the whole squadron to the Nore, but he seems not to have communicated this to his captains before the gale scattered the squadron for at daybreak on the 16th they set sail for their home anchorage, the Yarmouth Roads.[49] Over the course of the morning the *Russell*, *Triumph* (with the *Hercules* prize), *Monmouth* (towing in the *Alkmaar*), *Bedford* (towing the *Ardent*), *Belliqueux*, and *Agincourt* anchored in the roadstead. At 5.30 p.m. they were joined by the *Veteran*. The following morning the *Lancaster* arrived and in the early evening the *Director* anchored with the *Gelykheid* prize. By then the *Wassenaar* prize had already anchored. On the afternoon of the 18th the *Montagu* joined them and the following morning the *Vryheid* and *Haarlem* prizes came in. Later that same day, the *Adamant*, having briefly been aground in the Cockle Gat was brought to anchor. The remaining ship-of-the-line of Duncan's squadron, the *Isis*, had headed for the Humber, coming to anchor in Grimsby Roads on the 25th with the *De Vries* prize in tow. The frigate *Endymion* and the prize *Jupiter* were already anchored there.[50]

News of Duncan's victory and the arrival of his battered ships and the prizes quickly spread and the townsfolk of Yarmouth were soon streaming across the Denes, some eager to witness the return of the men-of-war they had less than a week ago waved on their way, others apprehensive, for many seamen from the port had sailed with the squadron. Over the days that followed people travelled from miles around to see for themselves the victors and the vanquished of the battle, with the *Norwich Mercury* reporting that, 'Yarmouth, as may be supposed, has been thronged ever since the arrival of the fleet, and parties continue daily to arrive; the Bishop of Norwich, the Dean, and many other families of distinction in the county have been here.'[51]

To the various agents of the support base, however, the sorry sight developing in the Roads could only have been a cause for concern for there had been no forward planning for such an eventuality and some of them would inevitably be found wanting. With Duncan and Onslow elsewhere, command of the depleted squadron fell to the most senior captain present, Henry Trollope of the *Russell*, the man who before the battle had commanded the small force shadowing the Dutch fleet. Aware that his superiors would not be returning to the Roads in the foreseeable future he set about the urgent task of dealing with the wounded, both friend and foe, sending them ashore as quickly as he could, but he was far from well himself. On 19 October he wrote to the Admiralty asking for a month's leave, claiming that he had such violent pains in his head he was hardly able to write and as a result he was granted a week's absence. In terms of seniority command should then have passed to Captain John Inglis of the *Belliqueux*, but he had been wounded in the foot and pronounced unfit for duty, so on the 22nd the next in line, Captain John Knight of the *Montagu*, became commander-in-chief at Yarmouth.[52]

By then a Sick and Hurt Board commissioner had arrived to take charge of the wounded (more of this later), enabling Knight to focus his attention on getting the ships and prizes ready for sea. The carpenters and others had done enough to get them into the Roads, but now, with assistance from the naval storekeeper, hulls, masts and rigging were further repaired. In addition all manner of victualling supplies were sent aboard. Priority was given to the British men-of-war, but by the 23 October it was possible to attend to the prizes. The Dutch crewmen were removed, being replaced by prize crews. As early as the 16th the Admiralty had chosen the *Bedford*, *Triumph*, *Montagu* and *Powerful* to transport the Dutch prisoners of war to Spithead and those at Yarmouth were transferred to the first three of those named.[53] Between the 25 and 28 October most of the ships set sail for one Royal Dockyard or another. The three ships designated to take prisoners of war set out for Spithead, the *Russell* was ordered to Plymouth, while the *Lancaster*, *Ardent*, *Monmouth*, *Belliqueux*, *Adamant* and *Director* headed for the Nore with the prizes *Hercules*, *Alkmaar*, *Wassenaar*, *Haarlem* and *Vryheid*. They were accompanied by the frigate *Circe* bringing the *Gelykheid*. On the 15 November the *Veteran* and the *Agincourt* set off for the Nore, the latter without her captain, John Williamson, for on the 26 October he had been arrested pending court martial for disobeying signals, not going into action, and cowardice.[54] With the departure of the last of the Camperdown ships the crisis was largely over although the lingering presence in the town of a great number of wounded men from both sides of the conflict, served as a vivid reminder of what had just occurred. The competence of the Yarmouth support base had been rigorously tested and while it had coped well enough, the experience had highlighted the need for improvements in service delivery especially in relation to medical care and the provision of naval stores.

3.

The Helder, Copenhagen and Peace 1798-1802

Although outstanding, Camperdown was not a decisive victory for seven of the Dutch ships-of-the-line had managed to escape into the Texel. Duncan struck his flag again on 1 November and shortly afterwards Onslow was also granted leave.[1] With both men in London and the North Sea Squadron out of action, alternative arrangements had to be made to monitor the Dutch anchorage. The man chosen as commodore to carry out the work was Captain Robert M'Douall with a squadron comprising the ships-of-the-line *Ganges*, *Agamemnon*, *Standard*, and *Repulse*, the frigates *Beaulieu* and *Hydra* and the sloops *Martin* and *Albatross*.[2] With this force he kept a close eye on the Texel and performed the port duties as the senior naval officer at Yarmouth.

After the momentous events of the previous year 1798 was a relatively quiet one for the North Sea Naval Station. Onslow returned to Yarmouth in early March, raising his flag on the *Monarch*, but he did not relieve M'Douall off the Texel until late April, shortly after the commodore had taken 26 Dutch fishing boats and sent them into Yarmouth harbour, after burning a further seven.[3] But for a short break in May, Onslow remained on Texel watch until relieved by Duncan in mid-August, in his newly built flagship *Kent* (74). The admiral had been unwell and had spent his leave recuperating in Edinburgh and London before arriving back in Yarmouth on 17 July.[4] He was a well-liked man in the town and his return had been eagerly awaited. In June the Yarmouth correspondent of the *Norwich Mercury* had reported that, 'Admiral Duncan is daily expected to hoist his flag on board the *Kent*; she is said to be the most beautiful ship ever seen in these Roads. The pleasure anticipated of seeing the gallant and venerable Admiral again here, is hardly to be described; for long before the ever memorable 11th of October he was much esteemed for his remarkable affability, which many of the common sailors here can witness. When on shore, nothing was more common than to see him, very early in the morning, with a spying glass in his hand, talking with every person he could make communicative, on the walls of the town; and with that ease and goodness of soul, that in the language of Shakespeare, he always appeared "full of the milk of human kindness".'[5]

This was followed in August with a further insight into his popularity, it being reported that, 'In consequence of a general invitation given last week by Admiral Lord Duncan, to all the fashionable visitors and residents at Yarmouth for three days, the *Kent* (a fine new ship, on board which the Admirals' flag was flying)was honoured by numerous parties. On Wednesday the Admiral accompanied a large party from the Jetty himself. On his going on board, the yards were instantly manned which was followed by every King's ship in the Roads. A salute of 13 guns was fired by the *Kent*, and three cheers given by the crew, which was returned by the other ships. On Thursday the company was still more numerous. Each day the elegant Miss Duncan honoured the party and the dance with her company, which was allowed to exhibit more beauty and fashion than have been seen at Yarmouth upon any similar occasion. A handsome cold collation was provided, and the company returned highly gratified with the hospitality and novelty of the treat.'[6]

Duncan and Onslow exchanged places again in mid-September, but the vice-admiral was unwell and like his predecessor, Macbride, succumbed to the rigours of the service. On 21 November he asked for, and was granted leave.[7] On 6 December Duncan also applied for leave and was told this would be granted once a replacement had been found. This proved to be Vice-Admiral Archibald Dickson who, having been appointed on 10 December, immediately travelled to Yarmouth.[8] In the meantime M'Douall returned to the Dutch coast with an enlarged force in order to intercept four Dutch ships-of-the-line and a frigate, said to be preparing to sail from Hellevoetsluis.[9]

That mixed blessing, the Russian warships, returned to the North Sea in the second half of 1798, following a change of heart by Tsar Paul. What was referred to as the 1st Division, under Vice-Admiral Mackaroff, joined the squadron watching the Texel, on 15 July, having convoyed British merchant ships thus far. The 2nd Division, under Rear-Admiral Tate, arrived at the Nore in late August and a frigate and five ships, under Vice-Admiral Kartzoff, anchored in the Yarmouth Roads in late November. Combined, these reinforcements amounted to 18 warships.[10] While they enabled Duncan to better rotate his forces they still presented him with the challenges experienced on their earlier tour of duty, especially in relation to accepting orders. On 20 August Onslow informed the Admiralty that he had spotted Tate's ships passing by Yarmouth, heading towards the Nore, and had sent the *Fox* cutter with orders for him to return to the Roads and place himself under his direction. The *Fox* caught up with the Russians in Hollesley Bay and delivered the order, but as soon as the tide was suitable the uncooperative Tate weighed anchor and continued on his way to the Nore, prompting Onslow to exclaim that his 'conduct astonishes me.'[11] While the Russians had been away, the servicing facilities at Yarmouth had been strengthened sufficiently for their needs to be satisfied there, enabling Tate and his squadron to be based in the Roads.

For the first four months of 1799 Duncan spent his time recuperating in Edinburgh, leaving Dickson in command of the North Sea Squadron in Yarmouth Roads. A skeleton force watched the Texel while M'Douall and his small squadron kept a close eye on Hellevoetsluis and its environs. In early May Dickson anchored off the Texel with the Camperdown veterans *Monarch*, *Veteran*, *Belliqueux* and *Ardent* where he was joined by M'Douall. Shortly afterwards Duncan returned to London from Scotland and, 'being at a loss to know where the Ships of the North Sea Fleet are at present,' requested from the Admiralty a copy of Dickson's last disposition return. It listed 15 ships-of-the-line (of which 10 were off the Texel), 10 frigates, 14 sloops, 14 armed vessels and 11 cutters, giving a total of 64.[12] On 2 June he arrived in Yarmouth Roads and hoisted his flag on the *Kent*, his health 'perfectly restored.'[13] Later in the month he was told in all secrecy that the second-in-command of the Dutch Texel Fleet, Van Braam, was prepared to bring his warships over to the British side provided he and his men were treated as allies. On the basis that knowledge of this plan should pass through as few hands as possible, Duncan was ordered to relieve Dickson off the Texel, which he did on 1 July, but Dickson did not return to the Yarmouth Roads until the 17th.[14] The defection did not take place but the future of the Dutch fleet was soon to become part of a much larger picture. Heartened by intelligence that the Dutch were ready to rise against their rulers in an Orangist counter revolution, on 22 June Pitt's government concluded a treaty with Russia for a combined invasion of the Batavian Republic as a diversion to assist the Austro/Russian armies of the Second Coalition operating in northern Italy, Switzerland, and Southern Germany. General Sir Ralph Abercromby was chosen to command the land forces and responsibility for all seafaring matters was given to Vice-Admiral Andrew Mitchell, who on 25 July was directed to hoist his flag on the *Isis*.[15]

In July and August an expedition force was assembled in Kent. In connection with this venture, on the 5 August, 10 revenue cutters arrived in Yarmouth Roads to transport the 17th Regiment of Foot, which was due to march in from Norwich. The soldiers duly arrived the following day, but on the 7th, in response to an order from the commanding officer at Norwich, they marched back again, leaving the cutters with a wasted journey.[16] Unfortunately it was to be a portent of what was to come. On 13 August Mitchell's flotilla set sail from the East Kent ports, laden with 13,258 'souls', comprising cavalry, infantry, staff and 750 women.[17] With no clear instruction where to land Abercromby decided to invade the Helder peninsula. This was easier said than done, however, for the fleet was soon engulfed in a series of violent westerly gales. It was not until the 27th that the troops began to disembark near Callantsoog under the protection of the guns of the fleet. The landing was eventually opposed by the Batavian forces, but these were soon driven off. The following day Major-General John Moore captured Den Helder with its naval yard, 97 guns and a large quantity of naval stores. In addition 13 warships (largely old and dismantled), three Indiamen and a sheer hulk were taken in the Nieuwe Diep.

Throughout July and August Duncan and the North Sea Squadron remained off the Texel, but being a full admiral he out-ranked Mitchell. Aware of the sensitivity of the situation the Lords Commissioners kept Duncan informed of their orders to Mitchell and advised him that

17. British troops landing on the Dutch coast between Petten and Callantsoog, just south of Den Helder, under the covering fire of Vice-Admiral Mitchell's squadron, 27 August 1799.

he was to take the vice-admiral under his command. Duncan, however, could read between the lines and Mitchell was pleased to report to the Admiralty that, 'his Lordship has, in the most handsome manner left the whole management and Direction of the Expedition to me, proposing not to interfere unless circumstances should render it necessary.' Duncan also reinforced the newly arrived force with nine warships from his own squadron.[18]

At the time of the invasion a major part of the Dutch squadron under Vice-Admiral Samuel Story, a Camperdown veteran, had retreated into the Vlieter Channel, removing the navigation markers as they went. On the 30th, after replacing the buoys, Mitchell's warships, in line-of-battle, entered the Mars Diep and demanded the surrender of the Dutch squadron in the name of the Prince of Orange. Fearing his largely Orangist crews would mutiny rather than fight Story capitulated. In all 12 warships were handed over, five of which had been at Camperdown. In a stroke the Dutch navy ceased to be an effective fighting force and Duncan's main objective, entrusted to him four years earlier, had been achieved.[19] It was, however, to be the only success of the campaign. Considering the job done Duncan released Mitchell from being under his orders and sailed for the Yarmouth Roads, arriving there on 2 September, but 'being at present much indisposed' he relinquished the port duties to Dickson. He was to recover, but never went to sea again.[20]

18. Rear-Admiral Samuel Story, Commander-in-chief of the Dutch Texel Squadron in August 1799.

19. Vice-Admiral Andrew Mitchell, Commander-in-chief of the British naval forces during the Helder campaign.

Back on the Helder things did not go well, despite a promising start. On 10 September Abercromby won an action at Zyper Sluis and shortly afterwards 33,000 reinforcements arrived, 12,000 of them Russians. With them came the Duke of York, as commander-in-chief, for it was thought a man of his status was necessary to ensure the Russians obeyed orders. On the 7th a substantial number of these Russians had arrived in Yarmouth Roads. They sailed a week later but not before taking on provisions and sending their sick ashore.[21] When all the troops had arrived the Duke of York had close on 50,000 men but the expedition was ill prepared and there was no Dutch uprising.[22] As he delayed his advance in order to organise his forces so the enemy strengthened their position and on the 19th defeated the allies at the battle of Bergen. The Anglo-Russians won the next encounter, at Egmont-op-Zee, on 2 October, but were defeated at Castricum on the 6th, forcing them to retreat behind the embankments of the Zype polder. With winter approaching and his position seemingly hopeless, on 18 October the Duke concluded a peace treaty with the Franco-Batavians, called the Convention of Alkmaar, by which, amongst other things, he was to remove all the British and Russian soldiers from Dutch soil by the 30 November.

In charge of the seaborne transportation requirements of the expedition was Captain Daniel Woodriff, the Transport Board's agent at the Norman Cross prisoner of war camp. Seconded for the role he established himself in the Nieuwe Diep, in the Dutch ship *Gouda*. Once it became clear there was going to be a rapid evacuation he gave Mitchell a list of transports under his orders and their proposed use. There were nearly 150 of them, mostly intended as troop carriers, but some were earmarked for the sick and wounded, ordnance, horses, women and prisoners of war. Others were to sail to the Elbe and Weser for oats and meal, while 17 were earmarked to sail for Harwich with 1,200 wounded British soldiers and 11 for Yarmouth, with sick and wounded Russian soldiers.[23] With Woodriff ready with his transports the Admiralty sent Duncan secret orders to place Dickson in charge of the evacuation. It was known that Duncan was too ill to carry out the task, but in his deputy he had a proven logistician with a good eye for detail who was perfectly able to fulfil such a challenging brief.[24] Dickson arrived at the Helder on 23 October and hoisted his flag on the frigate *Juno*. That same day he took Mitchell and his squadron under his orders and placed Captain Lawford of the *Romney* in charge of the actual embarkation process, assisted by Captains Sparks and Daniels. While transports formed the backbone of the evacuation fleet, many warships were employed, including ships from the North Sea Squadron.[25] Of the healthy British soldiers 20,000 were sent to Yarmouth and 6,500 to Ramsgate, Margate and the Nore, from whence they were forwarded to their regiments. The fit Russians amounted to just over 14,000 men and rather than inflict such a large number on one or more locality they were dispatched to the Channel Islands, via the Downs and Ramsgate. Nearly 1,000 Dutch volunteers for the Prince of Orange were also sent to the Nore and the Downs and 4,500 horses to Ramsgate.[26] With the embarkation complete, on 17 November Dickson set sail for the Yarmouth Roads, leaving Lawford in charge of completing the task. In the space of 25 days he had embarked nearly 42,000 men, 4,500 horses, and all the army's stores. Little wonder the Admiralty were 'very much satisfied with his zealous exertions & those of the Officers & Men employed under him.'[27]

For the third time in four years the townsfolk of Yarmouth were obliged to accept a sudden influx of fighting men, this time in much greater numbers than before. The British soldiers were quickly dispersed, but not before leaving behind a number of sick, for whom a military hospital was established. This also catered for the Russian wounded, the last of whom did not vacate the town until many months later. On 3 November, halfway through the embarkation process, the Duke of York and his suite arrived at Yarmouth in the *Juno*, Dickson having transferred his flag to the *Hecla* bomb to accommodate him. He was given a royal salute by the ships in the Roads and Duncan, together with an 'immence crowd of spectators', was there to receive him, the horses were removed from his waiting carriage, and he was hauled to the Admiral's lodgings, 'amidst loud loud and repeated acclamations.' At 12 o'clock he set out from the Bear Inn for Norwich. His rapturous welcome ignored the fact that he had once more failed in the Netherlands.[28]

With the surrender of the remainder of the enemy's Texel Fleet and the onset of winter, only a small naval force was sent to watch the Dutch Coast, with Hellevoet, where there were still seven enemy ships-of-the-line and several smaller warships, becoming the main focus of attention.[29] Duncan and Dickson remained together at Yarmouth until 10 April 1800 when the admiral struck his flag and proceeded to London. Indomitable as his spirit was he could not ignore the ill health that continued to plague him. He had withstood the rigours of the service better than most of his contemporaries, but being a wealthy man with estates in Scotland and being of the opinion that the North Sea no longer needed a squadron, he decided it was time to retire from active naval service.[30] Acceding to his wishes, the Admiralty formalised matters on the 26 April.[31] The same day Dickson was promoted to the North Sea command, a position he was to hold until the end of the French Revolutionary War.[32]

***

While Dickson was a good organiser he was not an enthusiastic sea officer. With the Dutch navy largely dealt with he was probably looking forward to a quiet time, carrying out little more than port duties, but it was not to be for as the year wore on so the Baltic began to emerge as a theatre of war, which had implications for the naval support base. On 25 July 1800 the Danish frigate *Freya* was sailing close to the Goodwin Sands, escorting six Danish merchantmen, when she was spotted by three British frigates. Their commander, Captain Thomas Baker of the *Nemesis*, hailed Captain Krabbe of the *Freya* to tell him he was sending a boat to board the merchantmen. The Dane replied that he would fire on any such boat. With Baker convinced right was on his side he sent the boat and it was duly fired upon. After a short action in which two Danes were killed and several wounded the Danish frigate and her charges were captured and taken to the Downs. Ever aware of the importance of the Baltic shipbuilding and repair materials to the British war effort the government decided to send Lord Whitworth to Copenhagen to try to diffuse the situation and Dickson, with a squadron of 20 ships and vessels, was to assist him with a not too subtle show of force.[33]

Dickson hoisted his flag on board the *Monarch* and the squadron left the Yarmouth Roads on 9 August. After receiving intelligence about the Danish Fleet, on the 15th he entered the Cattegat and eventually anchored in Elsinore Roads to perform his intimidatory role. On the 29th a convention was agreed and Dickson lost little time in making the Admiralty aware of the part he had played, writing on the 30th, 'that in consequence of the several movements, made by the Squadron by way of demonstration, the Negotiation has been happily closed, and in such a manner I trust, as will ensure to His Majesty, ample satisfaction for the past, and security for the future Conduct of the Court of Denmark.'[34] With this misplaced optimism Dickson set sail on 8 September and arrived back in the Yarmouth Roads on the 13th.[35] On the 25th he was given the Freedom of the Borough, 'as a mark of respect for his resolute conduct in defending the Rights of his Country, and also for the benefits the Trade of Yarmouth has received since he has had the command of the North Sea Fleet.'[36]

In November 1800 Horatio Nelson, arrived in the town. It was a chance visit brought about by his need, after an eventful two years in the Mediterranean, to return to England, via the safest sea route open to him, that from Cuxhaven to Yarmouth. On 1 October 1798 the brig-sloop *Kite* had arrived in the Roads carrying dispatches from his Lordship to the Admiralty concerning his recent victory at the Battle of the Nile (1 August). Since then he had been feted by the King and Queen of Naples and Sicily, became involved in Neapolitan politics and entered into a passionate relationship with Lady Emma Hamilton, the wife of the British ambassador, Sir William Hamilton. Both Nelson and Hamilton had been recalled and they and their suite had travelled overland from Vienna, before taking passage on the *King George* packet, as no warship was made available to them.

Landing at Gorleston on the 6th Nelson and his party boarded a coach and set off for Yarmouth, but news of his coming travelled fast and at the bridge over the Yare, 'the populace took the horses from the carriage, and drew it to the Wrestlers Inn, on Church Plain amidst the loudest acclamations of joy and attachment.'[37] Appearing at an open first floor window of the inn Nelson exclaimed to the idolising crowd that had quickly gathered, 'I am myself a Norfolk man, and I glory in being so.'[38] Shortly afterwards Vice-Admiral Dickson, Captain James Mosse of the *Monarch* and the Reverend Turner, came to pay their respects and at 2 o'clock, the Mayor and the Corporation arrived to present his lordship with the Freedom of the Borough. As he administered the Freeman's oath, Mr Watson, the town clerk, noticed that Nelson had placed his left hand on the bible and without thinking said, "your right hand, my Lord," to which Nelson replied "That is at Teneriffe!".[39] That evening at the Wrestlers, with

20. Vice-Admiral Nelson addressing the crowd from a first floor window of the Wrestlers Inn on returning from the Continent, 6 November 1800. It was then he exclaimed, 'I am myself a Norfolk man and I glory in being so'.

the town in celebration mood, his lordship entertained Captain Barker (the Mayor) and his company of volunteer infantry, talking warmly about the Battle of the Nile, his captains in that action and the Earl St Vincent, who had appointed him to his command. The following morning he and his party attended divine service at the parish church, entering to the strains of "See the conquering hero comes!".[40] Afterwards he took lunch at the Mayor's house before around 3 o'clock leaving for London. He was escorted as far as Lowestoft by the Yarmouth Volunteer Cavalry, commanded by Lieutenant William Palgrave, unaware that he would shortly be returning to the town on active service, for the country's relationship with the Baltic States was fast deteriorating.[41]

On the face of it relations between Britain and those countries (Russia, Denmark, Sweden and Prussia) were cordial enough, founded as they were on the mutual self-interest of trade and varying degrees of hostility towards France. Britain relied on imports from them, especially corn and shipbuilding materials (iron, hemp, pitch, tar, oak, fir, masts, and yards). But France and her allies also required access to these vital supplies, something the Royal Navy was instructed to deny them. To carry out their orders British warships stopped and searched neutral vessels wherever they found them, looking for cargoes destined for enemy ports or belonging to enemy owners. In response the masters of such vessels went to great lengths to falsify documentation, provoking even closer examination by the navy's North Sea cruisers. Unsurprisingly this high-handed interference engendered a simmering resentment, which the *Freya* incident had brought to a head.

Dickson's show of force at the entrance to the Baltic had also angered the Tsar, prompting him in September to mobilise his armed forces and sequestrate all British property in his domain. Although he lifted this edict three weeks later, when news reached him that Britain had retaken Malta without Russian involvement, he placed an embargo on all British shipping in Russian ports. This affected some 200 vessels and in the process their crews were ill-treated. Furthermore on 16 December he signed a defensive pact with Sweden, Denmark and Prussia, known as the 'League of Armed Neutrality'. Thereafter British merchant vessels were embargoed throughout the Baltic and in case there was any doubt about the League's intentions Hanover was occupied, representing a direct attack on the British Crown. To the British government these hostile acts removed all pretence of neutrality and could only give comfort to the French. The embargo threatened both the supply of grain, at a time when there were food riots in the country, and the procurement of naval stores. If diplomacy failed there could be only one answer, a major naval offensive.[42]

Determined to force the issue, in January 1801, a like for like embargo was placed on all Russian, Danish and Swedish vessels arriving in British ports, and all ships and vessels of every description belonging to the neutral powers found at sea were to be seized. Furthermore all Danish and Swedish seamen serving in the navy were discharged.[43] At the same time the Admiralty began assembling a Baltic Fleet and considering who should be its commander-in-chief. Dickson with the North Sea Squadron had handled his part in the *Freya* incident in a competent enough fashion, but the crisis had escalated beyond his rank, for if the navies of the Baltic states were to unite they would be able to field a combined fleet of over 40 ships-of-the-line, although it has to be said that this was thought extremely unlikely as the Russian ships were always ice bound until March. In the event around 50 ships and vessels were ordered to assemble in the Yarmouth Roads, under the command of Admiral Sir Hyde Parker with, as his second-in-command, Vice-Admiral Lord Nelson. They were to be assisted by Rear-Admirals Totty and Graves.[44]

Sir Hyde was a curious choice. His early career was promising enough. In 1776 he had distinguished himself at New York by breaking through the rebels defences on the North River, the action for which he was knighted. In 1781 he was briefly with the North Sea Squadron and was present at the inconclusive Battle of the Dogger Bank. But more recently he had spent four years as commander-in-chief in the West Indies where he was reported to have made over £200,000 in prize money without having to lift a finger. On returning to England in September 1800 he had been appointed second-in-command to Lord St. Vincent in the Channel Fleet and in December that year the 61 year old had married Francis the 18 year old daughter of Sir Richard Onslow, herself no stranger to Yarmouth.[45] Aware that Sir Hyde was little more than a safe pair of hands, the Admiralty appointed Nelson, the 'Hero of Nile,' to carry out whatever fighting might be required. Nelson, however, was every admiral's worst nightmare as a second-in-command; a well-connected predatory genius who successfully disobeyed orders and who was also an incorrigible self-publicist. Sir Hyde would have been only too aware that if he failed the blame would be his, but if he succeeded his popular subordinate would like as not be given the credit. It was not the basis for a good working relationship.

Sir Hyde was formally appointed commander-in-chief of a squadron, 'to be employed on a particular Service' on 31 January 1801.[46] He was on leave at the time, introducing his new wife to London society, with little desire to make haste to sea. On 17 February he received details of the officers and ships he was to command and issued them with orders the following day.[47] On the 27th he was directed by the Admiralty, 'to repair forthwith to North Yarmouth,' where he was to hoist his flag 'on board such one of H M Ships in those Roads as you may

21. Admiral Sir Hyde Parker, Commander-in-chief of the fleet assembled to break up the 'Armed Neutrality of the North'.

22. Vice-Admiral Nelson. He sat for this portrait by local artist Matthew Keymer while waiting to set sail for Copenhagen.

think proper until the arrival of the *London*.' He was also told to remain there until further orders.[48] As protocol demanded he was directed to take Vice-Admiral Dickson under his command together with the ships and vessels of the North Sea Squadron.[49] Arriving at Yarmouth on 28th he ordered his flag to be hoisted on board the *Ardent* then took lodgings with his wife at the Wrestlers where he was to remain until he sailed for Danish waters. Over the next ten days he busied himself with the paperwork and orders necessary to get the squadron to sea, including an order for his ships to complete their provisions to five months as he anticipated a lengthy stay in the Baltic.[50] On the 2 March he returned to Dickson the command of the North Sea Squadron, which was still watching the Dutch coast and protecting trade.[51]

23. The Wrestlers Inn, Yarmouth. Here Hyde Parker and Nelson stayed as did many other notables who had business in the town.

Expecting the preparations to take some time and with Rear-Admirals Graves and Totty not yet arrived, Sir Hyde allowed a ball to be arranged for his wife, to take place on Friday the 13th, even then an inauspicious date. There had never been so many warships in the Roads at any one time and the town became thronged with visitors eager to witness the preparations, even more so after the 6th when Nelson arrived from Spithead in his flagship *St. George* (98), the first three-decker ever to anchor there.[52] Bright and early the next morning Nelson, accompanied by Lieutenant-Colonel Stewart, who was to command the troops on the expedition, and Captain Thomas Hardy, called on Sir Hyde at the Wrestlers. To his surprise, although he was greeted politely enough, Sir Hyde soon departed to rejoin his wife in their suite, without there having been any mention of the forthcoming expedition, no word of the date the squadron would sail, nor any indication as to how the admiral intended to attack the Danes.[53] In fairness to Sir Hyde his behaviour can be interpreted as little more than an extreme example of the high command style of the day which relied on retaining rather than sharing information, but it can equally be seen as his way of trying to keep his, second-in-command at arm's length. Whatever his motivation it was to prove an unwise course of action, given Nelson's connections in high places. Back in his cabin on the *St. George* Nelson wrote to Sir Thomas Troubridge, an old naval colleague, who had recently become a member of the Admiralty Board, complaining about Sir Hyde's lethargy, but cautioning his friend not to, 'say a word of it to Lord St Vincent for he may think me very impertinent in endeavouring to dive into the plans of my C-in-C.'[54] Nelson knew full-well that this condition would be ignored, but by then the Admiralty was growing increasingly concerned that Sir Hyde had not sailed and the Lords Commissioners had also heard about the ball. On the evening of the 9th the *London* arrived in the Roads and on the following day she became Sir Hyde's flagship. Shortly afterwards he received strongly worded orders to proceed to sea the moment the wind would permit, without waiting for the remainder of his squadron to join him.'[55] Nelson's letter had done the trick, but it took a private letter from Earl St. Vincent to finally galvanise Sir Hyde into action. Cancelling the ball and sending his wife back to London he made the signal for all officers to return to their ships and prepare for sailing. As before Camperdown the signal caught many unawares, but nevertheless on the 11 March Sir Hyde went aboard the *London* (98) and on the following afternoon the crowd that had gathered on the beach watched as one by one the warships worked their way out through the St. Nicholas Gat and headed northward.[56]

Leaving before his rear-admirals had arrived, however, was to have tragic consequences. As they were soon expected Sir Hyde left orders at Yarmouth for them to join him off the Skaw.[57] The day after the squadron sailed Rear-Admiral Graves arrived from the Downs in the *Defiance* and was duly sent on his way. In the evening of the 14th Rear-Admiral Totty put in from the Nore, in the *Invincible* (74). On the morning of the 16th he too sailed to join the squadron, but instead of leaving via the St. Nicholas Gat the warship's pilot, despite objections from her officers, took her northward, through the Cockle Gat. Shortly after 2 p.m. she struck, and became stranded on the Hammond's Knoll sandbank.[58] After taking a battering for two hours her mizen mast fell overboard and her mainmast was immediately cut away to lighten the ship. Driven over the sandbank into deeper water she lost her rudder and became unmanageable before stranding again. By then a fishing boat from Yarmouth had hove to prompting the launch of two boats from the stricken warship, one of them containing Totty, the purser, four midshipmen and ten seamen. Both boats reached the smack safely. As darkness fell the seas were such that the smack could not get near the casualty, forcing her to anchor for the night. The following morning Totty took control of the smack, but was unable to get close to the *Invincible* and had to watch as she came off the sandbank and began to sink. Her captain, John Rennie, gave the order to hoist out the launch enabling another 70 men to be saved, but when the ship sank 400 men were still on board, nearly all of whom perished. This toll was more than the number of British sailors killed in the subsequent Battle of Copenhagen.[59]

Unlike Camperdown the Battle of Copenhagen was not a 'Yarmouth victory'. The successful force had been assembled in the Roads, but it was not the regular North Sea Squadron, so familiar to the townsfolk.[60] Sir Hyde's orders were to 'persuade' the Danes to leave the 'Northern Convention', either by diplomacy or by direct action, then to move on to deal with the Russians. In the event diplomacy failed and Nelson persuaded the over cautious Sir Hyde to let him attack the Danish fleet with ten ships of the line. The battle took place on 2 April 1801 and after three fierce hours of fighting Nelson received the submission of sufficient Danish ships to issue an ultimatum that he would burn his prizes without saving their crews if a ceasefire did not ensue. One was arranged and this quickly became a 14 week truce.[61] With his rear secure Sir Hyde led his squadron into the Baltic and opened negotiations with the Swedes, but on 23 April he heard that the Tsar had been assassinated. Unsure what to do he returned to the Danish coast where he received orders to hand over his command to Nelson and return home. Having done so he set sail for Yarmouth in the frigate *Blanche*.[62] Nelson immediately set off to ensure that the Russian fleet no longer posed a threat, but with the new Tsar, Alexander, refusing to negotiate under duress, the vice-admiral withdrew and two days later the Russian and Swedish crowns lifted their trade embargos and by so doing effectively dissolved the League of Armed Neutrality.[63] After the Battle all save one of the

24. Nelson writing his ultimatum to the Crown Prince of Denmark, on board his flagship Elephant, in the latter stages of the Battle of Copenhagen.

captured Danish warships were destroyed. There was to be no triumphant, prize laden, return to the Yarmouth Roads by the victorious British warships on this occasion. The urgent task of getting the wounded back home for proper medical treatment was entrusted to Captain William Bligh of the *Monarch*. To assist him he was given the *Isis* and the spared prize, *Holstein*, which was quickly converted into a hospital-ship to transport the wounded men, many of whom were landed at Yarmouth.[64] In June Vice-Admiral Charles Pole replaced Nelson in the Baltic and the 'victor of Copenhagen' sailed for England in the brig-sloop *Kite*, arriving at Yarmouth on the 29th. After a short but lively time in the town he set off for

London, escorted as before by the Yarmouth Volunteer Cavalry. He was never to return.[65]

While matters were being resolved in the Baltic a resurgent France was gathering a flotilla of vessels at Boulogne in order to invade England. This prompted the Admiralty to press Dickson to increase his personal involvement in watching the Dutch ports, a circumstance seemingly not to his taste after spending most of the previous year and a half ashore at Yarmouth. Throughout May, June and most of July he was constantly to and fro between the Roads and the Dutch coast, with the Admiralty wanting to know the reason why if he failed to sail.[66] With the fear of invasion rapidly returning, on 24 July, Nelson was appointed to command a naval force stationed between Orford Ness and Beachy Head, to help allay the public's fears and to take the fight to the enemy (which he did on 15 August with disastrous effect). As a result an area of sea and the port of Harwich were removed from the North Sea Naval Station and assigned to Nelson.[67] Just prior to this Dickson's ability to watch the Dutch was strengthened by the appointment of Rear-Admiral Sir Thomas Graves and Vice-Admiral Christopher Parker to his command.[68] Graves arrived from the Baltic on 19 July in the *Defiance* with 17 ships and vessels as reinforcements for the North Sea Squadron. The following day he sailed to join Dickson off Goree, enabling the admiral to return to Yarmouth.[69] On the 29 July Parker in the *Princess of Orange* (74) sailed for the Dutch coast in response to an Admiralty directive that two admirals should be at sea with the squadron at all times, but Parker was a sick man and on the 18 August he landed at Yarmouth and set off for London.[70] After a period of leave he tried to return to Yarmouth, but finding he was still not well enough, on 17 September, he resigned his command. By then peace was being negotiated so he was not replaced.[71]

In March 1801 Henry Addington became Prime Minister and one of the first actions he and his government decided to carry out was to bring the war to a close.[72] Fighting continued while negotiations took place, but on 1 October Britain and France signed the Preliminaries of Peace. When two days later news of this break-through reached Yarmouth there was a 'general burst of joy,' bells were rung and guns fired. A circular was immediately issued by the Mayor and magistrates recommending that 'the inhabitants of this Borough illuminate on Monday next.' As this was only two days away it is not surprising that the outcome was subsequently described as, 'as brilliant as could be expected on so short notice, it being impossible to prepare appropriate transparencies. But few could be displayed nevertheless the alacrity evinced by the inhabitants, was such as to manifest the unfeigned satisfaction, which the happy termination of our long and arduous contest must inspire.'[73]

With peace seemingly secured, orders were given for some early cost cutting measures. In November the Yarmouth column of the *Norwich Mercury* reported that, 'We are sorry to find the *Irresistible*, one of the finest ships in the service, commanded by Captain Bligh, is ordered round to Torbay, and not to return here again, which we think is the first breaking up of our North Sea Fleet.'[74] On the 25 March 1802 the Treaty of Amiens formally ended the war and with it came orders for a full demobilization, including the contraction of the navy to its peacetime establishment.[75] For the North Sea command and its Yarmouth support base this meant near total dismantlement, a process carried out in two phases. The first comprised the discharge of the naval personnel and departure of the warships; the second the closure of the civilian run services, which involved the removal of stores and the disposal of most of the fixed infrastructure.

On 1 April Dickson was informed by the Admiralty that once there was room his ships were to be sent to a King's port to be paid off and on the 6 April Rear-Admiral Graves was discharged.[76] Three weeks later Dickson was directed to reduce the complements of his frigates and other vessels, discharging those least fit for service first. He was to send the seamen so discharged to Sheerness to be paid and the marines to Chatham.[77] Before there was time to fully implement this order, however, on the 26th he was directed to proceed with all his remaining two decked ships to Gillingham Reach or to strike his flag at Yarmouth. Choosing the latter course of action he ordered Captain Cobb of the *Princess of Orange* to take the *Veteran* and *Monarch* to the Medway and on the 28th he left town, taking with him a glowing testimonial from the merchants and magistrates.[78] In turn he wrote to the Admiralty to express his appreciation of the shore based officers and officials who had served or worked with him.[79] With no naval officer remaining to relay orders he gave Robert Warmington, the Navy Board's agent, the responsibility of delivering to the captains of the absent frigate *Ariadne* and the ship-sloops *Lynx* and *Driver* the orders requiring them to reduce their complements.[80]

The date chosen locally for reading 'his Majesty's Proclamation of Peace' was 5 May, perhaps reflecting the fact that by the end of April the navy and the militia had left town. On that day the Mayor and Corporation, accompanied by the local volunteer corps, proceeded from the town hall to the bridge where, before a large crowd, the proclamation was read and the drawn sword, which preceded the procession, was symbolically sheathed. This ceremony was repeated at the church door, the market cross and outside the Mayor's house, to the accompaniment of 'God Save the King,' played by the bands of the Volunteer units. In the evening there was a more extensive illumination than that which had marked the first step in the peace process.[81] By the end of 1802 Yarmouth had returned to its pre-war role.

4.
The North Sea and Baltic Commands 1803-1814

The peace brought about by the Treaty of Amiens was generally met with euphoria by the British public. The First Consul of France, Napoleon Bonaparte, so recently demonised as a war-monger, was now praised as a peacemaker who had brought order to the chaos that was Revolutionary France. Everything French became fashionable, including visits to Paris by the British upper classes, especially those of the Whig persuasion.[1] But the peace was to last little more than a year and for much of that time the government was suspicious of Napoleon's intentions, a concern reflected in a precautionary request to Parliament, in December 1802, for funds to pay for 50,000 seamen, 20,000 more than the usual peacetime establishment.[2]

The terms of the peace treaty made clear who had actually won the war, for while the French were allowed to keep their Continental gains the British were obliged to return to their former French and Dutch masters the colonies they had seized. Emboldened by this perceived show of weakness Napoleon continued to pursue an expansionist policy, interfering in the affairs of Switzerland, annexing Piedmont and sending a large naval force to the Caribbean. In response Britain refused to return the strategic island of Malta to the Knights of St John.[3] Matters came to a head in March 1803 when Napoleon gave orders for Flushing to be made ready to receive a naval force to be called the 'Squadron of the North', which was to consist of ten 74-gun ships-of-the-line modelled on those of the Dutch. These ships were to be built in Flushing, Ostend and the French ports. Gun boats and flat bottomed craft were also to be constructed at the yards along the shores of the Schelde, the Weser and the Elbe. At the same time a troop laden fleet set sail for India.[4] Britain's response to this apparent duplicity came on 8 March in the form of a king's message stating that 'as very considerable military preparations are carrying on in the ports of France and Holland, [his Majesty] has judged it expedient to adopt additional measures of precaution for the security of his dominions.' The same day prime minister Addington asked parliament for permission to enlarge the militia and recruit more seamen as the navy was once more to be placed on a war footing.[5] On the 23 April the government gave Napoleon a final ultimatum to withdraw French forces from the Netherlands. With this not being heeded on the 18 May Britain formally declared war on France and the first phase of the Napoleonic Wars began.[6]

Soon after the declaration measures were set in train to re-establish the Yarmouth naval support base. A rendezvous for the impress service had already been opened and by the end of 1803 there was once more a naval store, hospital, prison, and a signal station link to the Nore. In addition a militia garrison had arrived and large numbers of sea fencibles had been raised at Yarmouth and along the adjacent coast. In the town itself the renewed threat of invasion revived the unease experienced in the previous war. Palmer recounts that, 'Many of the inhabitants [of Yarmouth] took lodgings in some of the inland towns for their wives and children, that they might escape the first ferocity of the invaders in case they effected a

25. Rear-Admiral Edward Thornbrough, 'Commanding Officer of his Majesty's ships at Yarmouth', 1803-4.

landing; for the license of the French soldiers over the peaceable inhabitants of conquered nations was well known.'[7]

As part of the 'additional measures,' on 12 March, Rear-Admiral Edward Thornbrough was appointed to a Downs based command, with a small force of frigates and gun vessels 'to hold themselves in constant readiness to put to Sea in case any circumstance should arise to require it.'[8] Thornbrough was no stranger to the North Sea having served there under Macbride and Duncan in the 1790's as captain of the *Robust*. Throughout March he remained in the Downs aboard a succession of flagships as the Admiralty built up his squadron, his captains being ordered to make good use of their time by pressing seamen from homeward bound merchantmen as part of the naval build up. By early April it was clear that hostilities would soon resume and he was ordered to cruise off Hellevoetsluis with a squadron of six ships and vessels to monitor the Dutch navy, which after Camperdown and the Helder campaign had been reduced to little more than seven ships-of-the-line and a few frigates. He arrived there on the 8th.[9]

When war was finally declared Thornbrough was considered insufficiently senior to have overall command in the North Sea. That responsibility was given to a reluctant Admiral Lord Keith. It was a role decided as early as November 1802, when Nelson was considered to be the best person to command in the Mediterranean. Being the senior man, and having held the latter command in the previous war, Keith naturally expected to do so in the present circumstances. Feeling snubbed he was furious at Nelson's impending appointment, but as Roger Knight observes, 'He [Nelson] had recently demonstrated that patience was not his strong suit his flair and judgement were of greater use in the Mediterranean. Keith's methodical personality was more suited to the defence of the Channel and the North Sea.'[10] On 17 May Keith was formally appointed 'commander-in-chief of his Majestys ships Vessels employed and to be employed in the North Sea and on the Coasts of England and Scotland, from Beachy Head to the Islands of Orkney & Shetland.'[11] On the same day he was ordered to proceed to Sheerness, raise his flag on the frigate *Ethalion* and take under his command Thornbrough and his squadron. The other ships assigned to him were all frigates, the *Clyde* at Leith, the *Fortune* in the Humber, the *Penelope* at Yarmouth, and the *Carysfort* and *Lapwing*.[12] This small force was rapidly expanded with both warships and subordinate admirals. By the time Keith relinquished his command, in May 1807, it comprised nearly 120 ships and vessels, although only 11 of these were ships-of-the-line.[13]

Largely unaffected in operational terms by Keith's appointment, Thornbrough continued his surveillance of the Dutch ports for much of the summer, but in early August he arrived at Yarmouth in the *Gelykheid* (64) and spent the next three months carrying out port duties as 'Commanding Officer of His Majesty's ships at Yarmouth.'[14] Aware of the dilemma that this command presented of having to be in two places at once, on 28 October, the Admiralty directed Rear-Admiral Thomas Macnamara Russell to proceed to Yarmouth and hoist his flag on the *Gelykheid*.[15] With Russell taking over the port duties Thornbrough shifted his flag to the *Ruby* (64), and on 9 December returned to the Texel to relieve Captain Rogers of the *Princess of Orange* (74), who, for seven weeks, had been cruising off that station.[16]

Another prominent naval officer to visit Yarmouth at this time was the flamboyant Commodore Sir Sidney Smith. In March 1803 he had been given command of a small squadron based at the Nore with orders to blockade Ostend and Flushing, his broad pennant flying on the *Antelope* (50). The 'Hero of Acre' had Norfolk connections through his father, which possibly explains why on 17 November the *Norfolk Chronicle* reported that, 'Sir Sidney Smith dined with Col. Patterson and the officers of the Norwich Volunteers at the Wrestlers, on Saturday last, and on the Wednesday following they were all to have returned to visit, by invitation, on board the *Antelope*, but there was so great a surf, that it was deemed advisable to defer it.'[17] In the succeeding months he frequently anchored in the Roads until in April 1804 he had to strike his pennant through being ill with rheumatism, opthalmia, fever and ague.[18]

Russell and Thornbrough continued in their respective roles until early October 1804 when it was reported that, 'On Saturday, the *Africaine* frigate, of 44 guns, Capt. Thomas Manby, arrived in these Roads, having on board Rear-Admiral Thornbrough, who instantly set off for Gloucester (through Norwich) in a post-chaise and four. This gallant and persevering Admiral looked far from well; which it is not to be wondered at, when we recollect he had not had his eyes once off the Texel since the 14th of November last. Capt. Manby sailed from these Roads three days ago, and carried out Rear-Adm Russell, whom he left on board the

Eagle (74). Our fleet, consisting of five sail of the line, three frigates, two brigs and five cutters, were all well, but now despair of meeting the Dutch fleet at sea till next summer.' Yet another North Sea Admiral had succumbed to the rigours of the service.[19] With Rear-Admiral Russell off the Texel the port duties at Yarmouth were performed by Captain George Hart of the *Monmouth*, which had become the port's receiving ship in May. In mid-December Russell returned to the Roads in the *Eagle* and in mid-January 1805 shifted his flag to the *Monmouth* after his former ship had been ordered to Portsmouth to refit for Channel service. Throughout much of that year he was forced to divide his time between Yarmouth and the Texel until in September the Admiralty saw fit to provide him with support in the shape of Rear-

26. Rear-Admiral Thomas Macnamara Russell, 'Texel Admiral' 1803-1808.

Admiral Billy Douglas, considered to be the first full-time port-admiral to be stationed at Yarmouth. He came from a command off Boulogne having been replaced there by Sir Sidney Smith.[20] Arriving on 8 October Douglas raised his flag on the *Roebuck* (44) which had been sent from Leith in July. This ship, variously described as the port-admiral's flagship, receiving ship or guard ship, was to serve at Yarmouth until July 1811. On 9 November 1805 both Russell and Douglas were promoted to Vice-Admirals of the Blue, shortly after the Battle of Trafalgar.[21]

Throughout the early years of the Napoleonic period action in relation to the war on trade was much the same as it had been in the previous conflict, with large numbers of prizes being sent in to the Yarmouth Roads by the North Sea cruisers, especially Dutch vessels of all descriptions, to be forwarded by the local prize agent to London for disposal. In addition warships had once more to be supplied to convoy merchant ships, not that the port-admiral's work in this respect was always appreciated. On 23 March 1804 the merchants of Leith wrote to the Admiralty complaining about the depredations committed by the enemy's privateers between that place and London. The Admiralty in turn wrote to Russell, on port duty at Yarmouth, directing him to give particular orders to his cruisers for the protection of coasting vessels. In reply the rear-admiral irritably informed their lordships that the gun-brigs *Snipe*, *Vixen* and *Censor* had for some time past been stationed to cruise for the protection of trade on that part of the coast before counter complaining, 'Permit me to add, that whilst these Merchants continue to decline sailing their Vessels in Numbers, to justify petitions for Convoy, but on the contrary endeavour, singly to outrun, and, I fear, circumvent each other, it will be impossible to protect them. As a case in point, I beg leave to state that the *Duncomb*, a Vessel lately recaptured by the *Beaver*, sailed from Harwich, bound to Hull, with a South easterly Wind; a Wind favourable for the Enemy's Cruizers to come out of Dunkirk and range along our coast, and instead of taking proper precautions, by keeping in Shore, and carrying Sail, to make the best of her Voyage, proceeded under easy sail, outside of Yarmouth Sands, (contrary to general Custom) where she was taken without making the least effort to get under the land, or to cause an alarm at the Signal Posts. This Statement Captain Petty had from one of the Crew left on board her, and I beg leave to repeat my opinion of the great difficulty or impossibility, of effectually protecting our trade, while such negligence, or worse conduct, is pursued by Masters of Merchant Vessels.'[22]

The scale of the Napoleonic Wars was such that the six home naval dockyards and the favoured shipbuilders on the Thames and the Solent could not cope with the demand for new warships, especially those classed as ship-sloops, brig-sloops, gun-brigs and schooners; the smaller vessels best suited for pursing the war on trade.[23] To solve this problem, in 1804, Lord Melville, the new First Lord of the Admiralty, decided to harness the resources of the civilian ship yards up and down the country in order to accelerate the building programme and between 1803 and 1815 a remarkable 84 per cent of warships (72 per cent by tonnage) were built in private yards. The Navy Board was not comfortable with this arrangement for it felt it had lost control over the quality of the ships built, but this was offset by the savings arising from competition between the yards and the quality control issue was dealt with by appointing Royal Dockyard shipwrights as overseers in the contributing yards.[24]

Yarmouth was one of the port towns to benefit from this policy. The building of merchant ships had long taken place on both sides of the river, and the repair of small naval vessels

27. The South Quay, Yarmouth. On the far bank of the river can be seen a vessel ready to be launched in similar fashion to the 20 naval vessels built in the town's shipyards between 1804-1810.

had recently been introduced, but between 1804 and 1810 some 22 new naval vessels were launched from the Yarmouth yards of Nathaniel Palmer, John Preston, Custance and Stone, James Lovewell, and Crane and Holmes. These vessels comprised two frigates, five ship-sloops, five brig-sloops, four gun-brigs and six schooners.[25] The first to be completed was the ship-sloop *Helena*, from John Preston's yard, on the west bank of the river. On 17 May 1804 the *Norfolk Chronicle* gave notice of her forthcoming launch, commenting that, 'the circumstance of her being the first ship of the kind ever built here, will, doubtless, induce much company to be present at it, Captain Losack is appointed to the command of her.' When launched on 26 May she suffered a small mishap when, 'The cable fastened under her stern, for the purpose of preventing her running against the quay head, snapped when she was about three quarters over, but the water not being of sufficient depth, she touched the bottom, which, with the tide occasioned her to veer round, without any further damage.' Several thousand spectators witnessed the launch which was claimed to be a good one considering the breadth of the river. On 5 June she sailed for Chatham to, 'immediately be fitted for service;'[26]

In a very similar fashion, on 16 August it was announced that the, 'very handsome vessel,' the ship-sloop *Cygnet*, would be launched from Nathaniel Palmer's yard on 23 August. Unfortunately the, 'many thousands of people, who had assembled to witness the launching were completely disappointed in consequence of the non arrival of the persons in the employment of Government, for furnishing her with cables and other stores.' She was finally launched on 6 September, 'amidst the acclamations of several thousand spectators; the Shropshire band played God Save the King, Rule Britannia, etc. on board, during the launch.

A number of persons having assembled on the scaffold of a vessel building in the adjoining yard, it unfortunately gave way, by which accident a woman had a rib, a youth his thigh broken, and a private in the Shropshire militia a leg much shattered; many others received severe bruises, but happily no lives were lost.'[27] These events were unpredictable affairs.

The launches of all the Yarmouth built naval vessels (except the schooners) were well reported by the local press, showing just how important these contracts were to the area. Of the 22 vessels built 14 were commissioned for the North Sea, or saw service there. Sadly nine of the total were wrecked, one was lost in a storm and one was burnt. This was the gun-brig *Exertion*, built in John Preston's yard and commissioned with her sister ship, *Redbreast* on 5 July 1805. They were together when on 8 July 1812 the *Exertion* grounded in the Elbe off Cuxhaven. The following day she was burnt by the captain of the *Redbreast*, to prevent her falling into enemy hands.[28] Another pair of Yarmouth built sister ships, the schooners *Woodcock* and *Wagtail* were both wrecked in the Azores on 13 February 1807.[29] It was not only the local ship yards that were in demand, for once again the navy cast a covetous eye on the town's shipwrights. In 1819 John Preston, who was Comptroller of Customs at Yarmouth, wrote, 'It is, perhaps, no less creditable than remarkable, that during the whole of the late war, very many of the best shipwrights, (indeed the strength of His Majesty's dock yards, particularly at Deptford and Chatham) were furnished from Yarmouth, the greatest number of them being freeman of the town.'[30]

Developments on the Continent in 1807 gave rise to the Yarmouth naval support base being expanded to its greatest ever extent, but not before the North Sea command had been restructured. It had been created in 1803 to combat a possible invasion, but in August 1805 Napoleon abandoned his Boulogne camps and sent his troops towards Germany and Austria thereby removing the immediate threat. Lord Keith continued to be responsible for watching the enemy coast, but by the spring of 1807 it was clear that his main task had become the war on trade, an activity requiring a more rapid, localised form of response than the cumbersome North Sea command could offer. Accordingly on 19 May 1807 Keith was directed to strike his flag and the component parts of his station became separate commands in their own right, under the direct control of the Admiralty.[31] At Yarmouth this had implications for both Vice-Admiral Douglas and Vice-Admiral Russell. Douglas was given command of 13 ships and vessels, 'employed and to be employed' from Harwich, to Newcastle. Other than his flagship, *Roebuck*, these consisted of gun-brigs, brig-sloops, schooners, hired ships and hired cutters. Russell's brief was much more extensive. He was to watch the enemy in the Texel and at Hellevoetsluis and 'in case any of the Enemys Ships should put to Sea you are to use your best endeavours to intercept them. If however the Enemys Ships should put to Sea & escape your Vigilance, you are in that case to follow them wherever they may go, according to the best Intelligence you may be able to obtain of them, either with the whole, or such part of your Squadron, as you may judge necessary, & upon coming up with them, to use your best endeavours to take or destroy them.' He was also to blockade the rivers Elbe, Weser and Ems. For this work he was given five ships-of-the-line, four frigates and 15 vessels of various classes.[32]

***

Through military genius and might Napoleon had taken control of much of mainland Europe, but he was forced to accept, like his predecessors, that, without the ability to invade, he could not defeat Britain by the same means. His answer to the problem was his own brand of economic warfare. In November 1806 he issued the Berlin Decree which prohibited continental trade with Britain and introduced what was called the 'Continental System' of embargo. Britain's response was to put in place a full blockade on all the ports under French control.[33] But Napoleon had not finished. In July 1807 he and Tsar Alexander signed the Treaty of Tilsit, a mutually beneficial Franco-Russian alliance, which confirmed all his gains and ceded to Russia considerable Continental territory, largely at the expense of Prussia. This enabled the French Emperor to give his full attention to defeating Britain, with the second strand of his strategy being an attempt to secure naval superiority.[34] He had already organised a vast shipbuilding programme in the French dockyards, but this on its own could not dislodge Britain's stranglehold on the oceans, so he set his sights on the shipbuilding capacity of his expanding empire, especially in the Schelde, and cast covetous eyes on the ready-made fleets of his neutral neighbours, Denmark and Portugal.[35]

In June 1807 Portland's government became convinced that Denmark was preparing for war with Britain. Intelligence suggested that the Danes had given the French permission to occupy Holstein, that the Danish fleet (20 ships-of-the-line) would be used to invade Ireland, and that France and Russia intended to form a maritime league to which Denmark and Sweden would be either invited or forced to join.[36] If true, such arrangements would help give Napoleon parity in warship numbers and Britain's vital interest in the Baltic, especially in

28. The French Emperor Napoleon and the Russian Tsar Alexander I meeting on a raft in the middle of the river Niemen, at Tilsit, to ratify their peace treaty, 7 July 1807.

51

relation to naval stores, would again be under threat. Taking no chances the British government decided to carry out a pre-emptive strike against the Danes and their navy, appointing Admiral James Gambier to carry out the task at the head of a strong naval force, which was to assemble in Yarmouth Roads.[37]

When in mid-July the naval ships and vessels began to arrive there was a strong sense of de-ja-vue in the town, for only seven years earlier Sir Hyde Parker's force had assembled there to pursue a very similar objective. On 23 July the *Norfolk Chronicle* reported that Admiral Gambier, Vice-Admiral Stanhope and Commodore Sir Home Popham had arrived that day and that the admiral had immediately hoisted his flag on board the *Prince of Wales* (98). Three days later he set sail for Copenhagen with an advanced force of 17 ships-of-the-line and 21 frigates, sloops, bomb vessels and gun-brigs. Prior to this, on 5 July, Lieutenant-General Lord Cathcart had set sail from the Roads for Stralsund in the frigate *Africaine*, from where he was to join Gambier to take command of the land forces being assembled to attack the Danish capital. Cathcart joined Gambier on 12 August. By then the expedition consisted of 25 ships-of-the-line, upwards of 40 frigates and smaller vessels, and 27,000 soldiers.[38]

With Yarmouth once more the springboard for naval operations in and around the Baltic it was decided to expand the support base's capacity to sustain the fleet established in that theatre of war. Even before the attack on Copenhagen, orders had been given for the permitted quantity of naval and ordnance stores to be augmented. Later in the year, when it was clear that the navy would be in the Baltic for some time, the port-admiral was connected to the Admiralty by telegraph and it was decided to appoint a master attendant and a master shipwright to provide extra support for the warships. In December the number of beds planned for the proposed naval hospital was greatly increased and the following year the workforce of the existing hospital was reinforced. In addition the victualling contractors were required to expand their operations to cater for the enhanced level of demand. With this flurry of activity the year 1807 proved to be the high watermark for the Yarmouth naval support base.[39]

On 2 August a naval squadron under Rear-Admiral Richard Goodwin Keats had completed the encirclement of the Island of Zealand and the Danes were given a final ultimatum to agree to deposit their fleet in a British port until the end of the war. As expected this demand was rejected and on 16 August a force under the future Duke of Wellington quickly defeated the Danes at the Battle of Køge. This was followed by a series of bombardments of such ferocity that on the 7 September the Danes capitulated.[40] As a result 17 Danish ships-of-the-line were confiscated along with 15 frigates, all of which were sailed to British ports.[41] It was not until 27 October that the fleet with its Danish prizes began anchoring in the Yarmouth Roads, with Gambier and ten sail-of-the-line arriving two days later, the same day King Louis XVIII, under the title Count de Lille, arrived in the town on board the Swedish frigate *Freya*. Gambier left for the Downs on 3 November and on 7th his subordinate, Rear-Admiral Sir William Essington, got underway in the *Minotaur* (74), taking with him the remaining ships and the transports.[42]

The main show had been at Copenhagen, but with the Danish Crown Prince declaring war on Britain, the opportunity was taken to capture Heligoland, a Danish island close to the mouth of the Elbe that could be used as a base to help break the Continental System. The task was given to Vice-Admiral Russell in whose operational area the island fell. He received

29. While the serviceable ships of the Danish navy were taken to Yarmouth as prizes, those being built or docked for repairs were dismantled or destroyed.

his orders on 3 September 1807, but by then he had sent the frigate *Quebec* with the ship-sloop *Lynx* and gun-brig *Sparkler* to establish an interim exclusion zone around the island. He was also informed that the troopship *Wanderer*, carrying 100 marines, and the bomb-ketch *Explosion* and gun-brig *Exertion* had been ordered to proceed from Yarmouth to assist him.[43] Sailing from at the Texel in the *Majestic* (74) Russell arrived off the island on 4 September and without waiting for his Yarmouth reinforcements prepared to attack. Realising his position was hopeless, the Danish commandant, Major Von Zeske, surrendered. With the island becoming a key player in the war on trade a number of naval vessels were stationed there and the task of keeping them supplied fell to the Yarmouth support base for the remainder of the war.[44] In March 1808 Mr Nicholas, the island's British agent, asked the Admiralty to arrange for a large and a small Yarmouth yawl to be sent there, as he considered them to be the most suitable boats to give assistance to vessels in danger of being lost on the coast. The support base's naval storekeeper was instructed to purchase two for that purpose.[45]

Another island to be taken by the British was Anholt, in the Kattegat, the lighthouse on which was important to shipping navigating the Sound. When the Danes extinguished its light, steps were taken in May 1809 to capture the barren place on which it stood and station a garrison there. Vessels supplying the island with men and materials sailed from Yarmouth, with the town often providing those making the journey with their last taste of civilised life before sailing from the Roads. In early September 1810 the *Norfolk Chronicle* reported that, 'Yesterday, arrived the *Alexandria* frigate, with Governor Maurice and his Staff, on their way to relieve the garrison in Anholt. The officers attended the Ball in the evening, where through the polite introductions of the Master of the Ceremonies, they soon joined in the gay dance with the Grace and Beauty of our neighbourhood.'[46]

After Tilsit/Copenhagen all the Baltic states, with the exception of the unstable Sweden, became hostile to Britain. Yielding to French pressure they tried to exclude British merchants from trading in the much needed naval stores. To counter this attempt at enforcing the Continental System, in early 1808, Vice-Admiral Sir James Saumarez was dispatched to the Baltic to take command of a fleet of seven ships-of-the-line and a number of vessels charged with blockading the Russian navy in port and convoying trade through the Sound.[47] On 30 April he sailed by Yarmouth in his flagship *Victory* (100) and in June four ships-of-the-line left the Roads to join him, followed in September by a further three in consequence of the Russian Fleet being at sea. Three more sailed in October. All these reinforcements took on supplies at Yarmouth, as did a number of ships of the Baltic fleet returning to a home port that winter.[48]

For some unknown reason in March 1809 the fleet heading for the Baltic 'passed at the back of the sands' off Yarmouth without pausing to be serviced, but in 1810 it was business as usual. In March, April, and May sub-divisions of the fleet arrived in the Roads to be re-supplied, before sailing for their northern station. Among them was Nelson's iconic flagship *Victory*, which was to be seen anchored in the Roads between 4 and 10 May.[49] All did not run smoothly, however, for in March the *Orion* (74), on coming through the St. Nicholas Gat at low water, ran aground and the view was expressed that that channel had been filling up for some time. Surveys were carried out and the following year a new channel was discovered, which was quickly named the Horatio after the frigate that had first negotiated it. Neither

30. Vice-Admiral James Saumarez's flagship Victory at anchor.

channel, however, was deemed deep enough to take ships-of-the-line, and no more attempted to take the risk for the remainder of the war. Although frigates and naval vessels of a smaller size were still serviced in the Roads, the loss of the ships-of-the-line considerably reduced the usefulness of the support base.[50] Yarmouth, however, remained the preferred port of embarkation/return for a steady stream of ambassadors, king's messengers, and deposed foreign royalty. It was also the destination of many fleeing German troops.

Saumarez was to remain in the Baltic (with winter breaks) for over four years. Early on he was involved in Sir John Moore's ill-judged expedition to assist Sweden, which sailed from Yarmouth Roads, and also an inconclusive skirmish with Vice-Admiral Hanikoff's Russian squadron (Duncan's old ally), but over time he was successful in breaking the resolve of the Baltic States with a skilful mix of force and diplomacy. His biggest challenge was having to deal with the many small Danish warships that preyed on British convoys, (known as the Mosquito War), which continued until hostilities with Denmark ceased in January 1814.[51]

While Britain was securing her interests in the Baltic Napoleon had become active in the southern North Sea. Since the failure of his earlier invasion plans he had decided to transfer his efforts from Boulogne to Antwerp and Flushing, on the River Schelde. The former was to become his principal naval base in the area. Faced with the need to extinguish this threat and take pressure off the Austrians, in July 1809, the government launched its ill-fated Walcheren Expedition, with Rear-Admiral Sir Richard Strachan in charge of the related naval forces. As it was based in the nearby Downs Yarmouth's involvement was limited to providing some naval stores and water for its ships and vessels, passing on prisoners of war to more permanent accommodation, and caring for a significant number of sick soldiers. The failure of the expedition resulted in a naval blockade of the entrance to the Schelde under Admiral William Young. Yarmouth continued to supply water directly to the ships at anchor there and serviced the vessels attached to the blockading fleet.[52]

In respect of blockading the Texel, the primary task of the North Sea Squadron for the past dozen or so years, Vice-Admiral Russell retained the Yarmouth based role until October 1808 when according to the *Norfolk Chronicle* the Lords Commissioners, 'have come to the determination of discontinuing the office and expense of a commander-in-chief of his Majesty's ships off the Texel.'[53] There must have been more to it than that for after a month during which Captain John Talbot of the *Thunderer* (74) monitored the Dutch anchorage Rear-Admiral Alan Hyde, Lord Gardner, once Russell's second-in-command, was appointed to the task in his flagship *Bellerophon* (74) with three other 74's.[54] In January 1809, the seemingly favoured Gardner left his command to attend his father's funeral and for the next six months the Texel was watched by Commodore Charles Pater in the *Princess Carolina* (74). Although Gardner returned to Yarmouth in June he soon became a subordinate rear-admiral in the Walcheren Expedition, before striking his flag in December that year.[55] Throughout 1810 the Yarmouth based frigates *Quebec* and *Desiree*, together with the gun-brig *Hearty* and brig-sloop *Britomart*, monitored the Texel, and similar vessels continued to do so until the end of the war. From 1811 they were supplemented by a small squadron detached from the Schelde blockading fleet under Rear-Admiral John Ferrier. Given the newly discovered problems of accessing the Yarmouth Roads this force was based in Hollesley Bay. Apart from the occasional supply of water it was not serviced from Yarmouth.[56]

Throughout this period it remained the duty of the Yarmouth port-admiral to keep merchant ships safe between Newcastle and Harwich. Billy Douglas remained in post until August 1810, when he was ordered to strike his flag and hand over to the aforementioned Rear-Admiral Lord Gardner.[57] As with Russell it is not clear why the change took place for the more junior Gardner proved to be an absentee again, leaving the port duties to Captain Richard Curry of the *Roebuck*. It was not a situation that was allowed to continue for long and in April 1811 Gardner was replaced by Vice-Admiral Robert Murray, who remained in command at Yarmouth for the remainder of this first phase of the Napoleonic Wars. The *Roebuck* was withdrawn in July that year to be replaced by the frigate *Solebay*.[58]

Part Two
The Support Services

SPRINGBOARD TO VICTORY

5.

Victualling

In order to keep the ships and vessels of the navy constantly at sea it was necessary for their crews to be regularly fed and watered. This was called victualling and was the responsibility of the Victualling Board, which maintained home yards at Deptford, Portsmouth, Plymouth, Chatham and Dover. The first of these was the most important, being directly under the eye of the Board in London. Vast quantities of agricultural produce were purchased from supply contractors and commission agents for processing at these yards, before trans-shipment to the various naval support bases, fleets and squadrons, at home and abroad. They represented a considerable investment in buildings, including storehouses, bakeries, breweries, cooperages, slaughter-houses and much else besides. At the smaller places like Yarmouth, fixed infrastructure for victualling could not be justified, so recourse was had to 'sea provisions contracts', whereby a contractor agreed to provide a range of commodities directly to the ships and vessels concerned. A typical sea provisions contract would include bread, beer, beef, pork, pease, oatmeal, butter, cheese, vinegar and 'bisket'. Other requirements, such as live oxen, fresh beef, rum, wine and spirits, tobacco and water were usually supplied under separate contracts or sourced directly by the pursers of the warships.[1]

Towards the end of 1790 the Victualling Board decided to seek tenders for a new sea provisions contract for Yarmouth, a process won in January 1791 by local merchant John Kerridge, who also acquired the contract to supply rum.[2] His tenure of these contracts did not last long, however, for in October the following year he suddenly died. Moving swiftly, Robert Warmington, as the administrator of Kerridge's effects, claimed that he had a responsibility to fulfil the contract, but the Victualling Board did not agree, pointing out that 'Mr Kerridge's engagement terminated with his life.' Initially the Board directed Kerridge's young clerk, Samuel Paget Jnr., to continue supplying provisions until a new contractor was appointed, but, possibly because of Warmington's activities, this direction was withdrawn in favour of the ship's pursers purchasing 'what may be absolutely necessary.' In the event the Victualling Board sought tenders for a new sea provisions contract, one for rum and another for fresh beef. In November 1792 Thomas Pinkerton, a London merchant, dealer and chapman, was awarded the sea provisions contract and also that for rum. At the same time local butcher, Thomas Martin Jnr., secured the contract for supplying fresh beef, which had previously been held by Pinkerton. This is how matters stood on the eve of war.[3]

Pinkerton was an experienced contractor, but for some reason his performance was soon deemed unsatisfactory for on 6 December 1793 he was given six months notice of the termination of his contract and the process of competitive tendering was once more set in motion for both sea provisions and rum. On 29 April 1794 the Victualling Board's tender box was opened, the four tenders contained therein were taken out, and a price per seaman calculated, so that a comparison of the submissions could be made. The highest, at 10.73d, was that of Warmington. He had already unsuccessfully tendered for the work in 1784, 1791 and 1792, and possibly earlier. Although employed in another naval capacity, victualling was to elude him. The next at 10.36d was that submitted by a prominent national contractor, John Grant. The second lowest at 9.25d was by the fresh beef contractor, Thomas Martin, but the successful tender, at 8.59d was that proposed by Kerridge's former clerk, Samuel Paget. The four men also tendered for the rum contract which was awarded to John Grant.[4] Paget's contract was to supply 'what Sea Provisions shall be demanded for twelve months certain from 6th of June next and further until six months warning (notice) shall be given at the prices of his tender of the 28th Instant, except for Bisket Bags for which he is to be allowed only one shilling and sixpence each.' By 2 June he had supplied the necessary security for performing the contract and was ready to provision his first warship in his own right, the cutter *Resolution*.[5]

31. Samuel Paget Junior, victualling contractor, brewer, and ship owner.

At face value, awarding the contract to the man submitting the lowest tender was no more than normal practice, but in point of fact it marked the start of the career of a rather astute entrepreneur. Paget's more famous son, surgeon Sir James, recorded the event in his memoirs thus, 'After leaving school, he became clerk to a Mr. Kerridge, a merchant of some kind in the town. When he was 17, his master, who held the contract for the supply of provisions to the North Sea fleet when they came into Yarmouth Roads, died suddenly. Here was an opportunity. At that time, lads of 17 were much nearer to full mental manhood than they are now, but even then it must have needed rare resolution for any lad to do as, I have heard my father did. He started at once for London. The journey was then nearly twenty four hours long, and he had never seen the huge place – as huge then in comparison with Yarmouth as it is now: seeming as boundless, as crowded and confusing. I have heard him say that when, on the first morning, he went into the Strand, he thought that the crowd he met must be coming from some great sight or public meeting; and he stood aside at a shop-door, that the people might pass and he be able to go on quietly. But the crowd continued, and he took courage and made his way to the Admiralty, and there showed such complete knowledge of his master's business, and pointed out so plainly the trouble that might arise from shifting the contract into others' hands, that he was allowed to hold it. He had to borrow money to begin with; and his mother went about, borrowing for him wherever she could; and they succeeded, in spite of opposition on political grounds and on account of his father's repute as being concerned in smuggling'.[6] Given that at the time this event took place Sir James had not yet been born it comes as no surprise that some of the details of this remarkable story are at variance with the official record. As we have seen, after the death of Kerridge, the sea provisions contract was awarded to Pinkerton, not Paget. It seems reasonable to suppose that being in need of a local manager Pinkerton employed the young bookkeeper in that capacity, drawing on his experience and local knowledge to carry out the work. The events outlined by Sir James would better fit the period immediately after Pinkerton had lost the contract, with Paget visiting the Victualling Office at Somerset House in the Strand (rather than the Admiralty) to plead his case, his boldness being rewarded with an invitation to tender. At 19 Samuel Paget was a young man eager to make his mark in business, especially naval business. In achieving this aim he was greatly assisted by his friend and business associate, local banker and patron of the arts, Dawson Turner. A year younger than Paget, Turner inherited his father's bank at the age of 18 and probably helped finance his friend's acquisition of the sea provisions contract. They were to be in partnership in a merchant shipping business and a brewery with, in each case, Paget as the managing partner. Both concerns would provide services to the Victualling Board.[7]

At the commencement of each contract the Victualling Office would inform the appropriate 'Commanders of His Majesty's Ships and Vessels' who they were now to apply to for provisions. When warships anchored in the Yarmouth Roads their pursers would approach the relevant contractor with lists of the supplies they required and the contractors would endeavour to satisfy their needs. Orders were usually given for ships to be victualled for a set period of time, a common one being for four months. At regular intervals the contractors would submit accounts to the Victualling Office for payment and these would be checked against the purser's returns. If these matched, bills of exchange would be issued in settlement of the accounts. Paget and Martin operated in this fashion until the middle of 1796, when the decision to supply the North Sea Squadron from Yarmouth brought major change to the way victualling was handled at the port.[8]

32. Dawson Turner, polymath and business associate of Paget Junior.

Earlier in the year the pair had successfully re-provisioned Rear-Admiral Pringle's small squadron, but several days had been lost through bad weather preventing the shore boats launching. On 28 February Pringle had informed the Admiralty that he had, 'sent an officer on shore to Assist the Contractor in supplying beer and water, particularly the last Article of which the *Asia*, *Repulse*, and *Inflexible* (64) are much in Want, but which it is exceedingly difficult to get off, There being so large a Surf on the Shore occasioned by this Easterly wind, that only one small Boat has yet got alongside since My Arrival'.[9] Unfortunately for Paget this report served to seriously weaken his position for when two months later the Victualling Board considered how best to victual Macbride's squadron it decided, not only to send a large quantity of provisions from Deptford and place them under the control of a member of its own staff, but also to store them in transports anchored in the Roads 'in order to obviate the difficulty which we understood existed in forwarding supplies from the shore, whenever there was any considerable surf on the Beach'.[10]

33. The entrance to the Deptford victualling yard. This facility provided a proportion of the food and drink that was issued to the ships and vessels at Yarmouth.

Thomas Pitt, the First Clerk to the Superintendent at Deptford, was the man chosen to manage this facility and on 17 May the Victualling Board made arrangements for 500 tuns of water, in various cask sizes, to be made ready to be shipped to Yarmouth. Ten days later warrants were issued for substantial quantities of bread, spirits, wine, beef, flour, raisins, suet, pork, pease, oatmeal, butter, cheese, and vinegar to be sent there too, once the Transport Board had provided vessels for that purpose.[11] Pitt arrived at Yarmouth on 15 June with access to £100 to cover his immediate expenses.[12] As the new arrangement had yet to be tested the contracted services of Paget and Martin were to be retained. In respect of the latter the Board wanted reassurance that he could increase his supply of fresh beef to meet the expected additional demand and wrote to him accordingly. For Paget, who was providing the same commodities as those being sent from Deptford, the Victualling Board drew up guidance setting out how he and Pitt were to co-operate. One suspects that Paget Jnr. was not overjoyed with this turn of events, although he must have taken comfort from the fact that his contract had not been terminated. As it happened being the local man with the ear of the town's business community his position was much stronger than it might at first sight appear and over the course of the French Revolutionary War he was to emerge as the key player in the victualling service at Yarmouth.[13]

The transports *Manchester*, *Prince of Orange* and *Christian* arrived on the same day as Pitt, with the allocated supply of water and provisions. Ten days later Vice-Admiral Macbride's squadron came to anchor in the Roads and remained long enough to adequately test the effectiveness of the new victualling arrangements.[14] It seems that Paget was required to provide the 'first supply' of sea provisions, but not expecting the ships to arrive so soon, he was 'not so well prepared' and, in accordance with an order from Macbride, Pitt was obliged to distribute all the provisions and water that had arrived in the three transports. Realising that his failure could jeopardize his contract Paget quickly reassured Pitt that he was now in a position to complete the victualling of the squadron 'to four months'.[15] Martin was also caught unawares, failing to provide fresh beef for more than two days a week, there being a scarcity of cattle in Norfolk and Suffolk. When in early July it became clear that the squadron would remain in the Roads longer than anticipated Captain Larcom of the *Russell* (Macbride's flagship) approached Martin to see if he could supply fresh beef at the rate of one pound per man, per day, only to receive a negative response. Ever the opportunist Paget offered to supply half the required quantity, an offer Macbride readily accepted given the urgency to complete. Informed by Pitt of the arrangement the Board wrote to Martin in terms that so alarmed him he paid Paget for the beef already prepared and also bought from him the remaining cattle, allowing Pitt to report that, 'The Fleet is now regularly supplied with Fresh Beef'.[16] Martin, however, was faced with another problem. Two or three days prior to sailing the irascible Macbride had ordered three quarters of beef, that he had seen hanging up in Robert Banyard's butchers shop, to be sent aboard the *Russell*, not because of failure to supply, but because 'it was fine Beef he wished to take to Sea with him.' An incensed Martin refused to pay for it.[17]

On 10 July the victuallers *Hope* and *Active* arrived from Dover with bread and beer. There then being more bread than the warships required, Pitt hired a warehouse to store the surplus and when the squadron sailed this was all the food that remained under his direct control.[18] Having for the first time completed the victualling of the North Sea Squadron Pitt could now reflect on how the system might be improved. His immediate thoughts concerned where best to store the food, how to ensure a steady supply of casks, where to source the required provisions and the water, the best method of transporting the goods to the ships and how to work effectively with the local contractors, especially Paget. Even before the squadron sailed Pitt was pondering these matters for on 19 July he had informed the Victualling Board that, 'Having conversed with the Admiral and Captn Larcom yesterday on the best method of victualling the Fleet they are of [the] Opinion that if warehouses were hired near the Mouth of the Harbour to deposit the Victg stores in as they arrive the ships would send their launches there for provisions and the Fleet would be victualled with a great deal more safety, expedition and correctness than from Victuallers laying in the Roads and desired me to propose this method to you. I therefore humbly submit it to Your Honours and if you approve of this Move I will endeavour to procure suitable Storehouses.'[19]

With the likelihood that provisions would be sent from Deptford and Dover on a regular basis it seemed sensible to the men on the spot to establish a safe and secure method of storage until the arrival of the warships that required them. The first three victuallers had lain in the Roads 10 days before they could discharge their cargoes directly into Macbride's ships, putting them and their goods at risk and rendering them inefficient in terms of their primary purpose. Notwithstanding its original intention to store the provisions in transports anchored in the Roads the Board directed Pitt to hire warehouses, but he was soon to find that nothing was available to him. Writing on 15 August he told the Victualling Board that, 'No such places are to be got at present as the Merchants of this Town have hired every Granary and Storehouse near the water side for depositing large quantities of Corn that is expected from the Baltic. Sir Edward Lacon the Mayor has a very large Storehouse conveniently situated that would answer every purpose (at present empty) but he does not seem inclinable to Let it. Mr Fisher Merchant and Agent to Claude Scott Esqr has another Warehouse that would answer extremely well but he is going to make a Granary of it for Corn to be received on acco[un]t of Mr Scott and has hired most of the other warehouses that were to be let for that purpose.'[20] Paget, of course, *could* find warehouses, offering to let them to the Victualling Board and to arrange cartage of the stored provisions to the waterside. By then, however, the commissioners had, 'given up the intention we had been entertaining of having storehouses in Yarmouth.'[21]

In case there should be any doubt about continuing to victual the squadron at Yarmouth Admiral Duncan took the unusual step for one of his rank, of attending a meeting of the Victualling Board to confirm his wish 'that His Majesty's ships under his command, may be continued to be victualled at Yarmouth from on board Victuallers, agreeably to the present mode.'[22] With the Board complying with Duncan's requirements, transports anchored in the roads continued to serve as victualling stores, with provisions being transferred between them, so as to free up as many as possible to return to Deptford to pick up more supplies. But as time went on, and with winter approaching, the harbour started to look like a safer option. In mid-September Commissioner Towry, who had been sent to assess the situation, ordered the *Princess* and *Caesar* into the haven, 'for the safety of delivering the Wine from the former to the latter vessel, it being very dangerous to trans-ship it in the Roads.' By the end of the month most of the other victualling transports had joined them.[23]

The place they chose to moor was at the bend in the river, near the harbour's mouth, known as the Brush, a location that presented the other river users with a problem. On 4 December Pitt informed the Board that, 'Some of the ship owners of this port having represented that the victuallers by laying at the mouth of the harbour are an obstruction to navigation of the river, the Mayor has peremptorill(sic) ordered them considerably higher up and threatened that if they do not come he will immediately order them out into the Roads. I believe the complaint to be without a cause as they were placed singly with their broadsides close to the quay agreeable to the harbour Masters direction, and the Masters say they have given every assistance to ships coming in or going out of the harbour. As it will be a great hindrance of the service for the Men of War to send their launches so high up the river I have to request Your Honours interference that they may be reinstated in their former births. It will be extremely hazardous for them to lay in the Roads at this time of the year.'[24]

The dispute was eventually settled in favour of the local ship-owners, with the victuallers obliged to moor at the town's quay, until that is Paget re-submitted his proposal. In March 1797 he again offered to let the Victualling Board, 'warehouse room for provisions except wine & spirits sufficient for 7 or 8000 men [for] four months and to find vessels to take the

34. A row of sailing vessels are moored against the strip of riverbank known as 'the Brush' in this allegorical painting by J. M. W. Turner. Victualling vessels that moored in this spot in 1796 were seen as problematical.

same on board His Majesty's Ships in the Roads at the rate of £165 p month.' He would also supply all labour and cartage.[25] Pitt was asked his opinion and readily agreed to the arrangement, having 'long been fully convinced from calculations which I have made that the hiring of warehouses for depositing provisions instead of letting them remain on board the victuallers would be a great saving to the Crown.' No doubt attracted by the thought of savings the Victualling Board accepted the offer, gave Paget a new contract and with it effective control of the provisions sent from Deptford. On 9 April Pitt was able to inform the Board that the *Acton*, *Christian* and *Eleanor* victuallers had been unloaded and their cargoes deposited in the storehouses.[26]

The importance of casks to the victualling service cannot be overestimated. Virtually everything came in casks of one description or another, but once they had been delivered to a ship they could end up anywhere in the world. Because of this the Victualling Board supplied and retained ownership of these containers, making the creation of a cooperage facility for their assembly repair and maintenance essential. When first he arrived from Deptford Pitt brought with him two coopers, establishing them in a stable. The Victualling Board, however, thought this facility poorly located and by late October Pitt had hired, 'a large carpenters shop for a cooperage in Mr Norfors rope yard within the paling exactly opposite the Dene well,' for £5.5.0 per annum. He described it as, 'in every way fitted for the purpose being large and roomy with a loft over it and floored and wanted nothing but what the coopers have done themselves to make it a complete coopers shop.' He also hired a piece of fenced ground close to the site to provide a secure store, 'As the casks by being exposed on the Denes are liable to be plundered of their Iron hoops and otherwise damaged.'[27] This arrangement seemed to have worked well enough until March 1797 when, following a dispute with Vice-Admiral Onslow respecting water casks, Pitt wrote to the Board suggesting that due to an expected increase in demand it would be prudent to send, '300 tuns of casks in packs – 200 tuns in butts and 100 tuns in punch[eo]ns, part of them as soon as possible.' To handle this 'flat-pack' provision he intended to use his two coopers together with an additional man who was prepared to set them up for 4s 6d per tun. The existing workers were to be given an additional 2s 6d per tun to achieve parity with the new employee.[28]

The provision of fresh water accounted for a great many casks. Prior to Yarmouth becoming the squadron's support base the pursers of the vessels in need made their own arrangements for water, sending seamen in launches to pump water from the well that the Corporation had sunk at the base of Gorleston cliffs, opposite the harbour's mouth.[29] In January and February

1796 Paget provided water to the Russian warships *Riga* and *Nickanor* and in March he started doing so for British ships and vessels, but initially the water for the squadron was shipped direct from Deptford.[30] Quickly realising that it would be more logical to source the squadron's water needs locally the Victualling Board turned to Paget and on 22 June awarded him a contract to provide and transport water. In September the rate was fixed at 7s 0d per ton for water from the river Yare and 7s 6d for spring well water, the difference reflecting the fact that Paget found it more expensive to extract the well water.[31]

There were teething problems, however, for on 25 September 1796 Pitt informed the Board that, 'The whole of the Fleet are nearly victialled…,' adding that, 'Above 700 tuns of water is now wanting altho' every exertion

35. A cooper at work. The importance of casks to the victualling service cannot be overstated.

has been made that circumstances would admit.'[32] Perceiving this to be a supply problem the Victualling Board directed Pitt to investigate whether the Gorleston pump could make a greater contribution. This he did and on 10 October reported that, 'there is not a possibility of filling more than thirty five tuns of water there p[er] day nor is the pump in its present state capable of producing more. It is situated about two hundred yards from the river and the casks must be roll'd over rough and uneven ground. The water by the present method of bringing it down the river in keels is procured in much larger quantities and with greater dispatch and being river water it is softer and will keep better. The delay arises from not having proper craft to take it out into the Roads in blowing weather. When the wind sets a swell on the bar at the mouth of the harbour the keels cannot get out and often an afternoon's tide is lost when it is moderate, as the keelmen will not go out into the Roads unless they are sure of

36. Known as Duncan's Pump this survival stands at the foot of the White Lion Steps in Gorleston. Sunk by the Yarmouth Corporation it helped to supply water to the warships in the Roads.

getting back into the harbour the same evening. They dare not trust their keels in the Roads all night, and are afraid of venturing with them in bad weather.'[33]

The keelmen had just cause for concern. On 29 September the *Elizabeth & Ann* ketch, on taking water out to the *Venerable*, struck Scroby Sands and was totally lost, despite the efforts of the beachmen to get her off and in late November a keel, bought three days earlier by Paget, got caught in a violent gale and sank alongside the *Director*. More losses were to follow.[34] It was not all bad news, however, for Pitt was of the opinion that, 'The pump would answer very well for the ships that are watered to send their own launch and men with empty casks to fill to keep up their stock while they lay in the Roads. If this mode was adopted a crane of sufficient purchase for a butt of water should be erected at the edge of the river.' He also thought that other wells might be sunk near the same spot.[35]

Concerning the problem of suitable vessels for trans-shipment he suggested that three larger vessels, such as Dover hoys or decked lighters could be employed to carry out the work.[36] Interested in this possibility the Victualling Board asked Pitt to find out what savings could be made on the existing arrangements, if this measure were to be adopted. Speaking directly to the keelmen (seemingly behind Paget's back) he discovered that, 'Mr Paget pays for the keels going up the river, filling the casks bringing it down and carrying it out into the Roads – nine guineas each…for the keels that are loaded at the quay with the spring well water taking it out into the Roads he pays four guineas & a half, so that he pays 4½ guineas for bringing it down the river and 4½ for sending it out to sea.'[37] In deciding to use its own vessels for the second stage the Board could reduce the rate paid to Paget by 2s 6d per tun.[38]

The vessels the Board intended to use to ferry the water from the harbour were the hired sloops *Fanny* and *Prince of Wales*, neither of which Pitt thought suitable for the work, but he did at least put them to the test before on 28 December informing the Board that, 'It does not appear practicable to procure any proper vessells by the trip to carry the provisions on board His Majesty's ships in these Roads as the keels are the only description of vessels that are employed by the merchants to carry goods into the Roads or lighter vessels that want to come into the harbour.'[39] No doubt allowing himself a wry smile Paget once more came to the rescue. Writing to the Board on 11 January 1797 he offered the use of a Dutch schuyt for the purpose of carrying provisions and water to the ships in the Roads. As usual Pitt's opinion was sought and he responded that, 'A vessel of an easy draft of water to go out at any time is much wanted. And it is my opinion that the vessel in question will answer very well.'[40] Paget had regained control of the transportation of water into the Roads and in early 1799 he strengthened his position still further by leasing land from the Corporation, 'east of the South Bleaching House for the purpose of sinking a well and erecting a mill to work it, with leave to pale in.' He then controlled his own water supply.[41]

Towards the end of 1796 Paget also acquired the transportation of fresh beef, undercutting Martin, the contractor in the process. On 14 October Pitt reported that, 'Mr Paget has not yet made up his mind respecting the price at which he will contract to take the fresh beef out into the Roads for. Mr Martin has come down to 1s p[er] cwt.' Six days later Paget had made up his mind, offering to contract for 10d per cwt, an offer that was quickly accepted.[42]

By March 1797 Pitt had been in charge of victualling his Majesty's ships at Yarmouth for nearly a year, in which time he had overseen the provisioning of the North Sea Squadron on six occasions, but had gradually ceded the operational management of the work to Paget. In addition to his sea provisions contract, Paget provided the majority of the fresh water and rum, controlled the warehousing of all the provisions and was responsible for their transportation to the ships in the Roads. The creation of this rather one sided relationship may have been the reason why later that month Pitt was promoted to the position of Clerk of the Cheque at Portsmouth and a more junior officer, Samuel Lewes, 'an Extra Clerk in the Cutting-house department at Deptford' was sent to Yarmouth to replace him.[43]

Lewes arrived on 6 April 1797. The following day he informed the Victualling Board that Mr Pitt thinks it will be necessary for him to stay, 'till all the victuallers now here, except the *Manchester* and *Princess*, are discharged before he can give me a true statement of what I am to take charge of.'[44] Pitt eventually left Yarmouth on 28 April.[45] In his letters Lewes comes across as an efficient enough administrator in his dealings with the wide range of victualling matters that came his way, but, like his predecessor, he was forced to accept that effective control lay with Paget. No sooner had Pitt left town than Lewes was presented with a demand from Paget for the cost of sending several keels out to the warships to retrieve empty water casks, 'by desire he says of the Admiral to expedite the watering [of] the fleet and which he says Mr Pitt used to settle with him for.' Seeking the Victualling Board's instructions re this demand he mentioned in the same letter that Vice-Admiral Onslow had returned a quantity of wine from the *Nassau(I)*, 'as the men were in a state of Mutiny and would have everything their own way.' Mutineers were one thing, drunken mutineers quite another![46]

37. Samuel Paget Junior built this house on South Quay, Yarmouth, in 1812-13, on the site of his previous house. Behind it stood a range of warehouses which he used in his victualling business before, in 1803, leasing them to the Ordnance Board.

Paget's reluctance to co-operate with Lewes became all too obvious in July that year when the Board received his account for provisions supplied to the warships. On querying this with Lewes he responded that 'I have complied with all the demands made upon me by His Brittanic & Imperial Majesty's ships and that I did not know the extent Mr Paget had supplied them with provisions at this place.'[47] On the 6th he wrote again to explain that the provisions supplied by Paget had, 'been made intirely without my knowledge except in the instance of the *Argo* and *Swan* transports for which I had your Honours consensus to apply to Mr Paget. I have never made any application to him for provisi[o]ns on any other occasion and being entirely unacquainted with the cause of such considerable supplies I have applied to him to know the reason and he has returned for answer that he shall write to the Board on the subject this post, when I hope your Honours will not consider me to have deviated from my instructions...' Paget did indeed write that day requesting under circumstances he outlined that, 'the Board will allow him to continue furnishing Provisions to His Majesty's Ships at Yarmouth, under the line of battle: and also those which casually come into Yarmouth Roads.'[48] As a result the Victualling Board sent commissioners Rodney and Hunt to review the situation. Nothing seems to have come of this visit, however, although Lewes tried to exploit the service. On 6 August he informed the Board that, 'my eldest son has lately assisted me in the receipt and issue of provis[io]ns at this place. Therefore [I] recommend him to your Honours as a competent and confidential person to attend the issuing of Mr Pagets provisions to see the demands are actually complied with.'[49] While it is clear Paget felt there was no need to involve Lewes in his business the reverse was not the case. When on 18 September the Board directed Lewes to hire a vessel 'on the best terms' to take a surplus of unserviceable stores to Deptford, he made an agreement with Paget (Messrs Turner and Paget) to hire the brig *Anson* for that purpose. In February 1798 Lewes also hired Paget's brig *Elizabeth* to transport condemned provisions.[50]

When Lewes first arrived in Yarmouth the North Sea Squadron was at anchor in the Roads, but on 26 May, fully provisioned, it set sail for the Texel and remained there watching the Dutch fleet for four months. In August quantities of beef, wine, water, vegetables and coal were delivered by victuallers to the ships where they lay off the Dutch coast, but when on 29 September Duncan received orders for the squadron to return to Yarmouth to re-provision the Victualling Board, 'conceiving that the multiplicity of business which will devolve upon Mr Lewes then Agent at Yarmouth, in consequence of the arrival of the Squadron of His Majesty's Ships at that place under the command of Admiral Duncan; will be more than he can be enabled to perform with requisite despatch; and being particularly anxious that the before mentioned Ships should be completed in their Provisions and Victualling Stores to the utmost expedition; have judged it expedient to order Mr John Slight, the First Clerk to the Superintendent at Deptford, to proceed to Yarmouth, for the purpose of affording Mr Lewes every assistance in his power, in the effecting of the business…' The fact that Slight was Pitt's replacement at Deptford and therefore senior to Lewes suggests that the real reason he was sent was because the Victualling Board had reservations about Lewes's ability to effectively carry out the work.[51]

The squadron arrived in the Roads on 3 October and two days later Lewes informed the Victualling Board that, 'all possible despatch is making to victual the Fleet under the Command of Admiral Duncan which [I] am in hopes will be nearly completed by Sunday.' On the 6th he wrote, 'I beg leave to inform you of Mr John Slight's arrival here yesterday in the mail coach and that we are making every dispatch possible to victual the Fleet…'[52] Lewes was fulsome in his praise of his superior's efforts, informing the Board on 8 October that, 'Mr Slight is now very busy in shipping off the remainder of the prov[ision]s due to each ship…every possible exertion has been made to victual the Fleet with the greatest expedition and that Mr Slight has been indefatigable both by night and day and has afforded me all the assistance he possibly could and by whose assiduity I am in hopes the Fleet will be quite complete by this evening or tomorrow morning.'[53] By the time the news arrived the following day that the Dutch Fleet had slipped out of the Texel, the North Sea Squadron had been re-provisioned and Duncan was able to give chase and cover himself in glory at Camperdown. Paget and the Deptford men had brought the re-provisioning time down from five weeks to five days, but Lewes, made no mention of Paget's involvement in victualling the Admiral's victorious squadron. In fairness the latter's accounts show little direct provisioning of the warships involved, but he had the management of the storehouses and provided the transportation, so his role must have been crucial, a contention borne out by Duncan's personal observations. According to Paget's son, 'after the victory the chief people of the town gave Lord Duncan a great dinner and drank his health. He, as I have heard, pointed to my father and said, "That's the man that won the battle." His merit is commemorated by a gold medal, which was given to him, I believe, by Lord Duncan…'[54]

In November 1797 Lewes took further swipes at Paget, on the face of it with just cause. He wanted to examine the warehoused stores to see if the quantities tallied with what Pitt had claimed were there before he departed, observing to the Board that, 'as Mr Saml Paget Junr was then and has been ever since in the habit of keeping the keys of the warehouses where they are deposited, makes me very anxious to know the state of the same, that if there should be any deficiency in any of the diff[eren]t species of provs[io]ns, your Honours may be acquainted with the same and be satisfied it must proceed from Mr Saml Paget Junr, who has always been in possession of the keys of the warehouse ever since the prov[ision]s were first deposited in them.'[55] In a similar vein, when a few days later the Board wanted Lewes to take particular care that Paget was not paid for the transportation of a certain consignment of fresh beef, he replied, 'as I have not the inspection of Mr Paget's accounts it will be impossible for me to know, when he makes a charge for the same, or when it goes off in the ship's boats, not being present at the delivery of the fresh beef.'[56]

38. The Duke's Head Hotel. It was here during a celebratory dinner, in 1798, that Admiral Duncan pointed at victualler Samuel Paget Junior and exclaimed 'That's the man that won the battle' (Camperdown).

In March 1798 Lewes thought his chance to clip Paget's wings had finally arrived. With the preparations being made to ready the squadron for its summer stint off the Texel, the Victualling Board, seemingly looking to break Paget's stranglehold, directed Lewes to report on what savings could be made if warehouses were hired direct, and to find alternatives for Paget's other services. On 16 March he gave an eager response only to follow it up two days later with a grovelling retraction which is very informative about Paget's operation. 'My first enquiry was with respect to procuring warehouses, and upon what terms as my estimate was only calculated to the terms which Mr Paget procured his, and which I find to be erroneous. In the strictest search I found only two for which from the knowledge of my being under the direction of the honble Board the terms were very high notwithstanding they were not well situated for despatch to the service as those occupied by Mr Paget, nor near large enough for the whole of the prov[ision]s. On second enquiery also into the charges paid by Mr Paget for craft for the conveyance of the prov[ision]s, beer and water, I found that instead of 2/6 being paid p[e]r ton, it averaged 4s. The cartage likewise considerably more, and if under the directions of your Honours, craft or cartage would not be procured at so cheap a rate. This erroneous information likewise prevents that saving to Government which I first estimated in the beer and water, and on reconsideration of the quantities of water demanded at this port,

I found on trial the four pumps at Gorleston was insufficient to supply even one fourth the quantity requisite, without noticing the labourage necessary to convey the water from the pumps to the craft with bungs, bung cloth &, and with respect to Sir Edmund Lacons ability to supply beer at 42s pr ton of the quality which would give satisfaction it is impossible for me to ascertain, but from every enquirey I could make, I find the beer supplied by Mr Paget is much approved of and issued by all the ships in the Roads. Upon the whole tho[ough] urged by my duty to represent circumstances as they offered to your Honours notice, I beg leave to intreat your permission to retract the estimate which I submitted, being now convinced I have been wrongly informed, which I hope the Honble Board will conceive arose from the extreme difficulty which an enquiery of that nature always occasions, and which is so subject to misinterpretation.'[57] Other than early references to supplies from Dover, beer is scarcely mentioned in the Pitt/Lewes letter book, seemingly because Paget provided it directly. It was around this time that Paget and his partner, Dawson Turner, bought a brewery, probably to meet this need. With the exception of water the provision of beer is the one commodity that consistently appears in Paget's accounts throughout the war.[58]

It is unclear whether Paget was aware of Lewes' attempt to weaken his position but, be that as it may, he continued to try to expand his victualling business. Having approached the Victualling Board with an offer to collect wine and spirits from Deptford, store it in his vessels in the harbour and deliver it as necessary to the warships he informed Lewes on 12 April that he intended to go to London that day, 'to wait on the Board to know their final determination respecting landing the wine and spirits onb[oar]d the vict[ualle]rs and putting them under

39. Paget and Turner's brewery.

40. By a contract awarded to Paget Junior, in 1798, he was to provide vessels to store wine and spirits which had to be moored with the merchant ships in the harbour.

his charge.' Up until then wine and spirits had been stored in the victuallers *Manchester*, *Princess* or *Caesar*, under the strict supervision of the local excise officers, a complication that was probably why Paget excluded these items from his earlier warehousing contract. In the event in September he was awarded a contract to provide, 'a sufficient number of proper Vessels capable of containing at one time a proportion of Wine and Spirits for Eight thousand Men for four months.' The vessels were to be moored in the harbour except when they went to Deptford for more supplies. He was also required to deliver the wine and spirits to the warships in the Roads, 'in such quantities as shall be demanded'. For this service he was to receive £40 per calendar month.[59]

If Lewes felt Paget was giving him the run around he was faring little better with Admiral Duncan. In early August 1798 the Admiral was preparing to return to the Texel and ordered Lewes to arrange for two of the water carriers to be fitted up to take bullocks to the squadron there and to inform the Victualling Board of his order. But when on 9 April he sought to receive fresh orders from Duncan he was fobbed off with the Admiral's secretary who told him that, 'it was his Lordship's pleasure I should go on fitting up those vessels for bullocks and that when he arrived off the Texel he should be better able to judge whether it would be necessary to continue them any longer for that purpose and that his Lordship would write more fully to the Honble Board on that subject.'[60]

In April 1798 the fully provisioned North Sea Squadron was back off the Texel and as in the previous year the intention was to keep it on station by sending out provisions when required. By July it was necessary to start the top up in this way, but three ships, the *Glatton*, *America* (64) and the *Veteran*, were sent back to Yarmouth to complete provisioning to four months. The *Glatton* was also loaded with an extra 300 tons of water to take back to the squadron.[61] On 2 August Lewes reported that, 'The 6 vessels employed by the Honble Board to convey water and bullocks to the Fleet off the Texel arrived here Tuesday afternoon from the Fleet and are now getting ready to carry out a fresh supply of the same to His Majesty's ships.'[62] Throughout August and September these six victuallers, *Eliza*, *Charlotte*, *Queen*, *Port Roseway* (replaced by the *Oak*) and two called *Providence*, beat their way under convoy, between Yarmouth and the squadron, with supplies of water, bullocks, vegetables and coal, but with the squadron returning to the Roads on 17 September their services were no longer required and they were sent back to Deptford.[63]

Paget's position was further strengthened on 16 October 1798 when Lewes had to inform the Victualling Board that, 'There being [a] very large demand for bread & butter & there being very little of the former and none of the latter in store, [I] have been under the necessity of entering into an agreement with Mr Saml Paget Junr for 1500 bags of the former at 220s 6d p[e]r hundred exclusive of the bags and 20000 pounds of the latter at 9d per pound, being the lowest terms I could make, which [I] hope will meet...your Honours approbation.'[64] How difficult it must have been for him to write the words, 'under the necessity.' Five days later, on sending a bread sample to the Board, he included in his covering letter, 'and beg leave to acquaint the Honable Board that the demands for that article & butter were so sudden I had it not in my power to make a better agreement at the time...'[65] He clearly felt he had let his superiors down. With a similar need arising on 20 October and beyond the Victualling Board decided to accept the reality of the situation and on 3 December Lewes was directed to conclude an agreement with Paget to provide an additional quantity of 1000 bags of bread to be delivered monthly for six months at the rate of 18s 10d per cwt and 1s 6d each bag to commence from 20 December. In doing so Lewes informed the Victualling Board that Paget, 'would not agree to supplying it on lower terms as he says the markets are getting up in price.'[66] The agreement was reviewed on 30 march 1799 and continued thereafter. In a similar fashion Paget provided butter, salt, bisket and coal, together with table money and necessary money for the Russian warships. He even paid the coopers their wages. The Victualling Board needed Mr Samuel Paget Junior.

The other local contractor, Thomas Martin Jnr., had not fared so well. Concerned about the high prices of fresh beef at Yarmouth, in September 1797, the Board employed Messrs Peter and William Mellish to investigate. Peter Mellish visited the town on 19 September and reported his findings to a Board meeting on 4 December. As a result Martin's contract was terminated as from 10 December, 'it appearing on mature deliberation, that it will be highly to the advantage of the Crown to employ Messrs Peter & William Mellish in the future performance of this service...' Unfortunately for Martin it seems that a touch of 'judge and jury' had come into play. These brothers were well established national commission agents who intended to employ a Mr Capon as their local agent to handle their affairs and John Kett to actually furnish the beef at a rate of 42s per cwt for one year from the 11th.[67]

The last entry in the Pitt/Lewes letter book is dated 16 May 1799 and from then we lose touch with much of the detail and colour that has lifted the description of this mundane topic, especially the nature of the relationship between Paget and the two Deptford men. Paget and Lewes continued to work together until the end of the Revolutionary War with Paget's role remaining much the same. His accounts show that from 1799 he largely concentrated on supplying beer and water and was paid for the hire of storehouses, the provision of 'craft' and cartage, together with the provision of, 'vessels for the Depot of Wine & spirits.'[68] He also continued to supply the Victualling Board with other provisions as the need arose, especially bread and bisket, taking full advantage of the prevailing market conditions. With the price of wheat rising through 1800 he was able to increase his prices and in early 1801, when Admiral Sir Hyde Parker's fleet gathered in Yarmouth Roads before setting off for Copenhagen, he was able to drive a hard bargain.[69] Once Parker's fleet had sailed, however, the Board seemed to try again to break Paget's grip by contracting with William Worts to supply bisket at 50s 6d, per cwt, less than was being paid to Paget, but Worts had difficulty fulfilling his contract and ceased doing so after 30 August 1801.[70] By then Samuel Paget's career in the victualling business had peaked. With peace looming the commodity prices started to fall and the Victualling Board decided not to purchase any more bread or bisket from him. He still had his sea provisions contract, but demand for his services began to fall away.[71]

On 4 June 1802 the Victualling Board directed Samuel Lewes to send the two coopers back to Deptford and, when the remainder of the casks had been shipped, to dismiss his clerk and resume his duties as a clerk under the Clerk of the Cutting House at Deptford. Paget was still providing storehouses and transport for the provisions delivered to the warships in the Roads, together with vessels to act as a depot for wine and spirits, but his services in this

41. Warships moored in Yarmouth Roads.

respect were discontinued on 5 June. He then reverted to providing sea provisions for the much reduced naval presence at Yarmouth, as he had done when first starting out, but the victualling accounts include no entries for him beyond December 1802.[72] While his relationships with Pitt and Lewes was always strained, that with the naval officers he served could not have been better. Like Duncan before him Admiral Dickson was fulsome in his praise. On leaving his North Sea command he told the Admiralty commissioners that, 'during the time I have Commanded His Majesty's Ships and Vessels in the North Sea, the conduct of Mr Paget the Contractor for Supplying the Squadron with Provisions, and Water has been so uniform, and exemplary, that nothing could have exceeded his exertions for the benefit of the public service, and I beg to recommend his Zeal, and attention to his Contract to their Lordships consideration, and notice.'[73]

***

In June 1803, at the start of the new conflict, the Admiralty ordered the Victualling Board to send a quantity of provisions to Yarmouth, Deal, Harwich and Leith, and the urgency for Yarmouth was quickly reinforced by a direction that, 'a proper proportion of Provisions of all Species be immediately provided and deposited at the Victualling Stores at North Yarmouth for the supply of the Cruizers belonging to the North Sea Squadron as may from time to time arrive there to prevent the necessity of their proceeding to the Nore for that purpose.'[74] Quickly responding to the first of these requirements the Victualling Board sent Samuel Lewes back to Yarmouth to manage its affairs there and on 27 May decided to dispatch commissioners George Phillips Towry and Robert Sadleir Moody to the town to examine prices and premises, 'in like manner as was agreed with Mr Samuel Paget during the late War.'[75] The two reported back on 9 June. By then stores had already arrived at the naval support base and a warehouse had been hired for their storage, but for some unknown reason the Victualling Board suddenly changed its mind, deciding instead to seek a sea provisions contractor rather than maintain its own victualling facility in the town.[76]

Although Samuel Paget's contract had lapsed towards the end of the last war he was still the man with the most recent experience of carrying out the work.[77] Invited to take part in the tendering process for a new contract he sent a total of seven letters to the Board and as he had done at the outset of his career travelled to London to make his case before submitting his tender on 13 June.[78] There was other interest, but at the close of the tender period, on 16 June, the choice lay between him and John Grant, the national contractor, who in the previous war had missed out on the Yarmouth sea provisions contract, but had held that for rum. After careful scrutiny Grant was awarded the contract. The two competing submissions were similarly priced but what separated them was the fact that Paget's included conditions whereby if, at the end of the war or in the event of unforeseen circumstances, he was left with a considerable stock of provisions, it would be taken off his hands by the government. Grant's tender contained no such attempt to minimise the risk and this seems to have resonated well with the Victualling Board. In addition the scale of Grant's operation enabled the Board to confidently, 'enter into a Contract for the Victualling of His Majesty's Ships upon that Station than to revert to the mode, which it was found necessary to adopt in the late War, of having a Temporary Victualling Establishment at that place.'[79] Grant's contract

42. Loading victualling stores on Yarmouth Quay.

required him to be at all times in a position to victual 8,000 seamen for four months. He installed an agent in a victualling office, local man John Walter, (Lewes was recalled to Deptford) and took over the storehouse that had been hired by commissioners Towry and Moody, together with the stores already deposited there. These he issued on a commission basis until June 1804, when there was none left.[80]

With Samuel Paget no longer holding a sea provisions contract the Victualling Board wrote to him concerning the future of his water contract, to which he replied that he was willing to relinquish it. This the Board readily agreed to having already sounded out Grant on the subject, for on 5 July the latter wrote offering to supply water at the considerably reduced rate of 6s/5d per tun. As a result he was awarded a contract to supply water on the usual terms. In addition in October 1803 Grant began supplying flour and raisons which were not items included in his sea provisions contract.[81] As far as the provision of fresh beef was concerned, the Mellish brothers continued to hold the contract, sub-contracting it locally to Messrs Lowden and Son, with the agreement of the Victualling Board. They also supplied live oxen to the ships and vessels watching the Texel. Vegetables were the only commodity not supplied by Grant or the Mellish brothers, these being provided from March 1804 by Richard Kemp.[82]

It was the duty of the port-admiral to ensure that all naval ships and vessels were ready to put to sea as quickly as possible and the key to this was efficient victualling. For Rear-Admiral Russell, however, this was not a smooth process. On his arrival in early November 1803 he was approached by John Walter with a complaint that keels were being unnecessarily detained alongside the men-of-war. In response he issued a general order stating, 'that all possible dispatch be used in expediting the Agent Victualler's Craft,' and to encourage compliance he required details of the keel's arrival and departure to be entered in the ships' logs.[83] In January 1804 it was Russell's turn to complain, writing to the Victualling Board on the 18th to report that there was no pork in store at Yarmouth. The Commissioners immediately asked Grant for an explanation which he forwarded to them on the 20th. On the specific reason for the complaint he wrote that he was, 'extremely sorry that the unusual demand for Pork, has exhausted the Stock I had in hand,' but that a vessel had sailed that day from London for Yarmouth with 5,058 pieces of pork which, 'I trust she will arrive in time to prevent any delay to the Service.'[84] Having said this he went on to outline the cause of the problem as he saw it. In his opinion he had established at Yarmouth sufficient quantities of stock to fulfil the requirements of his contract, based on previous demand, expecting that as the North Sea cruisers put in to complete their provisions, the stock would diminish, but (he alleged) that as the ships came in they were ordered to the Nore to victual, leaving him 'daily sustaining an heavy loss on the advance of Capital and a still heavier one from depredations of Vermin and natural decay.'[85] Because of this he had re-calculated what was needed to be stored and as a result he could easily be caught out, as was the case with the pork. For good measure he also complained that provisions were frequently sent back after the keels had been kept alongside the warships for a whole day.[86] In the event Russell dismissed Grant's claims as excuses and like Onslow before him expressed the view that, 'Being only an executive officer it must not be expected that I waste my time on altercations except this once.[87]

43. A wherry lightening the cargo of a brig in Yarmouth Roads to enable it to negotiate the harbour bar. Although neither a warship nor a keel the print gives a good impression of the victualling process carried on there.

Russell also had a problem with fresh beef supplies. On 8 April he informed the Admiralty that the *Hero* (74) could, now be considered to be a healthy ship, thanks to the, 'very Extraordinary zeal and Ability of Doctor Baird in only six days exertion,' and that she would sail the next day with 20 oxen for the Texel squadron, together with a week's fresh beef for her own crew.[88] On the 10th, however, he wrote to report that the *Hero* had been prevented by an easterly gale from sailing that day, but that she could have sailed the previous day, in moderate weather, had it not been for the fact that the 20 oxen, ordered by the purser on 30 March had not arrived. Furthermore he informed the Victualling Board that this was the third time that, 'the Agent to the Contractor for supplying fresh beef here has disappointed us and delayed the Service.' William Mellish, like Grant earlier in the year, disputed the facts, but by then the Admiralty had directed the Victualling Board to, 'take such measures as may prevent similar disappointments in future.'[89]

Despite such operational difficulties Grant, or more specifically his local agent John Walter, ran the victualling service at Yarmouth for the best part of seven years.[90] At the heart of this activity was the need to satisfy the demands of the various warship pursers for the food and drink set out in the sea provisions and water contracts, but there was much more to the role than that for the agency also carried out work on a commission basis, organised transport for others and took responsibility for the casks and other containers provided by the Victualling Board. The main commission work concerned those sensitive commodities wine and spirits and for a while tea. From May 1804 the contractor's accounts show regular entries for 'Commission & Expenses on shipping & storing Tea and Wine.' These items were kept in secure storage and replenished externally when required. In April 1808 Messrs Scott Idles & Co. were contracted to provide 50 to 60 tuns of Spanish red wine to be delivered 'into the Stores of Mr John Grant the Contractor at Yarmouth,' and when in May 1809 Grant informed the Victualling Board that 'the Wine which was received into Store at that place (Yarmouth) is all expended,' John Walter was sent a further 10,000 gallons from Deptford.[91]

In terms of transport, Grant hired the keels necessary to take his agency's provisions out to the ships in the Roads and he also provided the same service for the contractors supplying fresh beef and vegetables. In addition he played a part in transporting goods from Deptford. In August 1809 the victualling agent at that place, 'had used every endeavor in his power to engage a Vessel to convey the Wine and other Stores due on warrant for Yarmouth.' Grant immediately stepped in with the offer of a schooner to carry out the work 'at the rate of sixteen Shillings per ton.' The offer was accepted and an additional schooner was also hired from him at the same rate.[92] As far as casks were concerned Grant organised their assembly, repair and issue. They, as before, were sent from Deptford in kit form under orders such as that of 25 September 1810 which required 300 butts, 300 puncheons and 300 hogsheads to be dispatched.[93] To carry out this work he set up a cooperage, but by the autumn of 1807, with the opening up of the Baltic front, he needed to expand his operation in this respect and increase his access to fresh water. As luck would have it, four years after he had given up his water contract, Samuel Paget Jnr. still possessed the well he had sunk on the Denes, together with the yard and buildings that accompanied it. Grant promptly bought these premises and leased from the Corporation an adjoining piece of land to the south with permission 'to enclose the same and to erect a Cooperage thereon.'[94]

The year 1810 proved to be a difficult one for the country's leading sea provisions contractors. Early on Grant wrote to the Victualling Board regarding losses he had sustained

44. The brig-sloop *Chanticleer* was a familiar sight in the Yarmouth Roads from 1808 until the end of the war. An accomplished prize taker she was typical of the smaller naval craft victualled at the naval support base.

in fulfilling his contracts, but the Board was not prepared to offer him relief, pointing out that he could at any time have given notice to terminate his contracts.[95] The surviving documentation does not record which of Grant's contracts were proving unprofitable, but it seems clear from other sources that he was struggling at Yarmouth to carry out his obligations. The contractor's accounts show that he continued to provide sea provisions until October, but in March he had been given the customary six month notice to terminate his contract and in September found himself having to re-tender for the work. Three submissions were received. The most expensive was that of Benjamin Ogden, but Grant was pushed into second place by London based contractor Belcher Byles, who was duly awarded the contract on 20 September 1810. Perhaps because he owned the well at Yarmouth Grant retained the contract to supply water, but this too was taken over by Byles, just before the former's bankruptcy in December 1812.[96]

Although Byles was awarded a sea provisions contract the Victualling Board was no longer disposed to risk leaving the service entirely in private hands, so it decided once more to appoint an agent of its own to manage the victualling service at Yarmouth.[97] It is unclear exactly when John Crockford was sent to fulfil this role, nor how his work meshed with that of Byles, but he first appears in the Victualling Board's minutes for February 1811 and remained active until the service was wound up at the end of the war. The wisdom of the appointment was soon to manifest itself. In September 1812 Byles was obliged to win his contract again, suggesting that by then there were concerns about his performance and in

April 1813 he wrote to the Victualling Board 'Stating his inability at present from the embarrassed state of his Affairs to furnish the supply of Sea Provisions required under his Contract at Yarmouth and requesting that such Articles thereof as shall be demanded for the Service of His Majestys Ships at that place may be purchased, and the difference of price be charged against him…' By return Byles was informed that Crockford had been directed 'to purchase, on the best and most advantageous terms that can be obtained, whatever quantities of Provisions and Water, the Service of His Majesty's ships at that place may require…'[98] This interim measure remained in place for three months, but with Byles in the throes of bankruptcy the sea provisions contract had to be tendered again. The Victualling Board received five submissions the lowest of which was that from Sir William Fletcher who on the 20 July was duly awarded the contract. The highest bid came from prominent merchant and brewer Francis Riddle Reynolds, the first local man to throw his hat into the ring since Samuel Paget. The contract for supplying water was tendered separately with Andrew Belcher proving successful.[99]

The other main area of provision, fresh beef, was also problematical with there being a succession of contractors, almost on an annual basis. Mellish lasted until the end of 1804. He was followed by H. Giles, William Nutt and John Lowden(1805), John Kett & Robert Leeder(1806), John Lowden Junior(1807), Christopher Horrocks(1808), John Lowden Junior (1809-1810), Robert Leeder(1811-1812), David Cockrill(1813-1814) and Nathaniel Martin (1815). In the summer months these contractors continued to provide live oxen to the ships in the Roads, off the Texel and at Heligoland.[100]

While the prohibition of ships-of-the-line entering the Roads from the end of 1810 was not

45. Heligoland was serviced from Yarmouth from its capture in 1807 until the end of the war.

the cause of John Grant's problems it could not have helped the Yarmouth victualling contractors thereafter. At its peak in 1807 the contractors annual business amounted to around £160, 000. By the end of 1810 this had almost halved and by the end of 1813 it had almost halved again. It is difficult, however, to draw hard and fast conclusions from this data for there is no record of the in-house supplies provided by John Crockford during this latter period.[101]

6.
Naval Stores

Being made of wood the warships of this period needed constant maintenance. Major repairs and refits were completed at the Royal Dockyards or occasionally at smaller yards but, while at sea, ships and vessels in need of running repairs had to rely on their own carpenters to carry out the work. Such repairs often necessitated replacement naval stores which had to be sourced wherever the warship or vessel happened to drop anchor. To facilitate this the Navy Board maintained a network of agents in ports up and down the country. These were called 'naval officers', but contrary to what that term implies they were civilians who had the necessary contacts to acquire supplies rather than stock them themselves. They also acted as a point of contact for naval captains who needed any form of assistance.

At the outbreak of the war wine merchant Robert Warmington was the Naval Officer at Yarmouth, having performed the role for many years. In January 1796 the captain of the Russian ship *Nikanor*(66) approached him for stores of some kind (probably anchors). Reporting this to the Navy Board, he was directed to acquaint the captain, 'that he should inform us of the nature of his wants and when we hear from him shall take measures for supplying them.' But Warmington had already complied with the request, for shortly afterwards he was told that the Navy Board approved of what he had done and that, 'if the Bills are approved & signed by the Russian Admiral they will be paid.'[1] When he approached the Board for payment, however, he was told he would be allowed a commission of 2½ per cent for the supplies to the Russian ships-of-war, other than for those he personally provided, and also for payments he may have made for the salvage of anchors belonging to British warships, but in respect of the stores supplied for repairs to those ships, their captains were under instruction, 'to oversee and manage the whole business without putting the Public to the Expense of Commission to any Person.'[2]

With Warmington having drawn attention to Yarmouth in this way the Navy Board decided to raise the town's store-keeping profile, resolving on 10 February to, 'Desire Mr Warmington to let us know if it will be convenient to him to take charge of a few Anchors and Cables etc and if he can procure Warehouses.'[3] He was quick to respond to this request, couched as it was in the customary well-mannered style used when dealing with civilians. He felt, 'it would be of great use if some anchors & Cables etc were sent for the Ships Riding in Yarmouth Roads' and that he could procure warehouses to lodge them.'[4] On the 13 February he was informed that an 'account' of a small proportion of Stores,' would be sent to him in the post, with instructions as to how they were to be issued.[5] He formally became Yarmouth's naval storekeeper on the 16 February, the Board having already informed the Admiralty that, 'we have fixed upon a proportion of Stores [to be] kept at Yarmouth which will be sent there as opportunities may offer, but as Mr Warmington merchant of that place has for many years past transacted what Business we had to do there & very much to our satisfaction We propose

46. Robert Warmington, naval storekeeper at Yarmouth, 1796-1812.

consigning the stores to his care.'[6]

At the outset he took delivery of 13 anchors with their cables and hired a number of warehouses in which to store them. Scarcely had he done so, however, than the Navy Board felt it necessary to remind him of the limitations of the service he was to provide.[7] On 27 February he was informed that he should retain the Russian anchors he had acquired and to re-issue them to Russian ships. He should also inform the pursers of the *Glatton* and the *Brilliant* and any other officers who may apply to him that it is only intended to keep anchors and cables at Yarmouth and not any small stores. For those they must wait until they arrived at a King's port.[8] One suspects that part of the reason for establishing stores at Yarmouth, albeit of a limited description, was to keep the Russian ships away from the more significant naval bases as much as possible.

Curiously, but not by the norms of the day, Warmington had not been told how much he would be paid for his work as storekeeper. On 5 March 1797, over a year after his appointment, he wrote to the Navy Board to ascertain what salary he was to receive and also seeking a rent for a building of his that had been converted into a naval storehouse. In response the Board directed its secretary to, 'Acquaint Mr Warmington that the Board having repeatedly desired him to make up his accounts to the end of the last year and not having yet received them they cannot yet determine what Salary etc to allow him until they see his accounts and can ascertain what trouble he has had.'[9] It was not until 10 October that the Board fixed his salary at £200 per annum, back-dated to his appointment. His clerk's salary was set at £40 (raised in December to £60). There was to be a rate of twopence in the pound commission on disbursements.[10]

The aftermath of Camperdown greatly tested the ability of the naval store to provide what was needed for the damaged North Sea Squadron, with Captain John Knight, its senior naval officer at the time, directing that boatswain's and carpenter's stores 'be furnish'd as far as the Kings Stores at this Place will admit.' As a result in November 1797 the variety and quantity of stores was increased and on 31 January 1798 Captain Harry Hamood, a Navy Board commissioner, was 'desired to proceed to Yarmouth to enquire into the situation of the storehouses hired by Mr Warmington and the manner of furnishing stores to His Majesty's Ships there, and also to inform himself for the guidance of the Board, with the best method to be adopted for supplying stores there, and performing such slight repairs as may be thought necessary & proper to be done at Yarmouth.'[11]

Having carried out his investigation Hamood reported to the Board that, 'the stores are at present disposed of in different parts of the Town in very inconvenient situations and at high

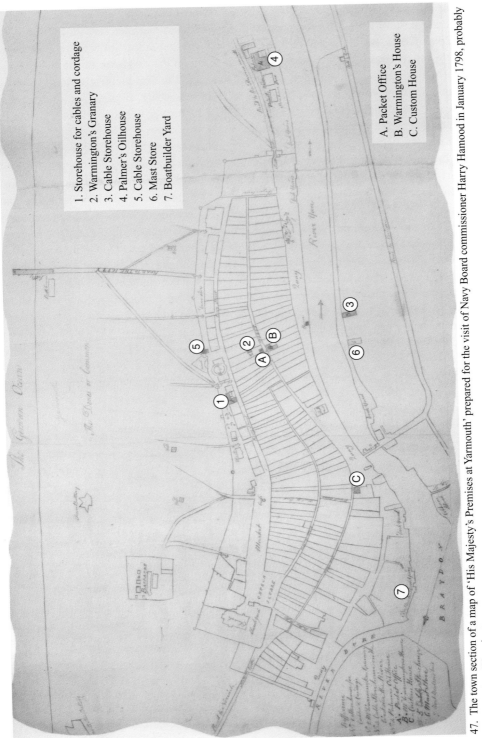

1. Storehouse for cables and cordage
2. Warmington's Granary
3. Cable Storehouse
4. Palmer's Oilhouse
5. Cable Storehouse
6. Mast Store
7. Boatbuilder Yard

A. Packet Office
B. Warmington's House
C. Custom House

47. The town section of a map of 'His Majesty's Premises at Yarmouth' prepared for the visit of Navy Board commissioner Harry Hamood in January 1798, probably by Robert Warmington.

rents, but that there is a capacious Store house of 108 feet in Length and 68 in breadth with a yard annexed to it which may be purchased for £400 and that the estimate for putting it into order will be £300 which will enable us to give up six out of the Seven Storehouses now hired at Annual Rents.'[12] The building identified stood on the east bank of the river, to the south of the South Gate. It was one of three constructed in that vicinity in the 1780's by different merchant consortia to pursue the Greenland whale fishery, ventures which, according to Warmington, ceased trading in 1794. This former 'whale oil house' was built on land owned by the Corporation and was subject to two leases, granted in 1784 and 1788. By 27 February Warmington had purchased the premises on behalf of the Navy Board and shortly thereafter the building was converted into a naval storehouse.[13]

As part of this upgrade the Navy Board decided to acquire a sailing lighter to transport stores from shore to ship and to collect them from Deptford. In April 1798 Yarmouth boat builders Preston and Son were contracted to construct her and on 26 November Warmington reported that, 'the Yarmouth Lighter has got in the Iron Ballast out of the Deptford Lighter, & will be ready for Sea in a few Days, but I have been able to get only One Man (for a crew), I beg to know whether any can be sent from One of the Kings Yards.'[14] The lighter needed a crew of ten but when approached the Deptford Yard could not find any men 'disposed to go to Yarmouth' on the terms offered. Having tried the kid glove approach the Navy Board now applied the iron fist. The Master Attendant at Deptford was directed to *order* men to perform the task. [15]

Between April and October 1798 the variety of small stores held at Yarmouth gradually

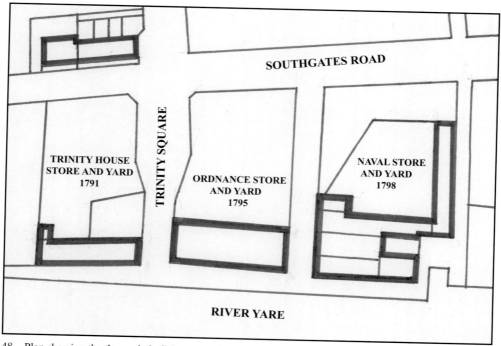

48. Plan showing the three whale fishery premises created in the 1780's and their subsequent use in the 1790's.

increased. These additions included coils of rope, leads, lines, beds and bedding and a full range of sea clothes.[16] In November the Navy Board decided to expand the facility still further. Having sent the Deputy Comptroller and the Surveyor of the Navy to review the situation, the Board wrote to the Admiralty stating that the new store building was 'perfectly proper for the purpose both with regard to its situation and size conformably to the Establishment of Stores there appropriated to Yarmouth but as it has since been thought necessary to augment the quantity of stores from the increase of Ships resorting to the Roads more particularly in Cables and Cordage and it is also intended to have a Depot of ready-made Topmasts and yards besides rough sticks that store has been found inadequate to contain the whole they have therefore recommended the purchase of a house and Premises contiguous to the Naval Storehouse belonging to a Mr Fisher which is estimated to be worth £400 or £420 which Sum or nearly so we shall be under the necessity of expending in building a shed to contain the Topmasts and Yards and making a proper way for hauling them up unless this house and Premises are purchased.' The Admiralty approved the acquisition.[17]

By January 1799 the amount of naval storekeeping business carried out in Warmington's office had increased to the extent that he had had to employ a second clerk. The man also acted as the warehouseman and was paid a salary of £50. Informed of this situation the Navy Board agreed to fund the cost of the man, but wanted him to live on the premises. As a result Warmington set about building a cottage in the naval yard.[18] In April 1799 he wrote again to the Board, highlighting a number of improvements that he considered necessary there. He had petitioned the Corporation for permission to erect a crane, the result of which was expected shortly, and he enclosed an estimate of £24.10s for 'making a Slip & a Crab without which we cannot get Spars and Masts into the Store house.' He also enclosed one for £12 for fencing the site and providing gates. By then the dwelling was nearing completion.[19] Both estimates were approved and in May nearly 60 lower yards and masts were delivered to the new mast store.[20]

By mid-1799 all the improvements had been completed and the yard was supplying a much wider range of stores and services to the ships and vessels in the Roads (in 1800 a further 43 sails were added to the itinerary). But Yarmouth was still dependent on the Sheerness and Deptford yards, the one for handling most ship repairs, the other for the provision of stores. In January 1801 the ship-sloop *Driver* arrived from off the Vlie Passage. Her defects were too substantial to be made good in the Roads, so she was ordered by Admiral Dickson to proceed to the Nore. In the event the Sheerness dockyard was too busy to take any more ships so the *Driver* was sent on a cruise off the entrance to the Elbe for a month prior to getting into Sheerness for a refit.[21] Such occurrences were not unusual.

In early 1801 Warmington approached the Navy Board for salary increases for his staff and additional expenses for himself. In respect of his clerk and clerk/warehouseman he explained that they were both married with families, but that the cost of provisions of all kinds were so expensive that they were unable to maintain themselves or their families. As a result the Board raised the salary of the clerk to £80 and the clerk/warehouseman to £65. For himself he pointed out that the business of the yard had greatly increased in the past three years and that he had never had an allowance for office rent or stationery. Sidestepping the issue of rent the Navy Board awarded him £10 per annum for stationery. All the increases were backdated to the previous 1 January.[22]

Things ran smoothly from then until peace removed the need for a naval store at Yarmouth. On 8 May 1802 the Navy Board gave orders for the stores to be removed to Deptford and for the storehouse to be let. The former proved to be a drawn out affair for on chasing progress in October, the commissioners were told that, 'the Deptford [lighter] is now in Loading, after which about two trips for each Vessel (that and the Yarmouth lighter) will clear all the Stores except the Spars mentioned in the Margin; the Lighters each of them take four spars alongside after they are loaded which is so many as they can take with safety; if they could stow the spars in the holds the whole might be cleared by the end of the year.'[23] In respect of letting the store Warmington informed the merchants of the town that the premises were available, but told the Board he had, 'little reason to suppose they will let, as there are several in the Town unoccupied.'[24] The Board informed him that if he was not able to let them he was to take care they were not damaged.[25] In the event Warmington's pessimism proved unfounded for on the 26 November Thomas & Edmund Hurry & Co offered to hire the premises for £25 per annum, with a three month notice period. The Board agreed to these terms, 'provided they keep the Wharf, and all the Premises in repair.'[26] In accordance with the Board's order of the 25 December 1802 Warmington dismissed his staff, but in respect of himself he wrote, 'I humbly beg leave to inform You that there are nearly as many Stores remaining here as will load the Lighter when She returns from Deptford, My Accounts of disbursements etc shall be forwarded to the Office the instant they are compleated but I beg leave to mention that it will take at least two months to finish all the Accounts and I hope Your Honors will be pleased to continue the Salary [for] that time.'[27] The Board agreed to pay his salary until the stores were removed, but as his accounts should have been regularly kept up to date they would not pay it, 'during the time they are compiling.'[28] On 8 January 1803 he informed the Navy Board that the 'magazines' were now clear except for the anchors he had been ordered to retain. He was paid until that date when his role reverted to that of Naval Officer.[29]

**

Less than five months later, on 26 May 1803, Warmington was re-appointed naval store-keeper, following the collapse of the peace. Soon after the storehouse and yard were returned to him, under the terms of Messrs Hurry's lease. As per a Navy Board warrant of 7 June he was sent an establishment book setting out those items he was to manage and shortly afterwards the specified stores arrived from Deptford.[30] He was soon to discover, however, that neither the Admiralty nor the Navy Board had any intention of re-establishing the service at its 1802 level and he found himself without a vessel to convey the stores, for in August the Navy Board decided that the Yarmouth lighter should be retained at Deptford for the duration of the new conflict.[31] A more fundamental problem was the cautious approach taken by the Navy Board to what could be stored. The allocation comprised 7 anchors, 12 cables, 140 coils, 30 hawsers, 21 yards, 13 topmasts, and 43 sails, together with some smaller items such as lead lines. It was a less than adequate provision for the needs of the ships and vessels resorting to the support base, as soon became apparent.[32]

In October Rear-Admiral Thornbrough was having difficulties in respect of stores, with several of his ships being 'under the necessity of going to sea at this season of the year without being supplied with slop Clothes or Beds.' In addition Rear-Admiral Russell's port duty letters to the secretary of the Admiralty make frequent reference to the inability of the store to provide what was required. On 20 November 1803 he wrote that, 'The *Galgo* being in great want of Sails and other Stores of which there is no Supply here…' (she also needed caulking and was sent to the Nore for that purpose) and on 22 January 1804 he acknowledged the fact that, 'their Lordships have been pleased to direct the Navy Board to Send without a moment's loss of time, the Sails and such other Stores to the *Antelope*, as She cannot be supplied with at Yarmouth.'[33] Responding to this situation, the Navy Board augmented the stores on nine separate occasions before, on 19 April 1804, greatly increasing the allocation to include more masts, spars, cables and hawsers, a large quantity of deals, boards and planking, boats,

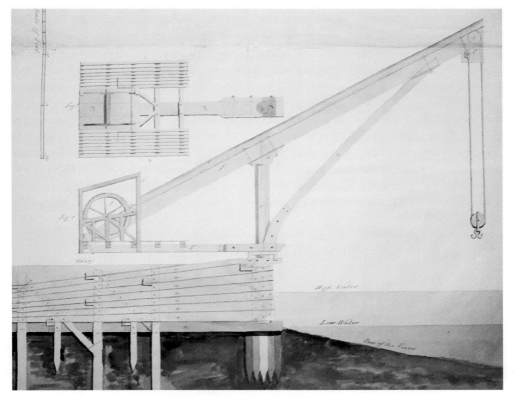

49. A drawing of the crane erected at the naval yard in early 1800.

blocks, boat hooks, nails and leather scuppers.[34] The improvement this represented was soon to bear fruit for in May 1804 Russell was able to report that, 'The *Mallard* has arrived from the Texel with the loss of three top masts, top-gallant mast, jib-boom, Bower Anchor and Cable Buoy and Buoy Rope… There are top masts Cables and Anchors in Store here, which I shall order her to be supplied with, the top-gallant mast and jib boom, shall be made for her on board the *Stately*' (his flagship).[35]

Not that predicting the demand for naval stores at an out-port like Yarmouth was an easy thing to do. In February 1806 Warmington wrote to the Navy Board in the following terms, 'The Establishment of 74 Gun Ships Sails being larger than is required for this Port, and having so little room to Store them, that they cannot be properly looked after in case of wet getting to them; and as I am fearful some of them may get injury before they can be brought into use, I beg leave to suggest for your consideration the reducing [of] the Establishment, for which purpose I enclose an Account of the Number now in Store and the Number proposed to be sent away leaving two of each sort in store which will be a Sufficient Establishment for carrying on the Service of this Port.' The Board agreed and 41 sails were sent to Chatham, leaving 34 in the store.[36] Nine months later, however, port-admiral Billy Douglas informed the Admiralty that, 'I have requested the Navy Board to send a proper proportion of Stores to this Place, as the Naval Officer has hardly a coil of Rope in store,… ' The Admiralty's response was to direct the Navy Board, 'to send a supply of small stores to North Yarmouth where they appear to be much wanted.'[37]

There were also other areas where Warmington felt under-resourced. In September 1804, he approached the Navy Board for an additional clerk and was told to justify the need. In response he said, '[I] beg leave to acquaint your Honors that when I applied to You [in the] last war for an Extra Clerk and Warehouseman You allowed me one on my representing to You the necessity of having a warehouseman to live on the spot to take care of the Stores, and to assist my Clerk in receiving and Issuing Stores; and having as much Duty to do this War as at any time during the last from the Number of Ships on this Station, I beg leave to acquaint you that this Service cannot be carried on with less assistance than Your Honors are pleased to allow me at this time, indeed I have more Duty to [do in] this War than [the] last, as your Honors had a Superintending Master here last war.'[38] The appointment was duly approved and William Nichols became 'warehouse-keeper to the Naval Store,' but not for

50. Activity at the naval yard's wharf. The warehouseman's cottage can be seen fronting the slipway

long for on 25 September 1806 he fell overboard from a vessel and drowned before he could be rescued. The forty-year old was described as a man 'much respected by his employers' and a subscription was opened for the relief of his large family.[39] Still playing catch up in April 1805, Warmington reminded the Navy Board that in the last war he had had a fire engine on site and that as there was a great number of prizes laying on the opposite side of the river to the store it would be prudent to have one again in case of an accident. He also asked for 30 fire buckets. A fire engine was duly sent.[40]

Warmington had been re-appointed on a salary of £200, with his clerk, Thornton Fisher, receiving £80, the same remuneration they had received during the previous war.[41] Thinking these sums inadequate to cover the work involved Warmington approached the Navy Board for increases. The Board was sympathetic and recommended that they should be paid the same as the equivalent officers at Kinsale and Leith i.e. £240 per annum for Warmington and £120 for his clerk. Unfortunately for them the Admiralty did not agree.[42]

The year 1807 was to prove a very active one for the naval yard. In addition to his usual day to day storekeeping duties, Warmington busied himself improving the store's facilities. In April he submitted a proposal for the addition of an upper floor on the masthouse, in order to create a sail-loft. On receiving his plan and estimate the Navy Board sent the Master Carpenter of the Sheerness yard to assess the scheme. His response was favourable and as a result a warrant for its construction was issued on 6 May.[43] The work progressed so quickly that on 13 June Warmington was able to report that the loft was ready to receive sails. But he had not acquired all he needed, for with his letter to the Navy Board, he had enclosed an estimate of £41-14-10, 'for making a Nail Room and a place under it for the Fire Engine, also a Necessary Contiguous to the Buildings which is very much wanted, and to repair the Boundary Fence and Crane etc.' As a means to save money his intention was to use condemned masts and yards for all the carpentry work. Permission was forthcoming, but he was chastised for not consulting the Sheerness Master Carpenter on the proposals when the latter had recently visited the yard.[44] On 18 July Warmington reported that all the works had been completed, but he also raised another matter, for at very high tides the river flowed round the buildings and at times it was difficult to keep the water out of the stores. Ever the man with a solution he informed the Board, that, 'the Engine for clearing the River is now at Work and I can have any quantity of Mud necessary for stopping the Breach and raising the Ground next the Stores by paying part of the labor of landing the same.' The Navy Board directed him to 'cause the Work to be performed.'[45]

At this juncture, events at Copenhagen and subsequently in the Baltic presented Warmington with a fresh challenge. On 13 August the Yarmouth correspondent of the *Norfolk Chronicle* reported that, 'The establishment for naval stores at this port is ordered to be increased equal to the supplying of 20 sail of the line, with a proportion of frigates and small vessels.'[46] By then Warmington had been notified and had been sent a new establishment book, under a warrant of 8 August, setting out the stores he was now expected to stock. It ran to 75 pages, listing large quantities of a wide range of naval stores.[47] Showing his concern Warmington informed the Navy Board that he found, 'the Magazines are not capable of receiving near the quantity of Stores intended to be sent particularly Cables and I have been obliged to prevail on Mr Davy to Let me a part of the Trinity Store for a short time to put some of the Cables received by the *Sussex Oak* Transport not having room for them in the Store.'[48] His remedy was to build a new two storey storehouse and accompanying his letter was a plan and elevation of the proposal, together with an estimate of £1,044-18-9½. It was a fine effort at such short notice, but the Navy Board did not react positively and the building was never built. Perhaps his recent capital expenditure was thought to be enough for the time being.[49]

There were other service upgrades including the return of the Yarmouth lighter and more significantly the appointment of a master shipwright and a master attendant. On 16 November

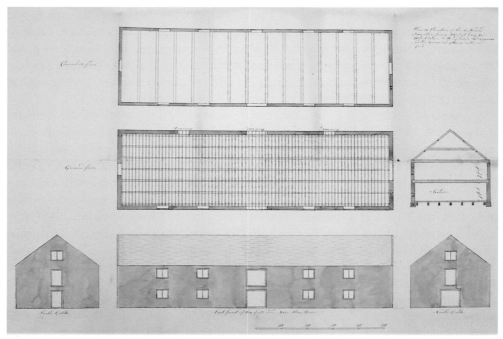

51. Plans and elevations of the new storehouse proposed by Warmington in August 1807 to cater for an increase in stock brought about by the events in the Baltic. In the event it was never built.

the newly appointed secretary to the Admiralty Board, William Wellesley-Pole, asked the Navy Board, 'whether it may not be proper to establish a Shipwright Officer with Shipwrights and Caulkers at Yarmouth.' The Navy Board's response was that while the appointment of a shipwright officer was considered advisable it felt that it, 'would be better to hire occasionally, such Shipwrights, Caulkers or other Artificers as may be necessary in addition to those which may be found on board the Ships of the Fleet.'[50] With the courtesies attended to, on 25 November, the Admiralty appointed George Kimber Cromwell to the post of Master Shipwright at Yarmouth, on a salary of £240 plus £50 for house rent, and he duly arrived in the town on 13 December.[51] Cromwell's role was to assess the repair needs of the warships in the Roads and decide how best these could be met. To enable him to perform this task port-admiral Douglas was directed to provide him with, 'the means of visiting the different Ships in want of repair.'[52] The Admiralty seemed less inclined to upgrade the management of the anchorage, for it was left to Douglas to identify the need. On 6 December he informed the Lords Commissioners that, 'as this Port is become more than ever frequented by His Majesty's vessels, the want of a Superintending Master to officiate as Master Attendant at this Naval Yard is every day more evident, such officer to be fully authorised to Inspect Survey and Condemn Stores from such vessels as may be refitting in their Haven, as sending Warrant Officers from Ships in the Roads to Survey Stores on shore or on board any vessel that may be ordered to refit at this Port is attended with considerable inconvenience and hindrance to His Majesty's Service.' By return Douglas was informed that James Russell was to be appointed to act as Master Attendant at Yarmouth.[53] He was to receive the same remuneration as Cromwell and in addition to the duties outlined above he was to relieve Warmington of the management of the navy's use of the anchorage. Despite being paid more than the storekeeper (soon to be a bone of contention) Cromwell and Russell were directed to place themselves under Warmington's orders and both were described as 'acting,' suggesting that the Admiralty saw these appointments as for the duration of the war only. To accommodate these men, in February 1808, Warmington submitted a plan and an estimate from Messrs Howes and Hodskinson, the builders he usually employed, for the construction of an office in the yard and this was duly built.[54]

Further service improvements followed. In January 1809 Russell was given permission to hire a boat with a crew of six to carry out his work.[55] Shortly afterwards Warmington, Cromwell and Russell jointly approached the Navy Board to hire a boathouse with a capacity for 20 boats, because the boats in store were constantly exposed to the weather. This too was approved.[56] In March 1809 Warmington received printed instructions for the implementation of new regulations that were to come into force on April 1. As this involved the completion of many new returns he used this as a pretext to re-approach the Navy Board for a salary increase. He cited, among other things, his greatly increased workload, having to pay a second clerk and provide an office, both at his own expense. He also highlighted the niggling fact that although the Masters were under his orders they were paid more than him, especially when their rent allowances were taken into account, and that he was paid less than his counterparts at Leith and Deal, even though they had less work to do. Accepting his argument the Navy Board recommended that Warmington and his clerk be placed on the same footing as the officers at Leith and Kinsale.[57]

In January 1810 permission was given for the erection of a temporary shed, 'for the purpose of refitting rigging in,' and in May the making of a saw mill was authorised.[58] With the completion of these works the naval yard had nearly reached its greatest extent. It comprised an enclosed riverside yard within which was a single storey warehouse, mainly used to store cables, a two storey building divided into a mast house on the ground floor with a sail loft over, a cottage for the second clerk/warehouseman, an office for the Masters, a fire-engine house with a nail room over, a privy, a sawmill and a temporary shed. On the waterfront was a wharf, on which stood a crane. There was also a slipway and a mooring for the lighter. The yard's permanent workforce was small, no more than the personnel already mentioned. Moderate ship repairs were carried out in the local yards and the loading and unloading of stores was carried out by the crews of the boats transporting them, especially that of the lighter under its master John Errington (later the crew of the guard-ship *Utile* carried out this work). The warehouseman did, however, have a labourer to assist him and another man, William Nichols, was given a protection by Master Shipwright Cromwell, on 17 September 1812, through being 'employed as a Mast Maker in His Majesty's Naval Yard here.'[59]

Robert Warmington died on 22 September 1812, at the age of 73.[60] He was the sole survivor

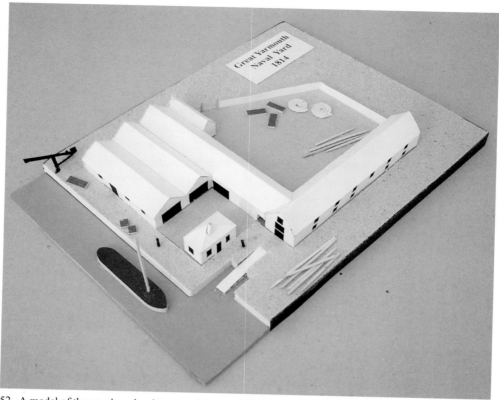

52. A model of the naval yard as it appeared in 1814.

of the locally employed civilian agents. Following a short period when his first clerk held the reins, he was succeeded by a long-service navy man, John Day, who arrived in Yarmouth on 9 December and remained for the remainder of the war. By the 15th he had assessed the operation of the yard and its perceived shortcomings. He pointed out that the office used by Warmington was on the former storekeeper's own premises, some distance away from the naval yard and that once this was no longer available he would want an office close to the store. He also felt that the clerks were underpaid, forcing them to take supplementary employment, which was not good for the naval service and, like Warmington before him, he considered his own salary to be inadequate, given what was paid to the Masters. The Navy Board referred these matters to the Admiralty,[61] and while there seems to have been no movement on the pay front, in September 1813 authorisation was given for the construction of an office in the yard for Day and his clerks.[62]

7
Ordnance Stores

David Jones had been the ordnance storekeeper at Yarmouth since 1788. He belonged to the civilian branch of the Ordnance Board's activities, which was responsible for the storage and issue of ordnance supplies to both the navy and the military. Some storage facilities already existed at the Fort and Jones had use of a storehouse hired by the Ordnance Board for £40 per annum, but these were deemed insufficient for the coming fray. In early 1793 Captain Sutherland of the Royal Engineers was sent to the town to assess the adequacy of the defences and the storage of ordnance supplies. Among his findings was the need for an additional gunpowder magazine, prompting an approach to the Corporation for land on which to build one.[1] On 1 February the Corporation's Committee of Liberties recommended, 'that a piece of ground near the South Battery by the Haven's Mouth should be taken for the purpose of erecting a magazine. This was confirmed by the Assembly on 25 February.[2] In March a Mr fortune was appointed acting clerk of works to oversee the project. He was to be paid by 'the storekeeper at that place.'[3] Sometime later this magazine was described as containing 'Gunpowder for Supplies to the Navy also Small Arm Ammunition for Sea and Land Service. It is calculated to contain 500 Whole Barrels; is a brick building with slated Roof…'[4]

Two years later, in early 1795, Jones was directed to find larger general storage premises. In March he identified another of the redundant whale fishery buildings, on the east side of the river, just south of the South Gate, as suitable for the Board's purposes.[5] It stood on land owned by the Corporation, but leased to a Mr Colls. He was prepared to dispose of his interest for £350 and the Corporation was also willing to grant the Board a new 21 year lease. The cost of fitting out the single storey building as a storehouse, 'for depositing Ordnance Stores of every Description, for the Sea Service' including the erection of a small lodge for a watchman, was £143-15-0. In March the Ordnance Board agreed to the proposal and the building was acquired.[6] With this facility and the newly built magazine Jones now had sufficient capacity to fulfil his duties in relation to providing the warships in the Roads with gunpowder and shot and the militia, volunteers and sea fencibles with small arms and ammunition for the duration of the Revolutionary War.

***

Unlike the other service providers the Ordnance Board seems not to have scaled down its operation at Yarmouth in 1802 and as a result a year later storekeeper David Jones was in a position to make supplies available at the same level as before. In July 1803, however, the Board's secretary wrote to 'desire him' to hire another storehouse at Yarmouth, 'it being probable that an additional Supply of Stores may be sent to that place.'[7] As luck would have it Samuel Paget had just lost his victualling contract and had buildings that were surplus to

95

53. The harbour fort, built in 1653, was the Ordnance Board's base at Yarmouth until the escalation of hostilities necessitated the creation of additional facilities.

requirements. By the end of the month Jones had acquired from him a fish-house complex which lay behind his South Quay house, for a rent of £30 per annum. As with the main storehouse it too was to be used for, 'depositing Ordnance Stores of every Description for the Sea Service.'[8]

By February 1804 gunboats created for the sea fencibles were ready for service and the Ordnance Board had sent large quantities of stores to arm and equip them. Unfortunately no consideration had been given to the storage of these items, nor who was to take care of them. Following pressure from his officers Captain Cobb, the officer in charge, wrote to the Admiralty, raising these concerns and as a result storehouses for this purpose were hired at Winterton and Cromer (19 March 1804), Yarmouth (26 May 1804) and Lowestoft (23 September 1805), with the stores being placed under the control of the sea fencible petty-officers at those places.[9]

In mid-1804 the Ordnance Board decided to construct a number of armouries, each designed to hold a specified quantity of arms and accoutrements for the cavalry and infantry. Orders were given for them to be built at Carlisle, Chatham, Chester Castle, Dover, Hull, Plymouth, Portsmouth, Tynemouth and Yarmouth.[10] The Yarmouth order, dated the 25 July, informed Lieutenant-General Morse, the Inspector General of Fortifications and Works, that it was the Board's intention to lodge 20,000 stand of arms there and he was to direct Captain George Whitmore, the Eastern Military District's Chief Engineer, to prepare plans and an estimate for an armoury, the workshops necessary for repairing and cleaning that number of arms, and a powder magazine. With extraordinary naivety the Board wanted the work completed before the winter set in i.e. within 3-4 months. Prior to the order being given storekeeper Jones had been asked to provide information in the form of answers to a number of questions.

He told the Board that there was no armoury at Yarmouth, but that there was a small room fitted up for cleaning and repairing arms. This work was carried out by an armourer. He also said that there were no buildings capable of being converted into an armoury, nor land on which to build one.[11] By 27 July, however, Jones *had* identified a building which would 'answer the purpose' and Whitmore was directed to assess this possibility as part of his deliberations. In the event it was decided to build a new complex on land situated on the west bank of the river, safely away from the built up area of the town.[12] By then the planned capacity had been reduced to 10,000 stand of arms and James Wyatt, the Board's architect, proceeded to produce a scheme for that number.[13] By the end of January 1805 the land had been leased from Lord Anson, the detailed plans had been approved and Captain Whitmore had been directed to proceed with the building work.[14]

The construction contract was awarded to a Mr Frost, but before he had got very far with the work the Ordnance Board made another alteration to the scheme. The magazine was now to be capable of holding 1,000 barrels of gunpowder rather than the 500 originally specified.[15] The complex as built was in the form of an east-west orientated 'H', partially closed at the western end. It contained an armoury, a magazine, six large storehouses, a carpenter's shop, a smithy, a shed for a fire-engine, a house for the Storekeeper and one for the Clerk of the Cheque, together with a barracks for 20 soldiers. A stone wharf was later added on the river frontage.[16] With the main building work completed by the end of May 1807 Captain Whitmore informed Lieutenant-General Morse that the storehouses would be sufficiently dry for the reception of stores by the end of June and that the houses and barracks only needed the necessary fixtures to render them habitable.[17]

54. The entrance to the Royal Arsenal as it looks today. To the right is the Storekeeper's house, to the left that of the Clerk of the Cheque and in the centre, the armoury.

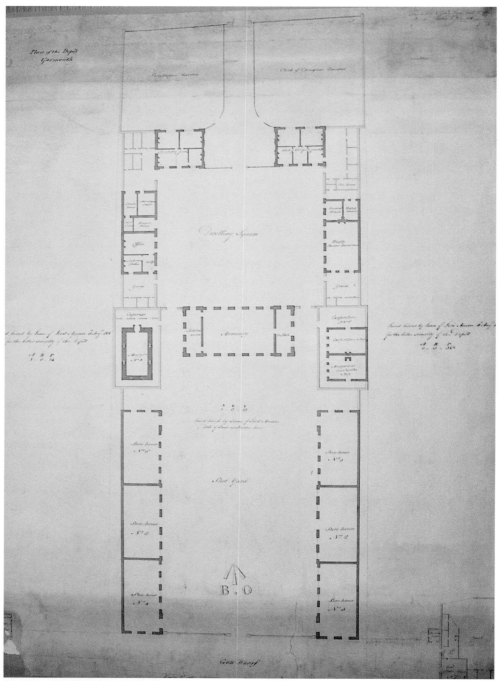

55. Plan of the Royal Arsenal built at Yarmouth between 1805 and 1807.

56. The barrel of this 18th century cannon served as a gatepost at the Royal Arsenal until 1983 when it was removed and mounted on a replica gun carriage. It now stands on Yarmouth's South Quay.

In October 1805 Richard Minty replaced David Jones as storekeeper and throughout the period of the building contract Captain Whitmore found it very difficult to work with the man, finding him quite obstructive. In July 1808 he wrote a private letter to Lieutenant-Colonel Rowley in which he confided that, 'I am sorry to be obliged to premise my Reply by Stating that I should be puzzled to recollect a Single instance wherein the Storekeeper at Yarmouth has not opposed (in some degree) my wishes or employment on the Depot under his Care. Mr Frost has experienced the same disposition and I think General Morse may have himself remarked it.' Clearly building the facility that became known at the Royal Arsenal was not without its challenges.[18]

Given the unpredictable nature of war, no sooner had the armoury been completed than events in the Baltic suggested that its capacity was insufficient. In August 1807 the Board decided to increase the quantity of ordnance stores to be held at Yarmouth, in order to sustain an additional three sail-of-the-line. Minty was given the task of finding suitable buildings for hire and Captain Whitmore was instructed to investigate land purchase, to enable the Board to consider whether to rent or build.[19] Whitmore immediately directed the clerk of works to survey the land on either side of the armoury site and a further two acres were subsequently leased from Lord Anson, the paper-work being finalised on 11 August 1808. As it turned out this land was not built on, nor were any more buildings hired, as Minty was able to accommodate the additional stores in the existing facilities.[20]

When Major Bryce visited the town in 1805 he had recommended the construction of an additional magazine and had even suggested a suitable site for it. In October that year the Ordnance Board had directed Lieutenant-General Morse to give the necessary orders for one to be built, with capacity for 500 barrels of gunpowder.[21] The following month Minty had sounded out the Corporation on what terms it would lease a piece of land, 'in case it was necessary to erect a powder magazine between the South Star Battery and the Gun Wharf,' another location safely away from the built up area of the town.[22] It was not until July 1807, however, when there was a need for additional storage, that a lease was concluded, 'with liberty to inclose the same and erect a powder Magazine thereon.'[23] The construction of this facility was the last major ordnance project to be completed at Yarmouth, but in November 1808 Minty petitioned the Corporation for permission to construct, 'a landing place or steps about 9ft square on the Yarmouth side of the River opposite the Ordnance Depot and before the house of Samuel Paget Esq,' to facilitate a connection between the Board's dispersed storehouses. A co-operative Paget gave his consent to this 'accommodation for the public service,' but the Assembly did not share his view and rejected the request.[24]

In August 1812 the civilian ordnance establishment at Yarmouth comprised 25 men, together with two who were described as not established. In charge was Storekeeper Thomas Gibson, who had replaced Minty on New Year's Day 1811. Next in line was the Clerk of the Cheque, George Lovell, who dealt with all financial matters. Assisting them both was a clerk, Robert Boult Fenn. These three men were salaried, whereas all the other employees were paid wages on a day rate. Of these the armourer was the most senior, followed by the carpenter, smith and the foreman of labourers. The remainder were assorted assistants and labourers, except for Henry Nicholas, master of the powder vessel *Lord Amhurst* and his crew of four.[25] On the military side Captain George Hoste of the Royal Engineers was described as in 'Command at Yarmouth,' John Green was the clerk of works and there was also a labourer.[26] In addition a small number of soldiers guarded the complex. Between them these men provided the ordnance service at Yarmouth until it was no longer required.

8.

The Roads Anchorage

With the constant flow of victualling, naval, and ordnance stores out to the warships in the Roads there was a requirement to manage the navy's use of the anchorage. This responsibility was vested in the Navy Board and its agent, Robert Warmington, carried out the duties in this respect as he had for decades in his capacity as the port's Naval Officer. It was a facility the warships shared with merchant ships and both needed servicing from the jetty, shore or harbour by the town's beachmen and keelmen. The former ferried people and light freight to and from the warships, while the harbour based keels transported the heavier loads, such as food and water. It can be supposed that Warmington had a good working relationship with these local boatmen and kept a close eye on their day to day activities in the Roads, work that largely goes unnoticed in the records.

The weather was not always kind to those using the Roads. Any strong wind, especially from the north-east round to the south-east, could play havoc with those dependent on sail or oar, often preventing the launching of boats from the shore and causing the stranding or sinking of ships and vessels, with consequent loss of life. It is these occurrences that *do* get recorded. In February 1796 Rear-Admiral Pringle complained that it was difficult for boats to be launched from the shore. Two weeks later he was still grumbling about the impact of the surf. In September that year Admiral Duncan was experiencing the same problem, informing the Admiralty that 'The Wind still continues to blow fresh from the ENE and the surf has been so great for these four days past that we have not made any progress in Victualling and Watering the Squadron and many of the boats have been stove in attempting it.'[1] This was a major drawback in using the Roads as a naval anchorage, but for the beachmen bad weather was a godsend for it enabled them to earn sizeable sums of money by assisting ships in difficulties. When the casualty was a warship they would approach Warmington to secure from the Admiralty or the Navy Board a one-off payment for their efforts. In January 1795 he forwarded a claim for the services 'performed by Persons in saving the Boats Crew of the *Scourge*.' The sum of 50 guineas was awarded to be distributed, 'in Such proportions as the Several parties may from their exertions merit.' In February 1796 he was dealing with claims for assisting the frigate *Apollo* and in March he was directed to pay Mr Boult (the master of a beach company) two guineas for his (unspecified) services.[2]

Bad weather also forced ships and vessels in the Roads to 'cut and run' before the wind, in the process leaving their anchors on the seabed. Retrieving anchors (termed 'swiping') provided the beachmen with a steady income via the Yarmouth Admiralty Court, which paid out salvage money on each item recovered.[3] In November 1798 an anchor lost from the frigate *Gayette* was entered into the Admiralty Court, much to the annoyance of the Navy Board. Warmington was directed to pay the claim of £25.15.9, but in future he was to take measures to prevent naval stores being processed by the Court by claiming them as soon as they were brought ashore. The following month the *Deptford* lighter's anchor was taken up and salvage was duly paid by the Navy Board.[4]

In January 1796 the Board had to deal with a 'young upstart' who was trying to usurp Warmington's position. This was the 21 year old Samuel Paget Jnr. who, seemingly emboldened by being awarded the sea provisions contract for the warships in the Roads, approached the Navy Board about a salvaged anchor and cable belonging to the brig-sloop *Zephyr*. He was informed that, 'Mr Warmington having already been employed by us [we] desire he will deliver the *Zephyrs* Anchor & Cable to him.' Warmington was told to send this anchor and those belonging to the brig-sloop *L'Espeigle* and the frigate *Circe* to one of the King's yards, if he could not return them to their vessels. Not giving up easily Paget took possession of two pieces of cable belonging to the *Circe*, but the Navy Board told Warmington to retrieve them and to 'inform us if Mr Paget makes any difficulty about doing so.'[5]

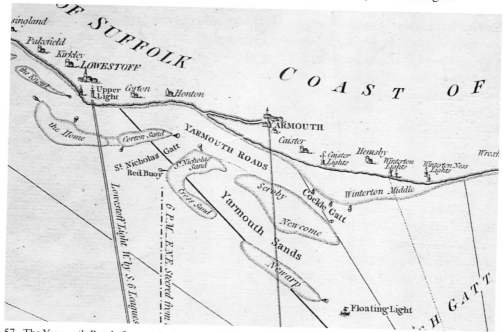

57. The Yarmouth Roads from a chart surveyed in 1796 on the orders of Vice-Admiral Macbride.

When in December 1798 Vice-Admiral Dickson arrived at Yarmouth he immediately reviewed the management of the navy's use of the anchorage. Concluding it was inefficient, he decided that what was needed was the appointment of an 'active' officer to superintend and direct the activities of the various boats. Writing to the Admiralty he highlighted 'the difficulty we find at this Port in supplying His Majesty's Ships with Provisions and Stores, heavy Stores such as Anchors, Cables, Beer and Water, particularly the two latter from the very great suspense frequently ships under Orders for Sea cannot proceed, tho' their Lordships Orders direct they should be always in a constant state of readiness to put to Sea at the shortest notice, those Defects are owing to the neglect of the Lightermen, and want of knowledge of those who employ them, in the event of the favourable opportunity which should be attended and carried into effect the moment it offers, to send the Lighters out with the Stores and Provisions. The *Saint Peter* one of His Imperial Majesty's Ships lost her Rudder a fortnight ago and with some difficulty got it finished(sic) this day, which might have been done in two days, had a proper person attended the work, the Ship was in great Danger for the want of two Cables, which were ordered to be sent off, her situation was such, had it come on to blow, it called for the greatest exertions to save the Ship; the inattention of those Boatmen, the difficulties by saying the surf was too high to get out, and no person to controul them, I directed Captain Deans of His Majesty's Ship *Monmouth* to get the men into the Boat, and use his best endeavours to get the Cables off, which he did with the greatest ease.' He went on to say that such an officer could survey those ships in need of repair, check their rigging and supervise the repair and refitting of cutters and small vessels in the harbour. In effect he was advocating the role normally performed by two officers, a master attendant and a master shipwright.[6]

Always concerned about getting ships to sea quickly, the Admiralty consulted the Navy Board (ignoring the ship repair aspect) only to receive the cool response that Vice-Admiral Dickson should 'let us know what particular duty he proposes to employ this person upon, and what are the craft he alludes to, as we have only one Lighter there.'[7] Undeterred, on 23 January, the Admiralty approached the Navy Board for an establishment for an officer and was told that, 'we are of [the] opinion he should be allowed the same salary as a Master Attendant of a Dockyard viz £200 p[er] annum, and that the Admiral or Commanding officer should furnish him with a Boat and Crew when it is necessary for him to go afloat.'[8]

Wasting little time, in early February 1799, the Admiralty appointed George Patterson 'to superintend the movements of the different Craft employed at Yarmouth in conveying Stores and Provisions to His Majesty's Ships and Vessels in the Roads.' He was to be the Master Attendant.[9] The choice of Patterson is not without interest. He was master of Duncan's flagship *Venerable* at Camperdown and is depicted on paintings of Admiral De Winter's surrender to the North Sea admiral. When the *Venerable* was paid off he was transferred to Duncan's new flagship, *Kent*, where he remained until gaining his Yarmouth appointment. He was well thought of by Duncan who after the battle recommended him for promotion (probably master attendant at Sheerness), but the Admiralty appointed someone else. Duncan was affronted and was still making complaint about it to Evan Nepean, the Admiralty's secretary, as late as October 1799. It seems likely that the appointment of Patterson to the Yarmouth post was a placatory gesture.[10] Warmington was not consulted on the appointment and was not placed in charge of the man who had supplanted him. Patterson took instruction from Dickson and carried out his own correspondence with the Navy Board. There is no evidence that the two men did not work well together and with Warmington having so many commercial interests of his own to attend to he was probably pleased to let Patterson 'be active.'

Although the main purpose of his appointment was to supervise the movement of people and goods to and from the warships Patterson also took on the normal duties of a master attendant in keeping the anchorage buoyed and clear of obstruction, as well as retrieving lost equipment, especially anchors, and assisting ships and vessels in distress. In June 1802 the soon to be outgoing Master Attendant submitted to the Navy Board, '*An Account of Anchors, Cables and Wrecks taken up in Yarmouth Roads by Mr. Geo: Patterson and along the Coast between the 9th March 1799 and 11th May 1802.'* This recorded 36 anchors, nine of which were sent aboard warships, the others into store. Also listed were 19 wrecks and a quantity of wreckage, some of which he deposited on sandbanks, away from the sea lanes.[11] The list did not include the wreck of the *Guernsey Lily*, an ordnance transport serving the Helder campaign, which sank off the Jetty in November 1799, in 'the best Anchorage in the Roads.'[12] Patterson sought to move her, but was told that, as she was a transport, the navy was not liable and it is the business of the Corporation to clear the roadstead. The Corporation, however, declined to take responsibility. In November 1802 Patterson managed to take up the stern of the vessel, 'which was full of Bolts and Nails.'[13]

His willingness to assist vessels in distress may have been another reason why he was chosen for the post. When the Russian man-of-war *St Peter*(74) lost her rudder and was blown ashore Patterson, still master of the *Kent* at the time, took out a launch and crew, boarded her and after weighing her anchors, and attaching cables from the next Russian ship in line, got her off and into safety. If, as seems likely, Dickson witnessed this sterling piece of work he might well have rewarded Patterson with a recommendation for the role he was trying to establish. This was not enough for Patterson, however, for, in June 1799, he petitioned the Navy Board for some kind of remuneration for the service, only to be told that 'we consider it to be the Duty of every King's Officer to assist the Ships of an ally serving with our own fleet when such ships are in distress, without expecting any pecuniary Reward for his services.' Undeterred Patterson tried again in September and this time the Navy Board awarded him ten guineas and half a guinea to each of his boat's crew.[14]

In November 1800 the safety of crews landing from the warships became the formal responsibility of Patterson when he was directed by Admiral Dickson to hoist a blue and yellow pendant on the Jetty, 'whenever you may deem it either unsafe or improper for the

58. The Roads Anchorage and the Jetty, 1801. In this painting local artist John Butcher has captured the essence of the role of Yarmouth in these wars.

Boats to Land.'[15] It proved to be a successful measure for, two years later, when the service was discontinued, Patterson was able to claim that there had been no accidents since its inception and that it has been the instrument of saving many men's lives and boats to the benefit of the Government.[16]

The jetty facilitated the ship to shore contact for the men-of-war and its constant use for this purpose greatly contributed to its deterioration. On 7 July 1801 the town's Haven and Pier Commissioners ordered the town clerk to 'make such application to Government as may be advised for an allowance or compensation for the use of the Jetty and the damage done thereto by the very great quantity of heavy materials continually put thereon for the use of the Navy.' The Mayor subsequently wrote to Admiral Dickson quoting a sum of £1,100 for the repairs.[17] Dickson in turn sent a letter to the Admiralty supporting the town's position. In it he outlined the causes of the damage, but when the matter went before the Navy Board, on 7 August, the commissioners could 'not find any precedent of our having paid any remuneration for the use of this Crane or Piers for His Majesty's Navy. We have no objection occasionally to supply a new Crane Rope, but we cannot without directions from the Lords of the Admiralty contribute to the Repairs of the Pier or Crane.'[18] Getting the ever cost conscious Navy Board to share financial responsibly was never an easy task. Shortly afterwards the North Sea Squadron was withdrawn, the anchorage resumed its predominantly commercial role, and nothing more was said about the government's potential involvement in Jetty repairs at that time.

**

For the first four years of the Napoleonic War Robert Warmington was again responsible for the navy's use of the anchorage, but, as mentioned earlier, in late 1807 this duty was passed to the newly appointed Master Attendant, James Russell. The day to day work of servicing the warships in the Roads was much as before and the fickle nature of the weather continued to wreak havoc, especially in winter, causing the naval authorities to once more rely on the skill and expertise of the local beachmen to assist naval ships and vessels in distress and save sailor's lives at a time when there were very few dedicated lifeboats on the coast. Brief mention has already been made of their activities, but the nature of their involvement with the navy becomes much clearer in the Napoleonic War. In terms of rewards for their work there was a significant difference between saving property and saving life, the one being a matter for the Navy Board, the other being handled by the Admiralty. Ships approaching and leaving the anchorage, from the south or the east, did so via the St. Nicholas Gatway, whereas those to and from the north could use the Cockle Gat. The Roads themselves were worked by four Yarmouth beach companies which at the start of the conflict comprised those led by James Boult, Edward Boult, Benjamin Eastmure and John Bickers. Their work was described in April 1803 as, 'assisting ships in distress, carrying off pilots, and at the Yarmouth Ferry.'[19] The northern end of the sandbank system, as far as the Haisborough sand, was serviced by beach companies at the villages of Winterton, Sea Palling and Happisburgh and the southern end by companies at Corton, Lowestoft, Pakefield and Kessingland.

Two examples will serve to give the flavour of what was involved. The first concerns naval property, the second the possibility of saving life. On the evening of 10 January 1808 the brig-sloop *Belette*, captained by John Phillimore, ran aground on the Haisborough Sand and yawls from four different beach companies combined to refloat her and get her into the Yarmouth Roads, taking three days to do so.[20] On 14 February Warmington duly informed the Navy Board of the service performed, as set out in a certificate signed by the vessel's captain, and asked for an indication of 'the Sum to be paid each boat separately as they belong to different Concerns.'[21] The Navy Board's response was to ask Warmington what would have been the hire rate of the boats for the three days to which he replied, 'it is not customary here to pay them by the Day, they are generally paid a lumped sum according to the service rendered.'[22] Accepting the point the Navy Board asked Warmington to give his advice on, 'what according to Custom would have been allowed,' for the services rendered. Referring to the fact that as a magistrate he had frequently been called upon to settle similar cases he recommended an award to each boat of four guineas per crewman together with eight guineas for the upkeep of the boat, making a total of £231. He also stated that the men who assisted in the launch of the yawls would also be entitled to a share of the sum awarded.[23] After six weeks deliberation, during which time the beachmen persistently pestered Warmington for news of the outcome, the Navy Board awarded three guineas per crewman and six guineas for each boat, amounting to an overall sum of £173-5-0.[24]

The other case concerned the brig-sloop *Skylark*, commanded by Captain Stuart, which, during an easterly gale on the night of 10 November that same year, was driven ashore at Yarmouth on the sand ridge that lay not far from the beach. Signals for assistance, consisting of lights and guns were made and a boat was hauled down to that part of the shore where it was thought the vessel would be wrecked. Some 16 men kept watch. In the event the vessel did not break up and the beachmen's assistance was not required, but the Captain signed a certificate, being appreciative of what they had done. As a result port-admiral Douglas approached the Admiralty to consider, 'allowing those Persons some trifling remuneration in addition to the Bill paid by them for hire of six horses which drew the boat down,' which amounted to £1-11-6. The Admiralty in turn directed Douglas to, 'make such remuneration as he may think reasonable.' He awarded each of the 16 beachmen one guinea and paid the bill for the horses.[25]

Being driven onto the ridge of sand that ran close to the shore was a major cause of shipwreck and loss of life and early in the previous year there had been a major catastrophe in this respect. In the early hours of 17 February 1807, without warning, a heavy gale sprang up from the north-north-east which caught and wrecked a great many vessels along the coast, leaving a total scene of devastation, both in terms of wreckage and corpses. At Happisburgh the revenue cutter *Hunter* was lost with all hands and in the Roads a large merchantman collided with the gun-brig *Snipe*, which had on board 93 people, including French prisoners of war, women, and children. The merchantman sank with the loss of all hands and shortly afterwards the *Snipe* was driven onto the sand ridge at Gorleston, just south of the harbour entrance.[26] It was impossible for help to come from the shore, just 100 yards away, and the large crowd that gathered could clearly hear the cries of those on board. Only 20 people survived, with 30 drowned and the rest dying of exposure on the gun-brig's deck.[27] Among those watching was the barrack-master, Captain George Manby, who later wrote that they were, 'as distant in effect as if she had struck a rock in the middle of the Atlantic Sea.'[28] Saddened by what he had witnessed this ingenious yet paradoxically self-absorbed man, set to work to develop the lifesaving mortar for which he is best known. This simple device, whereby a shot with a line attached was fired from a mortar from the beach over the vessel in distress, was the instrument of saving many lives around the coast until replaced by the rocket line later in the century.

The port-admiral was responsible for the safety of naval seamen landing at the Jetty and established rules to prevent them so doing when it was dangerous. In foul weather they were not to go off after sunset or when a warning flag was hoisted by Thomas Rummer, the beachman appointed to provide that service. Nevertheless there were accidents, some unfortunate, others avoidable.[29] On 21 March 1805, a boat from the *Antelope* in coming to the Jetty, overturned and an officer and four men of the eleven man crew were lost. The mother of one of the unfortunates had travelled 60 miles to see him and was standing on the Jetty when he drowned.[30] Similarly on the evening of 19 October 1808 Captain Charles Harford of the brig-sloop *Chanticleer* was drowned when a squall upset his boat, it being reported that having just arrived he was unacquainted with the rules of the port-admiral.[31] Five beachmen were paid one guinea each, 'for their services in taking the master of the *Chanticleer* off the bottom of that sloop's boat and going off to the assistance of the Survivors.'[32]

Crossing the harbour bar was equally as hazardous. On 29 June 1808 port-admiral Douglas informed the Admiralty that a boat from the recently arrived *Minotaur* (74), in attempting to come into the haven, took too much water on the bar and sank with the loss of three lives. He asked permission to establish a flag there, 'to indicate the impracticability of landing and of my engaging a Person at 4 guineas p[e]r annum to duly attend to hoisting the same when

59. The entrance to Yarmouth's haven where in 1808 port-admiral Douglas established a flag to give warning when it was not safe for boats from the warships to attempt to cross the bar.

needful.'[33] Towards the end of the war the 'harbour-duty man' was John Dillon of the *Utile* receiving ship. He also doubled up as the port-admiral's messenger.[34]

Stormy weather was also to claim another victim, the town Jetty. Although the structure was substantially repaired in 1801 the crane at the seaward end remained in a dilapidated state and was removed in 1804. The following year the landing stage itself was nearly destroyed by a 'great storm, accompanied by a raging tide' and in September 1807 it suffered further extensive damage.[35] Acting swiftly the Mayor ordered a temporary repair to be carried out, sufficient for the embarkation and disembarkation of men and stores. The cost of putting the structure into a proper state of repair was estimated at 'not far short of £4,000' but before consideration could be given to such a course of action fate dealt it a further blow. On 14 January 1808 another violent storm virtually destroyed what was left of the vital landing stage.[36] In reporting the implications of this disaster port-admiral Douglas informed the Admiralty that, 'almost all the planks and several of the piles and cross pieces have been washed away,' and that the tide was higher, 'than ever was known at this place.' More significantly it was his opinion that until something was done to repair the Jetty, any connection between the warships and the shore, apart from in the most moderate weather, would have to be from the haven, a circumstance 'which will considerably retard the service.'[37]

In June that year the local Haven and Pier commissioners took the bull by the horns and decided to build a new jetty as a like for like replacement of the previous one. William Jessop, the experienced civil engineer usually employed by the Commissioners, was instructed to prepare a plan and estimate for the work, which he duly completed in two weeks. The first pile was driven on 20 August and the finished structure was opened to the public on 13 January 1809 at a cost of £5,000.[38] With the destruction being an 'act of God' there was no liability on the part of the government to contribute to the cost of the work, but the Admiralty had been consulted and Jessop produced two plans, the other being for an extension by 50 feet with a 'T' shaped seaward terminal at an additional cost of £1,500. Because this represented an improvement beneficial to the navy the government was expected to pay for it and while there was support for the proposal from port-admiral Douglas and William Wellesley-Pole, the Secretary to the Admiralty Board, nothing seems to have come of it.[39]

The importance of the Jetty to the navy during these wars was explained by Preston in 1819 when he wrote that it was built in 1808, 'at a time when his Majesty's fleets, lying in the roads, were victualled and watered from hence, and at the heads of which were the late gallant Admirals Duncan, Nelson, Onslow, Russell, Douglas, Mitchell, &c. who at that time displayed their proud flags in these roads, and who not infrequently, with many other brave officers and seamen then fighting in their country's cause, honoured Yarmouth jetty with their presence.'[40]

Of course, as we have seen, the most fundamental problem with the navy's use of the Roads anchorage emerged in 1810 when the silting up of its main entrance channel ended its use by ships-of-the-line for the remainder of the war.

9.
Raising Seamen

Recruiting men to crew the navy's ships and vessels was a constant challenge, especially in wartime. Ideally the necessary recruits would be procured by bounty driven voluntary enlistment, but such was the navy's voracious appetite for seamen that this approach never produced enough and the coercive methods of the press gang had to be employed to make up the difference. There were two types of press gang; those regularly employed by the land based impress service and those assembled from a ship's company to press men to serve on board a particular ship or vessel.[1] Both types were active at Yarmouth, where they often worked together to achieve their goals.

With war seemingly inevitable, in December 1792, a number of half pay captains and lieutenants were directed to set up recruitment centres in the port towns and elsewhere. The man chosen to 'repair forthwith' to Yarmouth was Captain James Glasford. His task as regulating officer, as these men were called, was to 'superintend and regulate the Service of procuring Volunteer Seamen & Landsmen at (Yarmouth) & in the Neighbourhood thereof for His Majesty's Fleet…' In addition to his half pay he was to receive expenses of 20 shillings per day, out of which he had to fund all the activities of his office, accept the services of a clerk, who was to receive 20 shillings a week.[2] Lieutenants John Ellis and William Marsh were appointed to assist him, the latter described as 'Prevented from Serving on board His Majestys Ships after the Peace of 1783 by extreme Deafness.' Both had been lieutenants since 1778.[3]

Emphasising the carrot rather than the stick Glasford's instructions refer only to volunteers, but the organisation he was to set up was clearly designed to recruit men by whatever means possible. Having two subordinate officers enabled him to create two gangs of 10 men, each with two petty officers termed midshipmen. They operated from 'rendezvous' established in one or more of the town's taverns, under the auspices of the all-important press warrant. To encourage volunteers to come forward the government offered a bounty of five pounds and shortly after recruitment started the 'Magistrates Merchants and principal Inhabitants of this Town' (Yarmouth) supplemented this with an additional two guineas for able seaman, one and a half for ordinary seamen and one for landsmen. In February 1793 the Corporation matched these rates, but to encourage a quick response, the offer was to close on 1 May and was only to be given to those who enlisted voluntarily.[4]

From the start the designated destination for men enlisted at Yarmouth was the Nore, along with all the others raised on the East Coast. Tenders with recruits soon began arriving from the north, mooring temporarily in the Roads before continuing southward, but when the Admiralty asked Glasford to consider putting his raised men on board a King's Lynn tender, he replied, rather defensively, 'I am of [the] opinion that it will by no means answer the purpose for the Tender to call here as many difficulties may occur putting them on Board in

60. The press gang at work. Contrary to popular belief the gangs sought to procure experienced seamen rather than men who had never been to sea.

these Roads.' What he failed to mention was that he had already hired Warmington to arrange the conveyance of his intake. Later, when the number of recruits was much smaller, the men procured were sent to join the crews of the ships in the Roads.[5]

Whether through feelings of patriotism, lure of the bounty, or impressment, the first two years of the Revolutionary War proved to be the best for naval recruitment.[6] Glasford and his gangs were very successful, but in February 1795 he resigned his post, an event reported in the following terms, 'Capt. James Glasford, who has been employed in regulating the impress service at this port during the last two years, has resigned that situation, after furnishing his Majesty's fleet with 646 men. On Sunday last he left Yarmouth, and his absence will be severely regretted not only by a very numerous acquaintance, but by the inhabitants in general; for although he was zealous in the service in which he was employed, he never lost sight of the trade and interest of the Town.'[7] The circumstances surrounding his departure are not clear, but the death of his wife in January that year probably played a part and he might well have been a sick man himself if he is to be identified with the James Glasford who died at Saltash the following year.[8]

His replacement, Captain Laughlin Hunter, arrived on 3 March, but scarcely had he familiarised himself with his new posting than his rendezvous was the subject of an inspection.[9] Ever cost conscious the Admiralty decided to carry out a survey of all naval recruitment centres and directed five unemployed vice-admirals and rear-admirals to pay them a visit and report back. Of those chosen, Vice-Admiral Macbride and Rear-Admiral

Pringle have already been mentioned in relation to their later service in the North Sea and it was the latter who was allocated the inspection of Yarmouth as part of a group of 14 rendezvous along the East and West coasts of the country.[10] Pringle made his inspection on 26 March 1795 and in his report observed that 'Captain Hunter has been but a short time in direction of this Station, therefore could give me little information. But in my opinion the Regulating Captain, One Lieutenant, two Midshipmen and one Gang are sufficient for this Port, and the other might be discharged, or sent to Stockton upon Tees, or Scarborough.'[11] Attached to his report was a schedule of comparative facts and figures for those rendezvous' he had inspected, providing a useful critique of Glasford's performance. The number of men recruited at Yarmouth was given as 650, confirming the newspaper report. To this Pringle applied disbursement data to calculate how much each man had cost to recruit. Yarmouth, at £5-2-6, was average, but there is a telling note at the bottom of the page. 'This only includes the two Lieutenants Disbursements Capt Glasford having lately left that Rendezvous & carried with him his Accounts And Captain Hunter having just come to the Station.' With Glasford's disbursements added in, the cost per man looks expensive, hence Pringle's (ignored) recommendation to reduce the gangs to one.[12] No breakdown is given for Glasford's recruits in terms of seamen/landsmen, volunteers/pressed men, but such is the size of the figure that it is to be presumed that the majority were volunteers. It must always be remembered, however, that men faced with the inevitability of being pressed would often volunteer in order to gain the bounty, thereby distorting the figures.

With recruitment drying up the government introduced a new method of procuring seamen, the Quota Acts. The first of these (35 Geo III c5) set quotas for the counties and the second (35 Geo III c9) for the ports. The men were to be raised by the Justices of the Peace and taken before the regulating officers to be accepted or rejected. An able seaman was considered to be equal to two landsmen, and was to count as such in the calculation. Norfolk's quota was set at 260 and that for Yarmouth 506.[13] In February 1795 an embargo was placed on all British vessels in the country's ports in order to prevent seamen trying to avoid the quota by taking a berth on a merchant ship. It was lifted in December that year, by which time it can be assumed that the quotas had largely been met.[14] No returns seem to have survived for the Norfolk/Yarmouth contributions to this measure, but Hunter's involvement is echoed in a letter he wrote to the Admiralty on 20 July 1796. In it he claimed, 'that when the Quota men came in from Norwich and other places in this Neighbourhood, I was obliged to employ an additional Clark to whome I paid Twelve Pounds, Twelve shillings which the Commissioners of the Navy Object to paying without an Order from the Admiralty.' Presumably this expenditure related to the vetting process.[15]

From 1796 recruitment relied largely on the endeavours of the regulating officers and the warship captains, which more often than not proved unproductive. With so many exemptions under the Acts and with the magistrates and townsfolk conspiring to keep seaman from the gangs, it was a thankless task. In November that year, following a direction from the Admiralty, Hunter made arrangements with Captain Bowater of the frigate *Trent* for a combined press. More than 100 men were taken, but upon examination they were all found to be exempt, except for two mates taken on shore in public houses. Quickly arrested for alleged debt by the authorities the mates were taken to the town gaol, a common ruse in these circumstances, leaving Hunter and Bowater with nothing to show for their efforts.[16]

In addition to the standard exemptions the Yarmouth regulating officer had to be aware of one that was of great importance to the town. In September 1793 Glasford and James Hardy, Commander of the brig-sloop *Otter*, which was stationed in the Roads, received the following order; 'Whereas many of the Persons engaged in the Red Herring Fishery at Yarmouth, are Labourers only, come from distant Places and are employed during the Fishing Season, in ferrying, carting and curing the Fish, after which they return to their respective Abodes: And whereas we think fit that the Persons so employed (provided they are not seamen) should be permitted to follow the abovementioned Occupation during the Season for the said Fishery and afterwards to return to their respective Abodes without any hindrance or Molestation whatever; You are therefore, hereby required and directed to take notice thereof, and to give Orders to the same effect to the Officers employed under your Command, to the end that no Hindrance or, Molestation whatever be given by you, or them, to the said Persons, provided they are not Seamen accordingly.' Can the hand of the Yarmouth merchants be detected in this order and subsequent orders of a similar nature, or was it purely a matter of what was in the national interest? [17]

In early 1798 the local newspapers recorded a spate of 'warm' and 'sharp' presses in the Roads and on shore, 'by which means some good seamen were procured.'[18] These men were probably taken directly on board the warships for a return made by Hunter on 27 May does

61. Yarmouth's riverside town-hall. From here the Mayor and the Corporation sought to manage the delicate balance between supporting the navy and safeguarding the interests of the local merchants by thwarting the press gang.

not suggest such vigorous activity. It covers a period of nearly three and a quarter years, from 3 March 1795. Overall 251 men had been recruited, giving an average of a little over six per month. Of those that were seamen 86 were volunteers and 62 'prest men'. The remainder comprised 62 landsmen, 29 sent in by the civil authorities and 12 raised by the East India Company. They were disposed of 'as p[er] last Account', but since then Lieutenant Marsh had enrolled one volunteer and Lieutenant Ellis had pressed a man, both of whom had been sent aboard the *Lancaster*.[19]

Still concerned about the cost of raising men and with peace on its way, the Admiralty decided to carry out another inspection of the rendezvous.' On 8 July 1801 Rear-Admiral Arthur Phillip was instructed to perform the task.[20] At Yarmouth he found that over an eight month period 185 men had been raised, comprising 33 volunteers, 78 pressed men, 72 landsmen and two men received from the magistrates. The average cost per man was £15-10-0, which was very high, only three of the other 20 rendezvous he inspected being higher.[21] The Admiralty was not pleased with this outcome and in August instructed Hunter to break up the rendezvous and send the gangs aboard the warships in the Roads. Alarmed at what might become of them the men refused to comply.[22] Hearing this the Admiralty wanted to know from Hunter why he had not applied to the commander of one of the ships to secure them, at least those who were seafaring men and thus liable to be pressed. To this he replied that he had asked the Commander of one of his Majesty's ships to take the men, 'but his (the commander's) mode was to send them on board in our own Boat, which could not be done, as they were suspicious of something since Rear-Admiral Philip had mustered them. I had done my best Endeavours to prevail upon them to enter, they made me for answer that I well knew they would be cut to pieces on board any of His Majesty's ships afloat and they might as well be served so in forcing them on board, hoped their Lordships would consider them and that they were willing to serve in the Fencibles or Batteries. I am ready to assist any Party from the Line of Battle Ship's now in the Roads to take them up singly as several of them are inhabitants of Yarmouth if their Lordship's approve of it.'[23] Not wishing to prolong Hunter's stay at Yarmouth he was asked by the Admiralty for a list of those liable to be impressed, which in early September was passed to Admiral Dickson with the direction to try to impress the men named. Dickson was off the Hook of Holland at the time so he sent the direction to the senior naval officer at Yarmouth to implement, but what followed is not recorded.[24] Seems there was no trusting the Admiralty where recruiting seamen was concerned. With the town's rendezvous closed, on 11 October Dickson was directed to order his captains and commanders to discontinue impressment, much to the delight of those seamen in hiding in the town.[25]

***

When it became clear that the peace would be short-lived the necessary finance to raise additional seamen was granted and orders were given to re-establish the recruitment centres. Sea captains were also issued with press warrants to take the men they needed from merchantmen. At Yarmouth press gangs from the frigates *Leda* and *Penelope* procured a number of useful hands before, on 16 March 1803, Captain Thomas Campbell arrived to set up his rendezvous.[26] Campbell was another officer familiar with Yarmouth having commanded the hired armed ship *Wright* in the North Sea between 1797 and 1801.[27] To assist him he was given Lieutenant Mark Robinson Lucas, uncharacteristically a relatively young officer who later had a successful sea career.[28]

One of Campbell's earliest tasks was to assess the town's Greenwich out-pensioners to identify any who were fit enough for service, but on 6 May the work on which he would be judged commenced in earnest when he was directed by the Admiralty to carry out a press from all protections (i.e. ignoring them). Proceeding 'with the greatest Secrecy' he tried to do so in the early hours of the following morning, but failed to procure a single man. Initially he put this down to the probability that, 'the people here must have had some intimation, or at least a strong apprehension of the measure.'[29] When directed by the Admiralty to justify his contention he quickly backtracked, claiming that, 'This suspicion was the hasty idea of the moment occasioned by the disappointment I felt in not being able to get hold of any of the boatmen who had lately obtained Protections from Their Lordships.'[30] The details of the event, as he saw them, are informative in that they show, as was the case in the previous war, how difficult it was to press men at Yarmouth, something Campbell and his successors were to find very frustrating. On receipt of the order he had directed Lieutenant Lucas to conceal his gang among the boats on the beach before daylight, ready to press the beachmen as they arrived. But none appeared the whole morning, contrary to their normal behaviour, which was to arrive very early. This gave rise to Campbell's suspicions. His change of mind came about when he discovered that several letters had arrived from London stating the inevitability of war and on hearing this the beachmen had suspected that there might be a press from all protections (they had only received theirs on the 29 April). This, and the fact that they had spotted the concealed press gang, kept them away from the beach.[31]

There was more luck in Norwich a little later when Lieutenant Lucas, a petty officer and two men spent a few days there and in that time recruited 12 volunteers, four of whom were

62. Yarmouth beach where in May 1803 Captain Thomas Campbell hid his press gang in a vain attempt to surprise the local beachmen.

seamen.[32] When back in Yarmouth Lucas pressed two mates from different vessels and sent them aboard the frigate *Penelope*, thereby setting in motion the furore that always attended the impressment of mates. Mates were exempt from being pressed while going about their lawful seafaring business, but at Yarmouth, where merchant vessels moored against the quay this was something of a grey area. Campbell was usually flexible with his interpretation of the exemptions, but one of the men, Robert Howes, had been taken, 'in a public house drinking far from his vessel' and the other, Joseph Salmon, 'sauntering about the Market place.'[33] As usual the owners of the vessels concerned immediately petitioned the Admiralty for their release, claiming the mates possessed mate's affidavits and that at Yarmouth it was customary for crews to sleep ashore. In response Campbell informed the Admiralty that, 'eager as the Owners of the Vessels [are] to procure their discharge, it does not arise from any difficulty they would find in getting others to supply their places, for it is notorious that great numbers of Seamen are still concealed in this place, and its vicinity many of whom have been shut up so long, that it is said they are almost starving, but who would gladly come out of their hiding place cou'd they obtain the protection that a Mate's berth would afford them.' Unmoved by the owners' pleas the Admiralty would not allow the mates to be discharged.[34]

In July Campbell approached the Admiralty for permission to hire a boat for the gang on the grounds that while there had been warships anchored in the Roads he had not needed one as boats from those ships, 'took care to examine all ships coming into or passing thro' the Roads, but they now only came in for supplies, stay but a day in which time their crews are fully engaged with their own tasks.'[35] His request was granted.

The next general press took place on 7 November 1803. It was organised by the newly arrived port-admiral Russell, with the, 'advice and assistance of Rear-Admiral Thornbrough and all the Captains of His Majesty's Ships in this Roads.' Helped by the Mayor a large number of men were taken, but after they had been 'regulated' by Captain Campbell only four were detained. What's more Lieutenant Borough of the ship-sloop *Curlew* had violently beaten the constable sent to support him and had disobeyed the order to maintain silence. As a result he had been taken into custody by the Yarmouth magistrates.[36] On 27 November Campbell forwarded to the Admiralty a return of the 'recruits' he had procured since his arrival in March. In all he had raised 230 men, 114 of them volunteer seamen, 70 volunteer landsmen, 9 sent in by the civil authorities, and 37 described as 'Prest'. Despite the Admiralty 'exhorting him to use every means in his power to procure men' he had fallen well below expectations in respect of men pressed.[37] Another source of recruits was prisoners of war. In February 1804 Campbell reported that 12 prisoners, all seamen from Denmark, Sweden or Prussia, wanted to enlist in the navy and that in the past 20 such men had been accepted. The Transport Board was ordered to release them for that purpose.[38]

On 11 May 1805 the Yarmouth correspondent of the *Norfolk Chronicle* reported that, 'One of the sharpest presses took place on Monday night last, that was ever remembered here. About nine o'clock, parties from the different ships of war in the roads were landed at the Jetty, from whence they proceeded into the town, and began to stop every person they met, without discrimination or even respect to appearances. Not less than 300 persons were impressed in the course of the night, a considerable number of whom were volunteers and apprentices. Some of these they confined at the rendezvous of the town-gang, others were marched into the barracks, or conveyed to the boats lying in readiness at the Jetty. And the whole body during the night carried on board the *Monmouth*. The next morning, however, a regulation took place, and about 50 only were detained.'[39] While the reporter seems to have been disappointed with the ultimate outcome Captain Campbell was no doubt extremely pleased to have pressed in one night what normally would have taken him months to procure by his normal methods, especially as toward the end of August he was directed by the Admiralty to state the reasons why he had raised so few men during the past six months. He was very candid in his response, citing three main reasons for his apparent failure. The first concerned the nature of the Yarmouth vessels and the manner in which they were manned. He explained that they were small and were generally employed in the coasting trade. Each had a master, a mate, three or four apprentices and an old man, or one who was infirm or injured, or was a foreign seaman. All of them were exempt from being pressed. In addition the apprentices, when their period of servitude was up, would conceal themselves until they could procure a mate's berth, or employment in one of the numerous vessels hired by the government, or in a revenue cutter, as in such vessels they could leave when they pleased. His second reason was the existence of a great number of competing recruiting parties that were stationed in Norwich or scattered round the adjacent countryside, offering bounties which enticed potential naval recruits into the army. Last, but not least, was the establishment of the sea fencibles which kept a great many men out of the navy because they were exempt from impressment. In conclusion it was his view that, 'the probability that a considerable number of men more may be procured here in future, than has been done already, I think it is not likely to happen; the same causes which have operated against it before, will still continue to do so; and it would be deceiving Their Lordships were I to raise expectations, that I am pretty certain would not be realized.'[40]

Shortly afterwards Campbell was released from his purgatory for in January 1806 he was promoted to post rank. He was succeeded by Captain William James who seemingly making little headway was soon replaced by Captain Thomas Forrest.[41] Forrest, however, was to fare no better than his predecessors. In March 1807 the Admiralty directed him to 'cause the officers and men under his command to 'execute the duty intrusted to them diligently.' He assured the Lords Commissioners that he always did his best, and while he accepted that his returns showed fluctations, he thought his weekly average was more than three and that in the previous week he had raised 18 men, all able seamen under the age of 30. Nevertheless he cited the usual reasons for not managing to procure more.[42] In July he was ordered to arrange another general impress, which took place on the night of the 24th. It was carried out, 'with all possible secrecy not an Officer Employed was acquainted with it, until the very moment it commenced.' The boats of the squadron were involved and nearly 200 men were detained and taken to the 'French prison', which was empty at the time. But of these only 16 were forced to join the navy, the remainder being protected, through being foreigners, volunteers(soldiers), or sea fencibles. With a degree of understatement Forrest informed the Admiralty that, 'it has not however been so productive as I hoped for.'[43]

Having served three regulating captains, in August 1807 Lieutenant Lucas was rewarded with the command of the hired cutter *Swan*, which worked the North Sea and the Baltic. After pushing for a replacement, on 22 October, Forrest was given Lieutenant Thomas John Folds, who at the time was a patient in the Haslar hospital. He wrote to say he would 'join, as soon as the physician thought it would be safe for him to travel.'[44] Forrest too managed to escape the frustration of the impress service when in early 1808 he was 'removed afficat' to command the fireship *Prometheus*. He was replaced on 12 February by the then unemployed Captain Thomas Heddington, who from 1791 to 1795 had been a midshipman aboard the *Chatham* on George Vancouver's 'Voyage of Discovery & Round the World.'[45] The Admiralty was quick to put him to the test, ordering him to carry out a general press, which he did on 9 April. Having rounded up 115 men, however, he had to release all but three for seventeen different reasons. In addition to the usual exemptions many of the men were already employed by the government![46]

References to rendezvous by name are rare, but in August 1808 the (ale) house of George Cook was the base of the Yarmouth press gang, despite the fact that port-admiral Billy Douglas disapproved of such places being used for that purpose.[47] In December 1807 he had suggested to the Admiralty that it might be a good idea if a vessel no longer suitable for sea service was moored in the harbour, to act principally as a rendezvous for the impress service, instead of a public house, wherein the landlord was the midshipman of the gang. In his view this would prevent the many desertions that took place. As a result the Admiralty directed the Navy Board to propose a vessel, but it was not until 1 September 1808 that the ship-sloop *Utile* was chosen for the role. Under the command of Lieutenant William Gilchrist she was moored on the west bank of the haven.[48] It is unlikely to be a coincidence that the very same day the order was given, Heddington was having to explain why so few men had been raised at such a considerable expense, to which he replied that he had produced more or less the same as those before him and that he, 'should think that it is about the number that might always be depended on,' hastily adding that he would use every means possible to double that number.[49] This proved impossible and in November 1810 the Admiralty's patience finally ran out and he was ordered to discharge himself, his lieutenant and men and to break up the rendezvous. This he did the following day. In his final letter to the Admiralty he wrote with no hint of irony, 'I have sincerely to hope I have executed the service here to their Lordships' satisfaction.'[50]

Gilchrist was not without his own problems for his vessel was multi-purpose and in February 1809 he was forced to ask Douglas for a master of arms as, 'it frequently happens in stormy weather that there are on board New raised men from the Rendezvous, Prisoners of War from the Prizes, Recovered men from the Hospital, men belonging to other ships from liberty on shore from Prizes, several boats crews, the harbour duty men and my own ship's Company all mixed together.' As usual alcohol played a large part as many of the men came on board, 'in a state of inebriation, much confusion and mischief might often ensue.'[51]

For the remaining three and a half years of the war any recruiting that took place at Yarmouth was largely carried out by the crews of the warships in the Roads or from the *Utile*. There was, however, a growing 'spirit of resistance' to their activities and on 14 April 1811 Captain Curry, on port duty, reported to the Admiralty that as a result of the warship captains endeavouring to complete their complements by impressing men in the town and vicinity, 'where most certainly many proper and unprotected persons are likely to be found,' he had received representations 'from several of the most respectable Inhabitants' concerning the civil unrest the pressing had provoked, as manifested by the parading of many shipwrights and apprentices round the market place armed with bludgeons in defiance of the press gangs.

Curry had also received repeated applications to release persons impressed and sought the Lords Commissioners' guidance. By return the Admiralty told him not to grant protections or to liberate men, reminding him that his duty was to assist in raising men and to call on the military if necessary.[52]

While raising new men was the principal method of keeping warship crews up to strength, retaining those already on the books was also of great importance. In December 1811 port-admiral Murray was asked how many non-commissioned officers and privates he thought would be necessary to prevent men 'running' from the ships stationed in the Roads. Murray responded with a detailed appraisal and in March 1812 a small detachment of Royal Marines arrived from Woolwich under the command of Lieutenant Thomas Drury, 'to prevent desertion from His Majesty's Ships and vessels at this Port, as well as to endeavor to procure Men for the Service,' for which Drury was given a press warrant.[53] The detachment was the size of a pressgang, comprising a lieutenant, two sergeants and nine privates (two of whom could be corporals if required). They were stationed in four areas centred on Yarmouth, Lowestoft,

63. A Royal Marine, 1814.

Acle and Haddiscoe.[54] The unit had to face a number of challenges, including in July, the rescue of a deserter by a mob at Lowestoft.[55] This prompted the Admiralty to ask Murray whether he thought the marines, 'should be continued, as it does not appear that they apprehend any deserters.' Murray felt they were useful as a deterrent and sent an account of their performance between 29 March and 12 November 1812. In all 48 men were listed comprising 4 volunteer recruits, 15 pressed men, 6 deserters and 23 'stragglers'. As a result of this reasonable performance the marines were retained.[56]

In addition to the marines Lieutenant Gilchrist also sent out parties from the *Utile* to attempt to procure men and on one occasion in June a violent mob, which included local militiamen, stoned his sailors in order to rescue an impressed man but, 'Bloodshed was prevented by the Meritorious and Soldierlike conduct of the Corporal of the Guard, at the Ordnance Stores, who turned his men out to their support, and dispersed the Mob.'[57] Gilchrist was replaced by Lieutenant Edward Blaquire in May 1813 and he commanded the receiving ship until the end of the war.[58]

10.
The Sick and the Wounded

The Sick and Hurt Board was responsible for keeping seamen fit for service. The crews of most warships included a surgeon and, depending on their size, a number of surgeon's mates. Although the principal skill of these men was amputation they also had to act as physicians and apothecaries. They were in effect medical 'jacks of all trades.' This arrangement was not without its limitations for space aboard ship was at a premium, naval service was extremely arduous, and on board medical care was quite basic. Wherever possible, sick and wounded seamen were sent ashore to be cared for in sick-quarters or a naval hospital. When war broke out there were only two naval hospitals in England, those at Haslar, near Portsmouth and Stonehouse, near Plymouth. At all other places where naval ships and vessels had reason to call a retained agent of the Sick and Hurt Board, usually a local surgeon, arranged for those in need to be cared for in sick-quarters.

Surgeon Benjamin Fielding was the Yarmouth agent when the French declared war. To start with the number of patients he received reflected the limited role the town played in naval affairs at the time, although there was a threefold increase from the numbers landed in the immediate pre-war period. Between 1793 and 1795 some 162 men were sent to sick-quarters, mostly to the lodging house of Ann Briggs, but nine of them were officers and these were taken in by Mary Barber, presumably a more 'genteel' woman.[1] The majority were from the North Sea cruisers, although 27 came straight from the recruitment rendezvous, such was the desperate need for seamen. The commonest illness they suffered from was fever of one kind or another, accounting for a third of the total. Other medical conditions rendering them unfit for service included rheumatism, ulcers, epilepsy, diarrhoea, hernias, venereal disease and inflammation of various parts of the body. There were also six cases of scurvy and four of small-pox.[2] Because of the reactive nature of the work Fielding did not receive a salary for his medical duties, but could claim an allowance per patient termed 'cures.' He also had to arrange for the landladies to provide the board and lodgings, the cost of which he recharged to the Sick and Hurt Board.

When in 1796 the North Sea Squadron became established at Yarmouth the number of sick seamen sent ashore rose dramatically with just over 300 being landed between June and December that year.[3] By early 1797 the level of demand was proving unsustainable and with standards of care slipping, complaints were made to Admiral Duncan. On 6 May he ordered his second-in-command, Vice-Admiral Onslow, to inspect the sick-quarters, paying particular attention to the treatment of the patients and their diet. To advise him on medical matters Onslow instructed Robert Young, the surgeon of his flagship *Ardent*, and George Kelly, surgeon of the *Leopard*, to accompany him.[4] Two days later, against the backdrop of the Naval Mutiny, the inspection was carried out and Onslow wrote his report. He found that the sick-quarters hired by the agent comprised one principal and two lesser dwelling houses situated in different parts of the town, together accommodating about 150 men. Two of these houses, namely those of Mrs Robinson in White Lion Row and Ann King in Factory Lane, were overcrowded.[5] The contract with the agent for board, lodging and washing was at a rate of six shillings per man, per week. There was no supply of bedding at the quarters, such as would be expected in a contract for lodging, the patients being required to use their own beds and bedding (only those not bringing any bedding being supplied). They were with few exceptions without pillow cases or sheets and under these circumstances it was impossible for the bedding to be kept clean and wholesome. The patients had one clean shirt per week and the washing did not extend to much beyond this article. The vice-admiral and his advisors were, however, satisfied with the dietary regime and the medical treatment.[6] Drawing on this assessment he recommended that restrictions be placed on the number of patients per house and that the sick ought to be supplied with clean bedding and linen, with their own bedding being aired, cleaned and stored to avoid the danger of contagion when they returned to their ships. He advocated segregating the various categories of sick and the enforcement of their diet. He also highlighted the problem of discipline, especially among those who were convalescing, as they would not obey civilians, especially the landladies and their helpers. Theft was also commonplace.[7]

When forwarding Onslow's report to the Admiralty Duncan suggested that to preserve good order, particularly when the fleet was absent, an officer resident in Yarmouth should be appointed to superintend the sick-quarters and 'as Captain Hunter, employed in the Regulating Service here, is a steady good Officer, I beg leave to recommend him to perform that Service'.[8] After sending the report to the Sick and Hurt Board the Admiralty quickly appointed Hunter to superintend the sick-quarters, a role very similar to that performed at a later date by each hospital governor. There followed a flurry of correspondence between the Sick and Hurt Board, Fielding and the Admiralty which resulted in a member of the former being sent to Yarmouth 'to arrange the accommodations for the Sick and put them on the best footing that circumstances will admit of.' This was especially necessary as there was evidence that Fielding had been withholding part of the allowance made for the sick-quarters, something that the Sick and Hurt Board thought 'extremely improper.'[9]

Dr Blair, the Board's First Commissioner, duly travelled to Yarmouth, inspected the quarters and submitted his findings. These were sent to the Admiralty on 16 October. Three days later the Board forwarded its own views on Fielding's behaviour, perhaps prompted by the need for a change to cope with the aftermath of Camperdown. After reiterating several of the earlier findings the Sick and Hurt Board highlighted the main 'crime', which was that Fielding had been retaining three shillings and ninepence from the nine shillings and ninepence per week allowed for the quartering of each patient under the pretence of providing some items to the sick, which the quarters could not provide. He also claimed that the money made good the losses he had sustained from arranging funerals and also supplemented the inadequate allowance for cures.[10] Writing to the Admiralty on 19 October the Sick and Hurt Board sympathised with Fielding's dissatisfaction with the allowance for cures, but nevertheless recommended his dismissal, adding that 'In case the Service at Yarmouth shall hereafter be considerable, We beg leave to propose that a Navy Surgeon be appointed with an adequate Salary instead of Allowances for Cures.'[11] Given the crisis that existed at the support base the Admiralty delayed matters for the best part of a month, but permission was eventually granted on 23 November 1797 and Fielding was promptly dismissed.[12]

By then the nature of medical care at Yarmouth had dramatically changed. On 16 October the ships that had taken part in the Battle of Camperdown brought into Yarmouth Roads around 360 wounded seamen and marines. In addition the prizes they brought with them contained a comparable number of wounded Dutchmen.[13] The need to get the most seriously injured of these men ashore and under medical care presented Captain Trollope, the officer temporarily in charge, with an immediate challenge. Despite being very ill himself he set about the task with some vigour, although he observed three days later that he had had 'a great deal of pain & trouble with the Wounded.'[14] Keels were soon to be seen making their way out to the warships and prizes, to transport the casualties upriver to the town's quayside. Surgeon Robert Young of the *Ardent* logged his ship's involvement in this desperate activity, writing that 'those who had survived (the battle) to undergoe amputation or be dressed… were conveyed on Shore in a Keel in good Spirits cheering the Ship at going away, Smoking their pipes and jesting as they sailed along, and answering the cheers of thousands of the Populace who Received them on Yarmouth Key.' As for the Dutch wounded, on the 19th William Youell noted in his diary, 'Two Keels at the Wherry Key this Evening with wounded Dutchmen. I saw some of them landed.'[15]

On the 17th Trollope reported his immediate actions to the Sick and Hurt Board and to the Admiralty, informing their Lordships that, 'as there is only one Person here under Government to take care of our own wounded and that is more than he can possibly do, I have been forced for the present to give an order to a Mr Taylor Surgeon of this [town] to take care of the Dutch Prisoners who are most badly wounded…' He had also applied 'for

64. The Wherry Quay, Yarmouth. It was in this sheltered location on the river Bure that the wounded from Camperdown were landed and the victualling keels were based.

the use of the Barracks for the Wounded who are very numerous…' for as luck would have it this facility was vacant at the time.[16] The 'one person' was, of course, Fielding who, despite or because of being under a cloud, readily took charge of the British wounded. He already had 143 sick seamen in quarters, but he quickly found room for 156 more. Over half were taken in by Ann Briggs, Mary Robinson, Mary Scott and Ann Burke. Another nine women were recruited to receive the remainder. To his credit Fielding accomplished this difficult logistical task extremely quickly, writing to the Sick and Hurt Board that same day to report the steps he had taken, hoping, 'by my attention…to merit the approbation of the Board.' [17] Seemingly unaware of Trollope's arrangement with William Taylor Jnr. he also wrote to inform the Board that, 'Several of the Dutch Ships taken by Admiral Duncan in his late Action are just arrived, having on board a number of Wounded Officers and Men.' These he thought could be accommodated in the Barracks and had written to General Tonyn, the local military commander, on the subject.[18] His letters were immediately forwarded to the Admiralty.

With the problems at Yarmouth being self-evident the Admiralty directed the Sick and Hurt Board to send a commissioner to the town and Dr Blair once more found himself on his way to Yarmouth. Much to the relief of Captain Trollope Blair arrived on the 19th to find that the wounded were being treated by surgeons from the squadron, supplemented by medical volunteers. This was made difficult by their dispersal around the sick-quarters and Blair was of the opinion that there was a great risk of infection through overcrowding.[19] To remedy this he undertook three courses of action. On the 20th he wrote to Captain Trollope to ask him not to send any more British or Dutch wounded ashore. The same day he appealed to 'the respectable Inhabitants of Yarmouth as have room in their Houses' to lodge one or two of these men for a specified sum, (an entreaty that through fear of infection fell on deaf ears). The third measure was to send some of the men to Norwich. Having organised a survey of those in sick-quarters Blair discovered that many were fit enough to travel by road. Accordingly on 22 and 23 October 59 men were transferred to Norwich by post-chaise, 50 of them to the Oxley Barracks, the remainder, being the worse cases, to the Norwich County Hospital. With them went two naval surgeons, Bromley of the *Monmouth* and Mant of the *Adamant*.[20]

As far as the Dutch wounded were concerned by the 22nd some 250 had been lodged in the new hospital established in the barracks, together with 18 surgeons and mates from the prizes, but 32 of them remained on their ships. Those ashore were still under the care of William Taylor Jnr., whose appointment to oversee the 'Dutch Hospital' had been confirmed. He was helped by three assistants and the aforementioned surgeons and mates. No hospital register survives for these men, but as they recovered many were sent to the prisoner of war prison and registered there. Between 6 November 1797 and 15 February 1798, some 203 men were transferred in this way with many of the remainder making the shorter, but sadly more permanent, journey to the town's graveyard. With them in the hospital were the wounded from the *Triumph*, who had been taken directly there at the outset at the 'desire' of Captain Essington.[21]

At this point Blair realised that the Dutch prisoners in the hospital were receiving better treatment than the British seamen in quarters, so he directed Robert Young to carry out an assessment of the barrack facility. Young found that with there being 542 berths and only 268 Dutch and 24 British wounded actually accommodated, there was 'abundant' room for

65. Landing some of the Camperdown wounded on the Jetty, October 1797. (see note15).

the men now quartered, so Blair decided that they should all be moved to the hospital. The majority of these men were transferred by parties of militiamen, between the 24th October and 4th November, under the direction of Captain Hunter.[22]

The creation of a naval hospital in this way necessitated the appointment of a naval surgeon to take charge. Blair's eye fell on the already much involved Robert Young. He was to be assisted by surgeon Hills of the *Belliqueux* and a surgeon's mate, with nurses being chosen from the 'quarterers'. It was to be an 'establishment distinct from, and unconnected with that of sick-quarters under the Agent.' Finding it impossible to arrange victualling Blair gave William Taylor the task, with Captain Hunter to advise him. Sensing at this point that he was considered to be surplus to requirements Fielding 'expressed a desire of retiring on superannuation,' but as has already been noted he was soon to be dismissed.[23]

Doctor Blair wrote his report on 3 November. Anticipating that it would not be long before the wounded men started to be discharged he concluded by pointing to the need for the Sick and Hurt Board to decide 'whether the former system of sick-quarters is then to be reverted to or an attempt made to navigate the *Spanker* to Yarmouth, or some regular and permanent establishment formed at that port.' On 15 November the Sick and Hurt Board sounded out the Admiralty on the matter, expressing the opinion that, 'it will be far more advantageous for an hospital-ship to be Stationed there, or for permission to be obtained for the Barracks being given up to serve as an Hospital, than to have recourse again to sick-quarters.'[24] Preferring the hospital option the Admiralty requested the Sick and Hurt Board to recommend a suitable establishment, but was not pleased with the result (a surgeon, agent, dispenser, matron, assistant surgeon, clerk to the agent, a porter and a steward), commenting that they, 'intended the arrangement for the care off Sick and Wounded Seamen at Yarmouth should have been on a much more limited scale...'[25] Accordingly the Sick and Hurt Board suggested a smaller establishment of a surgeon, a dispenser and a porter, with assistant surgeons and assistant dispensers appointed as the service required. This the Admiralty approved on 2 December, specifying that victualling was to be contracted out at a rate per man per day, 'taking care that with a due regard to the Comfort and welfare of the Patients, the same be done on the best and cheapest Terms you can for the Crown.'[26] By then permission had been given for the barracks to continue to be used as a hospital, although the Barrack Office retained ownership of the premises.[27]

On the face of it Robert Young was the obvious choice to take charge of the newly created hospital. He was an experienced surgeon and had a good knowledge of the sick-quarters at Yarmouth, but he too was not a well man. His ship, the *Ardent*, had been in the thick of the fighting at Camperdown, sustaining the loss of her captain among her 41 killed and 107 wounded, more than any other British ship taking part in that action.[28] He had also been without a surgeon's mate at the time, as his had resigned during the Mutiny and had not been replaced. A melancholy entry in his log graphically describes his hardships; 'I was employed in operating and dressing till near four in the morning, the action beginning about one [in the] afternoon. So great was my fatigue that I began Several amputations, under a dread of Sinking before I should have secured the blood Vessels. Ninety wounded were brought down during the action, the whole Cockpit deck, Cabbins, wing Berths, and part of the Cable tier, together with my platform, and my preparations for dressing were coverd with them. So that for a time they were laid on each other at the foot of the ladder where they were brought down…'[29] Even before the battle Young was succumbing to bouts of typhus fever and given the fact that he had a hernia or tumour developing in his abdomen, the Admiralty decided against making him the permanent surgeon of the hospital, appointing instead John Snipe of the *Sandwich*.[30]

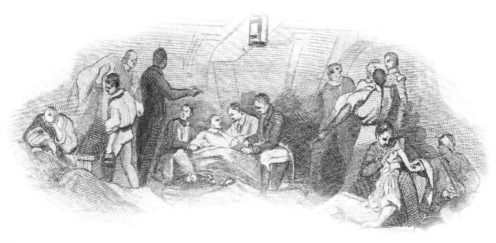

66. Attending the Camperdown wounded on the *Venerable*. Judging by surgeon Young's experience on the *Ardent* it was far more frenetic than this scene suggests.

Snipe was an energetic man. Within two weeks of his appointment he had assessed the situation at Yarmouth and together with Young had sent a critique to the Sick and Hurt Board. A number of concerns were raised, the solutions to which, in their opinion, warranted the visit of a commissioner from the Board.[31] Dr Blair travelled to the town again and submitted his report to the Admiralty on 3 January. At the same time the Sick & Hurt Board sent a letter dissenting from several of his recommendations for staff increases on the basis that, 'The great number of Patients at present in the Barracks at Yarmouth, are chiefly those wounded in the late Action with the Dutch Fleet, and Ulcers from the *Ganges*. The Seamen and Marines on their recovery will return to their Ships, or become Objects for being invalided. The Prisoners on their recovery will be removed to a Prison, and it appears by last weeks return that 29 were discharged to Prison, 133 remained on recovery, and 11 only very ill, from which it may be inferred that this Service will soon be nearly at an end.' In the event the establishment remained the same, although from then on Snipe styles himself surgeon *and agent*, having been given responsibility for all the patient's needs.[32]

The Board's analysis proved to be somewhat optimistic for on 17 June 1798 Snipe wrote , 'I do not expect to have fewer patients in the hospital than we have at present: there are fifty-three ships of war employed in the North Sea, and they never go to Sheerness but when in want of repairs. When the fleet comes in, I expect to get fifty or sixty fresh patients, and they are weekly sending in sick by the frigates and cutters. There are only two men in the hospital that were wounded in Lord Duncan's action, and the bad ulcers that were received last winter are mostly gone, yet the number is still kept up. There are more cases of ulcer received into this hospital, in proportion, than into the two royal hospitals...'[33]

John Snipe remained responsible for the medical care and welfare of the sick and wounded at the naval hospital until the end of the first war. While his medical work needs no explanation his agency accounts give an indication of the other matters that occupied his time. These included the payment of wages, the subsistence of officers in sick-quarters who maintained that privilege after the hospital had been established, acquisitions of dispensary necessaries, such as carrots for poultices, oranges, and leeches, shaving, conveyance of patients, including lunatics, and the repair of buildings, especially as the Barrack Office was keeping a close eye on their condition.[34] In September 1798 the Assistant Barrack Master General, 'represented to Us (the Sick & Hurt Board) that several repairs were much wanted at the Buildings lately given over by the Barrack Office for the reception of Sick and Wounded Seamen at Yarmouth particularly by some of them being undermined by Rats...' The repairs were carried out and Snipe was ordered to hire a 'proper person to destroy the Rats.'[35]

Duncan's North Sea Squadron was stationed in the Downs when in mid-1795 it was joined by Hanikoffs' Russian Squadron, prompting orders to be given for the Russian sick to be treated in a hospital-ship at the Nore.[36] When in mid-1798 the Russians returned, after a years' absence, a naval hospital existed at Yarmouth. After representations from Snipe the Admiralty directed that the sick Russian seamen should be received there and that a separate account of their cost should be kept.[37] The first of these men arrived in early August; 40 brought in by the Russian brig *Dispatch* from the warships off the Texel.[38] Thus began a very uncomfortable two years for the townsfolk of Yarmouth. Like their British counterparts the sick Russian officers were allowed to lodge in quarters, but Snipe soon found this inconvenient. In October the Sick and Hurt Board informed the Admiralty that, 'there are a

67. Bauleah House, Yarmouth. Its present appearance reflects the fact that it was remodelled after 1815 to provide a suitable residence for the manager of the nearby silk factory. In its original form it is where the sick Russian officers were cared for. It was later occupied by Captain Manby, the Barrack-master.

number of Russian Officers at sick-quarters (in Yarmouth) who hire Lodgings at a great distance from each other…which renders it impossible for him (Snipe) to attend upon them as their respective cases require.' Snipe's solution was to concentrate them in a house owned by the Barrack Office, which had been given up at the same time as the barracks.[39]

No muster books have survived for the Russian sick, but judging by the copious entries in the churchyard burial registers their numbers were considerable. The scale of these deaths was attributed to the unhealthy state of the Russian ships, it being suggested to the Admiralty that the Russian Admiral should be sent, 'a sufficient number of the printed Instructions for Navy Surgeons to enable him to furnish a Copy to each Ship as We conceive were the Regulations contained therein for the prevention of infectious Diseases by cleanliness, Ventilation, Fumigation etc carried into execution the same beneficial effects would be practiced in these Ships as are so evident in His Majesty's Fleet.'[40] Nothing changed, however, and such was the demand created by the sick Russian seamen that in December Snipe informed the Sick & Hurt Board that there were only four cradles unoccupied in the hospital. As a result he was instructed to identify additional premises that could be hired.[41] The problem of space still existed in March 1799 for on the 24th he again wrote to the Sick & Hurt Board expressing the view that, 'should an Action again take place in those seas, or should the Russian Auxiliary Squadron return to that Station, the Buildings now occupied as an Hospital would be far from adequate to the Reception of the Patients that may reasonably be expected from such an Emergency.' He went on to say that he found it impossible to obtain any accommodation in the town owing to the fear of contagion. In response the Sick & Hurt Board informed him that should such an eventuality arise a temporary hospital building would have to be erected.[42]

The war also placed a tremendous strain on the burial facilities at Yarmouth. Between March 1793 and the end of 1798 some 250 men of a naval or military description were buried in the churchyard, British sailors and militiamen, Russian sailors and soldiers, alongside French and Dutch prisoners of war.[43] Among the latter was Captain Gysbert Jan Van Rysvort of the *Hercules* who died on 28 October 1797 of wounds received at Camperdown. The *Norwich Mercury* reported that he was interred with military honours and that, 'The Oxfordshire Band played sacred Music; and, with the party of the Regiment who fired three vollies over the grave, preceded the Corpse. The Pall was supported by Four young Dutch Midshipmen, who had been in the Fleet. The corpse was followed by the Dutch Captains and Officers who were at Yarmouth, and also by the Captains of his Majesty's ships in the Roads, and the Officers of the Oxford Regiment of Militia, who by this voluntary mark of respect, paid the most honourable attention to the remains of a brave fallen enemy.'[44] He was one of 46 Dutch seamen from the battle who were buried there.

In the last four months of 1798 room was found for close on 50 Russian dead in the graveyard and it is probably this rapidly increasing death rate that prompted the authorities to conclude enough was enough. On 31 December 1798 the Corporation wrote to Snipe to inform him that, 'oweing to the smallness of their Burial ground in proportion to the number of inhabitants they find it impracticable to receive any more Corpses from this Hospital,' but to soften the blow they were prepared to grant a piece of land adjacent to the hospital's perimeter wall, 'for the purpose of Burying those who may Die in this Hospital or be sent on Shore from the Fleet.'[45] The offer was accepted and on 9 April 1799 Vice-Admiral Dickson informed the Admiralty that 'the Burial Ground for the interment of the Men belonging to His Majesty's Ships at this Station is perfectly compleat and fenc'd in, [and] only wants consecrating...'[46] On the 25th the Corporation caught up with the paperwork and granted a lease for the land in question, with, 'liberty to pale in and inclose the same for a Burial Ground.'[47] What followed was farcical. It was not until 4 October that the Sick and Hurt Board decided to execute the counterpart of the lease, 'it having been brought some time since to this office.' It was duly endorsed by Sir William Gibbons, Dr Johnston and Dr Blane, but it was the opinion of the Admiralty's solicitor, Charles Bicknell, that the document would not be legal, and that the ground could not be consecrated, until all the Board members had signed. This meant obtaining the signature of the 'Yarmouth expert' Dr Blair, but for some unknown reason he was reluctant to comply. Citing illness and decamping to various parts of the country he gave the Board's representatives the run-around, his prevarication being reported to the Sick & Hurt Board on no less than six occasions, before, on 25 October, he finally signed.[48] More delay was to follow for it took until 3 February 1800 for the counterpart to be sent to Dr Snipe with the direction to proceed to consecration as soon as possible.[49] The ceremony was duly performed by the Bishop of Norwich, but not until 26 September that year.[50] By then, however, there was no longer any urgency for such was the pressure on burial space that the unconsecrated burial ground had received its first interments on 9 December 1799. In the 11 months that had elapsed since the Corporation had banned new burials from the hospital, it had been obliged to take a further 224 deceased sailors and soldiers into the graveyard, 169 of them Russians.[51] Until the end of the war the new burial ground had its own register, in which is recorded 179 interments largely by name, but a note within it explains that, 'About 84 Russian Soldiers & 15 English (all whose Names are unknown) being of the Number of the Troops which returned from the Expedition to the Coast of Holland, were interred in the above Burial Ground.'[52]

The expedition referred to was that to the Helder. Although this Anglo-Russian venture lasted for less than two months, its impact on Yarmouth and the government's medical services there was to be felt for much longer. On 7th September 1799 four Russian men-of-war, armed *en flute*, three frigates, and a transport appeared in the Roads and were detained by contrary winds, prior to sailing for the Dutch Coast. On board were upwards of 8,000 troops. The *Norwich Mercury's* Yarmouth correspondent commented that, 'Four Admirals' flags are now flying in the Roads' and, that 'Our streets are crowded with Russians; Cossacs etc.'[53] General Erlon, the officer in charge, came ashore and asked for his sick troops to be taken into the Hospital. This Dr Snipe readily agreed to, despite being aware his instructions only allowed him to receive seamen. In writing to seek confirmation of his actions he informed the Sick and Hurt Board that, 'We have already One Hundred and forty Five Russian Patients in this Hospital, and I have this moment Sent an Official Report to the commander-in-chief, that I can accommodate Ninety three more. Should the Russian Squadron send more Patients to this Hospital than I can accommodate it is my intention provided you have no objections, to apply to the Commanding Officer for Spars and Canvas to erect Tents in the Hospital Yard…'[54]

The Board retrospectively approved his actions, but there were already moves afoot to create a hospital in the town for the expected sick and wounded from the expedition. The Inspector General of Regimental Hospitals had been ordered by the commander-in-chief to find a temporary facility to act as a military general hospital at Yarmouth, but he had been unsuccessful. As a result of high level talks it was decided to use part of the barracks hospital for that purpose and Dr Snipe was directed to, 'give up such part of the Barracks at Yarmouth as can be spared.'[55] Dr William Scott, Assistant Inspector of Hospitals, was placed in charge of this facility and his accounts date from 20 September.[56] On 19 October the first wounded soldiers arrived, 1,400 Russians aboard seven or eight transports. Evidently the sick and wounded were a priority as the campaign had only officially ended the previous day.[57] Two days later two more transports arrived with sick and wounded and on the 22nd it was reported that, 'This day several hundreds of the wounded from Holland were landed here; for whose reception many buildings are fitting up.'[58]

With the sick and wounded accommodated, large numbers of British soldiers began to arrive, some of whom were also sent to the hospital. Once fit again these men rejoined their units, but disposing of the recovered Russians was not so easy. On 19 November the usually uncritical Duncan wrote to the Admiralty, following an application from Dr Scott to remove about 300 such men to make way for others. In his letter the Admiral requested a transport, for in his opinion the Russians could not be sent in a King's ship without risk of infection. He was authorised to use one of the troop transports to take them to rejoin their units, then aboard ships at Spithead, and to fit out another to take the remainder. This he did. Soon after, on hearing that the Russian frigate *Riga* was now ready for service he requested, that she be ordered, 'to this Anchorage for the purpose of carrying the recovered Troops from hence to

68. The evacuation of the Anglo-Russian troops from Den Helder in September 1799, many of whom were Yarmouth bound.

their respective Regiments, as they wander about when they get better in health to the great annoyance of the Inhabitants.'[59]

But nothing relating to the Russians was easy. On 7 December the *Norwich Mercury* reported that the transport *Sensible*, with 450 Russian Troops on board had returned to the Roads having nearly been lost on the coast. She had been saved by the crews of some Harwich fishing smacks. The same newspaper reported that, 'Notwithstanding the great care and attention to the sick and wounded Russian[s] disembarked at Yarmouth, the mortality among then is still considerable.'[60] On 28 December upward of 470 Russians were embarked on board the troopship *Delft* for the Channel Islands, where it had been decided to send all the Russian soldiers.[61] The process of removing the recovered Russians continued until well into 1800. On 26 July that year two Russian warships and 24 transports anchored in the Roads. The sight of this fleet must have sent a collective shiver down the spines of the townsfolk, but fortunately the ships were on their way back to Russia and had only called in for provisions and water. Duncan speedily arranged for their needs to be satisfied and on the 2 August the Russian fleet sailed, leaving a frigate and two transports to remove those still remaining in the Russian Hospital, as it had become known.[62] Being a port town, the people of Yarmouth were used to mixing with foreign nationals, but the influx of so many Russian soldiers in such a short space of time tested their tolerance to the limit. Palmer caught the mood perfectly when he wrote, 'The dirty habits of the Russians at that time were obnoxious to the inhabitants, who were sometimes placed in partial darkness in consequence of the oil being abstracted from the public lamps by the Russians, who drank up that lubricant.'[63]

The removal of the Russians proved timely for within days Britain was effectively at war

69. Into the gentility of this King Street scene was thrust the anti-social behaviour of the convalescing Russian soldiers whose excesses included drinking the oil from the town's street lamps.

with Russia and the other countries that had formed the League of Armed Neutrality against her. This provoked the Battle of Copenhagen which produced another batch of wounded seamen for the hospital at Yarmouth. On 16 April 1801 it was reported that, 'As the wind is, we are in hourly expectation that some ships with some of our poor wounded Troops will come in *here*. Every preparation is making at the Hospitals.'[64] Admiral Dickson informed the Admiralty on the 20th that he had implemented the order that no more men from the squadron, who had venereal disease, should be sent to the hospital unless it was absolutely necessary and that those already there with that complaint should be removed, in order to make room for the wounded who may be expected from the Baltic.[65] Finally, on the 24th, the waiting was over when the *Isis* arrived in the Roads with the first casualties. A keel was sent out to collect 12 men, 11 of whom were taken to the hospital while the other man, an officer, was lodged in sick-quarters. Also on board was Captain Sir Thomas Boulden Thompson of the *Bellona* (74), who had lost a leg in the action.[66] Still awaited were the *Holstein* hospital-ship and the *Monarch*, with their consignment of wounded seamen. It is clear from Admiral Dickson's correspondence that the intention was for the *Monarch* to land her wounded at Yarmouth, while the *Holstein* was to take hers to Spithead. In fact the reverse turned out to be the case as Captain Bligh of the *Monarch* was not on the best of terms with the admiral. Early on the 25th, aware that the *Monarch* had sailed by without entering the roadstead, Dickson decided to leave the sick and wounded in the hospital, but directed the *Albion* and *Wright* armed ships to be ready to take them to the Medway, if that proved necessary.[67] When shortly afterwards the *Holstein* arrived Dickson ordered her captain to proceed immediately to Spithead, but he and the ship's surgeon informed the Admiral that the dressings for the wounded had been used up and with three men on board with gaol fever, it would be extremely hazardous to proceed. In view of this 96 wounded men were landed and taken to the hospital to be cared for by Dr Snipe, assisted by young surgeons sent from London.[68]

When in June Nelson returned to Yarmouth after Copenhagen he, 'immediately on his landing, went to the Hospital, to visit the brave fellows under cure there, who were wounded in the Battle off Copenhagen and gave each of the nurses a guinea for the care they had taken of the men. Those in a convalescent state formed a lane in the hospital yard, and gratefully cheered him.'[69] Palmer's account adds more colour; 'When Nelson landed at the Jetty from H.M.S. *Kite* he was welcomed with great acclamation. The populace surrounded him, and the military were drawn up in the Market Place ready to receive him; but Nelson making his way across the Denes through sand and dirt, crowd and clamour, went straight to the Hospital. There he stopped at every bed, saying something kind and cheering to each sufferer. "Well, Jack", said the hero, "what's the matter with you?" "Lost my right arm, your honour," replied the sailor, "Then," said Nelson, glancing at his empty sleeve, "You and I are spoiled for fishermen; cheer up my brave fellow." These and similar words had a magical effect on the sufferers. Their eyes sparkled with delight; and such acts of kindness rendered Nelson the idol of the fleet.'[70]

In a navy full of pressed men desertion was always a problem, with absconding from sick-quarters or naval hospitals being a favoured option. As a result naval hospitals resembled prisons, with high perimeter walls and armed guards. When in May 1797 Captain Hunter was appointed to superintend the sick-quarters, to improve discipline, the desertion rate immediately halved, dropping from 10 a month to five. It is not recorded how this was achieved, but deployment of guards might provide a partial answer.[71] The aftermath of Camperdown increased Hunter's involvement for he was then responsible for the security at a hospital rather than the less structured sick-quarters. This prompted him to solicit the support of Evan Nepean, the Admiralty's secretary, in seeking an additional allowance, 'for the supper Intendance of the sick and wounded men at Yarmo[uth],' but it is unclear if anything was forthcoming.[72] In September 1798 he complained to Vice-Admiral Onslow that, 'from the want of a Sufficient number of centinels, on duty at the Naval Hospital at this place, a great number of Men desert and are lost to the Service.'[73] He had repeatedly approached the commanding officer of the troops at Yarmouth for more guards without success, for it was the view of the military that the sentries were there to guard the stores belonging to the Barrack Board, 'as the Building is not yet given up to the Navy.' It was also thought that the Admiralty or Navy Board should provide the guard. The Admiralty was unwilling to mount a marine guard so the matter was referred to the army's commander-in-chief for resolution.[74]

Captain Hunter's performance could not have been considered entirely satisfactory for on 23 April 1801, shortly before the wounded arrived from Copenhagen, the Admiralty appointed Lieutenant Thomas Lynne as governor of the hospital, one of only four such posts in the country (the others being at Haslar, Stonehouse and Deal). This was a full time position, and it is clear from the preamble to his instructions that in many respects the hospital was not being well managed. 'We have appointed you to the superintendance and Charge of the Interior Arrangement and Oeconomy of H. M. Naval Hospital at Yarmouth, for the purpose of ensuring a proper attention to the Sick as also for preventing those inconveniences which have so frequently been felt from a want of proper Discipline & subordination.'[75] In summary he was to enforce all orders and regulations, keep a close eye on every aspect of the workings of the hospital, control all movements in and out, inspect accounts and supervise all contracts for stores and provisions. He was not to allow any liquor of any kind to be brought in and when the patients were discharged he was to get them to their ships as quickly as possible, taking 'affectual measures for preventing their obtaining in the intermediate time the means of Intoxication,' (drink, as ever, was the prime cause of indiscipline).[76] He could also punish irregularities by placing the perpetrators in solitary confinement. Finally he was told, 'as you will observe by the tenor of your Appointment that the entire management and superintendance of the Hospital has been committed to your care, you are to consider yourself not only responsible for the punctual performance of your own immediate Duty, but also for that of any person belonging to the Establishment.' One wonders exactly what Captain Hunter and Dr Snipe had not been doing to warrant such censure.[77]

The closure of the hospital at the termination of the French Republican War was a gradual affair. When the remaining ships of the North Sea Squadron sailed away, Captain Cobb took with him those seamen who were fit to be removed. Shortly afterwards Governor Lynne was discharged.[78] In late July Dr Snipe reported to the Board that there were now only nine patients in residence, eight of whom could be removed. The man who could not be was placed in sick-quarters under the care of William Taylor, who was then appointed surgeon and agent for the sick and wounded seamen at Yarmouth, the peacetime role previously performed by Benjamin Fielding.[79] On 1 August the frigate *Jamaica* arrived to take away the remaining men and the hospital stores. Four days later Dr Snipe closed the hospital and the buildings were returned to the Barrack Office.[80]

***

During the peace sick seamen continued to be landed at Yarmouth, to be cared for in quarters, but with the reinstatement of the naval support base the number of such men inevitably rose obliging the Admiralty to review the provision of medical care at there.[81] In order to avoid the expense of leasing buildings the Lords Commissioners initially decided to maintain the quartering system, continuing to rely on surgeon William Taylor to provide what was necessary.[82] However, by mid-October 1803, demand was such that the Admiralty decided to place a hospital-ship in the harbour. When asked to recommend a suitable candidate for the task the Navy Board consulted Warmington about the depth of water on the bar and in the haven. As a result of his detailed response the Navy Board abandoned its intention to suggest the frigate *Druid*, as she drew too much water, choosing instead the ship-sloop *Cynthia*, which, at the time, was laid up at Chatham.[83] By then, however, the Admiralty had had second thoughts about the proposal, opting instead for the very solution it had tried to avoid in the first place, the creation of a naval hospital.

In mid-November Dr Andrew Baird, a Sick and Hurt Board hospital inspector, was directed to, 'repair to Yarmouth for the purpose of providing an Hospital at that place.'[84] Shortly afterwards he was pleased to report that he had, 'succeeded in hiring a place as a temporary Hospital.'[85] The two storey building in question was owned by local brewer Sir Edmund Lacon and was probably a malt-house. It was 118 feet long and 22 feet wide with a narrow yard along its full length enclosed by an 8 foot high wall. Situated in the Rows it probably stood at the north end of the town, where Lacon's other brewery buildings were located. A number of modifications were needed to turn the building into a hospital, including the erection of partitions to sub-divide the two large floors into wards, glazing the windows, converting an adjoining shed into a cookhouse, dispensary, contractors storeroom and a store for hospital materials, constructing a privy and raising the height of the courtyard wall to discourage desertion.[86] In Baird's opinion the hospital, 'will give comfortable room for eighty Patients and on a greater influx sixteen more can be accommodated in the shed from which the kitchen etc are taken.' He also felt it could be ready to receive patients in a fortnight or less.[87]

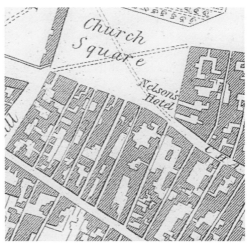

70. Sir Edmund Lacon, owner of the temporary hospital building.

71. The area of the town where the hospital building stood.

Having set the wheels in motion and sent in his report Baird departed for Norman Cross, leaving William Taylor to handle the details, which included negotiating the purchase of a small house close to the proposed hospital to provide accommodation for the dispenser or an assistant surgeon and matron. Baird was clearly impressed with the man for in the letter communicating his actions to the Sick and Hurt Board he added, 'Mr Taylor from whom I have derived much assistance in my numerous enquiries being well aware that he cannot succeed to the appointment of Surgeon to the Hospital would be ple[ase]d to accept the appointment of Dispenser, but is more particularly desirous of being appointed agent, an appointment [for which] he is extremely well suited.'[88]

With the conversion work underway the Admiralty turned its attention to staffing the new facility. In December Isaac Wilson was appointed surgeon, on a salary of £200, and in January he was joined by a clerk, Adam Glendenning, and a matron, Harriet Stratton. In February 1804 William Taylor did indeed become the dispenser, but the role of agent was given to the surgeon. By way of consolation Taylor was awarded the lucrative position of contractor for all non-medical services. The appointment of support staff soon followed, including an assistant surgeon (hospital mate), a porter, labourers and nurses.[89] In January 1804 Lieutenant Daniel Ivie was appointed governor, but his tenure did not last long for on 3 May he was ordered to sea aboard the *Glory* (98) and was replaced by Lieutenant William Larke, who had just arrived for service in the sea fencibles. He was to remain in charge of the hospital and its successor for the remainder of the first phase of the Napoleonic Wars.[90]

The first patients arrived on 20 January 1804, just two months after Baird had acquired the building. These comprised 28 sick seamen who had been landed from the warships in the Roads between 6 October 1803 and 18 January 1804. As befitted their rank those that were officers remained in sick-quarters.[91] For the following four and a half years the hospital served its purpose without any significant incident, the lowest number of patients mustered being 13, in October 1804, and the highest 86, in both April and August 1807. As a result the staffing level remained much the same throughout, the only alterations in personnel being the arrival in November 1805 of William Tait to replace Isaac Wilson as surgeon and the appointment of the Learmouth family as victualling contractors. Even the conflict with the Danes at Copenhagen in August/September 1807 only produced five wounded seamen for the hospital, in a batch of 13 sick and wounded landed from the hospital-ship *Frederikscoarn* on 29 October.[92]

In 1808, however, this comfortable state of affairs was disturbed by events in the Baltic. On 11 January the *Stately* and the *Nassau(II)*, both 64's, sailed from the Yarmouth Roads for Gothenburg carrying specie as a subsidy for the King of Sweden. Two months later, on 22 March, the two ships working in tandem destroyed the last surviving Danish ship-of-the-line, the *Prindts Christian Frederic*, in what became known as the Battle of Zealand Point. After a lively action the *Prindts* struck her colours and once her crew had been taken on board the British warships the grounded Dane was set on fire and subsequently blew up.[93] After returning to Gothenburg in early April the crews of the two British ships began to contract typhus. An entry for the 9 April in the captain's log of the *Nassau(II)* reads, 'about this time a Contagious fever with which the Danish Prisoners were afflicted – began to appear amongst our ship's compy'. The Danish prisoners were immediately sent on shore, but the damage had already been done. Riddled with the disease, on 20 April the ships set sail for the Yarmouth Roads. The voyage took two weeks and in that time close on 50 men died, their passing logged as 'committed the body of the deceased to the deep'.[94] On the 5 May, the ships arrived in the Roads with some 200 sick seamen, nearly all of whom had the fever. Most were immediately landed.[95]

Faced with a similar situation to that which arose after Camperdown, albeit on a smaller scale, surgeon Tait ordered the new arrivals to be sent to the hospital, but understanding the inadequacy of this facility to cope port-admiral Douglas quickly arranged for the hire of another building to accommodate them. On 9 May Tait was able to report to the Transport Board that, 'all the Sick from the *Stately* & *Nassau* except Seven Young Gentlemen were comfortably lodged in Sir Ed Lacon's Store House.' This overflow building probably stood close to the existing hospital. To facilitate the transfer 15 'extra' labourers were hired for up to two day's work and over 20 additional nurses were employed on a temporary basis. A Dr Jamieson was also involved for a short time.[96] Over the next three months most of the men recovered and were sent back to their ships or, in the latter stages, to the port receiving-ship *Roebuck* for reassignment. Nearly 20 died and three took the opportunity to desert. Among the intake were five who had been wounded in the battle, two of whom, being amputees, were discharged as unserviceable.[97]

Perceiving the need to increase the medical staff at the hospital the Transport Board acted quickly, appointing two more hospital mates before, on the 15th, promoting William Tait to the post of physician and replacing him as surgeon with J. D. Burke. Two days later the civilian dispenser, William Taylor, was replaced by Joseph Woolnough, who had acted in that capacity at the naval hospital in Madras, and he was given an assistant.[98] On the 8 June the Transport Board proposed to the Admiralty that, 'in consequence of the extent of the present service at North Yarmouth, the Medical Establishment of the Naval Hospital at that Port, should be put upon the same footing as at Deal...,' in effect the staffing level that had just been adopted. The Admiralty Board approved the proposal and sub-

72. This ex-Danish man-of-war landed numbers of sick and wounded seamen at Yarmouth on two separate occasions, as the Holstein after Copenhagen in 1801 and as the Nassau(II) in 1808 after Zealand Point.

sequently confirmed the appointments that had already been made.[99]

As the creation of the hospital was a matter of expediency it was never fully fit for purpose, its deficiencies being described in an inspection report by Dr John Weir, a colleague of Dr Baird's, in the following terms: 'On Account of the windows being few and small, the Wards are extremely gloomy and badly ventilated. At present the Petty Officers occupy one of these Wards; the other remains unoccupied. The second story is without ceilings, and forms two large capacious Wards, which at present accommodate the whole of the Sick in the Hospital, exclusive of the Officers; but as the Windows are very small like those of the under Wards, and as there are no Chimneys in either of the Wards, they of course are dark and unventilated. With a view to remedy these evils, I would suggest the propriety of enlarging, or augmenting, the number of windows in both stories, and of erecting two additional ventilators on the roof of each Ward on the upper Story. These in my opinion would tend greatly to promote Ventilation, and render the Wards more cheerful, and equally salubrious to those in our Royal Hospitals. The want of a sufficient extent of airing ground, for the patients to exercise themselves on is a local defect in this establishment, which cannot be remedied.'[100]

Nothing was done to implement Weir's recommendations for the leased building had always been seen as little more than a temporary solution pending the construction of a purpose built hospital and at the time of his report, in July 1806, moves were already afoot to provide such a facility. In fact as early as December 1803 the Corporation's Committee of Liberties had recommended to the full Assembly the granting of a lease to the Sick and Hurt Board, at the request of William Taylor, for a piece of land near the barracks on which to build a naval hospital. This proposal attracted complaints from the proprietors of the two nearby windmills, who claimed any such building, would 'take their wind.' Discounting these objections, on 13 January 1804, the Assembly offered to grant the Sick and Hurt Board up to three acres of land at the north-east end of the town, for £300.[101]

In the event the offer was not taken up and the long drawn out process that led to the construction of the substantial hospital complex that still stands today did not commence until mid-1806. In May that year the Transport Board directed port-admiral Billy Douglas to apply to the Corporation for an alternative piece of land and on 7 June its Committee of Liberties recommended that the Board, 'should have leave to inclose ground measuring 250 yrds by 150 yrds on the Denes south of the Signal Station in order to build a Naval Hospital and that they should have a lease.' This was subsequently confirmed by the full Assembly.[102] With the site identified the way was clear for the hospital to be designed and built, but the former activity proved much more challenging than it should have been due to fundamental differences between, on the one hand the men on the spot, supported by the Transport Board, and on the other the staff of the office of the Inspector General of Naval Works, backed by Dr Weir. Unhelpfully the Admiralty tended to prevaricate or veer from one to the other as proposals and counter proposals were submitted.

It seems likely that the newly appointed surgeon, William Tait, was the man who resurrected the stalled project. In July 1806 he prepared a sketch plan for a new hospital and sent it to the Transport Board for consideration. This was the context for Dr Weir's visit to the town, his task being to discuss the submitted proposal with Tait and port-admiral Douglas, but his brief also required him to give an 'opinion on the most economical plan to be adopted on this occasion.' Seemingly unenthusiastic about Tait's scheme, it was to the second part of his instructions that he devoted most of his time.[103] In assessing the proposed site he felt it, 'admirably calculated for a Naval Hospital,' being as it was only a quarter of a mile from the Jetty but, 'as it is greatly exposed to the North East Winds,' he recommended that the building should, 'front the West inclining a little to the South.'[104] Recognising that the size of any new hospital should be determined by the anticipated demand for beds he studied the recent patient records and concluded that the average at any one time was 40 to 60. In view of this he drew up an alternative scheme, 'similar to the one submitted to your consideration by Mr Tait, but on a reduced Scale.'[105] His design allowed for the accommodation of 110 patients and comprised three, three storey linked blocks in a straight line. He chose this configuration because he did not consider a quadrangular arrangement conducive to ventilation. Having sent his sketch plan to the Board he commissioned Joseph Stannard to draw up from it 'a regular plan and Estimate.' This was also to be submitted to the Board.[106]

On 1 August the Transport Board forwarded Stannard's submission, together with Tait's scheme, to Dr Weir for his opinion. Unsurprisingly the Board's inspector favoured that prepared by Stannard, which he felt, 'will be found the best calculated for promoting Cleanliness, Ventilation, Separation of Disease and finally a more expeditious Recovery of the patients.' Accordingly it was this plan that was referred to the Admiralty.[107] The wheels of bureaucracy, however, continued to turn very slowly and it was not until 12 January 1807 that William Marsden, the Admiralty Board's secretary, sent the Transport Board's preferred

73. The Royal Naval Hospital, Yarmouth.

plan to Samuel Bentham, the Inspector General of Naval Works, for his consideration.[108]

In late January Weir carried out another inspection of the temporary hospital and while he was satisfied with how it was run he was clearly concerned about the delay in building its replacement, writing in his report that because of, 'the smallness of the Scale on which this Establishment is formed; the total inadequacy of providing for any sudden influx of Patients, the hostile complexion of affairs on the Continent; the impracticability of securing a more eligible Building in the Town of Yarmouth and the being subject to the caprice and imposition of a Proprietor who can double or treble the Rent according to the pressing exigencies of the Service; it appears to me that the erection of an Hospital is become absolutely necessary.'[109]

On 8 April Governor Larke raised the stakes when he informed the Transport Board that, 'not having room in the Hospital to put up more than another Cradle and having understood that several Sick Men may be expected from the *Resolution*, on the arrival of that ship in Port, it will become necessary to hire Rooms in the Town for the reception of Patients.' On informing the Admiralty of this state of affairs the Transport Board took the opportunity to draw, 'their Lordships' attention to our Letters Dated as p[e]r the margin respecting the Building [of] an Hospital at the Port of Yarmouth.' There were eight of them, sent between 24 May 1806 and 7 January 1807.[110]

It was not until 6 June 1807 that the office of the Inspector General of Naval Works sent a response to the Admiralty, six pages written by Bentham's assistant Simon Goodrich, as the Inspector General himself was 'absent on service.'[111] To summarise, the whole scheme had been greatly expanded to provide for 238 patients. Although it was still based on three three storey hospital buildings it now included all the necessary ancillary structures and facilities such as a detached kitchen, wash-house, a porter's lodge, insane house, receiving house, soldier's guard house, privies in the airing ground, a dead house (mortuary), operating room, governor's office, dispensaries, clerk's and steward's apartments, cabins for eight nurses, a bathing room, a foul linen store, a laundry and a drying room, a store for seaman's bedding and clothing, together with a store room for the agent. The estimate for the work was £19,689-3-2½, more than twice that of the submitted scheme. This costing together with a set of plans, was sent to the Admiralty for approval.[112] Alarmed at the scale and cost of this latest proposal the Admiralty directed the Inspector General to reconsider both schemes, but with Goodrich suggesting only relatively small savings, on 10 August he was told to proceed with that for 116 patients, 'with the utmost expedition,' in a way that it could be extended if necessary. By late September revised plans had been prepared, with an estimate of £10,426-2-5½, and on the 24 September the Admiralty ordered the Transport Board to arrange for the hospital to be built.[113]

What followed can only be described as a desperate rear-guard action to overturn the Admiralty's decision. On 18 December 1807 the secretary to the Transport Board wrote to the Lords Commissioners to acquaint them that it was the opinion of Vice-Admirals Russell and Douglas and also Captain Bowen (a Transport Board commissioner), who had recently reported on the hospital site, 'that it would be most advisable that the Hospital should be only two stories high, and in which opinion this Board join.' It was also felt that it should be sufficiently large to receive about 300 patients, perhaps reflecting the anticipated demand from the naval operations in the Baltic. The letter went on to report that the approved plans had been returned to Mr Goodrich with whom the Transport Board had, 'had a conference on the Subject,' and that he had been given some other drawings prepared by Mr Tait, 'whose Opinion on the subject appears to us to merit attention.' To cover the possible rejoinder of delay it was pointed out that, 'no Works of any kind can at this Season of the year be undertaken.' On the assumption that the Admiralty would approve the new proposal a request was made for the Inspector general's Office to be instructed to prepare 'regular drawings' to enable a contract to be entered into.[114]

On this occasion the Admiralty acted swiftly, instructing the Inspector General, on 24 December, to comply with the Transport Board requirements, but when in April the latest drawings arrived, the buildings depicted were still three storeys high and what's more there were now basements. To overcome a Transport Board objection concerning the difficulty of carrying patients upstairs it was suggested that some form of a lift could be installed. The estimate for the work had risen to £32,242-10-1¾, but it was claimed that should the same amount of accommodation be placed in two storey buildings the cost would be increased by more than £7,000.[115] The Admiralty approved this scheme on 3 June and instructed the Transport Board to bring it to fruition. The latter, however, was not so easily thwarted. Objection was raised again to the three storey nature of the project because of the site's exposed position and doubt was expressed about the ability of the foundations to take the weight. There was also a concern that the low lying nature of the ground was not suitable for basements. Other criticisms included the absence of separation of contagious from non-contagious patients on the airing ground and the lack of a colonnade to shelter the patients from the summer sun, the winter damp and wet weather. Clearly dissatisfied with the performance of the in-house architects the Transport Board concluded its response by seeking, 'authority to employ an Architect that we may be enabled to carry into Execution the plan which We suggested.'[116] This long drawn out affair finally ended on 13 June 1808. Probably stirred into action by the recent medical crisis at Yarmouth the Admiralty returned to the Transport Board its plans with a direction to carry 'the same into execution with all possible dispatch as recommended in your letter of the 18th December last, accordingly, taking care that the Work be performed, on the best and cheapest terms.'[117]

The man chosen to design and manage the building works was William Pilkington, a London based architect of some standing. He made his first visit to the site on 18 June and over the next few months produced the necessary drawings for a hospital complex completely in line with the Transport Board's requirements.[118] As designed the main building comprised four two storey Georgian styled ranges set out as a north facing quadrangle. These were linked at the corners by single storey curved structures containing the 'necessaries' (toilets) and overall by a Romanesque style colonnade. The centre of each range was punctuated by a gabled projection, embellished with classical detailing. The northern (front) range, at ground floor level, was earmarked for support facilities such as the kitchen, bathroom, pantry, coal cellar, and stores for the agent and dispenser, together with a mess room for convalescents. The upper floor of this range contained rooms for commissioned officers, a ward for warrant and petty officers, staff sitting rooms and bedrooms, together with various stores. The other three ranges contained wards for seamen, with at the centre of the one to the east, a dispensary, that on the south, the operating theatre and 'dead' room, and that on the west the chapel, which, together with a burial ground, was consecrated by the Bishop of Norwich in August 1813, following the appointment of the Reverend John Homfray to the post of hospital

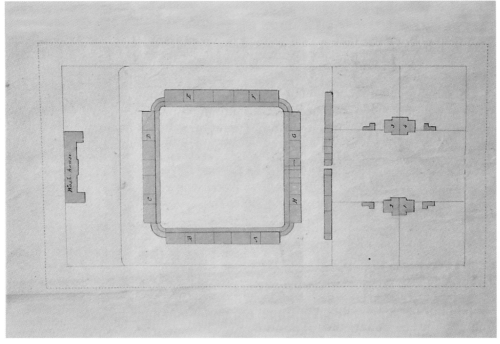

74. A plan of the Royal Naval Hospital, Yarmouth.

chaplain in October 1812.[119] A single storey block in front of the northern range stood astride the main entrance to the complex and contained a recovery room, porter's lodge, guard room, and an office. A similar block to the rear housed wash-houses. Facing each other across the driveway stood two pairs of substantial semi-detached houses for the use of the principal officers. The whole was enclosed by high walls and railings.[120]

The contract for erecting the main hospital buildings, at a cost of £66,798, was awarded to John Miles. A clerk of works, John Webb, was employed from 24 January 1809 and construction commenced on 6 February, the first brick being laid by port-admiral Billy Douglas.[121] Associated with Miles, in a subordinate capacity, was another contractor, Henry Peto, whose job it was to provide the bricks. At the Corporation's Assembly of 6 March 1809 he was given 'leave to burn bricks and lay materials on the South Denes for the erecting of a Naval Hospital.'[122] As luck would have it he had recently discovered brick earth when excavating a dock in Southtown (probably that of James Lovewell) which enabled him to, 'make a considerable sum.'[123] Peto, however, was somewhat cavalier in his approach to officialdom for on 29 March the Corporation's Committee of Liberties was told that he had exceeded the limits set out for burning bricks and placing materials on the South Denes and, 'had encumbered the whole open space between the ground granted for the Hospital and the moats near the Whale Fishery warehouses.' He was directed to work within the agreed limits while at the same time he was given permission to level part of the Denes and sow it with

75. A pair of officer's houses on the eastern side of the approach drive to the Royal Naval Hospital.

grass seed.[124] Undeterred Peto continued to offend. As a result on 14 August the Assembly ordered him to remove the materials placed by him on the South Denes[125] and on 2 July 1810 the Committee of Liberties directed the town clerk to give him notice to clear the ground by 1 September and thereafter to discontinue burning bricks.[126] With the Corporation's patience having run out, on 12 October 1810 his application to cut 'flaggs' on the Denes was refused.[127]

The first payment to the contractor was authorised by Pilkington on 13 July 1809. By then much of the northern service block had been com-pleted. The tenth and final payment was sanctioned on 18 May 1811, when the works were nearly complete. The officers' houses were built under a separate contract awarded to Peto on 30

76. The former Royal Naval Hospital today, a mixed complex of houses and apartments

September 1810. He commenced work later that year and by 2 December 1811 they were nearly finished. The whole project cost around £75,000.[128] When complete the pale yellow brick building must have been extremely eye-catching, prompting Preston to comment, 'The noble and massive appearance of the exterior cannot fail to arrest the notice of visitors, particularly when viewed from the high lands of Gorleston, or in approaching from thence towards Yarmouth.'[129]

The Royal Naval Hospital, as it was called, received its first patients in June 1811, but it was only operational for a little over three years in which time the highest number of patients mustered was 77, in December 1812. Dr Weir had been right in his assessment of need; a hospital for 110 patients would have been more than adequate for providing the medical care required for the remainder of the war, but he had not won the day. In the event, with room for 500 patients the hospital proved to be a costly white elephant.[130] Palmer commented that by the time the hospital was opened, 'The war…was then nearly over as far as the Navy was concerned. No "glorious victory" sent its victims to this hospital…'and Druery provided further explanation for its lack of use when he wrote, 'It did not, however, long continue an hospital, for in consequence of St. Nicholas's Gatt, the only safe entrance to the roads, shoaling its water, the passage became contracted, and unsafe for men of war and ships of burthen, and, in consequence, an order was sent from the Admiralty, to discontinue it as an hospital,...'[131] There was, however, a significant increase in the number of patients between 17 December 1813 and 3 June 1814, but these were Dutch ex-prisoners of war who had arrived to be repatriated. Over 130 such men were cared for by a number of nurses especially employed for that purpose.[132]

As in the previous war the naval and military presence in the town produced a requirement for burial space, the records from which reflect the pattern of events both at the naval support base and further afield.[133] Deceased naval personnel continued to be interred in the hospital burial ground created in 1799, with some 300 such men being laid to rest there between 1803 and 1812. At least 24 militiamen from the town's garrison were buried in the churchyard during the same period, as were close on 100 regular soldiers. Apart from a sergeant from the 54th Foot, who was buried in December 1811 having drowned, these regulars were all casualties of Continental expeditions.[134] In February 1806 troop transports had arrived in the Roads from the Elbe and Weser following an abortive expedition to Bremen and in October 1807 transports arrived from the more successful expedition to Copenhagen. In each case a small number of soldiers were carried to their final resting place in the town.[135] It was, however, the Walcheren expedition of 1809 that accounted for the majority of the regulars interred. After the British force successfully reduced Veere and Flushing in mid-August the French garrison capitulated. Unfortunately the Earl of Chatham, the commander-in-chief of the invading army, failed to follow up this advantage and while his troops tried to break out they succumbed to a type of malaria that was dubbed 'Walcheren Fever', with 100 men dying each day. Faced with this calamity, in December the troops were evacuated. For Yarmouth these events resulted in a period of medical activity which closely resembled what had happened ten years earlier when many of the sick and wounded from the Helder expedition had been landed in the town, to be cared for in a makeshift military general hospital established in the naval hospital. The evidence for this repeat performance, however, is somewhat sketchier. In January 1810 the *Norfolk Chronicle* reported that, 'We are happy to find, that between 80 and 90 convalescent troops marched from the general Hospital here, since Thursday, to join their respective regiments. We observed several of the 5th, 28th, and 32d, and there were some of the 8th, 42d, 71st, 77th, 85th, and a few of the 63d and 84th to be seen with them.'[136] There are no newspaper reports of the arrival of these sick men from Flushing (nor Harwich to where many of the evacuated troops were sent), but 62 ended up in the graveyard and taken together with the above report it seems likely that a large number of sick soldiers were cared for in the town.[137]

11.
Prisoners of War

At the start of the first conflict prisoner of war depots were re-opened at Bristol (Stapleton), Gosport (Forton), Plymouth (Mill Prison), and Liverpool. The following year Porchester Castle was added to the list. Between them they could accommodate around 20,000 prisoners. To supplement this provision hulks were fitted out at Chatham, Plymouth, and Portsmouth.[1] However, none of these prisons were conveniently placed to receive enemy seamen taken in the North Sea or the Baltic, prompting the Admiralty to direct the Sick and Hurt Board to create a number of reception prisons along the East Coast, at Harwich, Hull, North Shields, and Yarmouth.[2]

As part of this process the Sick and Hurt Board, who at the time was responsible for prisoners of war, instructed its Yarmouth agent, Benjamin Fielding, to find a suitable place for prisoner confinement. He quickly discovered that the prison created in the previous war was available at the same rate as before, £40 per annum, but that it would cost a further £340 to refit. This the Admiralty found acceptable and on 6 March 1793 gave the order for him to hire the premises with the usual caveat, 'taking care that the Works necessary to be done thereto, be performed in the best and cheapest manner for the Crown.'[3] The prison had its main frontage on Row 135 and comprised two fish houses with associated yards. It was owned by local merchant William Fisher and by the terms of a memorandum of agreement it was hired for one year and thereafter for such further terms 'as the service shall require.' By then events had overtaken the paperwork, for the premises were described as, 'now occupied and used by the said Benjamin Fielding as a Gaol for Prisoners of War.'[4] In fact the first prisoners had arrived on 27 February, the 26 man crew of the French privateer *Le Custine*, escorted to the prison by soldiers of the East Suffolk Militia.[5]

There is no full description of the prison, but visitation reports and repair records serve to give an impression of what it was like. On 19 August 1798 Transport Board commissioner, Captain William Otway, submitted a report following his inspection of the facility.[6] He observed that the buildings 'were originally used as Curing Houses for Fish and being substantially built will not I think, require any considerable repair for some time. The situation is certainly not such as I should have chosen for a Prison, being very confined, and in the midst of the Town, I should therefore have supposed it unhealthy but am assured the contrary is the case.' This he attributed to the custom of taking the prisoners for walks a short distance from the town.[7] The main rooms housed the prisoners in a similar fashion to how they lived on board ship. Mess tables were provided and posts with hooks supported hammocks. There was also a kitchen, some storerooms (with a separate one for the French agent's stores), a straw room, separate accommodation for the officers and men of the guard, and a 'bog house', as the privy was called. For security purposes sentry boxes were placed at the entrances to the Rows and at night lamps were lit in these alleyways. Initially when prisoners fell ill they

77. Row 135, looking east. It was here that the first prison for prisoners of war was located.

were transferred to sick-quarters in the town, but as they recovered so a number of them escaped, prompting the creation of a sick-room within the prison. It is to Fielding's credit that of the many prisoners who passed through his hands only 11 died.[8]

Fielding was responsible for the overall management of the prison, but the day to day handling of the prisoners was left to a turnkey and a porter. Even so, given his other commitments, Fielding found it difficult to find sufficient time for his prison work, prompting him to press the Transport Board for a clerk to assist him. This was one of the matters Otway had to assess during his visitation in 1798. In his report he concluded, 'I can only say that with the salary of £80 pr annum, it cannot be supposed that he devotes the whole of his time to the duty of Agent for Prisoners of War I therefore think if a Cartel for the exchange of Dutch Prisoners does not shortly take place, he should be allowed an assistant. I more readily give this opinion as your Agent for the Prisoners at Deal has a Clerk, where at all times there is infinitely less to do than here.'[9] With the case made Thomas Godsell was appointed clerk, on a salary of £50 per annum.[10] The reason for such a small staff was that the support services that were needed to sustain the prisoners were contracted out. The main contract was for victualling. This seems to have been let on a six monthly basis and the fact that the contractor was constantly being changed suggests that feeding and watering the prisoners did not always run smoothly. In addition the task of preventing the prisoners escaping fell to the military, not the navy. Guards were usually provided by one of the militia units stationed in or near the town, although when required the volunteer corps could be called upon to perform this duty. When neither were available it became necessary for the agent to hire 'proper persons' to guard the prison, as was the case in June 1798.[11]

Being a reception prison with accommodation for little more than 150 men Fielding needed to move the prisoners on as quickly as possible in order to make room for new arrivals. As time went on this proved to be quite a challenge.[12] By the end of 1793 the crews of eight French vessels had been received. Of these 14 men had been granted parole, one had been released to Lieutenant-General Johnston by order of the Sick and Hurt Board and one had died, leaving 129 men to be processed.[13] In February 1794 the Board released 20 who were fishermen[14] and in May gave orders for the remainder to be sent to Forton prison, notoriously unhealthy at the time. The first 50 left on 19 May, in a tender escorted by the brig-sloop

Scourge and another 50 followed on 11 June.[15]. Although the Yarmouth prison was then virtually empty it was not until 25 July that more prisoners were landed, the 56 man crew of the French cutter *Nareissa*, taken off the Dutch coast by the frigate *Aurora*. These were the only prisoners lodged that year. It was a similar story in 1795, when despite the arrival of over 60 prizes in the Roads no more prisoners were deposited in the prison for by then the *Hero* and *Bristol* prison hulks had been established at Chatham and crews from the prizes were taken directly there. At the end of the year the prison was emptied again, but this time by prisoner exchange. On 23 December the cartel vessel *Thomas and Sally* embarked 65 prisoners and sailed for Dunkirk. Five days later she returned with 65 English seamen who had been prisoners in France. This is perhaps the context for an anecdote recorded by Palmer whereby that year, 'an agent of the French Convention arrived in Yarmouth to arrange an exchange of prisoners. He wore a tricolored cockade, which was considered an insult by the sailors who quickly possessed themselves of it, and a tumult ensued.'[16]

In 1796 the prison started to fill again, with 80 men landed from six enemy vessels taken by the North Sea cruisers between January and November. There were no significant transfers, however, for by then the land prisons and hulks were becoming overcrowded. In response to this problem, the Transport Board set about finding a site for a new major prison, one that could be easily accessed from a port, was far enough away from the coast to inhibit escape, yet close to a main road to facilitate rapid troop movement, should it prove necessary to quell an uprising. The site chosen was at Norman Cross near Peterborough. Plans were drawn up in December 1796 and the construction work started shortly afterwards.[17] This decision was not before time for 1797 proved to be the peak year for taking prisoners at sea as a result of a dramatic increase in the number of enemy privateers. The previous year had generated 2,448 privateer crewmen for the British prisons, whereas in 1797 some 7,094 were brought in.[18]

Yarmouth was an obvious feeder prison for the new Norman Cross facility and in anticipation of it coming on stream landings of prisoners on the Jetty continued apace. Short of bedding for the new arrivals Fielding wrote to the Transport Board, only to be told on 16 February that, 'we do not at Present think it necessary to send you a Supply of Bedding as it is intended Speedily to remove all the French prisoners now at Yarmouth.[19] The following day the 82 man crew of the French privateer *Buonaparte*, taken in the North Sea by the frigate *Espion* and the ship-sloop *Martin*, were marched up Jetty Road to the prison door, taking the number of prisoners incarcerated to over 200. This prompted the Mayor, Dover Colby, to complain to the Transport Board about the overcrowding only to receive the reply, 'it is

78. A prisoner of war hulk at Chatham.

intended to remove all the French prisoners now at Yarmouth, with as little delay as possible to a Prison now completing in Huntingdonshire.'[20]

Norman Cross received its first prisoners on 7 April, but it was not until 6 June that the Transport Board informed Fielding that 'on account of the Insecurity of the Prison at Yarmouth, we intend to remove all the Prisoners from thence to the prison at Norman Cross… to which Place we direct you to send them.'[21] Given that there was an urgent need to alleviate the overcrowding it seems a little odd for the Sick and Hurt Board to have cited insecurity as the reason for emptying the prison, but around that time 10 prisoners had managed to escape. Proceeding to Lowestoft they had seized a boat and put to sea, but being without provisions they landed at Southwold just as a brig was leaving the harbour. Pursued by this vessel, they were observed from the town, whereby a group of volunteer seamen quickly manned a boat and after firing flares in the direction of the escapees, succeeded in re-capturing them.[22] It would seem that the Board could not resist having a dig at Fielding. Whatever the reason for the removals, the arrangements were made and on 17 June a column of 200 prisoners set out from Yarmouth, guarded by soldiers from the Inniskilling Dragoons and the Oxford Militia. They arrived at King's Lynn on 21 and at Norman Cross a few days later.[23]

79. The block-house at the Norman Cross depot for prisoners of war, 1809. It sported six cannon charged with grapeshot.

A standard procedure for the removal of prisoners to Norman Cross quickly became established. When there were sufficient to be transferred, the Board applied to the Commander-in-Chief of the army (the Duke of York) for a guard to take them to King's Lynn. Once this escort had assembled Fielding sent the prisoners on their way in the charge of a person termed a 'conductor', having taken care to provide any barefoot man with shoes for the journey. After each day's march they would be quartered overnight in roadside farm buildings. At King's Lynn they were met by the Transport Board's agent, Captain Woodriff, or his representative. Here they would spend the night on a receiving ship or in the large warehouse that stood on the King's Staithe, before being embarked in lighters and taken along the inland waterways to the prison camp.

The system worked well, but with the constant arrival of ever more prisoners, Fielding was always under pressure. Scarcely had the first party left when the Mayor was complaining again about the overcrowded state of the prison and on 31 July another 200 were sent on their way.[24] Further transfers occurred on 16 September and 1 November, but by the end of the year the strain on Fielding was such that on 18 December he tendered his resignation. This the Transport Board reported to the Admiralty and on 26 December he was informed that a person would be appointed to succeed him. His decision may have resulted from his earlier dismissal from his naval medical post, but whatever the reason he was persuaded to change his mind and continued to run the prison until the end of the war.[25] Dissatisfaction with his performance, however, continued to dog him. On 16 June 1799 Admiral Duncan, told the Admiralty that, 'the King's Service labours under great inconvenience for want of Orders being given to have the place appropriated here for the reception of prisoners cleared when it happens to be full, which is the case at Present, as there are twenty one French Seamen, now on board the *Circe* and thirteen in the *Jalouse*, without any place of Security to lodge them; I therefore take the Liberty to suggest that directions may be given to the Transport Board to have the prison (which will only contain 150) cleared when the number Amounts to a hundred, that Room may be left for any prisoners necessary to be landed from the North Sea cruizers.' It was not until 4 December that the Transport Board directed Fielding to give early notice when the number of prisoners reached that figure.[26]

Until mid-1797 the prisoners incarcerated at Yarmouth came almost exclusively from French vessels, but with the opening of Norman Cross there was a change of policy and in late June that year the first crew from a Dutch vessel arrived, 48 men from the 10 gun schooner privateer *Stiver*, which had been taken by the frigate *Astrea* on the 1 June. This required the prison to be divided into a 'French prison' and a 'Dutch prison', for it was government policy to keep the two nationalities apart. The French were generally seen as revolutionaries to a man whereas the Dutch were considered to be unwilling allies of their more powerful neighbour and as such received better treatment. In April 1798 a number of Dutch fishing schuyts were captured and the prisoners taken from them were reported to be 'unanimous in declaring their abhorrence of the French, who compelled them to come out in their Boats to fish for their Navy, which could not otherwise be victualled; they assert, that the French who pretended to come as Friends, have robbed them of everything...'[27]

The Battle of Camperdown produced Dutch prisoners of war of quite a different nature, naval seamen who had taken part in a fleet action. Most of these were transported to Spithead, but their wounded colleagues were landed at Yarmouth and, as we have seen, when well enough, were transferred from the hospital to the prison, apart from the officers among them who were quartered in the Ship Tavern. These included some of the surgeons who were employed attending the Dutch sick and wounded at the naval hospital. Not being well guarded, on 24 November six of them escaped on board a Dutch Hoy. When the Admiralty asked for an explanation the Transport Board responded that 'they (the prisoners in question) were never delivered into the Custody of the Board's Agent, nor ever were at Norman Cross.' As a result all the Dutch officers at Yarmouth were sent on parole away from the town.[28]

While the vast majority of the prisoners detained were ordinary seamen and as such spent their captivity in a land prison or a prison hulk, better treatment was afforded to their officers over a certain rank. If they would give their word of honour as gentlemen, in writing, not to escape they were allowed to reside in a parole depot where, subject to certain conditions, they could live fairly normal lives, until they were exchanged or the war ended. The officers held at Yarmouth were largely from privateers and to start with they were given parole at nearby Beccles under the supervision of a Mr Purvis, the agent there, but in September 1796 two of them tried to escape thereby breaking their parole. As a result it was decided that the parolees at Beccles should be moved 'to some place more distant from the sea'. The town chosen was Eye in Suffolk, under the care of Thomas Nash.[29] From then on no more privateer officer prisoners were allowed parole, but those from warships continued to be sent to Eye and, from August 1799, Peterborough. They were all Dutch, and included among their number 44 officers who were moved from Yarmouth, following the escape of the Dutch surgeons mentioned earlier.

Throughout the war prisoners were exchanged or sent home if they were no longer fit for service. A number also enlisted in the British navy and army with in January 1801, 20 enlisting in the 60th Rifles, a unit largely made up of foreign nationals. In all 16 prisoners were recorded as having escaped or 'run', but these were the ones that got clean away. Those that were recaptured, and many were, such as the group of 10 already mentioned, have nothing against their names to show that they had been at large for a short period of time. Only a handful of men died in the prison, but at least one died on route to Norman Cross. Jean de Narde (or Derinard), son of the notary public at St Malo, entered captivity at Yarmouth on 2 July 1799, as part of the crew of the French privateer *Anacreon*. On 2 October that year, with just over 130 other prisoners, he set out for Norman Cross. On the way he escaped, but was recaptured and confined in the bell tower of East Dereham Church. Attempting to escape again he was shot by a guard and his body was buried in the churchyard.[30]

Benjamin Fielding could be forgiven for thinking his work as agent was not appreciated for before the war came to a close he was to suffer one last indignity. On 12 August 1801 Commissioner Ambrose Serle delivered to the Transport Board a report on

80. The gravestone of Jean de Narde in East Dereham churchyard.

his inspection of the Yarmouth prison. Fielding had shown him round and he had met the clerk, turnkey and porter, all of whom he thought to be 'attentive to their Dutys.' There were 19 prisoners, 17 of them French, the other two Dutch, who were so old and infirm he directed Fielding to send them home. He observed that the contract for victualling was with John Grant, but delivered by a baker named Worts. He examined the food and was satisfied with what he saw and heard. He found no complaints respecting gambling (so rife in the prisons) and the buildings which form the prison appeared in good condition as to security.[31] So far so good, but there was another reason for the commissioner's visit and that was to investigate allegations made by, Francis Tresson, a former French prisoner, that Fielding and his clerk had been charging five guineas a time for passports issued by them to non-combatants and prisoners entitled to parole, who were permitted to return to France. Serle questioned Fielding and Godsell the clerk, separately and together. Both declared the allegations to be malicious. The clerk stated that Tresson had entered the prison on 20 January 1801, claiming he was a steward aboard the French privateer *L'Impressable* and as such would expect a passport as a non-combatant. But the vessel's papers showed him to be an ordinary seaman and he was treated as such. He apparently took offence at this and on several occasions expressed his 'Malice and wish for Revenge'. On being sent to Norman Cross, in May 1801, he made allegations to the agent there. After taking affidavits, Serle concluded that as Tresson was back in France nothing more could be done.[32] Fielding was no doubt unhappy with this outcome, as mud sticks, but there was to be a vindication of sorts when he received a letter from the Transport Board, with a copy of a declaration from the Captain and Second Captain of *Le Voyageur* privateer, late prisoners at Yarmouth, by which it appeared it was the clerk, Godsell, who had received money for obtaining passports. Fielding was told to investigate, but by then the war was drawing to a close and nothing further was done about the matter.[33] Later that month he was directed to take in no more prisoners and to send those he already had to Chatham. At the same time William Fisher was given notice that the prison building would soon be returned to him[34] During this first war some 3,340 prisoners had been held at Yarmouth of which nearly 2,700 had been transported to Norman Cross. The remainder had been sent elsewhere or been discharged via, repatriation, exchange, parole, enlistment in the British army or navy, escape, or death.

***

The renewal of the war on trade, in 1803, soon produced a steady stream of prizes and prisoners of war. Unfortunately, with the disposal of the prison used in the previous two conflicts, there was no proper place for these men to be incarcerated, nor was there a designated agent to manage them. It was a situation that would take the best part of six months to rectify.[35] In June that year the Transport Board received correspondence from John Fisher, the Mayor, asking for guidance on how to dispose of five French prisoners of war who had been lodged in the town gaol. In response he was given a letter to be delivered to, 'the Senior Officer commanding H.M. Ships at that Port.'[36] With no officer fitting that description present at the time it was handed to Captain Thomas Campbell, the newly arrived regulating officer. In this chance fashion Campbell (and his successors) became the Transport Board's agent at Yarmouth, being formally appointed on 4 August.[37] Having in early July forwarded the

Frenchmen to the Nore Campbell was directed by the Admiralty to examine all the Dutch prisoners he received with a view to sending the fit ones to the same place and the 'unserviceable' back home. On this basis he soon dispatched 20 'Aged Dutch Fishermen' to Holland in the Prussian ship *Aurora*.[38]

On 9 July the Transport Board received the Admiralty's order, 'to have a Building to serve as a temporary Prison at Yarmouth,' and to report when it was ready to take prisoners. Campbell, in turn, was directed to find out if the premises used previously were available and, if not, to find a similar building capable of accommodating 200 men.[39] Quickly discovering that the earlier prison was not for hire or sale, in mid-July Campbell sent to the Transport Board plans and particulars of two buildings which had been offered to him, the more central of them being available for 400 guineas. After correspondence concerning repair costs, the number of troops needed to guard the facility, the type of tenure and the nature of proposed adaptations, the more convenient of the two was chosen and on 27 July Campbell was directed to purchase the property for the slightly reduced sum of £400.[40] While this was being attended to Campbell was told that the Norman Cross prison was ready to receive prisoners and that any arriving at Yarmouth, being not less than 50, could be sent there under the well-established procedure involving a conductor and a militia escort supplied by the Commander-in-Chief.[41]

Although agreement to acquire the new building had been reached on 3 August, there were delays with the paperwork at the London end, prompting the owner to complain, but on 19 September the purchase was finally completed. With the need to carry out the refurbishment, however, the prison was not available for use until early November.[42] Even then Campbell was in no hurry to receive prisoners. On 9 November the Transport Board considered his request for a supply of bedding. In reply he was told that 200 sets had been ordered to be sent to him and he was to purchase straw for the paillasses. He was also informed that he was to be allowed £70 per annum for a clerk and that John Masters Bell would be arriving to take up that position the following day. Later in the month, however, when three French prisoners were brought to him, Campbell recommended that, as the bedding had not arrived, they be sent on board the flagship. The Transport Board was not amused, advising him that the bedding was on its way and in the meantime he was to purchase, 'what was absolutely necessary, for any prisoners delivered into his custody.'[43] On 22 November turnkey James Sibert took up his position and a month later a labourer arrived to assist him. As far as victualling the prisoners was concerned on 1 December William Worts was awarded a contract at 6¼d per man, per day, which he fulfilled until the end of the war.[44]

The first prisoners to be accommodated were five Frenchmen delivered to Campbell on 12 December by Lieutenant William Bamber, the officer in charge of the Winterton sea fencibles. They were a prize crew taken when a British merchant ship had been recaptured. The following day 54 prisoners were received from the privateers *Le Vigilant* and the *Lyonois*, captured by the *Vixen* gun brig and the *Badger* Revenue Cutter.[45]

The prison was situated between Rows 110 and 113 and consisted of two buildings which, although not conjoined, were reasonably close to one another. They had previously been granaries or malt houses associated with a brewery. Details of their sub-division are harder to come by than those for the previous prison, but it would be safe to assume that the component parts were much the same.[46] When in September 1805 Transport Board commissioner, Sir Rupert George, inspected the prison he pronounced it, 'perfectly substantial and secure, but too much confined from Situation, it nevertheless is well calculated for a temporary Prison.'[47] This was not a view shared by port-admiral Billy Douglas, for when in December 1808 he had to process a number of Dutchmen taken from fishing boats he commented that, 'with respect to sending them to Prison here it is such a miserable place, that I hope you will only send a few at a time as I can dispose of them.'[48]

Palmer was familiar with these buildings. Writing in the 1870's, he observed that, 'Every aperture towards this row [Row 110] was bricked up, except a door with an iron grating, through which the unhappy prisoners were supplied with bones, by carving of which into ornaments they endeavoured to while away the tedious hours of captivity. A sentinel was placed at each end of the row and after dusk no one could pass without a watch word. Notwithstanding these precautions the prisoners frequently escaped.'[49] The records do not bear out this contention, not in terms of permanent escape anyway, although at the very start of the prison's use, shortly after lamps had been placed in the Rows as a precautionary measure, Campbell reported that two prisoners had absconded. As a result alterations were made to the buildings to prevent escape through the roof.[50] This seems to be the context for another of Palmer's anecdotes. Apparently the house at the north-west corner of the Row, on which the prison abutted, was during the war the residence of Ives Hurry. His wife Margaret, 'took a most compassionate interest in these poor men, contributed largely to their comfort, and even went so far as to connive at their attempts to escape. On one occasion, as the nursery maid was putting one of the children to bed in an upper back room, she caught sight of a man's hand thrust through an aperture in the wall. She ran down terrified, and informed her mistress; but Mrs. Hurry concluding that a Frenchman was endeavouring to make his way

81. Supplied with animal bones through a grating in the door the prisoners of war at Yarmouth made a variety of ornaments for sale which helped to while away the time and provide a small income.

out of prison, and not wishing to molest him, ordered the child to be taken to another room, and in the morning it became known that a prisoner had escaped.'[51]

It was not only escapees who vandalised the buildings. In September 1808 the Transport Board approved Captain Heddington's actions in putting the prisoners on 'short allowance' to defray the cost of repairs as a result of damage they had inflicted on the prison and in November 1810 they received the same punishment, 'until the Parties actually Concerned in damaging the Prison Walls and Floors be given up.' Two weeks later the new prison agent was directed, 'to keep the Prisoners now in your Custody on Short Allowance, until the 20th of this month, to make good the Damage done to the Prisons.'[52]

The post of agent was only part time, as the role was performed by naval officers with other primary duties, mainly the regulating officers. The fourth of these was the aforementioned Captain Heddington, who shortly after taking over the agency queried the nature of his remuneration for the work, only to be told, 'the Allowance which has been made by this Department to your Predecessors was considered merely as a Gratuity.' He was clearly dissatisfied with this response for six weeks later it was stressed to him that none of the previous agents had been paid more than £50 and that no more could be paid but, 'Should you not therefore, wish to continue the Service on these Terms, and will let the Board know so, they will make Some other Arrangements for carrying on this Service.' Heddington backed down and when, in November 1810, the rendezvous was closed control of the prison passed to the Transport Board's other Yarmouth based naval officer, Lieutenant Larke, the governor of the naval hospital.[53]

There was a considerable turnover in the men running the prison, there being four different turnkeys, five clerks and eight labourers. In December 1808 turnkey Sibert exchanged places with Timothy Foley, a turnkey at the Norman Cross prison. Foley seems to have been a man to keep an eye on for in April 1809 the Transport Board asked Heddington for a report on his conduct and on 13 June 1812 he, together with labourer, Samuel Silvers, were dismissed for selling the prisoner's clothing and bedding. The following March his successor, Joseph Hubbard, was also 'discharged immediately,' probably for a similar offence.[54]

With the Yarmouth facility remaining a reception prison one of the main duties of the agent, as in the previous war, was to move the prisoners on. Captured officers were once more sent on parole, mainly to Northampton and Chesterfield, and significant numbers of the non-French seamen volunteered for service in the navy, but the majority were exchanged with British prisoners of war held by the enemy, or sent to places of more permanent confinement, such as the Norman Cross prison and the Chatham hulks. Very few French prisoners from the Yarmouth prison were exchanged during this war, but a large number of Dutch seamen benefited from this reciprocal arrangement. If anything, the view that these men were unwilling allies of the French, was stronger than in the previous conflict and a lively exchange by cartel was quickly established. In March 1804 the *Norfolk Chronicle* reported that, 'The Batavian Government appears very desirous to have a regular exchange of prisoners of war, with this country, as they have lately liberated through the request of some of the most respectable merchants of Amsterdam and Rotterdam, the masters and mates of several merchant vessels, and suffered them to proceed to their respective homes on their taking an oath and signing a declaration not to serve by land or sea against that government, during the war.' Two men had just arrived at Yarmouth under these terms and it was hoped that there would now be a regular exchange of such prisoners.[55] By January the following year the Yarmouth correspondent of the *Norfolk Chronicle* was able to report that, 'The exchange of prisoners between England and Holland continues to go on. The ship *Hazard* sailed from this port on Saturday with Dutch prisoners for the Texel.'[56] These exchanges continued apace until early 1810 when port-admiral Douglas informed the Admiralty that the Dutch commodore in the Texel had sent a message to Captain Hunt of the brig-sloop *Britomart* saying that there would be no more cartels as the French had marched into Amsterdam. In the event the repatriation continued until June that year, but not thereafter. The French annexation provoked a change in British attitudes for in March 1811 Larke was directed to record all 'natives of Holland' in the French general entry book.[57]

In 1804 and 1805 the prisoners not exchanged were sent in batches to Norman Cross but with that depot becoming full most prisoners of war were sent directly to the prison hulks at Chatham. This change of policy began in July 1806 when the Transport Board 'desired' port-admiral Douglas to send the prisoners taken in the captured French frigate *Guerviere* to Chatham, 'there not being room at Norman Cross for the crew of that Ship or any part thereof.' Douglas informed the Admiralty's secretary that as there were, 'about One hundred of those prisoners now in the small Prison at this place, I have to request you will please to suggest to their Lordships Ordering the *Romulus* to call at Yarmouth Roads for that purpose on her way from the Humber to the Nore.'[58] Douglas had to deal with a similar situation in April 1808, informing the Admiralty that, 'from the number of Prisoners there are in the Prison at this Port and by Captain Heddington's report there is more than the Prison can conveniently accommodate. I intend to employ HM hired armed vessel *Charles* to convey part of them to the Nore to be forwarded to Chatham immediately the weather moderates.'[59] Occasions like this were not infrequent.[60]

Most of the prisoners of war were seamen taken from captured privateers and merchant vessels, or had been members of prize crews aboard recaptured British merchantmen, but on two occasions they were soldiers. The first of these arrived on 25 May 1804 after Sir Sydney Smith's squadron had captured the French transport *90* off Flushing. The officer in charge was immediately sent to Lichfield on parole, but his men, 28 of them, were imprisoned at Yarmouth until 26 November when they became part of a batch of prisoners sent to Norman Cross.[61] The other intake of soldiers was on a much larger scale. Following the fall of Flushing on 16 August 1809 two warships carrying prisoners from its garrison arrived at Yarmouth, creating another of those challenging moments for the officers of the naval support base. On 20 August port-admiral Douglas informed the Admiralty that, 'the *Agincourt* having arrived here with One Hundred and Eighty Prisoners, I have filled the Prison and press room of the *Utile* and sent sixty of them to the Nore by vessels named on the Margin (*Diligence* and *Acute*) which convoy the Baltic Trade to the Thames. And the *Calypso* having arrived at this port also with fifty seven Prisoners I have ordered her therewith likewise to the Nore then to return to these Roads.'[62] He had also been made aware that a further 4,750 prisoners were to be embarked on nine other naval vessels and he asked where he was to send them if they turned up at Yarmouth. He was no doubt relieved when told to forward them to Spithead, but when on 27 August one of these ships, the *Monmouth*, anchored in the Roads, 200 prisoners, were landed and taken to the prison and a further batch of nearly 200 was brought in by the *Agincourt* in early September.[63] It is not clear what arrangements were made to confine these men but the 37 who were officers were quickly sent on parole to Northampton, Chesterfield and Chester. Of the other ranks 300 were sent to Norman Cross over the next month and nearly 40 to the Chatham hulks. A further 60, non-Frenchmen, volunteered to join the navy[64]

Napoleon's defeat at Leipzig, in October 1813, served to embolden the Dutch people to rise up against their French masters. On 20 November port-admiral Murray informed the Admiralty that James Fagee and Baron Perpencher had arrived in a Dutch schuyt with intelligence that their countrymen had completely taken possession of Holland for the Prince of Orange 'without the aid of Foreign Troops' and that the Fleet in the Texel was in a state of mutiny. From that moment Holland was once more Britain's ally and its incarcerated men no longer prisoners of war.[65] With the permanent freedom of their country not yet assured it was decided to recruit volunteers from those Dutchmen 'residing' in the various prisons, to serve the newly re-instated prince, with Yarmouth being chosen as their place of assembly. Over the next few months naval vessels brought in a steady stream of volunteers from Leith, Portsmouth and Plymouth to join those from Norman Cross. Inevitably this sudden influx of men presented port-admiral Murray with an accommodation problem, prompting him to ask the Admiralty, 'whence such of those Volunteers as may arrive here after the depot, which will receive about 70, and the "Utile" on board of which about 140 may be accommodated, are filled, are to be kept.' He did helpfully add that, 'the "Solebay" may without any particular inconvenience receive about 80 or one hundred for a short time.' In response he was told to lodge them in the barracks, but with the all too common lack of co-ordination, on 24 December he complained that, 'The Military have not yet receivid orders to remove from them upon the appearance of any more Dutch Volunteers.'[66]

It was decided to raise a battalion of soldiers from these Dutchmen, but many of them were seamen. Of the first 269 volunteers, 120 were seafaring men and they wanted, 'to be employed under the Dutch Government in the line of their profession.' Captain Mackay, the man appointed to organise the volunteers, did not think they were, 'fit to be trained to the use of Small Arms or to enter the ranks with soldiers.' He also reported that they were impatient to get to Holland, a sentiment shared by Colonel de Panhays, the officer in charge of the newly raised soldiers, who did not want the two groups 'in conversation with one another.'[67] By March 1814 a battalion of 620 men had been trained, clothed and equipped and were ready to sail for Holland. Once the necessary transports had assembled at Yarmouth the unit embarked.[68]

In the ten and a half years this prison was operational around 4,000 prisoners of war had been confined there. About half of them were French, or counted as French, with the remainder being either Dutch or Danish in roughly equal proportion.[69]

12.
Communication

Effective communication was an important factor in the successful prosecution of the wars. For Yarmouth this involved facilitating contact between the Admiralty and its sea officers, monitoring the movement of warships, especially those of the enemy, and maintaining the country's links with those parts of Europe not under French control. Much has been written about the Admiralty's telegraph system, but it was the humble letter that enabled the Lords Commissioners to closely manage the activities of their home waters based naval officers, both on land and at sea. The many bound volumes of correspondence to and from Evan Nepean, secretary to the Admiralty Board, and his successors, bear testimony to this close control, with letters being exchanged, via mail coach, within a day or two. If the officer was at sea the link would be maintained by one of the busy little vessels that were attached to squadrons to fetch and carry. Letters which start, 'since my letter by the *Phoenix*' or 'I forward this by the *Grace* cutter…' are commonplace in these books. The Admiralty, however, was not comfortable with having to rely on the postal service, nor with the time taken to relay urgent messages so, when details of the French telegraph system crossed the Channel, the Lords Commissioners were quick to set up similar shutter based systems in England. They was designed by Lord George Murray and on 25 September 1795 a surveyor called George Roebuck was appointed to select sites for stations on lines to link London with Deal, Sheerness and Portsmouth. These were all operational by the end of 1796. Initially Murray was the man in charge, but by April 1798 he had been superseded by Roebuck as 'Inspector of Telegraphs'.[1]

At the time these lines were being established Yarmouth was in the process of becoming the support base for the North Sea Squadron, but its long term future in this respect was too uncertain to justify the expenditure needed to create a telegraph link with the Admiralty. Camperdown and the Helder campaign came and went without any suggestion that one was necessary, but in early 1801, with Sir Hyde Parker's reluctance to set sail in pursuance of the government's Baltic objectives and with the growing importance of that theatre of war, Roebuck was directed to find a route for a Yarmouth line. Having examined all the possibilities on 18 April he reported that he considered a direct line impracticable 'on Account of the great quantity of Trees and the want of Elevations'. Instead he suggested a route via Shooter's Hill, crossing the Thames to Aveley and then on to Laindon and Norton Cold, in Essex, before following the line of the existing coastal signal stations to Yarmouth. With the onset of peace, however, the idea was shelved. It would be another seven years before Roebuck was directed to try again.[2] Presumably he intended to erect separate telegraph stations alongside the east coast signal stations rather than combine them, for these systems had little in common. The telegraph employed a combination of shutters to spell out messages, almost letter by letter, while the signal stations used a system of balls and flags to convey

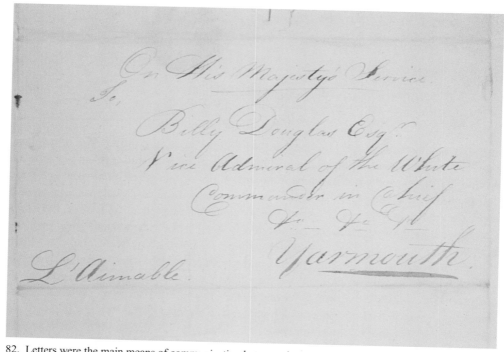

82. Letters were the main means of communication between the Admiralty and its naval officers, as it was between those officers and their out-port subordinates.

fixed signals from a signal book.

The earliest English signal stations were established to help counter the depredations of French privateers on British merchant shipping. In 1794 a line of posts was constructed along the south coast, from Land's End to Ballard Down, north of Swanage and the following year this system was extended to the North Foreland of Kent.[3] Towards the end of 1797 the possibility of invasion seemed very real and the package of countermeasures put in place in early 1798 included a line of signal stations between Shoebury Ness and Yarmouth, connecting the Nore anchorage with that in the Yarmouth Roads. Preliminary work was carried out and the locations for nine signal stations were identified before, on 27 January, Captain John Clements was directed to survey the line and gain the consent of the proprietors of the land on which the stations were to be erected. The choice of Clements seems a curious one for less than two weeks earlier he had been placed in command of the gunboats on the east coast of Scotland under Duncan and had already arrived at Leith, but he was to return to that command once his signal station commission had been completed.[4] Although presented with a scheme his orders required him to suggest further 'intermediate places' if he thought them necessary for the line to work efficiently and this soon proved to be the case. By the 9th he was at Lowestoft from where he reported that he had 'been detained upon the Coast much longer than I at first expected owing to the situations for signal stations (as marked in the reports given to me) by no means answering the intended purpose, many of them cou'd not possibly be seen, one from the other, for many Miles,...'[5] As a result the nine stations became 21, terminating at Yarmouth where Clements was to be found on 10 February at the Wrestler's Inn, writing to the Corporation, requesting permission 'to erect a small temporary building on the Dean, for the communication of Intelligence by signal, to accommodate a naval officer and four men.' Two days later the Assembly granted the government a piece of land south-east of the town and, with his work done, Clements submitted his report to the Admiralty and returned to Leith.[6]

As far as constructing the flag staffs and the temporary buildings for the accommodation of the officers and men was concerned, Nicholas Vass, the Master House Carpenter at the Portsmouth Dockyard, was ordered to carry out the work at the locations Clements had identified, with a deadline of the 10 March. In the event it was not until 14 April that the *Norwich Mercury* reported that, 'The beacon masts and watch-houses, are now completed on the Eastern coast, by which the approach of an enemy's fleet can be announced from Yarmouth to the Nore in less than five minutes.'[7]

On 4 May the Admiralty appointed a number of lieutenants to take charge of these stations and as was usual with shore based naval appointments the men chosen had held their rank for some time and were generally no longer fit for sea service. The exception was James Anderson who was appointed to the Yarmouth Dean (Dene) station. He had been a lieutenant for less than a year, but was not a young man having joined the navy as an able seaman in 1780. By the time of his appointment the sea fencibles had been established and with the decision taken to place the signal station lieutenants under the command of the sea fencible captains, Anderson found himself responsible to the Southwold based Captain Edge, not the senior naval officer at Yarmouth.[8] With his notice of appointment came instructions. Anderson was told that, 'You will find upon your arrival at the station a Temporary Building or Signal House, consisting of two Rooms with necessary Furniture vizt One for the accommodation of yourself, the other for your Assistants which you are to take into your Charge; as also a Telescope, One Red Flag, One Blue Pendant, and four Signal Balls; the Colours and Balls to be housed and the Yard secured up and down the Signal Staff when they are not in use.'[9] The signal staff was a 50 foot topmast fitted with a cap, crosstrees and a fid to secure the flagstaff. Various combinations of pennant and flag at the masthead and balls on the crosstrees indicated the coded messages, for example the pennant flying on the mast while three balls hung from the gaff signified 'enemy landing to the westward.'[10] For his assistants he was to engage one 'intelligent' Petty Officer who was to be paid as a fourth rate midshipman, with two shillings a day subsistence and two 'trusty' men at two shillings per day each. Anderson himself was to be paid five shillings per day plus two shillings and sixpence subsistence.[11]

The reason for erecting the signal stations was given as, 'conveying to the Commanding Officers at the several Ports and to His Majesty's Ships and Vessels, Information of such of the Enemy's Ships as may be discovered from any of the said Stations.' This was amplified by stating that, 'no Ship or Vessel of the Enemy shall be able to approach the Coast without being discovered to be such from one of the Posts, and you are therefore upon discovering any of the Enemy's Ships or Cruizers, instantly to make it known by shewing the Signal for that purpose, or repeating it if made by others; and as Signals are appointed to denote the principal Stations along the Coast, you will be careful to make the Signal for the Principal Station from whence the Enemy were first seen (or where the Signal originated) immediately after the first Signal has been repeated by the next Signal Staff to you, in order that the Commanding Officers at the different Ports, and His Majesty's Ships and Vessels may be informed at what part of the Coast the Enemy are likely to be met with and intercepted.'[12] There was more about dealing with the enemy, such as warning trading vessels if an enemy cruiser was on the coast and lighting fires and firing guns if the intelligence arrived at night. There were also instructions about identifying British men-of-war, using the private signals of the day.

No station log book or other document has survived to give an insight into the day to day operations of what must have been a very tedious activity, especially as the feared invasions never materialised, but there was an incident in 1801 which highlighted a problem a signal station lieutenant could face. In May that year Anderson had the temerity to write directly to the Admiralty complaining, it seems (the letter has not survived), that in Admiral Dickson's absence from the port, the signal book was not being left with the 'senior officers for the time being' and that some vessels were not answering his signals, through not being supplied with the relevant books, in particular the ship-sloop Ann, captained by George Delanoe. Forced to defend himself against a far more junior officer, Dickson informed the Admiralty that he took great care to pass the signal book on and that he would be surprised if Captain Delanoe had not been given the signals as he had been four years on the Yarmouth station. It comes as no surprise, therefore, that when Dickson relinquished his North Sea command the only Yarmouth based naval officer not to receive his 'perfect approbation,' was Lieutenant Anderson, although this may be because he was not directly in charge of the man.[13]

Just before Dickson left the town at the end of the war the signal station officers had been directed by the Admiralty to discharge themselves and their men, and to hand over the keys of the signal houses to the landowners.[14] For Lieutenant Anderson this was easier said than

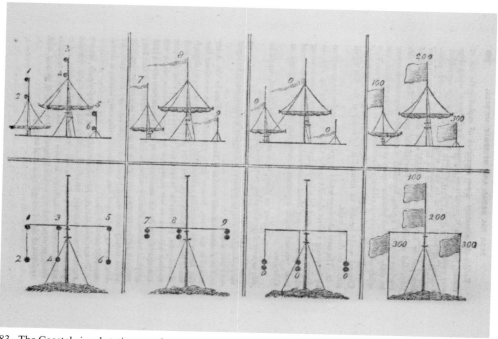

83. The Coastal signal stations used a system of balls and flags to convey fixed signals from a signal book.

done for when the lords commissioners wrote to the Corporation, notifying it of their intention to relinquish possession of the Dean signal house they added, in a rare moment of foresightedness, that 'as the said house will be again wanted for the same Service in the Event of a War, We wish to know if you are inclined to keep it in repair and on what terms you will engage that it shall be habitable when it may be wanted.' After initially declining to become involved the Corporation took possession of the building.[15] In order to complete the closure Dickson was directed to send vessels to call at the signal stations to collect the balls and flags and other moveable stores and convey them to the nearest King's port, whereupon he dispatched the ship-sloop *Pylades* to those stations between Yarmouth and Leith, and the cutter *Trial* to those between the port and Orford Ness, with the stores so retrieved being taken to Sheerness.[16]

Meaningful contact with Continental Europe was essential, especially for intelligence gathering, the maintenance of diplomatic relations, the dispatch of orders, and the transfer of bullion and specie. Added to this merchants and private individuals had travel requirements and a considerable volume of mail needed to be delivered. While the navy played its part in this respect the main carriers to and from the Continent were the post office packet boats, with services running between Dover and Calais and Harwich to the Dutch port of Hellevoetsluis. Shortly after France declared war the former had to be suspended and the Dover packets were transferred to Harwich. The post office was faced with the same dilemma when in early 1795 the French overran Holland and occupied Hellevoetsluis. Having once more to move the service northwards it made the decision to use Cuxhaven, at the mouth of the Elbe, as its continental packet port, 'whence the post branched off in two directions, one with letters for Holland, Frankfurt, Switzerland, and Italy by way of Bremen; the other with letters for Germany and the North of Europe, passing through Hamburg.'[17] At the English end it was decided to move the packet boats from Harwich to Yarmouth as the former was then, 'rather southerly for the prevailing winds on the homeward run.'[18] Events moved fast. By late February 11 packets had moved from Harwich to Yarmouth, comprising the original boats from that port, the *Diana*, *Dolphin*, *King George*, *Prince of Orange*, *Prince of Wales* and *Princess Royal*, together with the *Carteret*, *Courier*, *Diana*, *Express* and *Union*, which had previously been at Dover.[19] These packets were privately owned, but under charter to the post office, with the Harwich boats being schooner rigged, of 70 tons, each carrying a crew of 17, whereas the Dover vessels were smaller, with crews of 10 or 16.[20] The transfer was organised by a Mr Walcott who had previously been the agent at Dover and had concluded the postal treaties with Hamburg and Bremen. He continued to play a part at Yarmouth until July 1798 when ill-health forced him to retire.[21]

The man chosen to be the local agent for packets was the soon to be naval storekeeper, Robert Warmington. He was the logical choice as he had good contacts with northern Europe through being, 'Vice-Consul for Prussia and Denmark and represented other powers with whom Great Britain was at amity.'[22] Conscious of the fact he, 'will regularly require some instruction in the duties in his situation,' the post office commissioners were advised to, 'send Mr Saverland, who is conversant with all packet duties to proceed to Yarmouth to give Mr Warmington such help as he may stand in need of.'[23] Warmington, who was to be paid a salary of £220 for the work, established a packet office in a house at the south-west corner of Row 102, opposite his own dwelling in Middlegate Street, where he employed a clerk at a salary of £40.[24] According to Palmer, 'A packet sailed from Yarmouth every Sunday and Thursday at 9 a.m.; two packets returning weekly from Cuxhaven. There was also a by-boat, called the *Duke of York*, plying between Yarmouth and Hamburg.[25] The new route was around 350 miles, nearly three times longer than the old one. The average crossing took about five days in reasonable weather, with the packets being given permission to sail without the need of convoy.[26]

The forced relocation of the packet captains was not without its problems. At the outset they were unfamiliar with the new route and the nature of the Yarmouth Roads. To address this Inspector Saverland proposed that the captains, 'be given charts of the North Sea and sea charts of the St. Nicholas and Haisborough sands, as they were extremely dangerous to sailors who did not know them well.'[27] But the problem ran deeper than that. The men of Harwich, especially the members of the Deane family, had lived there for generations and had commitments in relation to the governance of that town. As a result they would deliberately land the mail at Harwich rather than Yarmouth.[28] In May 1795 it was reported that, 'There was no need for Deane and the *King George* to pull into Harwich, the wind was perfectly fair for Yarmouth. He must give reasons for the delay…if not watched this Captain will make every opportunity for Harwich and not Yarmouth.'[29] More such reports followed and in December the commissioners, were, 'very sorry to note that of late the Yarmouth packets have come to Harwich without any necessity for so doing. The *Diana* Packet belonging to Dover and the *Diana* belonging to Harwich sailed together for Cuxhaven. The Dover vessel though smaller is arrived at Yarmouth. The second is not, and the *Prince of Orange* under Capt. Deane who arrived at HARWICH on Nov. 26th is not yet back at her proper station, at Yarmouth although the wind has been favourable ever since. The excuse that he had to land the messenger is not admissible… having been decided that all the packets formerly at Dover and Harwich should be stationed at Yarmouth it is with surprise and disapproval that the Post Master General hears that the captains should evade their orders with such frivolous excuse. The agent is to express this in the strongest possible manner to the captains of the Harwich *Diana* 2nd, *Prince of Orange* and *King George*. The most implicit obedience is expected, only wind and weather may prevent orders being executed.'[30]

The primary purpose of the packet service was to transport post office mail, but the conveyance of passengers, kings messengers and for a time, bullion and specie, was also important. The working relationship between Warmington and Thomas Seaman, the local postmaster, must have been a close one in respect of the dispatch and receipt of 'ship letters', but little evidence exists to confirm the point. At the outset the novelty of having the 'great and the good' arrive in the town to travel to the Continent caused a bit of a stir. In February 1795 the Gressier Fagel, his brother, an officer in the Dutch navy, and Count Bentinck arrived to take passage in the packet *Courier*. They dined with Warmington and met the Mayor (William Taylor Snr.), Sir Edmund Lacon, Captain Horsford, Aid-de-Camp to General Leland, and the general himself, who they dined with the following day.[31] A steady flow of notables were to follow including, the Prince of Orange, Princess Caroline of Brunswick, Wordsworth, Coleridge, and the French writer Chateaubriand, but more usual were the merchants, bankers and others going about their daily business including the King's messengers. In August 1799, 'Sailed the *Prince of Orange* packet, Captain Bridge, with Mr Basilico, King's Messenger, in consequence of which the *Prince of Wales* packet takes the mails and passengers for

Thursday.'[32] The speedy conveyance of the King's messengers, carrying Foreign Office dispatches, took precedence over the scheduled departures of packets and when one or more arrived at the port they were accorded immediate priority.

According to Palmer Warmington's office frequently contained gold bars, boxes of coins and other treasure in course of transit and that on these occasions the building was well guarded by soldiers.[33] The first mention of gold arriving at Yarmouth occurred in late April 1797 when it was reported that, 'The *Hawke* sloop which conveyed Mr. Hammond, to Vienna, is returned to Yarmouth and brings intelligence of his landing at Cuxhaven on the 20th inst. – The *Diana* packet Captain Dean arrived yesterday and both vessels have brought home a considerable quantity of gold.'[34] In August that year the frigate *Brilliant* arrived from Cuxhaven with 600,000 guineas and, 'The packets, we are also informed, have brought over very considerable remittances to the Merchants.'[35] The following year, in July, the *Prince of Orange* packet brought over some £600,000-£700,000 of specie, in August she brought a further £30,000-£40,000 of specie and in September the *Diana* packet arrived with £40,000 in specie and bullion.[36] But it proved to be a short-lived business opportunity for the post masters general were not in favour of the packets transporting bullion, because of the extra work and the documentation involved.[37] His Majesty's ships, however, continued to carry valuable cargoes, but not without loss. On 9 October 1799 the frigate *Lutine* sailed from the Yarmouth Roads carrying specie to the value of £140,000 to pay the troops on the Helder expedition. Some 12 hours later, during a heavy gale at north-north-west, she was wrecked on the outer bank of the Vlie Island Passage, off the Dutch coast. Two men, the sole survivors,

84. The frigate Lutine, having sailed from Yarmouth, was wrecked on the outer bank of the Vlie Passage, off the coast of Holland, on 9 October 1799.

were picked up by the brig-sloop *L'Espeigle* and were taken to Yarmouth, where one of them died. Much of the bullion was salvaged as was the ship's bell, which famously hangs in the offices of Lloyds' of London and a cannon which stands on the ramparts at Windsor castle.[38]

The packet service also sustained losses, but through captures rather than shipwreck. On 23 September 1796 Admiral Duncan reported to the Admiralty that, 'several armed Luggers and Boats are fitting out by the Enemy for the purpose of intercepting the English Packets between Yarmouth and the Elbe.'[39] By then Captain Anthony Deane had lost the *Princess Royal* packet to the French (14 March 1795) and in June 1796 the same captain was unlucky enough to be captured by the French frigate *Republican* and a 'Brig Cutter' when in command of the packet *Prince of Orange*. Deane and his men were landed as prisoners at Flushing, where they were kindly treated. On 10 August 1797 Captain Matthew Flynn was becalmed in the packet *Dolphin* when he was attacked by a Dutch row galley privateer. Beating her off twice the packet finally succumbed and was carried into Delfzyl.[40] The *Union* packet was taken on 25 November 1797 and on 29 June 1800 the *Dolphin*, Captain Flynn, was captured by a French privateer and taken into the Texel after an engagement lasting an hour and three-quarters, but not before the mail had been thrown overboard. On landing, all the passengers were set free at the behest of the French consul at Amsterdam.[41]

If dodging the enemy was difficult, beating the elements could be near impossible. The move to Cuxhaven brought with it the operational difficulty that in winter the Elbe and Weser would freeze over, making mail delivery extremely challenging. This was the case in the severe winter of 1798/9, when ice blocked both rivers for the best part of three months. In December the post office found itself in difficulties as the movement of the packets became very irregular. With no reliable foreign news being received Prime Minister William Pitt, became concerned enough to impress on Sir Francis Freeling, the secretary of the post office and master spy, the importance of such mail. As a result a sloop of war, carrying post office

85. This depiction of the capture of the Dolphin packet in 1782 by a Dutch privateer was echoed in 1797 and 1800 by the capture of two other packets of the same name.

officials, a lugger, and the *Prince of Wales* packet, were dispatched. While the sloop and the packet were to venture no further than Norden, in Friesland, the lugger was to go to Heligoland to fetch the mail. In the event it proved impossible to land at either place and after ten difficult days at sea the officials reported that no mails could be expected until the weather broke.[42] Of the packet masters, only Captain Bridge of the *Prince of Orange* managed to get the mail through. Taking on board two sacks on 9 December he lay wind-bound in Yarmouth Roads for a week, during which time three other packets loaded. Eventually the four boats put to sea together, but soon after ran into fog, then a gale, with showers of snow and sleet. After four nights heavy sailing the four packets gave up and ran back to Yarmouth. Two days later they tried again and a strong west-sou'west breeze took the Prince of Orange within sight of Heligoland. Receiving no response from a signal for a pilot, at daybreak Captain Bridge took his packet into the Elbe. A shift of wind had broken up the ice and by the afternoon of Christmas Eve he was close to Cuxhaven pier and even had a line ashore, but the ebb tide brought down pack ice, which swept him away. Landing at the village of Doos, Bridge carried the mails to Cuxhaven in a hired cart, bringing back the English mails the same way. Back at Yarmouth he received great credit, the congratulations of the Admiralty and a gold medal from the merchants of Hamburg.[43]

Conditions continued to worsen, prompting a flurry of anxious initiatives as the service broke down completely. Warmington was in the thick of it. On 28 December he was instructed by secretary Freeling to send the mail directly to Heligoland, in the hope that it could be landed at Cuxhaven, on the coast, or at Tonningen, by that island's boats. The better informed Warmington responded that it was 'absolutely impossible to land the mails.'[44] This view was reinforced when on 3 January three packets arrived at Yarmouth from Heligoland, without mails or passengers, not having been able to get up to Cuxhaven.[45] A month later it was reported from Yarmouth that, 'The packet and passengers are still detained.'[46] Various measures to break the deadlock were put forward including the use of balloons to carry mail across the North Sea with Lord Auckland, the Post Master General, proposing that the man in charge should be made 'Comptroller of Balloons.' On 6 February Warmington was 'ordered to buy an ice boat and send Captain Hammond, plus ten men who were used to the Greenland trade, with the three Continental mails which were still at Yarmouth with all speed.'[47] On 4 March, however, it was reported that nine packets had arrived at Yarmouth and shortly afterwards normal service was resumed.[48]

One event was to characterise the extreme difficulty of reaching the Continent at this time. In November 1798 Tom Grenville, brother of the foreign secretary, was chosen to carry out an important diplomatic mission to Berlin. On his arrival at Yarmouth, on 18 December, thick fog stopped him getting on board the frigate *Champion* and, once he had, an easterly wind prevented her from sailing. When the ship eventually reached the Elbe she sustained such ice damage that she was forced to return to Yarmouth, reaching the port on 29 December.[49] Several weeks later, on 28 January, Grenville and his suite set out again for Cuxhaven, on board the frigate *Proserpine*, accompanied by the *Prince of Wales* packet. Picking up a local pilot at Heligoland, the frigate anchored overnight. The following day, in fine weather, she continued on her way, but in late afternoon, when only four miles from Cuxhaven, it began to snow heavily and they were obliged to anchor again. Throughout the night the *Proserpine* was battered by the snowstorm and the ice brought down by the ebb tide. Next morning, spotting a small opening ahead, and seeing the *Prince of Wales* on shore, James Wallis, the frigate's captain, decided to make for the coast of Jutland, but shortly afterwards the ship ploughed into a sandbank. After strenuous efforts to get her off, the following morning, on a proposal by Mr Grenville, it was decided to cross the ice to Neuwerk Island. After a journey of six miles in the severest weather, often up to their waists in snow and water, the bedraggled party arrived at the island. The following morning, guided by a local fisherman, an exhausted Grenville, together with half the frigate's officers and crew arrived at Cuxhaven.[50] Grenville had suffered in vain, however, for he failed to achieve his diplomatic objective of an alliance between Austria and Prussia.[51]

Under the deft hand of Robert Warmington the packets continued to provide a vital service from Yarmouth until November 1801 when the Post Master General decided to return them to Harwich, although the occasional packet did arrive at Yarmouth throughout the following year and thereafter.[52]

***

In May 1803 the signal stations created in the last war were re-commissioned and lieutenants and signalmen were appointed to staff them under the same terms as before.[53] The officer assigned to the Yarmouth Dean Station was the extremely deaf William Marsh, an old Yarmouth hand who had previously served in the town on the impress service.[54] During the peace, however, the Admiralty had allowed many of the houses attached to the signal stations to be acquired by the owners of the land on which they stood. As a result George Roebuck, the Superintendent of Telegraphs, was directed to investigate and report back on their current status. On 10 June he presented his findings on those between Shoebury Ness and Yarmouth and in respect of Yarmouth Dean he wrote, 'House situated on the Beach, proprietors the Corporation of Yarmouth who have given it up to Mr Seaman the Chamberlain. Mr Seaman has made great Additions to the building the expense of which he states to amount to £69.17.9 this sum he expects to be repaid and then is willing to give up the house.' The money was forthcoming and Marsh had the good fortune to move into a dwelling of superior quality to those of his fellow officers at other stations.[55]

As before the signal stations and their officers were placed under the command of the senior sea fencible captain in the district in which they were situated. Accordingly when Captain Cobb arrived in Yarmouth he found he was not only responsible for that at Yarmouth Dean, but for those to the south, at Gunton Common, Kessingland, and Easton Cliff.[56] There were, however, no signal stations in the northern part of his district, between Yarmouth and Cromer, and perceiving this to be a weakness in the system Cobb informed the Admiralty on 25 July 1803 that 'I have prevailed on the Parish Officers to erect Signal Staffs at different Stations.' He also reported that he intended to 'form a small code for the use of the District under my command, not in the least interfering with the Coast signals...'[57] By return the Admiralty asked to see a copy of this 'small code,' prompting Cobb to reconsider his proposal as, 'a confusion would follow that might be highly detrimental to the Public Service.' Instead he decided to give each parish officer a red flag to be hoisted if the enemy were sighted. He went on to observe that, 'as the Signal Posts on this coast terminate on the Denes here that their being carried North is the only sure mode of conveying intelligence of such consequence as the approach of the enemy, or the calling together the force situate at, or encamped near the Shore to draw it either North or South by the direction of the General of the district, or for the purpose of drawing the Sea Fencibles into a large body.'[58] Accepting his assessment in October the Admiralty ordered the erection of signal stations at Winterton, Happisburgh and Cromer, although in respect of the latter the lieutenant was actually stationed at the existing post at Trimingham, six miles south of the place specified. He was initially responsible for the posts at both places.[59]

On 30 November Cobb reported that the lieutenants had 'joined some days back, and the masts and stores are arrived; but as yet no House [has been] erected for the Lieutenant and his men at Winterton.' He also highlighted the need for a signal station on the 'Heights of Caister' to connect those to the north with Yarmouth.[60] As far as the Admiralty was concerned the primary purpose of these new signal stations was to communicate with the interior (Norwich) rather than with each other and Yarmouth. Mindful of the printed instructions, however, the Lords Commissioners directed Cobb to report on whether, 'both purposes might be answered by fixing the Station on Caister heights instead of Winterton.'[61] Cobb's response was both comprehensive and persuasive. After restating the arguments for and against the Admiralty's suggestion he pointed out that in the event of an alarm the Norfolk coastal signal stations, if in sight of one another, could pass information to the manned signal staff erected on Yarmouth church by the county lieutenancy for the purpose of communication with Norwich via Ormesby, Filby and Strumpshaw. This integrated system would also, 'have the benefit of the whole code of signals from the River Thames and only such part of the Signals

86. A view of Caister Heights where in 1804 a signal station was erected to link that at Yarmouth to those further north. The signal house is the building to the left of the beach company lookout that stands on the high ground in the centre of the print.

87. It was on the tower of the parish church of St. Nicholas, at Yarmouth, that in 1803 the Lord Lieutenant
of Norfolk erected a manned signal post.

which relate to the enemy's actual approach and appearance need be communicated to the
interior...' As a result an order was given for an extra signal station to be erected at Caister
to which a lieutenant was appointed in December.[62]

The man given the task of completing the infrastructure of the new signalling system was
Nicholas Vass, the carpenter who had constructed the Nore-Yarmouth line in the previous
war. In essence he had to establish a station at Caister and build a house there, together with
houses at Winterton and Happisburgh. He also had to construct houses on the North Norfolk
coast, at Blakeney and Holkham.[63] Vass received his orders on 10 December and by the 16th
he had travelled to Yarmouth to consult Captain Cobb and had agreed with local builder, John
Green, to complete the necessary work by the latter part of February 1804.[64] Later that year
the problem of the lieutenant at Trimingham having to also manage the signal post at Cromer
led to Vass arranging with John Green to build a house at the latter place, which was ready
to receive a lieutenant by mid-October.[65]

Set up in this way the signal stations in the Yarmouth district successfully carried out their
coast watch role until the end of the war with only one significant change. In 1812 it was
decided to update the stations between Sheerness and Yarmouth by replacing the old flag and
ball arrangement with the more modern French style semaphore system. To facilitate this
some of the stations were modified and others were replaced.[66] At Yarmouth the Dean Signal
Station was retained, but by then the Royal Naval Hospital had been built and it was decided
to place the semaphore facility on the clock-tower of the new building. 'Mr Pilkington, the

Naval Architect at North Yarmouth,' was consulted and in August 1812 the Transport Board was ordered to erect the structure.[67] With there now being two signal stations, close but not contiguous, Lieutenant Charles Woodger, who earlier that year had replaced Marsh, found his resources somewhat stretched, prompting him in May 1813 to complain to the port-admiral. Although he had responsibility for both stations he still only had one midshipman and one signalman to assist him. This he felt was an inadequate staffing level, especially if one of the men was away or was off sick, as had recently been the case. Accordingly he asked for an additional signalman 'as it is not the intention of the Admiralty for the officer, to take his turn, with the Midshipman, in looking out, which it has been the case with my Self, since the Semaphor Has workt…' The matter was referred to the Lords Commissioners who took the view that he 'Should look out with his people', but that if the port-admiral so wished he could provide temporary assistance.[68]

Drunkenness was not confined to the non-commissioned ranks. In April 1805 the lieutenant at Trimingham, Andrew Cheap, was transferred to the port-admiral's flagship, 'a situation he dislikes very much, and he is much surprised at it, as it was unsolicited on his part.'[69] His replacement, Lieutenant Caleb Infield, arrived at Cromer on 18 April 'dead drunk' and according to Captain Tremlett (the officer in charge of the signal stations north of Yarmouth), 'the next morning he drank 4s worth of Rum & milk before he got out of bed, has been constantly drunk since he took command of the Post, leaves the Signals exposed to the petty officers man etc, and has made no remarks, he appears to be deranged.' Tremlett reprimanded him, but on 26 May he reported that he had again visited the Trimingham station and was 'sorry to say that I found Lieut. Infield in a state of inebriety and was concerned to learn, that he had been so frequently.' After another reprimand Tremlett was able to report that 'he [Infield] has conducted himself better.' The improvement seems to have been sustained for Infield remained there for the duration.[70] This was not to be the outcome for Lieutenant Graham at nearby Happisburgh. On 23 June 1804 a mistake was made in the signalling, prompting Tremlett to visit all the stations in his sub-district. At Happisburgh he found the lieutenant 'in a state of inebriety and that he refused to obey the orders he gave him, and treated him with the greatest contempt and insolence,' as did his wife, who was giving orders to the men. Graham was dismissed and replaced by Lieutenant Henry Harford, a steadier man who was soon to lead a heroic rescue of seamen from a ship stranded on the Haisborough Sand.[71]

When in 1805 port-admiral Douglas arrived at Yarmouth he quickly came to the conclusion that there was no effective way for him to communicate with the naval vessels in the Roads, especially when the sea was running too high for a boat to go off. Considering the Yarmouth Dean signal post unsuitable for his purpose Douglas requested the Admiralty to direct the Navy Board, 'to cause the Naval Officer at this Place,' to erect a signal box for his use.[72] With his good local contacts Warmington soon came up with a proposal and on 4 November sent to the Navy Board a plan and an estimate for a signal box to stand in the carpenter's yard of Lombe Simpson, a site said to possess,' the most Commanding Sea View.' Simpson agreed to erect the box for £27, but he also wanted a ground rent of £13 per annum.[73] Considering this sum exorbitant the Board asked Douglas whether a sentry box attached to the existing signal house would suffice, but the port-admiral prevailed and on 9 January 1806 Warmington reported to the Navy Board that the box had been completed. It was staffed by two signalmen borne on the books of the naval yard.[74] Its usefulness was again queried in late 1812, when port-admiral Murray tried to claim for the cost of the coal consumed by the fire in the signal box, something his predecessor, Lord Gardner, had paid for out of his own pocket. By so doing Murray provoked the Admiralty into directing him, to make a new arrangement, by which communication with the *Solebay* would be either by the semaphore post or from his office, instead of having, 'a multitude of separate stations so inconvenient to the Public Service.' In reply Murray justified the need for the box, said he intended to continue to use it and would pay for the coal himself.[75]

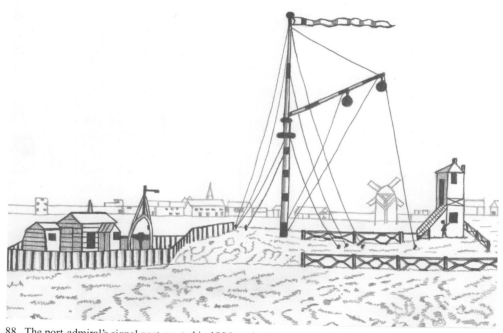

88. The port-admiral's signal post erected in 1806 on the shoreline.

At the start of the new conflict the Admiralty still had in place its shutter telegraph system linking the Lords Commissioners in Whitehall with the port-admirals at Portsmouth, Deal and Sheerness. In 1806 Plymouth was added to the system, but it was not until the middle of the following year, when affairs in the Baltic raised the profile of Yarmouth, that orders were given for it too to be connected to London by telegraph. Accordingly George Roebuck was directed by the Admiralty to survey a suitable route. His 1801 proposal had favoured a hybrid coastal option, but six years later, conscious of the interruption that could be caused by London smoke and coastal fog he came up with a workable alternative. The line he now suggested headed south-west from the Admiralty building to the roof of the Chelsea Hospital, from there it progressed north-west via St Albans to Dunstable Downs where it took a north-east turn to Norwich, before heading due east to Yarmouth.[76] In all there were to be 18 stations on the line (excluding that at the Admiralty) and work on their construction seems to have progressed from the southern end. By mid-September 1807 Roebuck had selected the site for the terminus at Yarmouth and had contracted John Green to carry out a survey, seek agreement with the Corporation for a lease and build the necessary structure. The half-acre site lay on the Denes, between the North Mill and the North Battery and was held under a lease dated the 27th of that month.[77] In November 1807 the Yarmouth correspondent of the *Norfolk Chronicle* reported that, 'The chain of Telegraphs between this port and the Admiralty will be completed in a fortnight.'[78] Be that as it may, there was still much work to be done, especially in relation to staff appointment and training. It was to take another seven months before Roebuck was able to report that following a successful practice run the Yarmouth line was ready.[79] In the event it was not officially used until the 24 August 1808 when port-admiral Douglas telegraphed the message '*Calypso* ready for sea.'[80]

Each station comprised a building divided into two rooms, one for operational use, the other a living space. On the roof stood the shutter frame held in place by heavy timber baulks. This was divided into a number of rectangular apertures containing shutters which, when opened and closed in various combinations, could communicate 63 letters, numbers and small phrases.[81] A crew of three men was the minimum needed to operate each repeater station, two of whom were on constant 'glass duty', training telescopes on the stations ahead and behind, while the third man hauled on the ropes to change the shutters. In addition there was usually a fourth man, the keeper, who entered messages into the log and provided backup where necessary. As the crew at Yarmouth only had to observe the shutter movements of a single station, that at Strumpshaw, there was only a need for one 'glassman', but there was a requirement for a man to carry the telegraph messages to and from the port-admiral's office, a mile and a half away. This proved problematical for port-admiral Douglas for the Admiralty expected him to supply these messengers from his own boat's crew. In order to avoid this imposition he reminded the Lords Commissioners that his flagship had but the complement of a sloop-of-war and that on occasion needed the services of every man, but his plea fell on deaf ears.[82]

One of the key features of the telegraphic system was a requirement for the content of each message to remain secret, with only the port-admiral and the Admiralty being able to read them. To achieve this aim a code was devised to prevent the telegraph operators knowing the meaning of what they were relaying, but at Yarmouth, in early April 1811, this precautionary measure was found to have been breached. On Sunday the 7th Captain Curry of the *Roebuck*, deputising for the absent port-admiral, Lord Gardner, arranged for a message to be sent to the Admiralty, reporting a failed attack by the Danes on the island of Anholt. Following this up with a visit to the telegraph station he found that the keeper, Mr Thackray, had deciphered the message and had written it down. When asked to explain how he had come by the cypher or otherwise had worked out the message he could not give a satisfactory explanation. With the matter reported to the Admiralty, George Roebuck was instructed to investigate.[83] Roebuck did so and reported to the Admiralty (rather naively) that Thackray had no knowledge of the cypher, and that what he had written down was a note of what was commonly known in the town. He had no idea it was similar to the message sent to London.[84] On receiving a copy of Roebuck's letter an incensed Captain Curry informed the Admiralty, 'that Mr Thackra[y] had written down upon his Slate the message alluded to, in the Identical words and in the Order they were Sent from the Admirals Office, as follows viz. "Anholt Attacked; "Enemy Defeated; "500 Prisoners taken; "Officer on his Way to Town with

89. The shutter telegraph on Dunstable Downs, a design adopted for all the free-standing stations on the London to Yarmouth line.

Dispatches," Which, upon my perceiving, he instantly, in a hasty Manner, Wiped from the Slate, under evident Embarrassment – he had previously informed me, that two of the Signals sent him (as I understand from the Admirals Office) were wrong, and that he had corrected them. – With respect to the News being known in Town at the time, I can hardly think it possible, for a very short time only elapsed after the Officer's Landing with the intelligence, before the Message was Sent to the Telegraph, which is Detached some Distance from the Town, and the Man sent with the Message has been questioned by me, and says he knows Nothing of the News from Anholt, or the circumstances to which the said Message related at the time of taking it to the Telegraph on Yarmouth Denes.'[85] Sending him Curry's letter the Admiralty told Roebuck that if, 'the man does not immediately and unequivocally declare by what means he became possessed of the key their Lordships are to order his dismissal,' but Roebuck's surviving letters give no clue as to what happened next.[86]

Although the London to Yarmouth telegraph was operational for six years its usefulness is open to question. No keeper's records have survived save for two journals from the Gog Magog station. From these it can be deduced that in clear weather the system was efficient, but hardly a week went by without reports of fog holding up the transmission of signals. In fact, in the two month period between December 1813 and January 1814, on seventeen days in each month, no messages at all could be sent because of fog.[87] It has to be concluded that while the naval telegraph was useful on occasion for relaying urgent messages letters carried by the royal mail remained the principal means by which the Admiralty was kept in touch with events at Yarmouth and in the North Sea and the Baltic.

13.
Defence

With Yarmouth once more vulnerable to seaborne raids and invasion the measures that had previously been relied upon to deter or counter such incursions were reinstated. Central to the defensive strategy were the seashore batteries constructed a decade earlier. These were quickly re-commissioned and with minor improvements sufficed for the duration of both main conflicts. Along the shoreline, with their guns facing the Roads, stood the North Star Battery, the Town (or Central) Battery, the South Star Battery and the Haven Battery. The North and South Star Batteries were, as their name suggests, both star shaped and of a similar design, each with a tenaille trace surrounded by a wide ditch, revetted with timber. The gorge to the rear was defended by a ditch and a small wooden blockhouse, similar to those erected in North America. The former mounted eleven 24 pound cannon and the latter 14. The Town Battery was smaller and of a more simple design than its neighbours, with no facility for ditch flanking. It mounted four 24 pounders.[1] The harbour's mouth was protected by the Haven Battery, the Fort, and the Gorleston Cliff Battery. The Haven Battery was similar in shape and size to the Town Battery and mounted five 32 pounders and ten 24s. Behind it stood the Fort which contained facilities for a small garrison, including a house for a master-gunner and one for a quarter-master-gunner. It had its own magazine and mounted eight 24 pounders and four long sixes. The Gorleston Cliff Battery was a linear earthwork mounting eight 24 pounders. It also contained a gunner's house.[2]

   The Board of Ordnance was responsible for these defences, with their maintenance being carried out by the engineers of its military branch. As has already been noticed in early 1793 Captain Sutherland of that corps was sent to assess the adequacy of the Board's deployments and it was his opinion that the earthworks of the batteries should be repaired. This led to an application to the Corporation for material to carry out the work.[3] On 1 February 1793 the Corporation's Committee of Liberties recommended, 'that the Board should be permitted to cut flaggs from the Denes to repair the batteries, provided they sow the ground with hayseed and make compensation for damage.' This was confirmed by the Assembly on 25 February.[4]

   In 1795, following the formation of the alliance between the French and the Dutch, the distinguished military engineer, Captain Sir Thomas Hyde Page, arrived to gauge the capability of the town's defences to resist an invasion from across the North Sea. As a result a number of improvements were made to the batteries, including the erection of six foot high palisading, store rooms, privies, wood houses and, at the North Star Battery a gunner's house. The most significant improvement, as far as invasion was concerned, was the construction at each of a furnace for heating shot, to enable the gunners to try to set fire to any enemy warships that might venture into the Roads.[5] While in the town Page prepared a plan for additional defensive measures, as part of an overall scheme commissioned by Norfolk's Lord Lieutenant, Marquis Townshend, to protect Yarmouth and cover the approaches to Norwich.

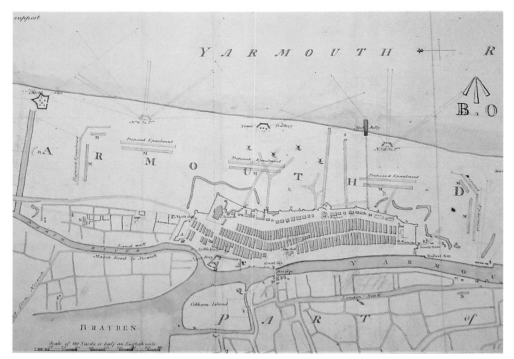

90. An extract from the plan prepared in 1795 by Captain Sir Thomas Hyde Page for additional defensive measures at Yarmouth.

The proposals included three new batteries interspersed between the four existing ones, to enable overlapping fields of fire into the Roads. Each was to mount six 24 pounders. In addition a series of temporary epaulments or breast-works was to be established between the batteries and the town, behind which troops could muster in the event of an invasion. He assumed that sufficient troops would be stationed south of Gorleston to protect the town's southern flank and for that to the north he proposed deploying a force of field artillery. None of these measures actually came to fruition.[6]

The fear of invasion never quite went away, it becoming more heightened in 1797/8 following General Tate's landing at Fishguard and again in 1801 when there was a build-up of enemy landing craft and troops at Boulogne, Dunkirk and Ostend. As a result, between 1794 and 1801, there was a steady stream of reports recommending various counter measures in the event of an invasion along the coast of the Eastern Military District, of which Yarmouth formed part. The most significant of these for the town was that prepared by Major Thomas Reynolds of the 30th Foot, entitled '*A Military Report of the Principal Part of the Eastern District.*' It bears the date 1797, but internal evidence suggests that the 32 page Yarmouth/Norwich section at least was compiled earlier. Under the heading, '*Yarmouth Roads, & the City of Norwich,*' it covers the eventuality of enemy attacks on the town, as one off raids, and also the possibility of one as a prelude to capturing Norwich.[7]

As was usual with such reviews he first considered the effectiveness of the batteries. As far as the Haven Battery was concerned he could not see its usefulness. It was too distant from the St. Nicholas Gatway to prevent an enemy force entering the Roads, and the mouth of the

Yare was sufficiently well defended by the Gorleston Cliff Battery. In addition, if its purpose was to repel a landing, the shoal water before it would force an enemy to land elsewhere. Turning to the other end of the beach, he could not understand why there was such a large undefended gap between the North Star Battery and the Caister Heights. His solution was to move the guns from the Haven Battery to an intermediate position between those two points. As for the beach batteries as a whole he was critical of the fact that none of the guns faced along the shore so that, in the event of a landing, crossfire was not possible along the beach. At a detailed level he was at a loss to know how the ditches could be kept clear of sand, given the windy nature of the weather and he thought it, 'a pity tho' it seems unavoidable that the Furnaces lately erected for Heating Shot should intercept in places the Fire from the Block Houses, & serve as Cover for the Enemy.'[8] In the event of a landing he envisaged that after spiking the guns in the batteries the defending troops would retire into the town and set about defending the medieval town wall. This was the last time this ancient structure was considered to have any defensive value. As far as troops were concerned he felt that 1,000 cavalry and 2,000 infantry 'cannot occupy a better situation than Hopton Common. It is near the Shore and Centrically situated with respect to the Samford(sic) & St Nicholas's Gatways. The remaining 1,000 inf[antr]y may be stationed as usual close to the Beach near Caister, ready to fall back on the Main Road to Norwich, or throw itself into Yarmouth as Circumstances shall require.'[9] After outlining the measures to be taken to defend the town, including the deployment of the townsmen and seamen in a fighting capacity and the destruction of the Jetty, he concluded that, 'this Plan of Defence could not be carry'd into Effect at present for want of Arms. It is therefore recommended to establish a Depot of 5,000 Stand of Arms, Accoutrements Ammunition etc at Yarmouth to be in readiness on such an Emergency.'[10] As was the case with Page's report few, if any, of Reynold's recommendations were implemented and after Camperdown a landing at Yarmouth was considered unlikely.

With most of the regular troops needed overseas it fell to the militia to provide home defence. This led to militia units being stationed at Yarmouth for that purpose. In addition to providing a military presence, militiamen manned the guns of the batteries and guarded the naval hospital, the naval store, the ordnance store and the prison. They also escorted the prisoners of war part of the way to the depot at Norman Cross.[11] Raising these territorial units, keeping them up to strength and making recommendations for officer appointments was the responsibility of the county lord lieutenants, but in wartime deployment of the militia was a matter for the army Commander-in-Chief.[12] In December 1792 the militia as a whole was embodied (called to arms), primarily as a precautionary measure, as the government feared insurrection prompted by the expression of the ideals of the French revolutionary government.[13] But being predominantly young manual workers these militiamen were thought likely to share the same radical political views of the section of society from which they were drawn. In view of this militia units were rotated on a regular basis to avoid close ties forming between the soldiers and the population they were policing. In addition a barrack building programme was quickly devised to remove the necessity of quartering these troops on the local people, with the familiarity this could engender. As the war progressed so the threat of invasion rather than controlling civil unrest became the main concern for home defence. Nevertheless the militia units continued to be kept on the move.

Having been embodied at Yarmouth the East Norfolk Militia marched to Essex in mid-

February 1793 to take up winter quarters at Colchester, Wetham and Kelvedon. At the same time six companies of the East Suffolk Militia arrived in the town, the other two being quartered at Lowestoft.[14] At the beginning of July the first spring rotation took place with the East Suffolks moving to Harwich to be replaced by the East Riding of Yorkshire Militia who encamped at Caister, after a short spell in quarters in the town to await the arrival of their tents and equipment. At the same time the West Middlesex and Leicestershire Militias encamped at Hopton.[15] In September all three units were reviewed by Marquis Townshend prior to a society ball and a supper.[16] In early October the camps were broken up with the Leicestershires moving into winter quarters in Yarmouth and the other two units to quarters elsewhere. In respect of the East Yorks it was reported that, 'To the private men in this regiment much praise is due for their orderly and peaceable behaviour, but to the officers, and to the Colonel Commandant in particular, the grateful acknowledgements of the inhabitants of Caister must justly belong; not only for their strict attention to military discipline, and rigid regard for good order and the peace and security of the neighbourhood, and the liberality with which they have rewarded all persons that have been employed by them, but more especially for a munificent donation of 5 Guineas left by the Colonel with the Rector for the use of the poor.'[17] By then Lieutenant-General James Johnston had been placed in charge of all the troops in the Yarmouth area. In November detachments of the Leicestershires were stationed at Bacton and Happisburgh to assist the revenue officers in suppressing smuggling.[18] In 1794 the spring and autumn rotations were repeated. In May the Leicestershires moved to Danebury Camp, after leaving sufficient men to guard the prisoners

91. The East Norfolk Militia re-enactment group standing to attention on the South Quay, Yarmouth.

of war. The East Suffolks encamped at Caister and the West Kent Militia on Gorleston Common. In October the West Kents marched to quarters at Bury St Edmunds and Thetford, the East Suffolks were quartered at Yarmouth and its vicinity, and the Pembrokeshire Militia, a unit of only two companies, marched in to join them.[19]

In the second half of the year moves were afoot to create a barracks in the town.[20] In the previous war the Duke of Richmond, Master-General of the Ordnance, had tried to acquire for this purpose a distillery, which stood to the east of the parish church, just outside the town wall.[21] It was on this complex that Colonel Oliver De Lancey, the newly appointed Superintendent of Barracks, focused his attention. The distillery buildings were purchased from David Simpson for £2,000 and to enlarge the site, a piece of land to the east was leased from the Corporation, upon an application by Captain Barbara, with a commencement date of 29 September1794. The work involved converting the distillery into barracks, constructing a new barrack block for the rank and file, with officers' quarters attached, and building an officers' mess. A small hospital and a cookhouse were also created. The whole was to be capable of accommodating 1,600 men.[22] In March 1795 it was reported that the, 'Government has purchased the extensive building on the Denes called the Distillery, which is now converting into barracks and will soon be ready for the reception of troops.'[23]

The following month the first militiamen took up residence, the South Lincolnshires and the Bedfordshires, but scarcely had they arrived when there was an urgent need in the town for barrack accommodation to house regular troops. Fortunately this occurred at the time of year when winter quarters were giving way to summer camps. In mid-May the East Suffolks and the Bedfordshires were sent to Warley Camp, the South Lincolnshires and probably the Pembrokeshires to a camp at Gorleston and the newly arrived East Riding of Yorkshire Militia to a camp at Caister. In addition another newcomer, the North Lincolnshire Militia, was sent to Hopton Camp.[24] Cleared in this way the barracks became available for a proportion of the Duke of York's evacuated Continental army. On 7 May it was reported that, 'On Monday (4th) arrived at Yarmouth, under convoy of the *Leopard* man of war, and 3 frigates, 100 transports with 20 regiments of infantry, besides the guards and artillery, with Hon. General De Burgh, from the Continent; the 63d commanded by the Earl of Balearres, are gone into our barracks, the other regiments sailed on Wednesday for Harwich and Portsmouth, and the guards and artillery go for the river.'[25] General Johnston had already been warned to expect these troops and he was to, 'march them into Temporary B[arra]cks at Norwich & Yarmouth, such part as can be accommodated therein.'[26] With the 63rd Foot accommodated at Yarmouth the 3rd, 53rd and 80th Foot were sent to Norwich.[27] The townsfolk responded well to the plight of the 63rd. A subscription was opened for their relief and Lieutenant-Colonel Gower, the commanding officer, 'was requested to apply the amount, in the manner he thought most conformable to the purpose of the subscription.' He wrote a letter of thanks on 3 June, the day after the battalion had been ordered to be quartered in Suffolk.[28]

In October the South Lincolnshires moved from the Gorleston Camp back into the barracks for the winter, where they were joined by the Huntingdonshire Militia. The other three encamped units moved into barracks further afield.[29] Unfortunately the Huntingdonshires proved to be an unruly unit, its soldiers not taking too kindly to discipline. In early December they rioted and smashed up the barracks. The authorities attributed the cause, 'to their frequenting low Ale houses where they are instigated by the Dissenters of which there are

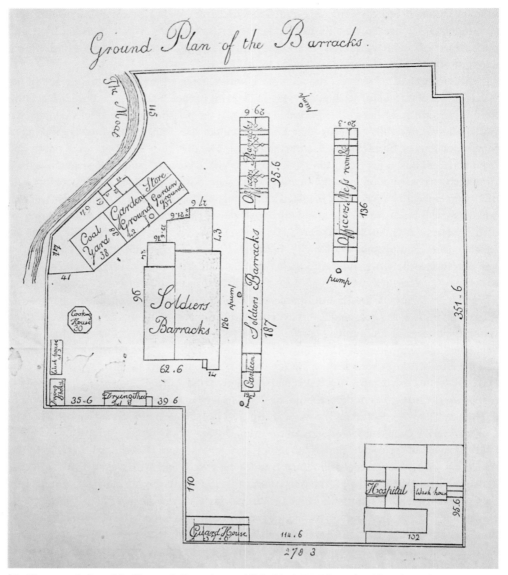

92. The ground plan of the Yarmouth Barracks, established in 1795. It is undated but shows the complex at its greatest extent.

many in the Regiment, and that is the opinion of the Mayor as well as many others.'[30] The soldiers claimed that the reason for their behaviour was the closing of the barrack gates an hour earlier than usual, a measure requested by the Mayor as 'several depredations' had been committed. More damage would have been inflicted if it had not been for the prompt action of a number of officers, including Colonel Sibthorpe of the South Lincolnshires, Sir Thomas Hyde Page and Captain Hook of the Royal Artillery, who directed his field guns at the rioters before the arrival of two troops of Inniskilling Dragoons from Norwich finally restored order.[31] An Inquiry was held and the Huntingdonshires were hastily packed off to Colchester, to be replaced on 14 December by the Cambridgeshire Militia from Norwich who earlier had expressed, 'great readiness to be employed in supressing this outrage.'[32] Ten days later the Cambridgshires were sent back to Norwich and were succeeded in the barracks by the East Kent Militia.[33]

In 1796 the spring rotation took place in April. The South Lincolnshires moved to Blatchington Barracks and the East Kents into Suffolk, but there had been a change of policy for no units moved into the adjacent camps, the Durham and the Oxfordshire Militias marching into the barracks. The camps were not occupied again.[34] In July the Oxfordshires were ordered to vacate the barracks, 'to Encamp on the Ground contiguous thereto until the Barracks undergo some Repairs; the Regt preserving the use of the Barrack Kitchens & other Conveniences, & continuing to receive the Barrack allowances.'[35] Instead the unit seems to have moved to Norwich, leaving a small detachment in the town (until June 1798). Later in the year the troops were reviewed by Major-General Loftus (one of the town's members of parliament) and, on a separate occasion, by Marquis Cornwallis.[36] In October a fire broke out at the barracks, but the militiamen quickly extinguished it.[37] Sometime in early 1797 the Somerset Militia moved into the barracks until May when they marched to Ipswich; 'the inhabitants in general regretted their leaving them.'[38] Shortly thereafter the Durhams went to Hull.[39] For some unknown reason no replacement unit was sent, which meant that when the wounded seamen from Camperdown arrived the barracks were a convenient place to lodge them.

With the threat of invasion being greatly reduced by Camperdown, in November 1797 it was reported that, 'Several of the regiments of infantry, which before the defeat of the Dutch fleet, were ordered in the counties of Essex, Norfolk and Suffolk, etc, are now ordered to Kent, Sussex, and the Western Counties.'[40] But if the local threat had largely dissipated the fears nationally were still very real and among the defensive measures taken in 1798 was the raising of the sea fencible and volunteer corps. The sea fencibles were established in March 1798 to, 'assist in the Defence of this Kingdom against Invasion.'[41] They were in effect a nautical home guard raised as volunteers from the coastal seafaring men, such as the fishermen and boatmen. The coast between Land's End and Yarmouth was divided into eleven districts and there was another on the east coast of Yorkshire. In charge of each district was a post-captain, who had subordinate officers to assist him.[42] Each sea fencible was paid a shilling a day while actually serving, with the added incentive that they were immune from impressment and from the militia ballot. The Suffolk Coastal district stretched from Harwich to Yarmouth, under the command of Captain William Edge, who had his headquarters at Southwold. No sea fencibles were actually raised at Yarmouth, but a unit was enrolled at Gorleston, to cover the harbour's mouth. In April 1798 it was reported that, 'On Tuesday, Capt Killwick, attended by the excellent Band of the 49th Regiment, colours flying, and 120 SEA FENCIBLES of the little, but loyal parish of Gorleston, after parading a considerable time through the High-street, proceeded to the Battery on Gorleston Cliff, where they exercised the 24 and 32-pounders, in the most able and spirited manner.'[43] These men were mainly boatmen and pilots who serviced the harbour and the Roads. For two and a half years they dutifully turned out once a week for training until October 1801, when they were disbanded. By then there were nearly 250 men on the muster roll.[44]

On 6 April 1798 Henry Dundas, Secretary of State for War, wrote to Marquis Townshend, the Lord Lieutenant of Norfolk, stating, that, 'Whatever confidence I place in the actual security of these kingdoms, in consequence of the decided superiority of our Navy, and of the amount of the land Forces already embodied, or now collecting for the protection of the country against the menaced invasion of the enemy, I should not feel that I discharged my duty, if our system of defence did not embrace such further means of security as appear to be evidently within our reach.'[45] The 'further means' meant the raising of more volunteer corps in the county which had been a bit tardy in this respect. At that time Yarmouth had no such corps, nor troops to man the batteries. A general meeting of the Deputy Lieutenants and magistrates was arranged at which General Sir William Howe, commander of the forces in the Eastern Military District, explained what was required.[46] On 25 April the Yarmouth deputies formulated proposals for the raising of a troop of cavalry and two corps of infantry, one of which was for manning the batteries. The troop was to consist of a captain, a lieutenant, a cornet, together with 40 non-commissioned officers and privates. Each was to be armed with a sword and a pistol and was to be given an allowance by the government of £3 per man for clothing. They were to exercise one day a week. The volunteer infantry corps would consist of 200 or more 'respectable Inhabitants of Yarmouth' who would use small arms and pikes. They were to choose their own officers and not be under military law as all expenses would be paid for by public subscription. The corps for manning the batteries would consist of 300 men trained by Captain O'Brian of the navy.[47] They almost got it right. On 30 April a Yarmouth volunteer troop of cavalry, 50 strong, was raised under the command of Lieutenant William Palgrave. The men were to provide their own clothing, but the government would furnish them with arms and pay for a sergeant and a trumpeter. In the event of an invasion it was to serve in the town and neighbourhood. On the same day a company of 60 volunteer infantry was formed under Captain Samuel Barker. It too was to be provided with arms from the government and was to serve locally. Six weeks later a second company of 60 volunteer infantry was raised under the command of Captain Samuel Paget Jnr., with the same characteristics as the first. It was called the Apollonian.[48] In August the three units received their arms and Lady Bacon presented the cavalry troop with its colours. In December 1800 the two infantry companies were accorded the same honour by the Corporation.[49]

Throughout the remainder of 1798 and on into 1800 the volunteer units were the effective garrison of the town, performing all the duties the militia had hitherto carried out, including firing vollies in the Market Place to mark the anniversary of the accession of the King and attending various church services. In January 1799 the conditions of service of the cavalry troop were described as, 'To assist the Civil Power of Yarmouth within the distance of 12 Miles, and escort Prisoners of War the like distance.'[50] This requirement was put into practice in April when the town, was,' infested with a gang of the most nefarious villains.' The volunteers were called out to assist the constables and watchmen almost every night for a week without effect, but stolen goods were eventually found concealed in a dogger and suspicion fell on some Russian sailors.[51]

In November 1800 it was reported that, ' The Yarmouth Volunteer Cavalry and Infantry will be reviewed by Major-General Loftus on Thursday or Friday next, when, should the day prove fine, the largest assemblage of beauty and fashion is expected to be on the ground, as the inhabitants intend to pay the greatest respect to their patriotic and volunteer defenders.'[52] When in November 1800 Lord Nelson arrived, he 'honoured Captain Barker's Volunteers

93. Yarmouth Market Place in 1799. One of the companies of volunteer infantry can be seen standing to attention at a time when they were performing garrison duty.

(who were assembled at the Wrestlers) with his company. He stayed with them more than an hour, enlivening the conversation with the most pleasant, unaffected language.' As we have seen when he left town he was escorted to Lowestoft by Palgrave's' cavalry troop.[53] The two volunteer infantry companies do not seem to have survived the signing of the Preliminaries of Peace in October 1801, but following ratification in March 1802 the cavalry troop unanimously offered to continue their service and this was accepted.

A small militia presence was resumed in 1800. It is not clear when it arrived, but in early June the Durham Militia and the volunteers, both cavalry and infantry, 'fired three excellent vollies,' to mark the King's birthday, 'followed by sumptuous dinners.'[54] In February 1801 the Durhams were ordered to march from their Yarmouth quarters to Northallerton and Boroughbridge. Before leaving Major O'Callaghan asked the volunteers to do duty in the town until another militia unit arrived. The two volunteer infantry companies immediately stepped forward and the following morning took up garrison duty, but a detachment of the East Essex Militia arrived in the afternoon and relieved the volunteers in the evening. It was reported that, 'those at the Batteries, Gorleston, etc did not reach home till very late.'[55] The correspondent went on to complain that, 'It is much to be regretted, at a crisis like the present, when France and all the Northern Powers are at War with us, and this part of the United Kingdom standing as it were in the midst of the Enemy, that hitherto so little public spirit should appear in this flourishing town, as may be imagined by only 1 Troop of Cavalry, and 2 Companies of Infantry, consisting altogether of 100 men, should be formed out of 18,000 Inhabitants.'[56] In March the East Essex detachment rejoined its parent unit at Colchester and was replaced by the Anglesea and Westmoreland Militias. They in turn were relieved by the Montgomeryshire Militia in July, which was succeeded by the Cambridgeshire Militia in November. This unit remained in Yarmouth until the end of the war. To complete the circle the East Norfolk Militia returned to the town and was disembodied on the 23 April 1802.[57]

***

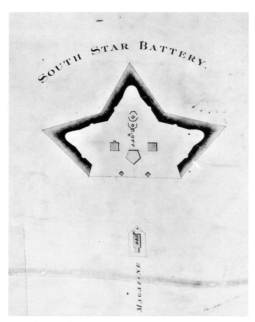

94. The South Star Battery and Magazine

The resumption of hostilities revived the fear of invasion and the town's batteries were once more made ready to resist a landing, although General Craig, the commanding officer of the Eastern Military District, was sceptical about their usefulness, observing that, 'one thing is certain, that the Batteries now in existence do not in the slightest degree tend to give any security to the Place.'[58] He recommended replacing them with more permanent works and the construction of four Martello towers was mooted.[59] Nothing so radical was forthcoming, however, and when Major Alexander Bryce, commanding officer of the Royal Engineers in the district, cast his experienced eye over the town's defences he only ordered that the Fort be repaired and a store room and gunner's shed be added to the Town Battery, work that was completed in 1805.[60] With the threat of invasion receding again the batteries were allowed to deteriorate and by 1808 they were in a parlous state, with their moats choked and the timber structures rotten. Three years later their condition had worsened and it was suggested that they either be rebuilt with brick revetments, as drifting sand and the sea air had all but destroyed the original turf work, or as previously suggested, be completely replaced by Martello towers.[61] Again nothing was done and they remained in this state for the remainder of the war. It is perhaps fortunate that the batteries were never put to the test.

With the barracks once more under military control they were made ready to receive the militia units posted to the town and on 3 August 1803 George William Manby was appointed barrack-master to manage the complex.[62] Brief mention has already been made of this man in relation to his best known achievement, the invention of the lifesaving mortar, but his pre-Yarmouth days gave no reason to suppose he would make such a valuable contribution to the welfare of seamen.[63] Norfolk born, at the age of five he attended a school at Downham Market, overlapping briefly with the 12 year old Horatio Nelson. This was enough for him to later claim an intimate childhood friendship with the victor of Trafalgar. After a failed attempt to become an artillery officer (he could not cope with the necessary maths) he settled for a commission in the Cambridgeshire Militia, serving in that unit until the outbreak of the

French Revolutionary War. After contracting an unwise marriage, squandering his patrimony of an 8,000 acre estate and being shot in the *back* of the head in a dual, his creditors had him arrested and thrown into gaol. It was a degradation he did not have to endure for long, however, for his younger brother, Thomas, had just been given command of the frigate *Bourdelois* and Manby was released to become the ship's lay chaplain.[64] In April 1800 the frigate sailed for Dublin and in foul weather grounded on the Arklow Bank. After her crew threw everything portable overboard she survived and managed to limp into port. The deep impression this near catastrophe made on Manby was probably what fostered his interest in saving life at sea. While ashore at Plymouth he became gravely ill due to the after effects of his duel, but when back at sea he made a remarkable recovery. On his return

95. Captain George Manby, barrack-master at Yarmouth from 1803.

he received a small legacy from his deceased sister's estate, but this was soon taken by his creditors, leaving him almost destitute.

By then Britain was once more at war with the French and being of the opinion that the proposed defensive measures being taken were totally inadequate, Manby became convinced that the only way to stop an invasion was to assassinate Napoleon. Promoting the idea in a pamphlet he offered to do the deed himself, but the government considered it too unstatesmanlike. Down to his final few shillings he decided on one last desperate gamble to earn himself fame and fortune. By then an officer he had known in his Cambridgeshire Militia days, Charles Yorke, had become Secretary-at-War. Spending the last of his money on the fare Manby set out for London, determined to persuade his old friend to allow him to go to France to kill Napoleon. He was well received by Yorke who expressed genuine sympathy for what had befallen him in the ten turbulent years since last they had met, but he would not sanction the murder of the French leader. What he did do, however, was appoint Manby to supervise the barracks at Yarmouth, an act of patronage that however bizarre it may now seem, was quite normal for the time.

The role was perfect for Manby. It was not quite a sinecure, but the management of the barracks could be left to his (long suffering) barrack-sergeant, enabling him to pursue his inventions and social asperations.[65] In these endeavours he found a willing patron in a man we have already met, local banker, Dawson Turner, who, for whatever reason, doggedly kept him financially afloat. Manby, however, could not delegate all his work and, as the representative of the barrack office, in 1808 he had to negotiate with the Corporation the acquisition of additional land to extend, 'the (barrack) hospital towards the east, removing the kitchen and out offices.' Eventually agreement was reached for a lease to the government

96. These original barrack buildings were not demolished until 1959.

of a piece of land, with permission to 'pale and erect buildings.'[66]

At the start of the previous war the militia provided the only units serving at Yarmouth but, as we have seen, as time moved on they were supplemented by volunteer corps and sea fencibles (at Gorleston). With these arrangements tried and tested, in early 1803, all three were re-formed for service in and around the town. The East Norfolk Militia was embodied at Yarmouth on 21 March and in early June departed for quarters at Beccles and Bungay, in Suffolk.[67] The first of the county militia units to march into Yarmouth was that from Cheshire, arriving in late May for a short stay before leaving for Colchester. The Shropshire Militia was next to occupy the barracks, to perform a spell of garrison duty that lasted over a year.[68]

The nature of this work was very monotonous and was only relieved by 'spit and polish' events, such as parades, exercises, inspections and, for the officers, social gatherings such as balls and formal dinners. Notices of these activities usually found their way into the columns of the local newspapers, but it is the coverage of the unusual occurrences that serve to illustrate the highs and lows that could accompany service in the militia. In January 1804 it was reported that, 'Capt. Dickens, of the Shropshire Militia, undertook, for a considerable wager to walk from the Angel Inn, at Yarmouth, to the Angel Inn, at Norwich, and back again, (47 miles) in 12 hours, which he performed, with apparent ease, in 11 hours and a half - considerable bets were laid for and against.'[69] Unfortunately the following month it was noted that, 'two brothers, privates of the Shropshire Militia, were interred here, the death of one was occasioned by excess in drinking *spirits*; the other, who had measles, by drinking too freely of cold *water*.'[70] Providing entertainment could also turn out disastrously for some. In July 1804, 'several battles' were fought on the Denes by soldiers of the same unit and unhappily one of these bouts had fatal consequences. It was between a soldier and an officer's servant, who was considered to be the '*best man* in the regiment.' After a number of rounds fought 'with great fury' the soldier, George Griffiths, was carried off the field so much injured that he died three hours later. The verdict of the coroner's jury was manslaughter and the servant, John Kent, was arrested. Tried in September he was sentenced to one month's imprisonment and was ordered to pay a fine of one shilling.[71] The Shropshire's left Yarmouth on 30 October 1804, as usual, 'much to the regret of the inhabitants.'[72] Waving them off were two women with extra reason to lament their departure for both were domestic servants who had married soldiers from the unit. A year and a half later these men came to visit their wives but, on not being allowed to return with them, the following morning, the heartbroken women tied themselves together with ribbon, walked into the sea, and were drowned. The *Norfolk Chronicle* described this sad act as, 'A strong instance, among many others, of the strength of female attachment, too often inhumanely slighted by the object of regard!'[73] Sadly these women were the victims of the policy of militia rotation which took no account of matters of the heart.

The Shropshire's were replaced by the militia from Fife, which served at Yarmouth until June 1805. Three weeks later a fleet of transports arrived from Leith carrying the Ross-shire Militia. Unfortunately their service at Yarmouth started inauspiciously when as a result of a sudden gale three of its soldiers fell overboard and drowned, together with several others who had put off in a boat to assist them.[74] The presence of these Scotsmen in Yarmouth, for the best part of three years, presaged what was to come during the latter part of the nineteenth and first six decades of the twentieth centuries when each October large numbers of Scottish men and women migrated to the town to take part in the autumn herring fishery.

In June 1807 the Ross-shires were succeeded by the Cambridgeshire Militia, commanded by the aforementioned Lieutenant-Colonel Yorke, the man who as Secretary-at-War had appointed George Manby to the post of Barrack-master. Since then Yorke had been Home Secretary and Manby no doubt exploited this piece of serendipity in the drawing rooms of the town's polite society.[75] Not so satisfactory was the behaviour of one of Yorke's soldiers. In March 1808 the military in the town was suspected of circulating forged one pound notes. On carrying out a search, William Hardy, a private in the Cambridgshires, was found to have some in his possession. He claimed that he had bought them from a Mr Shorten, a Norwich hawker. Both Hardy and Shorten were arrested and taken to Yarmouth gaol. Subsequently appearing at the Norfolk Assizes Hardy was found guilty and was sentenced to 14 years transportation. Shorten was acquitted.[76]

There seems to have been a period between the middle of 1808 and early 1809 when no militia regiments were stationed at Yarmouth, garrison duty falling to the volunteer and local militia units, but by June of the latter year the Berkshire Militia was in residence. It was officers from this unit who started the horse racing at Yarmouth, still a feature of the town's social and sporting calendar today. Preston records that, 'In the year 1810, during the stay of the Berkshire Militia here, some of the officers happened to have two or three private racing matches upon the Denes, which were conducted with much spirit; this induced a few active individuals to meet for the purpose of having, if possible, annual races...'[77]

In late September 1810 the Berkshires left Yarmouth to perform guard duty at Norman Cross, their departure causing 'general regret.'[78] They were replaced by the West

97. Horse racing on the South Denes was started by the Berkshire Militia in 1810. The meeting depicted here took place in 1840 when, as can be seen, the military still had an involvement.

Norfolk Militia who in mid-1811 shared the barracks with four companies of the 54th Foot, their line regiment namesake. This coincidence was exploited when the annual period for the militiamen to volunteer for service in the line regiments came around, for over 100 men chose to transfer from the one to the other.[79] By September 1811 the West Norfolks had moved to Woodbridge, making way for the Dorset Militia. In May 1812 this unit left for Bristol to be replaced by the militia from South Lincolnshire, which was followed, in mid-1813, by the Bedfordshire and the North Mayo Militias.[80] In early February 1814 this Irish unit was replaced by a detachment of their fellow countrymen from the Wexford Militia, who remained in the town until the end of the war,[81] when the East Norfolk Militia returned from Plymouth to be disembodied.[82]

Unlike in the previous war the call to arms for men to join the volunteer infantry received a good response at Yarmouth. Officially formed on 19 August 1803, a battalion sized unit was established, which numbered 480 officers and men. Command was given to an experienced soldier, Lieutenant-Colonel William Gould, and the captains of the two volunteer companies disbanded in 1802, were re-commissioned; Samuel Paget Junior becoming the unit's major and Samuel Barker serving as a captain of one of the six companies.[83] On 10 November the unit was presented with its colours by the Mayoress, 'after which the battalion fired three excellent vollies.' Later Gould and his officers hosted a celebratory dinner for the Mayor, the town's principal inhabitants and prominent military and naval officers.[84] In December it was inspected by Lieutenant-Colonel Metzner who observed that. 'This is one of the Steadiest & best Corps in the County, (the Lieut-Colonel) an Old Officer of the Line.'[85] By the end of the year Norfolk's volunteer companies had been grouped into eleven battalions, with the Yarmouth Volunteer Infantry being large enough to stand alone as the sixth battalion. The unit performed regular periods of service/training of two to three weeks duration until late 1808 when it transferred *en masse* into the newly created local militia as the Third Eastern regiment. In this form it continued to serve in the town, especially when there were no regular militia units present, until disbanded at the end of the war. The Yarmouth Troop of Yeomanry Cavalry, commanded by Captain Edmund K. Lacon, served until late 1803 when it became part of the Third Norfolk Cavalry. Metzner described this unit as 'An Excellent Troop complete & well appointed. Steady in Evolutions, charges bold & well.' By 1805 at least, Captain Brown's Yarmouth Company of Sharp-shooters had become their close associates.[86] In addition to these units some thirty other Norfolk volunteer troops and companies performed garrison duty in the town, especially during the early invasion scare, as did the various local militia regiments at a later date.[87]

Nationally the sea fencibles were re-introduced in an expanded form, with nearly 40 districts created in the United Kingdom and over 30 in Ireland, covering the whole coastline of the British Isles. The Yarmouth District stretched from Cromer in Norfolk to Easton Ness in Suffolk and at the outset was under the command of Captain Charles Cobb, a North Sea veteran, who had commanded the *Glatton* and the *Princess of Orange* in the previous war. With the resumption of hostilities looming, on 11 March 1803, he wrote to the Admiralty from his Portsea home, offering to serve, 'anywhere I may be thought useful,' although he pointed to his five years North Sea service as an indication of where his preference lay. Receiving no reply he wrote again on the 22nd, but it was not until 9 July that he heard that his persistence had paid off, as he had been given command of the Yarmouth Sea Fencible

District.[88] Arriving in the town on 12 July he found Captain William Tremlett and Captain Martin Hinton waiting for him and by the 25th Lieutenants John Ellis, Alexander Home and William Bamber had joined them. Tremlett was posted to the Cromer sub-district which included Winterton where Bamber was to take charge. Home remained in Yarmouth to assist Cobb and Ellis was established at Gorleston. Captain Hinton was given the Lowestoft sub-district where he was shortly joined by Lieutenant Edward Bennett, who was placed at Benacre.[89]

Enrolment began immediately and given the terms and conditions of service there was no shortage of willing recruits. The main inducement was, as before, protection from impressment.[90] In addition they were not to be treated as if they were regular naval seamen, nor soldiers for that matter, Cobb being instructed to direct his officers, 'to treat the men with proper attention, and to avoid all harshness and unnecessary severity which may teach them to be dissatisfied with the Service they have engaged in; always recollecting that as it is a voluntary service, quite new to them, and different from anything to which they have been accustomed, it may require more than common attention to reconcile them to the degree of control that may be absolutely necessary.'[91] Somebody at the Admiralty understood the nature of these free spirits. By the end of July over 500 had been enrolled in the Yarmouth district and such was the demand to join in the country as a whole that in early 1804 Rear-Admiral Philip, who had overall command of the sea fencibles, instructed the captains to cease recruitment.[92] As could be expected most of those enrolled were fishermen or men who had reason to work from the beach. At Gorleston a great many of those recruited were pilots and at Yarmouth there were significant numbers of beachmen, keelmen, and shipwrights, together with such men as Thomas Morley, master of the ordnance craft, Thornton Fisher, clerk to the naval store and William Nichols who also worked there.[93]

The duties performed by these men were much as before. They were exercised once a week (on a day least likely to interfere with their normal work), trained in the use of the pike and cannon, and taught how to charge an enemy. They were also to watch the beach, 'whenever the Wind and Weather shall be favourable for the Enemy to attempt a landing,' and not leave the coast, unless the enemy made, or was expected to make, a landing somewhere else. Lastly they were to man gunboats or other armed craft to protect merchant ships when enemy armed vessels were in sight.[94] The Winterton men were quick to comply with this last mentioned requirement. On the morning of 12 December 1803 Lieutenant Bamber received word that during the night an enemy privateer had taken a sloop and that she was now in the offing. Gathering what firearms they could he and his men launched boats and proceeded beyond the sandbanks where, in thick fog, they came across the sloop *Dutton* of Wells, with a cargo of barley and pease. Seeing she was in enemy hands they promptly re-took her from her French prize crew. As previously mentioned, these Frenchmen were sent to Yarmouth gaol.[95]

Cobb's command more or less coincided with what can be termed the 'Beachmen's Coast' along which, in each settlement, there existed one or more beach company, formed to carry out salvage work at sea and on the sandbanks. All these companies owned yawls which were capable of being converted into gunboats by the simple addition of slides fore and aft, on which could be mounted 12 or 18 pounder carronades from the Yarmouth ordnance store. In this fashion some 35 gunboats were created.[96] Cannon in the hands of some amateurs, however, could prove problematical. In February 1804, while the Cromer sea fencibles were exercising, a shot was fired from the recently constructed Eastern Battery by the Cromer Battery volunteers. This caught Captain Tremlett in the foot before striking the town surgeon in the leg. Tremlett recovered, but the unfortunate medical man had to have his damaged limb amputated.[97]

From then until disbanded the sea fencibles in the Yarmouth district operated without reportable incident. Captain Cobb was promoted to rear-admiral in April 1808 and was replaced at Yarmouth by Captain Joseph Larcom, who had been Vice-Admiral Macbride's flag captain in the *Russell* when first a naval squadron had been based at Yarmouth. In December that year he was replaced by Captain Thomas Surridge.[98] Of the subordinate captains Hinton stayed at Lowestoft for the duration, but Tremlett, through overzealousness 'became obnoxious to the inhabitants of Cromer,' and in September 1805 was moved to the rendezvous at Whitby with Richard Poulden, the captain there, replacing him. In June 1809 Poulden in turn exchanged with Nelson's former subordinate and friend, Sir Edward Berry, who was with the sea fencibles at Margate.[99]

The sea fencibles had been created as part of the response to the threat of invasion. With that possibility receding by February 1810 their cost could no longer be justified and accordingly they were disbanded. With their usefulness untested the real beneficiaries of this coastal defence measure was the men themselves, through being exempt from impress, much to the frustration of the local regulating officers. They did, however, perform one useful task outside the scope of their normal duties and that was to help bring back to the Medway ports the Danish warships captured at Copenhagen, in September 1807. By the terms of the surrender this had to be completed within six weeks. With Admiral Gambier unable to provide prize crews the call went out to the seafaring communities for volunteers, with each man being offered a bounty of £2 10s together with able seaman's pay. At Yarmouth Cobb set about encouraging his sea fencibles to step forward while port-admiral Douglas made arrangements for the transportation of all the volunteers from along the East Coast. There was an understandable suspicion amongst these men that the proposal was a ruse for them to be pressed, with Cobb informing the Admiralty that, 'The Volunteers express great apprehension at being put on board the Flag Ship till they are sent forward…' They also expressed the hope that men belonging to the same places would be kept together.[100] Their suspicions proved groundless and between 22 September and 4 October Douglas sent close on 700 men to carry out the task, including a significant number of sea fencibles from the Yarmouth District.[101]

Part Three
Victory and its Aftermath

SPRINGBOARD TO VICTORY

14.
Peace and Closure

The supremacy of the Royal Navy had kept Britain in the war, but it was the allied military success on the Continent that finally defeated Napoleon. Forced to abdicate on 6 April 1814, the Treaty of Fontainebleau granted him sovereignty over the island of Elba and on the 28th he was taken there in a British warship. Two days later the Treaty of Paris was concluded between the victorious allies and the restored Bourbon monarch, Louis XVIII, thereby formally ending the war. News of the Emperor's abdication reached Yarmouth on 10 April and with the town buzzing with 'exultation', Jacob Preston, the Mayor, called a meeting of the inhabitants 'to take into consideration the best mode of celebrating the late glorious event'. What they proposed and brought to fruition in the space of a week was quite remarkable, it being proudly claimed later that, 'no city or town has celebrated its rejoicings in a more rational, benevolent, or novel manner, than the ancient burgh of Great Yarmouth.'[1] The central idea was for the townsfolk to be treated to a dinner on the quayside, on the 19 April. Those at the meeting raised £400 to start a subscription fund (which eventually topped £1,100). Participation would be by ticket only, but these would be freely available. It was thought that some 4,000 people would attend, seated at 40 tables with 100 diners to each. In the event 8,023 people sat down, at 58 tables. In addition the people in the fisherman's hospital, workhouse, children's hospital, charity school and prison were to be fed where they were living. The event was to be concluded in the evening with the ceremonial burning of an effigy of Napoleon, and 'to prevent any disorder or confusion which might arise from so many persons, stimulated by strong ale', donkey races and pig hunts were to be staged on the Denes between the dinner and the lighting of the bonfire.

The day started with the ringing of bells and 'the town early exhibited a delightful scene of bustle and activity'. The warships in the Roads and every ship in the harbour had their colours flying and a great many flags were suspended across the quay, from the attic windows of the houses, to the masts of the ships moored in the river. At 12 o'clock three decorated barges left the *Solebay* and after passing by the brig-sloops *Portia*, and *Chanticleer*, and the frigate *Unicorn*, 'whose riggings were manned', came ashore 'under a constant salute.' In the first boat was Neptune attended by Tritons; in the others British sailors, Cossacks and a sledge on which was the effigy of a chained Napoleon. On landing Neptune was greeted by 50 nymphs dressed in white and after parading round the town, he and his followers arrived at the port-admiral's house, where they waited. At one o'clock, when the diners began to arrive, it was raining, but by the time the food and drink was served it had stopped. Each person was served a beef main course, a plum pudding dessert and a penny loaf, all washed down with copious amounts of ale, which was also given to the children. Tobacco was supplied together with, 'a portion of snuff for their elderly female visitors'. During the meal the bands of the Wexford Militia and the Third East Norfolk Local Militia marched up and down, playing martial music and it was estimated that 20,000 spectators paraded round the tables while the meal was in progress. At 5 o'clock, alerted by a signal gun Neptune and his party departed the port-admiral's house and, with Napoleon's effigy, proceeded round the town before passing through the North Gate to a spot near the telegraph, where the bonfire had been erected. They were followed by an immense crowd. After two pig hunts and three donkey races, at 8 o'clock, the bonfire was lit, much to the enjoyment of the 30,000 people gathered there. With the bills paid the committee found it had a balance in hand of £35-15-11, which it decided to give towards the 'Relief of the Prisoners returning from France, belonging to Yarmouth.' It was not until 6 July that the civilian authority formally announced the peace, with the Mayor reading the pro-clamation at the customary places. That evening the houses were 'brilliantly illuminated and a great number of appropriate transparencies and mottos were displayed.'[2]

As far as the naval presence was concerned port-admiral Murray was heavily involved in the 'Grand Festival', as the dinner was called, but it was to be his swan song, for on 25 May he struck his flag and left town.[3] His departure marked the formal closure of the North Sea Naval Station and its Yarmouth support base, thereby setting in motion the measures necessary to remove the warships and dismantle the infrastructure that had sustained them. Having prepared the *Utile* receiving ship for sea, Lieutenant Blaquire sailed her to Deptford to be paid off. The port-admiral's flagship *Solebay* was also ordered to Deptford, but before arriving there she made a number of trips between Leith and Calais to return released French prisoners of war to their homeland.[4]

The prison had already been emptied when on 26 May the Transport Board directed Lieutenant Larke to 'abolish the Establishment for Prisoners of War at Yarmouth,' and to give advice on how best to dispose of the empty building. He was also asked for his view on how much it would fetch if sold at auction. Four days later he was told to transfer all the prison stores to the Naval Hospital.[5] Larke ceased to be the Board's agent for prisoners of war on 30 September, but a year was to elapse before he was paid anything for his work. Having made application in October 1815 for some remuneration, he was awarded an allowance of £50 per annum, which resulted in a payment of £173-13-8, after tax for the time he had managed the prison.[6] The disposal of the building, however, proved problematical. On 2 May 1815 it was put up for auction and bought by the highest bidder, Robert Pickis, a Norwich oatmeal maker, for £190, but the title deeds could not be found and it was not until 28 May 1818, following a special Act of Parliament, that the premises could be properly conveyed to the purchaser.[7]

Lieutenant Larke was also in charge of the Transport Board's other facility, the Royal Naval Hospital, but with only fourteen patients remaining, on 28 July, he was ordered by the Admiralty to 'discontinue the Establishment' and turn the building over to the Barrack Department.[8] By 6 August there was no one left in need of care enabling the principal medical staff to be discharged. Larke, however, retained the services of the agent, the dispenser and the porter, to prepare the medical stores for removal, a task brought to a close in early September when the transport vessel *G. T.* arrived to take the supplies to Portsmouth. Once empty the hospital was closed.[9]

The departure of the port-admiral rendered surplus to requirements his personal signal box and the telegraph link between him and the Admiralty in London. In October 1814 the Corporation considered a letter from George Roebuck enquiring if it would be willing to purchase the telegraph house. The answer was negative, but after further discussions, on 30 November, it was decided that 'if a moderate Price is asked for the surrender of the Lease the Corporation will purchase the Same and if otherwise will insist that the Covenants in the Lease which require the buildings to be left be performed.' The lease was not due to expire until 1821 and what became of the building is unclear.[10]

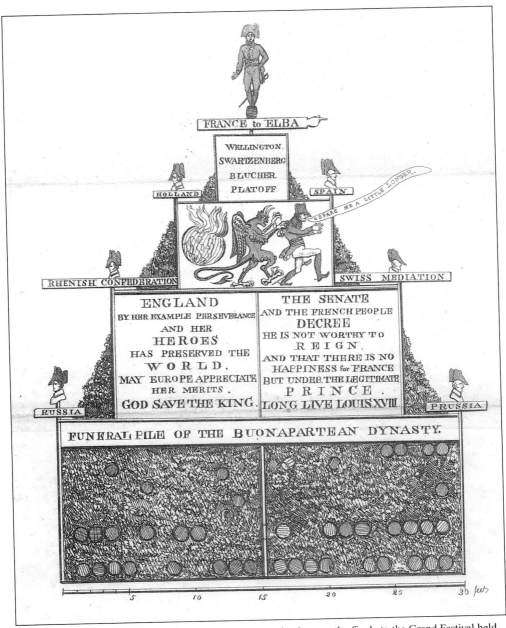

98. 'The funeral pile of the Buonapartean Dynasty,' erected to burn as the finale to the Grand Festival held at Yarmouth on 19 April 1814 to celebrate the end of the war.

For some unknown reason the signal stations between the Nore and Yarmouth remained in commission until 14 November, when the Lords Commissioners gave the order for each lieutenant to discharge himself and his men, and to send his signal code books to their secretary. Telescopes were to be sent to the navy office and the flags and other stores to the nearest King's yard. The stations on the Norfolk coast, north of Yarmouth, had already been closed under a similar order of 3 May.[11] The Admiralty decided that the redundant signal station houses should, where possible, be offered to half-pay lieutenants and on this basis Lieutenant Woodger applied to the Corporation for permission to continue his occupation of the house at Yarmouth Dean. This the Assembly approved and he was given a tenancy dating from 29 September at an annual rent of 5s, provided he kept the building in good repair and took responsibility for Manby's lifesaving apparatus, which was stored there.[12]

Once the barrack function had been transferred to the former naval hospital the old facility became redundant. In October 1814 the town clerk reported to the Assembly that the Inspector General of Barracks had offered to sell to the Corporation the leases under which the buildings were held. Initially the Assembly decided not to purchase, but, as with the telegraph house, discussions took place and in late November the government's interest in the buildings was acquired for £400. In 1815 the Corporation sold the premises to crepe manufacturers Grout Bayliss and Co for use as a factory.[13]

Regarding the victualling service Sir William Fletcher made his last deliveries under his sea provisions contract in November 1814 and Andrew Belcher supplied water until July 1815. Charles Green, who had taken over the vegetable contract from Kemp in April 1814, was allowed to fulfil his one year contract. Thereafter the pursers of visiting warships had to make their own arrangements. This did not apply to the supply of fresh beef, however, for in December 1815 Nathaniel Martin was given a new contract.[14] In September 1814 the Victualling Board requested the Transport Board to, 'give Directions to the Master of the *Jane* Transport now loading at Deptford with Provisions for the Garrison of Heligoland to call at Yarmouth on his return from that Island for the purpose of bringing to Deptford such Casks Staves and other Victualling Stores as are from the alteration of Political circumstances no longer wanted at Yarmouth.' Crockford was duly directed to load the vessel when she arrived. This was done in early October, but not all the stores could be accommodated on board the transport. In November Crockford informed the Board that there still remained 639 butts at Yarmouth and in May 1815 he was still organising transport for the remaining stores before vacating his post.[15]

Throughout the summer months the Yarmouth lighter made several trips to Deptford to transfer the naval stores, but it was not until 21 November that the Navy Board received an Admiralty directive to close the naval yard itself. As a result storekeeper John Day was ordered to 'load Such Craft as may be sent in addition to the Yarmouth Lighter, with the Stores etc in these Magazines for conveyance to Deptford Yard.' The additional vessels sent were the Deptford and the Medway lighters and it took the three vessels until the 26 April 1815 to remove all the naval stores, following which the remaining workforce was discharged. On the 27th storekeeper Day departed for London, handing over the care of the storehouses to his late first clerk, Thornton Fisher.[16] As far as the storehouses were concerned on the 24 November 1814 Day had received a warrant directing him to find tenants for them and he had subsequently placed advertisements in the county newspapers for that purpose.

Unfortunately only one tender was forthcoming, that from Messrs Hurry & Co, who had hired the storehouses during the short-lived peace of 1802/3. When sent to the Board in early January 1815 this tender was immediately rejected and Day was asked to explain why the rent offered was so much lower than had been paid before. The main reason he gave was that there had been an increase in the various taxes and charges that were now applicable. He also pointed out that, 'at a time in the late war when Prizes were constantly coming into Yarmouth, many storehouses were erected which are at this moment (& likely to continue so) lying empty:- making therefore the value of such Premises much less at the present time.'[17] Day was directed to try again, but he was no more successful it being his opinion that the uncertainty of tenure was another reason the merchants of the town were not interested. By the time of his departure the naval store had still not been let and what's more repairs were needed to the roof and the masthouse floor. Some repairs were carried out and in 1818 Samuel Paget Jnr. offered to hire part of the premises, but it seems terms could not be agreed. It remained in naval ownership for many years afterwards, being let on occasions.[18]

The ordnance depot survived the immediate post-war service dismantlement, but within five years the staffing level had been greatly reduced. In 1830 the former clerk, Robert Boult Fenn, was living on site as the acting storekeeper, but by then most of the buildings were let for other purposes, making him little more than a caretaker.[19]

***

By the end of 1814 the naval support base had been dismantled. It had been in existence for the best part of 20 years and in that time had successfully fulfilled its primary purpose of sustaining the warships operating in the North Sea and the Baltic. Despite the difficulty of getting boats off the beach or out of the harbour when there were strong winds from all points east, the Admiralty stuck to its decision to station a squadron in the Roads, even when the Peace of Amiens offered the opportunity for a rethink. This points to the navy being satisfied with the performance of Yarmouth as a support base, but if this is not enough proof the facts speak for themselves. The war on trade was vigorously pursued by Yarmouth based cruisers and hundreds of prizes were sent into the Roads. Convoys of merchantmen were also protected by these vessels. In addition the North Sea Squadron, through its blockade of the Texel, prevented the Dutch Fleet linking up with its French counterpart to facilitate an invasion and managed to defeat that fleet when it did venture out, all of this supported by the facilities at Yarmouth. The anchorage also provided a convenient assembly point for naval and military expeditions to northern climes, such as those that achieved success at Copenhagen, as well as being the first port of call for returning troops from less successful European ventures. The naval support base was also reasonably cost effective. The shore-based naval personnel were mostly no longer fit for sea service and as they were on half-pay, to employ them in this way was a sensible use of resources. Most of the buildings required were leased with any alterations that were necessary being carried out as cheaply as possible, with the exception of the two major building projects, the Royal Naval Hospital and the Royal Arsenal, which proved to be costly mistakes, although the fact that they were built at all demonstrates the importance accorded to the Yarmouth naval support base in the prosecution of these wars.

But how did the town fare as host to the navy? Fluctuations in population and housing stock provide good indicators of economic health. There is no reliable data for 1793, the year the French Revolutionary War broke out, but given that there was no stimulus to growth in the previous decade the population is unlikely to have risen much above the 12,608 recorded in 1784 and might well have been less. In 1801, when the first nationwide census was taken, the town's population was given as 14,845, not including those men who were at sea or with the military. Nor could it include any growth that might have occurred in the last year of the war. From these figures it is reasonable to suppose that there was a population increase of around 2,500 during the first war. By 1811 the population had risen to 17,977, an increase of just over 3,100 over the previous decade. This will no doubt have risen further by the end of war, in 1814. Taken as a whole the figures suggest that during the course of the wars the population of Yarmouth rose by some 6,000 people with a proportionate rise in the housing stock to accommodate them. This extraordinary level of growth was well above the national average and shows that the existence of the naval support base had a very positive affect on the town's economy.[20]

Being a seaport with no adjacent farmland virtually all the town's employment related to the sea and all the people benefitted from the spending power of the navy, including merchants, bankers, brewers and shipbuilders, the various shipbuilding tradesmen, such as shipwrights, ropemakers, block-makers and sailmakers, the carriers, including the beachmen and keelmen, the everyday town tradesmen, and an assortment of labourers. The merchants did particularly well from government contracts, property sale and rental, and the ability to buy prize cargoes at knock down prices. Little wonder there was an influx of workers to the town. Another source of income that increased as a result of naval ships lying in the Roads was that to be had from those attending the summer season. In July 1801 the *Norwich Mercury* reported that, 'Yarmouth now exhibits a very lively scene and is not to be equalled by any other Watering Place owing to the great number of passengers passing and repassing by the Packets,[and] the beautiful prospect of the Ships of War in the Roads. The town is filling very fast with company of the first distinction.'[21]

There was, however, a price to pay for this prosperity in the shape of alcohol fuelled anti-social behaviour that inevitably accompanied the arrival of large groups of sailors and soldiers. When the militia units moved out it was customary for the local newspapers to report that the town regretted their departure, but if the Huntingdons behaviour in 1795 is anything to go by, it would more likely be with a sigh of relief, unless it was a question of 'better the devil you know.' As we have seen the worst offenders were the Russian soldiers returning from the Helder expedition, who went as far as drinking the oil from the street lamps. There was another downside, the seamen's ever-present fear that they might be pressed into the navy, which prompted many of those without the necessary documentation to hide in the town for long periods. This presented the merchants with a dilemma. As members of the Corporation, and from a commercial point of view, they supported the navy, needing its protection to pursue their merchant ventures, both trading and fishing, but they also required seamen to man their vessels and would go to great lengths to prevent them being pressed. On balance, though, the presence of the navy was a good thing for Yarmouth and most of the townsfolk were poorer for its departure.

Epilogue

Confirmation that the status quo had returned to Yarmouth was provided by an event reported in the *Norfolk Chronicle* on 18 September 1814 in the following terms; 'Last Sunday being what is commonly called Dutch Sunday, was observed here by the arrival of Schuyts from Holland, previous to their going a fishing – It being twenty years since the day was last kept for this occasion, it attracted a numerous assemblage of visitors from the neigh-bourhood.'[1] But five months later Napoleon was once more in a position to inflict war on Europe. Escaping from Elba on 26 February 1815 he landed in France and on 20 March entered Paris at the head of an army. This provoked a further period of conflict, known as the 'Hundred Days', which eventually ended in his defeat at Waterloo. Being largely a land based crisis and with the Dutch once more Britain's allies, there was no immediate need to re-establish the Yarmouth naval support base, but as a precautionary measure, for the navy as a whole, orders were given to bring warship crews up to strength, much to the dismay of the townsfolk. From April 1815 the brig-sloop *Cadmus* and the gun-brig *Hearty* frequented the Roads and in early May it was reported that, 'A very sharp press has commenced here this week, by the *Cadmus* sloop of war.' Soon after there was more; 'Last night, the boats from the above vessels (*Cadmus* and *Hearty*) came on shore to press, and a number of men were taken, but the greater part of them were cleared before being taken on board; not more than two or three were carried on board. A scuffle took place about six o'clock this morning, between the shipwrights, chaulkers(sic), and others, and the boats' crews, upon which the latter retreated down the haven, with their boats, followed by the former assailing them with showers of stones, and at the ferry at Gorleston, the mob seized the gig of the *Cadmus*, and literally knocked her in pieces, and at the same time doing considerable damage to another boat. It is much to be regretted this affair should have happened, as the officers suffered no persons to be taken who could give a tolerable account of themselves, and ordered their men to behave in the most peaceable manner.'[2]

The following month there *were* moves afoot to re-establish the support base and it was reported that Admiral Drake had been appointed port-admiral. He was to have at his disposal a naval force comprising six sloops of war and several cutters, presumably to resume the war on trade, but with Napoleon's defeat shortly afterwards, nothing came of it.[3] In the event what involvement the town had in this brief period of war did not emanate from its potential as a naval support base, but from the fact that it sported a brand new and virtually empty former naval hospital. In anticipation of casualties from continental land battles in mid-May steps were taken to fit out the building to accommodate 500 wounded soldiers, 'whenever they arrive' and in early June it was reported that, 'the gentlemen belonging to that department are said to be appointed, viz. two physicians, two surgeons, and thirteen medical assistants.'[4]

News of Waterloo reached the town on 23 June and on the 27th the *Telegraph* coach arrived with colours flying, bringing word of Napoleon's abdication, providing yet another cause for celebration throughout the day.[5] Shortly afterwards the annual Water Frolic 'concluded with a *spectacle* allusive to the present eventful times. A fire ship was launched from the slip in a builder's yard, having an effigy of the Fallen Usurper of France, standing on its poop. This vessel was towed round the flotilla, and then being moored in the middle of them, a match was laid to the train by the representative of Neptune and his attendants; and Buonaparte was quickly enveloped in flames and blown up into the air, amidst the acclamations of the assembled multitude.' Such events were becoming a habit.[6]

The first of the Waterloo wounded arrived from Ostend in two transports on 13 July, some 240 of them. They were ferried to the quayside in keels and taken to what had now been designated the Yarmouth Military General Hospital. On 10 August four more transports arrived from the Belgium port with a further 270 wounded. These soldiers came from 40 different army units.[7] Less than two months later most of the wounded had been discharged, enabling the Yarmouth correspondent of the *Norfolk Chronicle* to comment that, 'It gives us real pleasure to learn, that a great number of the brave soldiers, who were wounded in the late battles in the Netherlands, and brought to our Naval Hospital, have been discharged cured and have joined their respective regiments:- indeed out of nearly 450 only 14 of the Heroes of Waterloo have "sunk to rest", since their arrival at this noble asylum, where every attention has been paid to their comfort and relief.'[8] An old wall plaque at the former naval hospital marks the interment there of the deceased Waterloo soldiers, together with a sergeant from the 55th Foot. A detachment of that regiment had arrived in the town in November 1814 to perform garrison duty. It remained until August 1815 when it was replaced by the Cambridgeshire Militia, which in turn left for Colchester in November 1815.[9]

As we have seen the townspeople benefitted from hosting the naval support base, but not everyone considered it to have been a blessing, for in September 1815 it was reported that, 'The town has not for the last ten years been so full of visitors as at present; having ceased to be a Naval station it is now become a most respectable and genteel bathing place: improvements are every year visible, and the new walk and carriage-way to the beach (Regent Road), when finished, will not be found amongst the least of them. – The Jetty and Bath-room are thronged every evening with company, and the Band of the Cambridgeshire Militia enliven the *promenade* - The attendance in the Race week is expected to be immense; almost every lodging house and accommodations at the inns having been already secured.'[10]

Soon to complement these improvements was the 'Norfolk Pillar', a monument erected to commemorate the victories of the nation's best known naval officer, Vice-Admiral Lord Nelson. It predates the more famous column in Trafalgar Square by 24 years and although its purpose was to honour the 'Norfolk Hero' its location at Yarmouth can be seen as recognition of the town's role in the conflicts of his day. In October 1805, shortly after his death at Trafalgar, a county meeting held at the Shirehall in Norwich resolved, 'to open a subscription for erecting a memorial to perpetuate the memory of Lord Nelson's victories.' Sites were suggested in Norwich and in the church at, Burnham Thorpe, but this early attempt to commemorate his battles soon petered out.[11] It took the peace of 1814 to prompt the county's Grand Jury to resurrect the idea and despite the Norwich Corporation offering a contribution of £200 for a monument to stand on Castle Hill, it was decided by the subcommittee appointed to consider the matter that a coastal location would be more appropriate. As a result Yarmouth was chosen with perhaps the Corporation's offer to, 'grant a sufficient quantity of land on the South Denes for the erection of the same,' having a bearing on the choice.[12]

The column was designed by Norfolk born architect William Wilkins and was similar in style to his ill-fated monument to Nelson erected in Dublin, in 1808. It comprises a fluted Doric column of white Mansfield stone 144 feet high with an internal staircase of 217 steps leading to a small observation platform. The original intention was to surmount it with a classical triumphal galley, but in January 1818 the Yarmouth Corporation granted a further £50 to change this to a statue of Britannia.[13] The foundation stone was laid on 15 August 1817 at a ceremony attended by 'an immense concourse of people,' including persons of 'rank and respectability,' some 350 of whom attended a celebratory ball that evening. The monument was completed on 1 June 1819 when the statue was hoisted to the top.[14] Curiously the statue was placed facing inland rather than towards the sea as might have been expected. There is no recorded reason for this, but one theory is that she looks towards Nelson's birthplace, Burnham Thorpe. Be this as it may the story soon spread that the workmen had made a mistake and when the architect saw what had been done, he threw himself from the top of the Pillar to his death. This was untrue, but what did happen was that the then Borough Surveyor and superintendent of the works, Thomas Sutton, while at the summit directing the workmen in their endeavours to raise the statue, 'complained of a giddiness, was seized with a spasm, and instantly expired.'[15] Subsequently a cottage was erected nearby, 'for a sailor to reside in, and to shew the monument; one who has fought under the banners of the immortal hero is intended to be selected.' The man chosen was James Sharman. Born in 1785 he was working at the Wrestler's when at the age of 14 he was pressed into the navy. He joined the *Victory* in 1803 and was present at Trafalgar, claiming to have helped carry the wounded Nelson down to the cockpit. When Charles Dickens visited Yarmouth in 1849 he was so taken with Sharman that the old sailor entered the pages of *David Copperfield* as Ham Peggotty, or so it is said.[16]

While the monument on the Denes represented the formal recognition of the Vice-Admiral's exploits, in the streets of Yarmouth itself a proliferation of new inn and alehouse signs paid popular tribute to him and several other key figures of the recent wars, especially those who had been involved with the North Sea Naval Station. Of the 135 such establishments listed in 1819 three featured Nelson's name (including for a short time the Wrestlers) and three the name of the Earl St. Vincent, the town's former Member of Parliament. Others honoured in this way were Admiral Duncan, Admiral Onslow, Lord Collingwood, Sir Sydney Smith and Sir Samuel Hood. The army was represented by the Duke of Wellington. The majority of these eating and drinking establishments belonged to the breweries owned by Samuel Paget Jnr. and Sir Edmund Knowles Lacon, men who in one way or another had played a part in ensuring the success of the naval support base.[17]

***

Two hundred years have elapsed since those heady days of Duncan, Dickson and Douglas, and during that time the memory and physical evidence of Yarmouth's involvement in the last great wars with the French have slowly disappeared. Bomb damage, slum clearance and new roads have all but destroyed the town's unique Rows, in the process sweeping away anything which might have remained of the two prisons, the temporary hospitals and the premises and houses of the local participants, not to mention the townscape so familiar to the officers of the North Sea Squadron. Some of the original barrack blocks survived for many years in silk factory use, but after the latter's closure in the 1970's, the site was cleared to make way for a supermarket. Likewise nothing remains of the naval store and the adjacent ordnance store that were established in the redundant whale fishery buildings. The seashore batteries have also long gone. While the telegraph building seems to have been removed shortly after the wars, the house belonging to the Yarmouth Dean signal station stood until the middle of the nineteenth century, when it was demolished and replaced by a more permanent brick residence. This in turn was taken down in the 1950's to make way for a small housing development called Seafield Close.

The timeless anchorage remains, but where the billowing sails of wooden walled warships could once be seen there now turns sails of quite a different character, those attached to the 30 electricity generating turbines of an offshore wind farm. The Jetty which for centuries symbolised the town's relationship with the sea was demolished in January 2012, when the Borough Council decided it could not justify the cost of refurbishing this heritage asset. Its existence has been marked by the installation of an interpretation panel and three of its old piles are to be seen in a flower bed on the seafront, placed there by Great Yarmouth in Bloom. Along the seafront only two buildings survive from the period covered by this book, The Marine Hotel, (formerly the Admiral Onslow public house) and the mid-eighteenth century

99. All that remains of the old Jetty, three piles erected in a seafront flowerbed by Great Yarmouth in Bloom.

bathhouse, now part of an amusement arcade. Of course, in the parish churchyard lie hundreds of naval seamen, soldiers, and prisoners of war of all nationalities, but there are now no individual or collective memorials to mark their interment.

There are, however, some notable exceptions to this disappointing tale. Although the complex was bomb damaged, significant parts of the Royal Arsenal are still to be seen on Southtown Road and in 1983 a cannon barrel from the site was provided with a replica gun carriage and now stands on the South Quay. At the base of the cliff, below Gorleston's White Lion steps, stands what is called Duncan's Pump, marking the site of one of the spring wells used to supply water to the warships during the wars. The most significant survival, however, is the former Royal Naval Hospital. After the Waterloo wounded had departed, the building reverted to barrack use, but was seldom occupied. In 1846 it became a military lunatic asylum before, in 1854, being refitted for its original hospital purpose when Sir Charles Napier's fleet sailed for the Baltic, during the Crimean War. In 1863 it became a naval lunatic asylum and during the Second World War a naval base under the name HMS *Watchful*. The officer's houses suffered bomb damage in that conflict and were later demolished to make way for new buildings when, in 1958, the hospital was transferred to the National Health Service. It served as the St. Nicholas Psychiatric Unit until its closure in 1993.[18] Recognising the importance of this grade II listed building, a planning brief was prepared by the Borough Council in July that year and the complex was bought by Historic Buildings Rescue. Under the guidance of architect Kit Martin it was sensitively converted into apartments, town-houses and cottages, the first of which were occupied in 1996. It now stands as a fitting memorial to the time when Yarmouth played an important part in the defence of the realm.

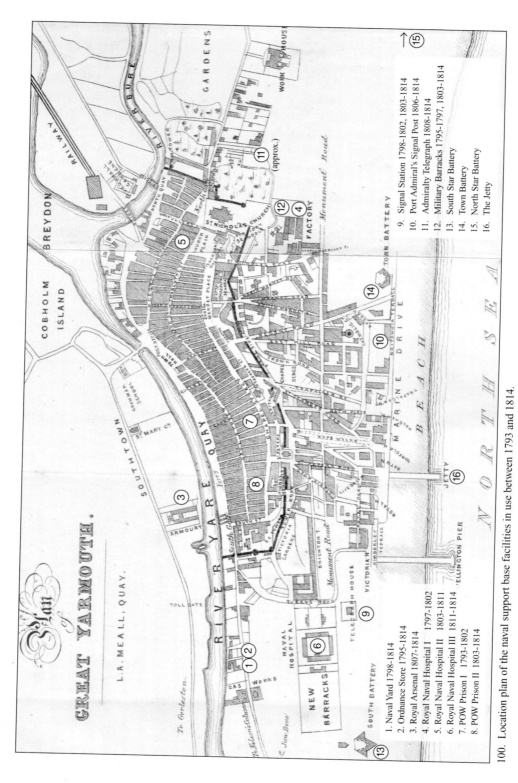

PLAN

GREAT YARMOUTH.

L. A. MEALL, QUAY.

1. Naval Yard 1798-1814
2. Ordnance Store 1795-1814
3. Royal Arsenal 1807-1814
4. Royal Naval Hospital I   1797-1802
5. Royal Naval Hospital II 1803-1811
6. Royal Naval Hospital III 1811-1814
7. POW Prison I 1793-1802
8. POW Prison II 1803-1814

9. Signal Station 1798-1802, 1803-1814
10. Port Admiral's Signal Post 1806-1814
11. Admiralty Telegraph 1808-1814
12. Military Barracks 1795-1797, 1803-1814
13. South Star Battery
14. Town Battery
15. North Star Battery
16. The Jetty

100. Location plan of the naval support base facilities in use between 1793 and 1814.

Notes and References

Prologue: No Stranger to Conflict

1. Brooks, *The Cinque Ports' Feud with Yarmouth in the Thirteenth Century*, p.27.
2. ibid, p.48.
3. ibid, p.27.
4. ibid, pp.43-45.
5. Ecclestone, *The Rise of Great Yarmouth*, p.110.
6. Saul, *Great Yarmouth and the Hundred Years War in the Fourteenth Century*, pp.107,113.
7. ibid, pp.108-9.
8. Palmer, *The Perlustration of Great Yarmouth*, Vol.I, p.202.
9. Davies, *Pepys's Navy*, p.10.
10. Kent, *Fortifications of East Anglia*, pp.202-205.
11. ibid, pp.205-6.
12. Davies, *Pepys's Navy*, pp.14-15.
13. Kent, *Fortifications of East Anglia*, pp.206-7.
14. Davies, *Pepys's Navy*, p.195. TNA, SP46/116/27, 61, SP46/119/88d.
15. Davies, *Pepys's Navy*, p.195.
16. ibid, p.201.
17. ibid, pp.34, 109. *The Second Dutch War*, quoting NMM, DAR/3. Kent, *Fortifications of East Anglia*, p.208.
18. TNA, ADM 106/1018/266, ADM 106/1050/213.
19. Palmer, *Perlustration*, Vol.II, p.192.
20. Swinden, *The History and Antiquities of the Ancient Burgh of Great Yarmouth*, subscribers list.
21. Palmer, *Perlustration*, Vol.II, pp.110-111. TNA, ADM 106/1231/66.
22. TNA, ADM 2/96/32-3, 40-1, 160-2. Palmer *Perlustration*, Vol.III, p.295, quoting Ives.
23. Edler, *The Dutch Republic and The American Revolution*, pp.42-62, 95-138, 163-6.
24. Dirks, *De Nederlandsche Zeemagt in Hare verschillende Tijdperken Geschetst*, p.291.
25. ibid. pp.306-9. TNA, ADM 2/111/41.
26. TNA, ADM 2/112/266, 475-80.
27. TNA, ADM 2/113/27-28, 30-31, ADM 2/114/141-2, 377.
28. It was while on convoy duty with the frigate *Albemarle* that Captain Horatio Nelson first visited Yarmouth in a naval capacity, being anchored in the Roads from 17 to 31 December 1781, TNA, ADM 51/21. Knight, *The Pursuit of Victory. The Life and Achievement of Horatio Nelson*, pp.66-8.
29. TNA, ADM 2/111/291.
30. TNA, ADM 2/110/316-7, NRO, Y/C 36/20/18.
31. TNA, ADM 97/123/4.
32. TNA, ADM 2/100/79, ADM 2/113/45-6.
33. NRO, Y/C 36/20/9.
34. Kent, *Fortifications of East Anglia*, pp.209-10.
35. *Norfolk Chronicle* 12 December 1781.
36. Palmer, *The History of Great Yarmouth designed as a continuation of Manship's History*, pp.262-3.

1. The North Sea Naval Command 1793-1797

1. Knight, *Britain Against Napoleon*, pp. 3-6, 10-17.

2. Gardiner, ed., *Fleet Battle and Blockade*, pp.14, 86.
3. The sources for this figure are the victualling account ledgers, TNA, ADM 112/179-182, the sick-quarters muster books, TNA, ADM 102/825, and the *Norwich Mercury* 1793-96. It does not include the ships-of-the-line of Rear-Admiral Pringle's squadron, which briefly anchored in the Roads in early 1796.
4. Lavery, *Nelson's Navy*, p.282. That these predators had been successful in earlier wars is part of the reason why on the 25 February 1793 the Corporation's loyal address included the words, 'We of this commercial Town are well aware that we may suffer severely in our Trade during the Contest but We should Ill deserve the name of Britons, were private Considerations to lessen our Zeal in a Cause where the honor of the Crown and the safety of the people are so materially concern'd,' NRO, Y/C 19/15/108.
5. TNA, ADM 7/328/2-3. The captains were Thomas Riches of the *Hunter* Revenue Cutter and Matthew Gunthorpe of the *Lively* Excise Cutter.
6. *Norwich Mercury* 27 April 1793.
7. ibid 2, 16 March 1793.
8. ibid 30 March 1793, 24 May 1794, 2, 23 May 1795, 13 June 1795.
9. ibid 23, 30 March, 6, 13 April 1793, 19 April 1794.
10. For the prize system see Hill, *The Prizes of War*.
11. Lavery, *Nelson's Navy*, pp. 305-10.
12. ibid.
13. *Norwich Mercury* 22 July 1797.
14. ibid 2 March, 6 April 1793.
15. TNA, ADM 2/124/34.
16. *Norwich Mercury* 21 September 1793, 20 September 1794. Palmer records that, 'The Sunday before Michaelmas day was called "Dutch Sunday"; when a kind of fair was held. An eye witness, writing in 1785, describes the Dutchmen as easily distinguished by their round caps, short jackets, capacious breeches, and wooden shoes. They might be seen on the Saturday making their purchases. On the Sunday, he says all the country people round as far as Norwich, flocked in to see the Dutch, who on the occasion decorated their vessels with flags in the gayest manner; the whole length of the Quay being crowded with people of all ranks in their best apparel.' *Perlustration*, Vol.III.p. 226-7.
17. *Norwich Mercury* 8, 29 October 1796.
18. Fortescue, *A History of the British Army*, Vol. IV, Part 1, p.66.
19. *Norwich Mercury* 30 March, 6 April 1793.
20. ibid 23 November 1793.
21. ibid 3 May 1794.
22. Fortescue, *A History of the British Army*, Vol. IV, Part 1, p.324.
23. Palmer, *Continuation of Manship*, pp. 271-3.
24. ibid.
25. ibid. The Mayor was William Taylor Senior.
26. The popular account of this event has the hussars thundering over the ice to take the fleet at sword-point, but de Jonge, in his *Geschiedenis von het Nederlandse zeewezen*, shows it to have been a far less dramatic affair. De Winter was a former Dutch naval officer who since 1787 had been in the service of France. He was to command the Dutch fleet at Camperdown.
27. On 16 May 1795 France concluded a formal alliance with the Batavian Republic the terms of which required the Dutch to provide 12 ships of the line and 18 frigates in support of her neighbour together with half the troops under arms, Earl of Camperdown, *Admiral Duncan*, p.37.
28. TNA, ADM 2/127/287-8, 384.
29. Earl of Camperdown, *Admiral Duncan*, p. 37. Between August 1794 and January 1795 Rear-Admiral Henry Harvey commanded a squadron in the North Sea, but this was largely concerned with the defence of Flushing.
30. TNA, ADM 6/25 11 March 1795.
31. TNA, ADM 2/128/116.
32. ibid 95.

33. ibid 8. The ships and vessels where the *Venerable* (74), *Minotaur* (74), *Asia* (64), *Scipio* (64), the frigates *Ambuscade, Sibyl, Squirrel* and *Camilla* and the cutters *Trial* and *Black Joke.*
34. Turner, *The Russian Squadron with Admiral Duncan's North Sea Fleet*, pp. 213-4.
35. ibid p. 219.
36. Earl of Camperdown, *Admiral Duncan*, p. 44.
37. TNA, ADM 1/523/79.
38. ibid 82. Earl of Camperdown, *Admiral Duncan*, p. 62.
39. TNA, ADM 1/523/106.
40. TNA, ADM 2/130/343.
41. Earl of Camperdown, *Admiral Duncan*, p. 63.
42. TNA, ADM 1/523/114.
43. TNA, ADM 2/1350.
44. TNA, ADM 2/130/380.
45. TNA, ADM 1/523/116.
46. TNA, ADM 2/942/273.
47. TNA, ADM 1/521/131. The Dutch ships were commanded by Captain Von Dirking who secretly favoured the House of Orange. He wanted to hand them over to the British, but in a manner that looked as if they had been taken in action. This was achieved on 7 May by the frigate *Phoenix*, Earl of Camperdown, *Admiral Duncan*, p. 64.
48. TNA, ADM 1/523/134.
49. ibid 137.
50. ibid 142, 143, 146, 147.
51. TNA, ADM 111/139, 17 May 1796.
52. TNA, ADM 1/523/174.
53. ibid.
54. *Norfolk Chronicle* 2 July 1796. *An Historical Guide to Great Yarmouth in Norfolk*, p. 67. This work contains the statement that, 'From this time, these Roads became the active station of a North Sea squadron'. By then Admiral Duncan had 58 ships and vessels to carry out his duties in the North Sea, TNA. ADM 1/523/190.
55. TNA, ADM 1/523/269. Turner suggests that having to work with the Russians was the cause of his indisposition, *The Russian Squadron*, p.217.
56. TNA, ADM 2/132/354. While holding his North Sea command Macbride commissioned a chart of Smith's Knowl which includes the Yarmouth Roads. Surveyed in 1796 it was published by Laurie & Whittle on September 21st 1798, TNA. ADM 352/6.
57. Earl of Camperdown, *Admiral Duncan*, p. 67.
58. ibid p.90.
59. TNA, ADM 1/523/357-65.
60. TNA, ADM 2/132/74.
61. Duncan resumed his command for a brief period in February 1797.
62. TNA, ADM 1/524/32.
63. TNA, ADM 1/524/26.

2.   Mutiny and Camperdown 1797

1. Earl of Camperdown, *Admiral Duncan*, pp. 91-93.
2. TNA, ADM 1/524/110.
3. ibid.
4. Earl of Camperdown, *Admiral Duncan*, p.100.
5. ibid pp.101-2.
6. ibid pp.110-11, quoting Ralfe's *Naval Biography*.
7. TNA, ADM 1/524/131.
8. ibid 125.
9. ibid 120, Earl of Camperdown, Admiral *Duncan*, p.109. The other ships were the *Standard, Trent, Lion, Glatton, Montagu* and *Repulse.*
10. TNA, ADM 1/524/136.

11. Earl of Camperdown, *Admiral Duncan*, p.113, quoting the *Annual Register* for 18 May 1797.
12. ibid pp.116-20.
13. TNA, ADM 1/524/146.
14. ibid 147a, 149. The latter letter was endorsed at the Admiralty with the words, 'acquaint him (Duncan) that their Lordships are inclined to think they have deceived Lt. Reddy in order to prevent their detention.'
15. Earl of Camperdown, *Admiral Duncan*, pp.120-1.
16. ibid.
17. ibid p.127. Bligh's report is to be found on pp.133-4.
18. ibid p.128.
19. ibid p.125.
20. NRO Y/D 87/30 24 May 1797.
21. TNA, ADM 1/524/146. These were the two ships stopped from going to the Nore to be paid off.
22. ibid 147.
23. TNA, ADM 50/39.
24. ibid.
25. *Norwich Mercury* 3 June 1797. Palmer *Perlustration*, Vol. III, pp.171-2.
26. Earl of Camperdown, *Admiral Duncan*, pp.141-2, quoting Ralfe's *Naval Biography*.
27. ibid p.147.
28. TNA, ADM 50/39.
29. Parker was hanged from the yardarm of the *Sandwich* on 30 June 1797.
30. Earl of Camperdown, *Admiral Duncan*, p.172.
31. ibid p.175.
32. ibid. Turner, *The Russian Squadron* with *Admiral Duncan's North Sea Fleet*, pp.215-6. They were to return, but missed the Battle of Camperdown.
33. Earl of Camperdown, *Admiral Duncan*, p.181.
34. ibid pp.185/6.
35. ibid p.174. TNA, ADM 1/524/187.
36. Earl of Camperdown, *Admiral Duncan*, p.184.
37. ibid pp.188-90.
38. TNA, ADM 1/524/223.
39. Earl of Camperdown, *Admiral Duncan*, pp.191-3.
40. ibid p.195.
41. ibid pp. 204-6. Duncan's account of the battle is contained in these pages.
42. ibid pp. 203-4.
43. ibid pp. 232-3.
44. Captain's logs, TNA, ADM 51/1213 *Adamant*, 1196 *Agincourt*, 4411 *Ardent*, 1207 *Bedford*, 1207 *Belliqueux*, 1195 *Director*, 1254 *Isis*, 1211 *Lancaster*, 1211 *Monarch*, 1231 *Monmouth*, 1232 *Montagu*, 1196 *Powerful*, 1235 *Russell*, 1212 *Triumph*, 1214 *Venerable*, 1210 *Veteran*.
45. TNA, ADM 51/1207.
46. James, *The Naval History of Great Britain*, Vol. 2, pp. 76-7. TNA, ADM 1/2597/76.
47. Earl of Camperdown, *Admiral Duncan*, p. 214. TNA, ADM 51/1214.
48. TNA, ADM 1/524/244.
49. Earl of Camperdown, *Admiral Duncan*, p. 207.
50. Captain's logs, TNA, ADM 51/- series, as note 44. *Norwich Mercury* 21 October 1797.
51. ibid.
52. TNA, ADM 1/2597/76-9, TNA, ADM 1/2017/141-3, 145-6.
53. TNA, ADM 2/134/174.
54. While De Winter's flagship *Vrieheid* was anchored in the Roads her bowsprit was cut away and subsequently salvaged by the Caister beachmen opposite Paine's Gibbet. Entered into the Admiralty Court on 24 October it was opportunistically purchased by J. Keymer and exhibited in the Pantheon, Norwich. 'Ladies and Gentlemen' paid one shilling and ' Tradespeople, etc' sixpence to see ' The greatest curiosity of its kind ever exhibited in the city,' NRO, Y/C 16/3,12. *Norwich Mercury* 4 November 1797.

3. The Helder, Copenhagen and Peace 1798-1802

1. On 10 November 1797 both men were granted the Freedom of the Borough of Yarmouth, 'as a Testimony of the Sense this Corporation entertains of the most important and eminent Services they have rendered in their Country by their most glorious brilliant and decisive victory over the Dutch fleet on the memorable eleventh of October last...' NRO, Y/C 19/15/199.
2. TNA, ADM 1/524/255.
3. *Norwich Mercury* 21 April 1798.
4. TNA, ADM 1/525/145, Earl of Camperdown, *Admiral Duncan*, p.300.
5. *Norwich Mercury* 16 June 1798. Palmer, *Perlustration*, Vol. I, p.383 for where Duncan and Onslow lodged.
6. *Norwich Mercury* 18 August 1798. The presence of warships in the Roads gave a great boost to the town's season when the 'great and the good' came to stay.
7. TNA, ADM 1/525/359. Onslow never returned and was officially discharged on 20 February 1799, TNA, ADM 2/137/171.
8. TNA, ADM 1/525/380, ADM 2/136/524.
9. *Norwich Mercury* 13, 27 October 1798.
10. TNA, ADM 1/525/143, 358.
11. ibid 202, 205.
12. TNA, ADM 1/526/250.
13. ibid 293.
14. Earl of Camperdown, *Admiral Duncan*, p.306. TNA, ADM 1/526/348, 386.
15. TNA, ADM 2/138/78.
16. TNA, ADM 1/527/428, 430.
17. ibid 422.
18. ibid 474.
19. ibid 489, 490.
20. TNA, ADM 1/527/494.
21. ibid 506, 510, 525.
22. The Duke's behaviour was mocked in the nursery rhyme 'The Grand Old Duke of York'.
23. TNA, ADM 1/527/625, ADM 108/63.
24. TNA, ADM 1/527/622, ADM 2/1356.
25. TNA, ADM 1/527/631, 634,716.
26. ibid 625, 716.
27. ibid 716.
28. ibid 662. *Norfolk Chronicle* 9 November 1799.
29. TNA, ADM 1/528/275. In July 1800 the Dutch ships and vessels at Hellevoet were the *Brutus* (74), *Jean De Wit* (68), *Dogger Bank* (68), *Hercules* (68), *Neptunus* (68), name unknown (64), *Endrought* (44), *Juno* (30), *Phoenix* (30), and the *Fly* brig.
30. Earl of Camperdown, *Admiral Duncan*, pp.337-341.
31. TNA, ADM 2/139/375.
32. TNA, ADM 6/27 26 April 1800.
33. Pope, *The Great Gamble*, pp.60-61. *Norwich Mercury* 16 August 1800. TNA, ADM 1/529/361.
34. TNA, ADM 1/529/367.
35. ibid 383.
36. *Norwich Mercury* 4 October 1800.
37. ibid 8 November 1800.
38. Palmer, *Perlustration*, Vol. I, p.185.
39. ibid.
40. ibid p.186.
41. This account of Nelson's visit is drawn from those in the *Norwich Mercury* and Palmer. Where they differ I have favoured the more contemporary newspaper version. Before leaving town Nelson gave £50 to the Mayor and 10 guineas to the minister to be distributed among the poor, sums seemingly covered by the £100 he asked Robert Warmington to advance him at the time. He also asked Warmington, as agent of the packet service, to settle Captain Deane's account for

transporting him and his party from the Continent, NMM AG/C/17/18. While at the Wrestlers the landlady, Mrs Suckling, asked Nelson for permission to change the name of the inn to the Nelson Arms, to which he replied, 'That would be absurd.., seeing that I have but one.' It became the Nelson Hotel instead. Palmer, *Perlustration*, Vol. I, p.186. The Newspaper has him saying to the innkeeper 'that he was perfectly welcome to change the name of his Inn - but that he must be sensible he had no arms to spare.' *Norwich Mercury* 29 November 1800. Captain Mosse was killed in the battle.

42. Gardiner, ed., *Nelson Against Napoleon*, pp.169-70.
43. TNA, ADM 2/141/30-31.
44. ibid 134, 427. TNA, ADM 6/27 31 January 1801.
45. *Dictionary of National Biography*, Sir Hyde Parker, 1739-1807.
46. TNA, ADM 6/27 31 January 1801.
47. TNA, ADM 50/65.
48. TNA, ADM 2/141/170.
49. ibid 158.
50. TNA, ADM 50/65.
51. TNA, ADM 1/530/221.
52. TNA, ADM 51/1371.
53. Pope, *The Great Gamble*, pp. 185-6. Nelson commented in a letter that, 'Dickson came on board today to say all were scandalized at his (Sir Hyde's) gross neglect..,' Pope, p.190.
54. ibid p.187. Troubridge was an M. P. for Yarmouth from 1802 to 1806.
55. TNA, ADM 50/65.
56. Pope, *The Great Gamble*, pp.193-9.
57. Pope considered the ensuing tragedy to be Sir Hyde's fault for not sending Totty's orders to Nepean to be forwarded to Sheerness, thereby negating the Rear-Admiral's need to call at Yarmouth on his way to the Skaw (p. 239). This is a somewhat harsh judgement as Sir Hyde had no way of knowing how close Totty and Graves were to Yarmouth when he was obliged to leave without them.
58. Pope, *The Great Gamble*, p.238.
59. ibid pp.238-9. A mound in Happisburgh churchyard marks the burial place of 119 of the sailors who were lost.
60. Four of the ships of the North Sea Squadron took part in the battle, the *Ardent, Monarch, Isis* and *Russell* and there were other connections, Pope, p.358.
61. Gardiner, *Nelson against Napoleon*, p.170. Nelson famously disobeyed Sir Hyde's signal to stop fighting, but the story that he put his telescope to his sightless eye and exclaimed, ' I really do not see the signal,' is considered to be apocryphal.
62. ibid.
63. ibid.
64. *Norwich Mercury* 2 May 1801. Pope draws attention to the fact that Bligh and Dickson did not get on and that this was the reason for the change of plan in respect of landing the wounded, p. 481.
65. *Norwich Mercury* 4 July 1801.
66. TNA, ADM 1/531/411-565.
67. TNA, ADM 6/27, 24 July 1801. Ever in a hurry Nelson wanted to attack and burn the Dutch ships at Hellevoet for if successful, 'he would probably [be awarded] medals and an earldom'. Hellevoet, however, was Dickson's responsibility so St. Vincent blocked the idea. Coleman, *Nelson*, p.274.
68. TNA, ADM 2/142/10, 231.
69. *Norwich Mercury* 25 July 1801. TNA, ADM 1/531/621.
70. *Norwich Mercury* 1, 22 August 1801.
71. TNA, ADM 1/532/906.
72. Knight, *Britain Against Napoleon*, pp. 215, 525.
73. *Norwich Mercury* 10 October 1801.
74. *Norwich Mercury* 14 November 1801.
75. Knight, *The Pursuit of Victory*, p.437.

76. TNA, ADM 1/533/137, ADM 2/143/86.
77. TNA, ADM 2/143/139.
78. TNA, ADM 1/533/165, *Norwich Mercury* 17 April 1802.
79. TNA, ADM 1/533/166.
80. ibid 167.
81. *Norwich Mercury* 8 May 1802.

4. The North Sea and Baltic Commands 1803-1814

1. Davey, *In Nelson's Wake*, p.4.
2. Knight, *Pursuit of Victory*, p.441.
3. Davey, *In Nelson's Wake*, pp.5-6.
4. James, *The Naval History of Great Britain*, Vol. 3, pp.175-6.
5. Knight, *Pursuit of Victory*, p. 444. Davey, *In Nelson's Wake*, p.6.
6. ibid.
7. Palmer, *Perlustration*, Vol. III, p.186.
8. TNA, ADM 6/28, 11 March 1803, ADM 2/144/358, 362.
9. TNA, ADM 1/534/61. James, *The Naval History of Great Britain*, Vol. 3, p.177.
10. Knight, *Pursuit of Victory*, p.446.
11. TNA, ADM 6/28 17 May 1803.
12. TNA, ADM 2/145/71.
13. *Steel's Navy List* May 1807.
14. *Norwich Mercury* May-October 1803. 'He [Thornbrough] was frequently to be seen on Yarmouth Jetty.' Palmer *Perlustration*, Vol. III, p.186. NMM ADM/A/2969.
15. TNA, ADM 2/146/200. In his Memorandum of Service Thornbrough does not acknowledge that he served under Keith, TNA, ADM 9/1/21.
16. *Norfolk Chronicle* 22 October, 17 December 1803.
17. ibid 19 November 1803.
18. TNA, ADM 1/1424/257, ADM 2/144/360. Pocock, *A Thirst for Glory*, p.159.
19. *Norfolk Chronicle* 13 October 1804. Thornbrough did not return to Yarmouth. In March 1805 he became Captain of the Fleet to Lord Gardner.
20. The exact date Douglas was appointed is not recorded.
21. *Norfolk Chronicle* 10 October 1805. Syrett and DiNardo, *The Commissioned Sea Officers of the Royal Navy*, pp.128 (Douglas) and 390 (Russell). Billy Douglas resided ashore in a house in the Market Place, at the south-east corner of Row 22. During the wars 'many of the rooms over the shops in the Market place were let as lodgings; and were frequently occupied by military and naval offerers', Palmer, *Perlustration*, Vol. I, pp.197, 201.
22. TNA, ADM 1/1424/190.
23. Knight, *Britain Against Napoleon*, pp. 357-64 for the shipbuilding section.
24. In 1804 a 'Mr Beck' was an overseer at Yarmouth, NMM, ADM/B/213.
25. The Naval vessels built at Yarmouth were the frigates *Boreas* and *Comus*, the ship-sloops *Cygnet*, *Ariel*, *Helena*, *Hyacinth* and *Raccoon*, the brig-sloops *Musquito*, *Pandora*, *Cephalus*, *Procis*, *Sparrow*, the gun-brigs, *Redbreast*, *Exertion*, *Fancy* and *Havock* and the schooners *Cuckoo*, *Woodcock*, *Wagtail*, *Crane*, *Quail*, and *Pigeon*, Winfield, *British Warships in the Age of Sail*.
26. *Norfolk Chronicle* 19 May, 2, 7 June 1804.
27. ibid 18, 25 August, 8 September 1804.
28. Winfield, *British Warships in the Age of Sail*, p.344.
29. ibid p.361.
30. Preston, *The Picture of Yarmouth*, p.109.
31. Davey, *In Nelson's Wake*, p.86, 138. TNA, ADM 2/152/276.
32. ibid 291, 297.
33. Davey, *In Nelson's Wake*, p.148.
34. ibid p.149.
35. ibid pp.150-1.
36. ibid.

37. ibid pp.151-2.
38. *Norfolk Chronicle* 11, 25 July 1807. James, *The Naval History of Great Britain*, Vol.4, pp.284-6.
39. *Norfolk Chronicle* 15 August 1807. TNA, ADM 106/3160, WO 55/733 28 August 1807.
40. Davey, *In Nelson's Wake*, pp.153-6.
41. See page 186.
42. *Norfolk Chronicle* 31 October, 7, 14 November 1807. Palmer, *Perlustration*, Vol. I, p.197.
43. Drower, *Heligoland*, pp.14-16.
44. ibid, pp. 17-19. James, *The Naval History of Great Britain*, Vol. 4, pp. 295-6.
45. *Norfolk chronicle* 12 March 1808.
46. Woodman, *The Victory of Seapower*, pp.119-21. *Norfolk Chronicle* 1 September 1810. The island had recently become a 'stone frigate.' notionally classified as a 50 gun ship.
47. Davey, *In Nelson's Wake*, pp.186-7. *Norfolk Chronicle* 7 May 1808.
48. ibid, *Norfolk Chronicle* 4,11 June, 17 September, 8 October 1808.
49. *Norfolk Chronicle* 1 April 1809. TNA, ADM 51/2934.
50. TNA, ADM 1/1429/142,149,440,441,445,605, ADM 1/1430/679,709,720.
51. Knight, *Britain Against Napoleon*, p.395. Woodman, *The Victory of Seapower*, p.135.
52. ibid, pp.136-140. A stickler for detail, on 20 February 1810, storekeeper Robert Warmington sent to the Navy Board, 'An Account of expenses incurred at North Yarmouth on account of the late Expedition to the Scheldt, as would not have been incurred in the Ordinary course of Service had not the Expedition taken place.' In it he detailed stores provided to gunboats 1, 57 and 64 and the pilotage of gunboats 1,3,31,46 and 57, for the total sum of £37-13-9, TNA, ADM 106/1976 20 February 1810.
53. *Norfolk Chronicle* 8 October 1808.
54. ibid 5 November 1808.
55. ibid 14 January, 25 February, 5 August 1809.
56. *Norfolk Chronicle* 1810, 1811, 1812,1813.
57. TNA, ADM 2/158/494, 498.
58. TNA, ADM 2/160/332. Murray lived in a house which stood next to the town wall, on the south side of what was to become Regent Road. Palmer relates that, 'Lodgings were then scarce in the town; and there were but few houses "on the Denes". Ludicrous stories are told of the shifts to which the hospitable admiral was driven by the smallness of his residence; post-captains being, it is said, sometimes obliged to sleep two in a bed!' *Perlustration*, Vol. III, p.89.

5. Victualling

1. For an overview of this subject see Knight and Wilcox, *Sustaining the Fleet*. This book contains a specific chapter on the victualling service at Yarmouth.
2. TNA, ADM 111/121 3 January 1791, ADM 112/160/70.
3. TNA, ADM 111/125 6 November 1792, ADM 112/140. Knight and Wilcox, *Sustaining the Fleet*, p.146.
4. TNA, ADM 111/129 6, 13, 21, 23, Dec 1793, ADM 111/131 29 April 1794, ADM 112/160/79.
5. TNA, ADM 111/131 30 April 1794, ADM 112/180.
6. Paget, ed, *Sir J. Paget, Memoirs and Letters*, pp.1-3.
7. For the background on Dawson Turner see Goodman, ed, *Dawson Turner*. Turner's letters are held in the library of Trinity College, Cambridge. The relationship between Paget and Turner would repay further study.
8. John Grant lost the rum contract in early 1796.
9. TNA, ADM 1/523/86.
10. TNA, ADM 111/140 16 August 1796.
11. TNA, ADM 111/139 17, 27 May 1796.
12. PLLB 16 June 1796. TNA, ADM 111/139 9 June 1796.
13. PLLB 19 June 1796. A copy of the guidance was entered into the Common Letter Book, but this document does not seem to have survived, TNA, ADM 111/139 9 June 1796.
14. PLLB 16 June 1796, TNA, ADM 51/1130.
15. PLLB 1 July 1796.

16. PLLB 1,5, 14 July 1796.
17. PLLB 31 July, 4 August 1796.
18. PLLB 14, 19 July 1796.
19. PLLB 19 July 1796. This is at odds with Pitt's letter to the Victualling Board of 17 November 1796 in which he states that, 'Many of the Captains of the Men of War object to sending their launches for fear of loosing their men'.
20. PLLB 15 August 1796.
21. Knight and Wilcox, *Sustaining the Fleet*, p.195.
22. TNA, ADM 111/140 20 August 1796.
23. PLLB 11, 29 September 1796.
24. PLLB 4 December 1796.
25. PLLB 23 March 1797. TNA, ADM 111/142 30 March 1797.
26. PLLB 26 March, 9 April 1797. TNA, ADM 111/142 30 March 1797. The whereabouts of these storehouses is not recorded. Paget owned warehouses behind his house on South Quay which he later let to the Ordnance Board (see pp.95-96). Lewes mentions two cheese stores, one on the east, and the other on the west side of the river, PLLB 7 December 1797.
27. PLLB 19 October 1796.
28. PLLB 17, 22 March 1797.
29. The pump for this well is still to be seen at the foot of the White Lion Steps in Gorleston. PLLB 10 October 1796.
30. TNA, ADM 112/182.
31. Knight and Wilcox, *Sustaining the Fleet*, p.197. TNA, ADM 111/140 20 September 1796, ADM 112/140.
32. PLLB 25 September 1796.
33. PLLB 10 October 1796.
34. PLLB 3 October, 20 November 1796. In respect of the *Elizabeth & Ann* Mr 'Paget has sent to the different places along the coast and offered the salvage - for such of the casks as might come on shore, but has not yet heard of any of them...'
35. PLLB 10 October 1796.
36. ibid.
37. PLLB 5 November 1796.
38. TNA, ADM 111/14 11 November 1796.
39. PLLB 28 December 1796.
40. PLLB 14 January 1797.
41. NRO, Y/C 19/40/76 2 March 1799. The lease was formally granted on 10 June 1799, NRO, Y/C 32/2/80.
42. PLLB 14, 20 October 1796.
43. PLLB 7 April 1797. Knight and Wilcox, *Sustaining the Fleet*, p.194, note 6. TNA, ADM 111/143 4 April 1797.
44. PLLB 7 April 1797.
45. PLLB 28 April 1797.
46. PLLB 4 May 1797.
47. PLLB 2 July 1797.
48. PLLB 6 July 1797. TNA, ADM 111/144 7 July 1797.
49. Knight and Wilcox, *Sustaining the Fleet*, p. 200. PLLB 6 August 1797.
50. PLLB 24 September, 4, 5 October 1797, 11, 27 February 1798.
51. NA, ADM 111/145, 4 October 1797.
52. PLLB 5, 6 October 1797.
53. PLLB 8 October 1797.
54. Knight and Wilcox, *Sustaining the Fleet*, p. 203-4. Paget, *Memoirs and Letters*, pp. 3-4. This dinner took place on 11 October 1798 at the Duke's Head to celebrate the Battle of the Nile and the first anniversary of Camperdown, Earl of Camperdown, *Admiral Duncan*, pp. 374-7.
55. PLLB 12 November 1797.
56. PLLB 19 November 1797.

57. PLLB 16, 18 March 1798.
58. Palmer, *Perlustration*, Vol. I, p. 234.
59. PLLB 12 April, 24 June 1798. TNA, ADM 111/148, 15 September 1798.
60. PLLB 8,12 August 1798.
61. PLLB 15,25 July 1798.
62. PLLB 2 August 1798.
63. PLLB 23 September 1798.
64. PLLB 16 October 1798.
65. PLLB 21 October 1798.
66. PLLB 9 December 1798.
67. TNA, ADM 111/145, 7 December 1797. PLLB 12 September 1798. Thomas Martin became a Freeman of the Borough of Yarmouth in 1785 and died in 1801, aged 40.
68. TNA, ADM 112/185, 186, 187.
69. Knight and Wilcox, *Sustaining the Fleet*, pp. 205-6.
70. TNA, ADM 112/141.
71. Knight and Wilcox, *Sustaining the Fleet*, p. 206.
72. TNA, ADM 111/163 4 June 1802, ADM 112/188.
73. TNA, ADM 1/533/166.
74. TNA, ADM 2/145/188-9.
75. Knight and Wilcox, *Sustaining the Fleet*, pp. 206-7. TNA, ADM 111/167 27 May 1803.
76. ibid p.207.
77. TNA, ADM 112/189.
78. Knight and Wilcox, *Sustaining the Fleet*, p. 207.
79. ibid pp. 207-208. TNA, ADM 111/167 10 June 1803.
80. Knight and Wilcox, *Sustaining the Fleet*, p. 208, quoting Wellcome 6815/144 5 May, 6815/159 6 July 1803. TNA, ADM 112/189.
81. TNA, ADM 111/168 5 July 1803. By the time Samuel Paget Jnr. retired from naval victualling he had become a successful businessman in shipping and brewing. He also held a commission as a Lieutenant-Colonel in the local volunteers. Between 1800 and 1813 he had 11 children, including the eminent surgeon Sir James. In 1817 he served as Mayor. Later in life he lost his fortune and , 'at the last was very poor.' He died in 1857.
82. Knight and Wilcox, *Sustaining the Fleet*, p.130. TNA, ADM 111/169 27 December 1803. Peter Mellish was dead by then. ADM 112/189.
83. TNA, ADM 1/1424/52.
84. ibid.
85. ibid.
86. ibid.
87. ibid.
88. ibid 222.
89. ibid 239, 251.
90. John Walter was in effect the Victualling Agent at Yarmouth and as such was in direct contact with the Victualling Board. In addition to his agency duties he ran his own side-line in valuing live oxen. He died in 1811, aged 50.
91. TNA, ADM 111/187 16 April 1808, ADM 111/191 26 May 1809.
92. TNA, ADM 111/192 22 August 1809.
93. TNA, ADM 111/196 25 September 1810.
94. NRO, Y/C 19/43/75, Y/C 32/2/196.
95. Knight and Wilcox, *Sustaining the Fleet*, pp. 149-153.
96. TNA, ADM 112/161, ADM 112/198. Knight and Wilcox, *Sustaining the Fleet*, p.153.
97. TNA, ADM 111/198.
98. ibid 12 February 1811, TNA, ADM 111/205 2 October 1812, ADM 111/207 23 April 1813.
99. TNA, ADM 112/161 20 July 1813, ADM 111/208 23, 24 July 1813.
100. TNA, ADM 112/190-201.
101. TNA, ADM 112/193-200.

6. Naval Stores

1. TNA, ADM 106/2657 4,7 January 1796.
2. ibid 9 February 1796.
3. ibid 10 February 1796.
4. ibid 13 February 1796.
5. ibid.
6. ibid 16 February 1796, ADM 12/70.
7. TNA, ADM 106/3158.
8. TNA, ADM 106/2657 27 February 1796.
9. TNA, ADM 106/2660 10 March 1797.
10. ibid 10 October 1797.This put him on the same footing as the storekeepers at Deal, Leith and Kinsale, NMM ADM/A/2877.
11. TNA, ADM 106/2661 31 January 1798, ADM 1/2017/146, ADM 106/3158.
12. TNA, ADM 106/2661 13 February 1798, TNA, MRQ 1/17.
13. Palmer records that these whaling ventures, 'were encouraged by the legislature, for, under conditions made in pursuance of the 26 and 28 George III., if five vessels sailing from Yarmouth to Greenland returned within fourteen months and produced a certain quantity of oil, the owners were entitled to bounty.' In 1794 the bounty was refused on some pretext, but Sir Edmund Lacon brought a successful action against this decision, *Perlustration* Vol. III, p. 230-1.
14. TNA, ADM 106/1976 21 April, 26 November 1798.
15. TNA, ADM 106/2661 4 December 1798.
16. TNA, ADM 1063/3158.
17. TNA, ADM 106/2661 16 November 1798.
18. TNA, ADM 106/1976 12 January 1799, ADM 106/2662 15, 29 January 1799.
19. TNA,ADM 106/1976 23 April 1799.
20. TNA, ADM 106/3158.
21. TNA, ADM 1/530/6.
22. TNA, ADM 106/1976 20, 28 January 1801, ADM 106/2664 30 January, 31 March 1801.
23. TNA, ADM 106/1976 11 May, 11 October 1802. For a list of the stores remaining on 30 April 1802 see NMM, ADM/B/204/371.
24. ibid 11 November 1802.
25. TNA, ADM 106/2665 16 November 1802.
26. TNA, ADM 106/1976 26 November 1802, ADM 106/2665, 30 November 1802.
27. TNA, ADM 106/1976 29 December 1802. The staff at that time consisted of the storekeeper, his clerk, and the extra clerk and warehouseman. Labourers were hired as and when required NMM, ADM/BP/22A.
28. TNA, ADM 106/2666 4 January 1803.
29. ibid 11 January 1803.
30. TNA, ADM 106/2670 23 June 1807, ADM 106/1976 22 April 1805, ADM 106/3159.
31. TNA, ADM 106/2666 12 August 1803.
32. TNA, ADM 106/3159.
33. NMM, ADM/A/2969 20, 21 October 1803. TNA, ADM 1/1424/25, 50.
34. TNA, ADM 106/3159.
35. TNA, ADM 106/1424/282.
36. TNA, ADM 106/1976 3 February 1806.
37. TNA, ADM 1/1425/570.
38. TNA, ADM 106/1976 20 September 1804.
39. *Norfolk Chronicle* 4 October 1806.
40. TNA, ADM 106/1976 11 April 1805, ADM 106/2668 16 April 1805.
41. NMM, ADM/A/2964 24 May 1803.
42. TNA, ADM 106/2668 26 November 1805.
43. TNA, ADM 106/2670 14 April, 1 May 1807.
44. TNA, ADM 106/1976 13 June 1807.
45. ibid 18 July 1807. Preston refers to this dredger as the 'Didelling Engine' which he says was built

by order of the Corporation 'about twenty-six years since' i.e in 1793. He gives a good description of its method of operation, *Preston, The Picture of Yarmouth*, p.160.

46. *Norfolk chronicle* 15 August 1807.
47. TNA, ADM 106/3160.
48. TNA, ADM 106/1976 13 August 1807.
49. ibid 27 August 1807.
50. TNA, ADM 106/2670 17 November 1807.
51. TNA, ADM 106/1976 14 December 1807.
52. TNA, ADM 12/127 2 December 1807.
53. TNA, ADM 1/1426.
54. TNA, ADM 106/1976 17 February 1808.
55. TNA, ADM 106/2672 10 January 1809.
56. TNA, ADM 106/1976 6 February 1809.
57. ibid 14 March 1809, TNA, ADM 106/2672 21 March 1809.
58. TNA, ADM 106/2674 12 January, 22 May 1810.
59. NRO, FX 200/6. The Yarmouth Naval Yard pay-lists for 1807-1815, TNA, ADM 42/2061, only cover the lighter crew and the two men at the port-admiral's signal station. If there were other lists they do not seem to have survived.
60. Seemingly of humble origins Robert Warmington established himself in Yarmouth as a prominent wine merchant, local politician and consular representative. When it came to maritime and mercantile business in the town he was the man to go to. His obituary in the *Norfolk Chronicle* reads '1812 Sept 22. Died at Yarmouth aged 73, Mr Robert Warmington. He served the office of Mayor in 1790 and 1808 and was Prussian, Swedish, Danish, Hamburgh and American Vice-Consul, and naval Store Keeper at this port.' He was interred in the parish church.
61. TNA, ADM 106/1976 15 December 1812.
62. ibid 21 September 1813.

7. Ordnance Stores

1. NRO, Y/C 19/37/161.
2. NRO, Y/C 19/15/109.
3. TNA, WO 47/2364 28 March 1793.
4. TNA, WO 55/2357.
5. TNA, WO 47/2366 31 March 1795.
6. ibid, TNA, WO 55/2357/7.
7. TNA, WO 47/2389 13 July 1803.
8. ibid, WO 55/2357.
9. ibid items 14-17, TNA, ADM 47/2395, ADM 47/2397, ADM 47/2413.
10. TNA, WO 55/974 27 December 1805, WO 47/2399 25 July 1804.
11. ibid. For Morse see Knight, *Britain Against Napoleon*, pp. 274-5.
12. TNA, WO 55/973 28 July 1804.
13. ibid 23 August 1804.
14. TNA, WO 55/974 28 January 1805.
15. ibid 1 May 1805.
16. TNA, WO 55/2357.
17. TNA, WO 55/733 20 May 1807.
18. ibid 24 July 1808.
19. ibid 28 August 1807. According to Preston the Royal Arsenal 'was originally designed and constructed to contain a sufficient quantity of stores for sea service during war, to equip two sail of the line, four frigates, and six sloops and, for the land service, to furnish ten thousand stand of arms.' He went on to say that the cost of the building was between fourteen and fifteen thousand pounds, Preston, *The Picture of Yarmouth*, p.1.
20. TNA, WO 55/733 2 September 1807, WO 55/2450.
21. TNA, WO 55/974 9 October 1805.
22. NRO, Y/C 19/42/366.

23. NRO, Y/C 19/16/113.
24. NRO, Y/C 19/43/73, Y/C 19/16/154.
25. TNA, WO 54/512. On 25 June 1804 the Board ordered Jones to hire a vessel to take ordnance stores out to the Texel bound transports anchored in the Roads. The vessel he secured was the *Elizabeth* owned by Thomas Morley.
26. George Hoste was the Norfolk born brother of the celebrated naval officer Captain Sir William Hoste of 'Remember Nelson' fame.

8. The Roads Anchorage

1. TNA, ADM 1/523/86, 93, 296.
2. TNA, ADM 106/2653 29 January 1795, ADM 106/2657 23 February, 17 March 1796.
3. Higgins, *The Beachmen*, pp.133, 149-59.
4. TNA, ADM 106/2661 20 November 1798, ADM 106/1976 21 December 1798.
5. TNA, ADM 106/2657 28 January, 18 March 1796.
6. TNA, ADM 1/526/2.
7. TNA, ADM 106/2662 8 January 1799.
8. ibid 25 January 1799.
9. TNA, ADM 1/526/64.
10. Earl of Camperdown, *Admiral Duncan*, pp. 380-2.
11. TNA. ADM 106/1976 20 June 1802. The letter is endorsed 'Was Mr Paterson directed to send this account ' with the answer 'no' written against it.
12. TNA, ADM 106/1976 6 November 1799.
13. ibid 30 November 1799.
14. ibid 26 June, 24 September 1802.
15. ibid 11, 12 November 1800.
16. ibid 15 November 1802.
17. NRO, Y/C 36/20, 21.
18. TNA, ADM 1/531/674, ADM 106/2664 7 August 1801.
19. Higgins, *The Beachmen*, pp. 27-28, quoting TNA, ADM 7/386.
20. TNA, ADM 106/1976 14 February 1808.
21. ibid. The boats were the *Lord Duncan* and *Benjamin* (Winterton), *Percis* (Palling), *Elizabeth* (Happisburgh).
22. ibid 7 March 1808.
23. ibid 21 March 1808.
24. ibid 28 April, 3 May 1808, TNA, ADM 106/2671 3 May 1808.
25. TNA, ADM 1/1427 13, 18 November 1808.
26. Malster, *Saved from the Sea*, p.19.
27. ibid.
28. Walthew, *From Rock and Tempest*, p.28.
29. TNA, ADM 1/1433/252.
30. Grocott, *Shipwrecks of the Revolutionary & Napoleonic Eras*, p.196.
31. ibid p. 262.
32. TNA, ADM 1/1427 3 November 1808.
33. ibid 29 June 1808.
34. TNA, ADM 1/1433/253.
35. *An Historical Guide to Great Yarmouth*. Palmer, *Manship*, p. 331. *Norfolk Chronicle* 1 October 1807.
36. TNA, ADM 1/3527 5 January 1808, ADM 1/1427 17 January 1808.
37. ibid.
38. NRO, Y/PH I, pp. 234, 239, 242. Finch-Crisp, *Chronological Retrospect of the History of Yarmouth*, p. 65.
39. NMM, ADM BP/29B 11 July 1809, ADM BP/28 18 July 1809.
40. Preston, *The Picture of Yarmouth*, p.13.

9 Raising Seaman

1. Lavery, *Nelson's Navy*, pp.120-8.
2. TNA, ADM 2/123/6-9, 25.
3. ibid 26-27, TNA, ADM 9/6/1667. Glasford had commanded the sloop *Alderney* at Yarmouth in the final months of the Fourth Anglo-Dutch War.
4. NRO, Y/C 19/15/108 25 February 1793.
5. *Norwich Mercury* 6 April 1793. TNA, ADM 1/1841.
6. Dancy, *The Myth of the Press Gang*, p. 34.
7. *Norwich Mercury* 14 March 1795.
8. Jane Glasford was buried in the churchyard at Yarmouth 9 January 1795, aged 46.
9. Palmer makes reference to Hunter's arrival in the following terms, ' One of the Miss Hunters became the wife of Admiral Hunter under peculiar circumstances. The admiral then Captain Hunter, was appointed to a command at Yarmouth. By some mistake his luggage was taken to Miss Hunter's house, she being the only person of the name known to the porter. She was no relation to the captain; but this occurrence led to an introduction and ultimately to a marriage.' Their wedding took place at the parish church on 25 September 1798. *Perlustration*, Vol.II, p. 378.
10. TNA, ADM 2/127, pp. 299-302.
11. TNA, ADM 1/579, 2 April 1795.
12. ibid, TNA, ADM 30/34 for Glasford's disbursements.
13. Lavery, *Nelson's Navy*, pp. 126, 128.
14. ibid p.128.
15. TNA, ADM 1/1915 20 July 1796.
16. ibid 28 November 1796.
17. TNA, ADM 2/124/450.
18. *Norwich Mercury* 3 February, 19 May 1798.
19. TNA, ADM 1/1919 27 May 1798.
20. TNA, ADM 2/141/525. Philip is best known for founding the first penal colony in Australia and serving as its governor.
21. TNA, ADM 1/579 5 December 1801.
22. TNA, ADM 1/1925 26 August 1801.
23. ibid 30 August 1801. Hunter was appointed to command the Cromer to Fosdyke Wash Sea Fencible District in 1805 and was superannuated in 1808, having been promoted to the rank of rear-admiral. He lived in Southtown, Yarmouth, until his death in 1830, aged 98. Palmer records that, 'He had sailed with the former Captain Cook; and being a man of much simplicity, the wits had an opportunity of saying that like Commodore Anson the worthy admiral had been "round the world but never in it." *Perlustration*, Vol. III, p. 267.
24. TNA, ADM 1/532/846.
25. TNA, ADM 1/532/1009.
26. *Norfolk Chronicle* 19 March 1803.
27. TNA, ADM 9/2/331 (Campbell).
28. TNA, ADM 9/7/2109 (Lucas).
29. TNA, ADM 1/1633 8 May 1803.
30. ibid 12 May 1803.
31. ibid.
32. ibid 15 May 1803.
33. ibid 27 May 1803.
34. ibid.
35. ibid 6 July 1803.
36. TNA, ADM 1/1424/5.
37. TNA, ADM 1/633 23 June, 27 November 1803.
38. TNA, ADM 1/1637 29 February 1804.
39. *Norfolk Chronicle* 11 May 1805.
40. TNA, ADM 1/1641 24 August 1805.

41. TNA, ADM 9/2/331 (Campbell), ADM 11/15/134, ADM 1/1994 16 October 1806.
42. TNA, ADM 1/1805/124.
43. ibid 127.
44. TNA, ADM 9/7/2109 (Lucas), ADM 11/15, ADM 1/1805 1 November 1807.
45. TNA, ADM 11/15/232, ADM 9/4/992 (Heddington).
46. TNA, ADM 1/1934 17 April 1808.
47. ibid 2 August 1808.
48. TNA, ADM 1/1426 11 December 1807, ADM 2/155/18, ADM 9/7/2120 (Gilchrist). Palmer, *Perlustration*, Vol. III, p. 294.
49. TNA, ADM 1/1934 1 September 1808.
50. TNA, ADM 1/1942 7 November 1810. Heddington went on to become agent for prisoners of war at the Valleyfield Depot from January to June 1811, agent for prisoners of war at Edinburgh Castle from June to August 1811, and regulating captain at King's Lynn from July 1813 to April 1814.
51. TNA, ADM 1/1428/60.
52. TNA, ADM 1/1430/880.
53. ibid 1420, ADM 1/1431/188.
54. ibid.
55. ibid 355, 364.
56. ibid 616.
57. ibid 298.
58. TNA, ADM 9/7/2284 (Blaquire).

10 The Sick and Wounded

1. TNA, ADM 102/825.
2. ibid.
3. ibid. Of this total 208 were lodged with Ann Briggs, 59 with Mary Bullock and 16 with Mary Sheerman. Some 21 officers were taken in by Mary Barber.
4. TNA, ADM 1/524/128.
5. ibid.
6. ibid.
7. ibid.
8. ibid.
9. TNA, ADM 98/18/293, NMM, ADM/F/28 28 September 1797.
10. TNA, ADM 98/18/300, 303-6.
11. ibid.
12. ibid 331. NMM, ADM/E/46 23 November 1797. Between February 1793 and his dismissal in November 1797 Fielding provided for around 1200 sick and wounded seamen of which some 530 were discharged as unserviceable, 290 went back to sea, 170 ran (deserted) and 80 died. Most of the remainder became the responsibility of his successor, TNA, ADM 102/825. He retained his position as agent for prisoners of war until the end of the conflict, but for this role he was responsible to the Transport Board.
13. James, *The Naval History of Great Britain*, Vol.2, p.380.
14. TNA, ADM 1/2597/77.
15. TNA, ADM 101/85/7. NRO Y/D 87/30 19 October 1797. On 22 October Thomas Rowlandson published an etching entitled ' GLORIOUS DEFEAT of the DUTCH NAVY.' It depicts a view of the six Dutch prizes anchored in the Roads 'DRAWN on the SPOT' with in the foreground a line of men carrying wounded seamen. He could not have prepared his sketch earlier than the 19th when the last prize arrived. By then the majority of the British and Dutch wounded had been landed at the wherry quay. The small number of men shown on stretchers are probably the last of the Dutchmen. Surprisingly he got the date of the battle wrong and mistakes the sunken *Delft* for the *Haarlem*.
16. TNA, ADM 1/2597/76.
17. TNA, ADM 98/18/306. NMM, ADM/F/28 18 October 1797. TNA, ADM 102/825. Of the

wounded 43 came from the *Ardent*, 40 the *Belliqueux*, 36 the *Triumph*, 27 the *Bedford*, four each from the *Russell* and *Monmouth* and one each from the *Veteran* and *Agincourt*. No wounded were landed from the *Lancaster* as the captain and surgeon of that ship did not think the shore accommodation good enough. The variety and severity of the wounds bare testimony to the fierceness of the fighting.

18. TNA, ADM 98/18/306. NMM, ADM/F/28 18 October 1797.
19. NMM, ADM/F/28, Blair's report, 3 November 1797. One of these volunteers was surgeon and anatomist John Bell (1763-1820). As a result of his first-hand experience at Yarmouth he wrote a *Memoir on the Present State of Naval and Military Surgery*.
20. NMM, ADM/F/28, Blair's report. *Norwich Mercury* 28 October 1797. TNA, ADM 102/825.
21. NMM. ADM/F/28, Blair's report. TNA, ADM 103/458. NRO, Y/PD 28/21. All the Dutch prizes were represented except the *Jupiter*, with 46 coming from the *Alkmaar*, 37 from the *Gelykheid*, 34 from the *Wassenaar*, 31 from De Winter's flagship *Vryheid*, 30 the *Haarlem*, 16 the *Hercules*, six the *Admiral de Vries* and three from the *Delft*.
22. NMM, ADM/F/28, Blair's report. TNA, ADM 102/825.
23. NMM, ADM/F/28, Blair's report.
24. ibid TNA, ADM 98/18/317.
25. ibid 333.
26. ibid TNA, ADM 2/134/430-1.
27. The relevant Barrack Office records have not survived. That permission was given is to be deduced from subsequent events.
28. James, *The Naval History of Great Britain*, Vol. 2, p. 380.
29. TNA, ADM 101/85/7.
30. TNA, ADM 2/134/387. Young took exception to being superseded by a man a hundred places below him in the seniority list, seeing it as a 'tacit censure' of his conduct. Nevertheless he respected Snipe and worked well with him before re-joining his ship. If Snipe was aboard the *Sandwich* at the time he would have witnessed the main events of the Nore Mutiny from the decks of its leader's 'flagship'.
31. TNA, ADM 98/18/349. NMM, ADM/F/28 15 December 1797.
32. TNA, ADM 98/18/366-71. NMM ADM/F/28 3 January 1797.
33. Smyth, *The Effect of the Nitrous Vapour, in Preventing and Destroying Contagion*, p.152.
34. TNA, ADM 102/825.
35. TNA, ADM 98/19/58. ADM 2/136/231. NMM, ADM/F/29 5 September 1798.
36. TNA, ADM 2/129/32.
37. TNA, ADM 2/136/95, ADM 98/19/37-8.
38. ibid.
39. ibid 73, TNA, ADM 2/136/405. This was probably the dwelling that later became Bauleah House.
40. TNA, ADM 98/19/120.
41. ibid.
42. ibid 181-2.
43. NRO, PD 28/19-21.
44. *Norwich Mercury* 4 November 1797.
45. TNA, ADM 1/526/1.
46. ibid 188.
47. NRO, Y/C 19/15/230.
48. TNA, ADM 99/52 25 October 1799.
49. ibid.
50. *Norwich Mercury* 4 October 1800.
51. NRO, PD 28/21.
52. NRO, PD 28/22. As it is written in one neat hand this document appears to be a copy prepared at a later date.
53. *Norwich Mercury* 14 September 1799.
54. TNA, ADM 99/52, 11 September 1799.
55. ibid, 20 September 1799.

56. TNA, AO 1/1522/227, AO 1/1524/286.
57. *Norwich Mercury* 26 October 1799.
58. ibid. It is unclear where these buildings stood, but one of them, hired from Sir Edmund Lacon to house sick and wounded Russian soldiers, became the temporary hospital in the subsequent war, NMM ADM/E/49 24 November 1803.
59. TNA, ADM 1/527/714, 739.
60. *Norwich Mercury* 7 December 1799.
61. ibid 4 January 1800.
62. TNA, ADM 1/528/286, ADM 1/529/304, 310.
63. Palmer, *Perlustration*. Vol. III, p. 123.
64. *Norwich Mercury* 18 April 1801.
65. TNA, ADM 1/530/374.
66. ibid 391.
67. ibid 395. Pope, *The Great Gamble* p. 481.
68. ibid 396. TNA, ADM 51/1333 *Monarch*, 1358 *Isis*, 4458 *Holstein*. The wounded men from the *Holstein* comprised 29 from the *Edgar*, 18 from the *Ardent*, 13 each the *Bellona* and *Defiance*, six from the *Glatton*, five the *Polyphemus*, four each the *Monarch* and *Alcemene*, three the *Elephant* and one from the *Ganges*. The Danish prize used as a hospital ship was laid up in ordinary at Yarmouth until October 1802 when it was moved to Chatham. TNA, ADM 102/827. Palmer records that one of the young surgeons was Martin Tupper who afterwards became an eminent surgeon in London, *Perlustration*, Vol. III, p.78.
69. *Norwich Mercury* 4 July 1801.
70. Palmer, *Perlustration*. Vol. III, p.78.
71. TNA, ADM 102/825.
72. TNA, ADM 1/1917 26 October 1797.
73. TNA, ADM 1/525/235.
74. ibid.
75. TNA, ADM 2/141/308-15.
76. ibid.
77. ibid.
78. ibid 165, ADM 9/6/1776 (Lynne). In July 1803 Lieutenant Lynne became governor of the naval hospital at Deal and remained there until April 1804 when he transferred to the Greenwich hospital.
79. TNA, ADM 98/20/290. William Taylor Jnr. had been working as an assistant surgeon at the hospital.
80. ibid 292. In March 1803 Doctor Snipe was appointed to inspect seamen raised in the neighbourhood of London, but in May that year he became physician to Nelson's Mediterranean Fleet. Did their chance meeting at Yarmouth in 1801 influence this appointment? He died in 1805 as a result of an illness contracted while visiting Messina in order to negotiate a supply of lemon juice.
81. TNA, ADM 102/829.
82. TNA, ADM 1/3526 9 June 1803.
83. TNA, ADM 106/1976 3 November 1803 and an undated letter. To gather the information Warmington consulted Thomas Watson, the pier master.
84. TNA, ADM 2/146/308-9.
85. TNA, ADM 105/20 24 November 1803, NMM, ADM/E/49 23 November 1803.
86. ibid TNA, ADM 105/20 24 November 1803.
87. ibid.
88. ibid. It was necessary to be in the navy to be surgeon at a naval hospital.
89. TNA, ADM 2/146/420, ADM 104/1.
90. TNA, ADM 6/28, ADM 2/146/473, ADM 11/14 3 May 1804. Larke had joined the navy as an able seaman in January 1796 aboard the frigate *Hebe*. As a midshipman on board the *Prince George* (98) he took part in the battle of Cape St. Vincent and received the naval general service medal for that service, ADM 9/7/2397 (Larke).

91. TNA, ADM 102/830. It is unclear how these patients were cared for from October 1803 as no musters survive for the period.
92. TNA, ADM 102/830-2, ADM 104/1, ADM 101/101/3.
93. *Norfolk chronicle* 14 January 1808. James, Vol.5, p.31. The *Nassau* (II) was the former Danish ship of the line *Holstein*, taken at Copenhagen in 1801 and refitted in 1805 for naval service.
94. TNA, ADM 51/1757 (Nassau), ADM 51/1740 (Stately).
95. ibid *Norfolk chronicle* 5 May 1808. TNA, ADM 102/832.
96. TNA, ADM 99/61/83-88, ADM 102/838, ADM 102/832.
97. ibid.
98. TNA, ADM 99/61/106, ADM 104/1.
99. TNA, ADM 2/154/364.
100. TNA, ADM 105/22 19 July 1806.
101. NRO, Y/C 19/41/100, 109, 112, Y/C 19/16/43-4. NMM, ADM/E/49 15 November 1803.
102. NRO, Y/C 19/42/373, Y/C 19/16/115.
103. TNA, ADM 105/22.
104. ibid.
105. ibid.
106. ibid.
107. ibid 2 August 1806.
108. TNA, ADM 1/3527 6 June 1807.
109. TNA, ADM 105/22 31 January 1807.
110. TNA, ADM 98/24/46.
111. Bentham was absent in Russia, assessing the possibility of the dockyards there building warships for the navy. While he was away Goodrich, an engineer by profession, deputised for him. On his return, in October 1807, Bentham found that his post as Inspector General within the Admiralty had been abolished, but on 3 December 1808 he was appointed Chief Architect and Engineer in the Navy Office, Knight, *Britain against Napoleon*, pp. 378-9. This change has complicated the unravelling of the design process for the new hospital.
112. TNA, ADM 1/3527 6 June 1807.
113. ibid 8-10 August, 23 September 1807, ADM 2/153/102, ADM 98/24/154.
114. ibid.
115. TNA, ADM 1/3527 16 April 1808.
116. TNA, ADM 98/24/228.
117. TNA, ADM 2/154/368. This must have been confirmatory because the *Norfolk Chronicle* of 11 June 1808 had already announced that the order had been made.
118. Pilkington's involvement in the project is recorded in an inscription over the south entrance to the north range which reads: GUILEMO PILKINGTON ARCHITECTO A.D. 1809.
119. *Norfolk chronicle* 28 August 1813. TNA, ADM 104/1.
120. TNA, ADM 140/393-425.
121. TNA, ADM 102/840, Preston, *The Picture of Yarmouth*, p.6.
122. NRO, Y/C 19/16/158. Peto (1780-1830) was the uncle of the better known Samuel Morton Peto, entrepreneur civil engineer and railway constructor.
123. Preston, *The Picture of Yarmouth*, p.104. Palmer, *Perlustration*, Vol. III, p. 206.
124. NRO, Y/C 19/43/113.
125. NRO, Y/C 19/16/162.
126. NRO Y/C 19/43/348. The following day Dover Colby and Simon Smith were given permission to make bricks on the North Denes, transport them to the South Denes, and burn them there.
127. ibid 378.
128. TNA, ADM 102/840. Preston in his *The Picture of Yarmouth* says the works cost £120,000.
129. ibid.
130. TNA, ADM 102/833.
131. Palmer, *Perlustration*, Vol. III, pp. 206-7. Druery, *Historical and Topographical Notices of Great Yarmouth*, p. 89. As secretary to the Haven and Pier Commissioners Druery had first-hand knowledge of the problem.

132. TNA, ADM 102/835, ADM 102/839.
133. NRO, PD 28/136, 137. The burial register for 1813 to June 1819 does not appear to have survived.
134. ibid.
135. ibid *Norfolk Chronicle* 15, 22 February 1806, 31 October 1807.
136. ibid 20 January 1810.
137. NRO, PD 28/137.

11. Prisoners of War

1. Chamberlain, *Hell Upon Water*, pp.58-60,81.
2. TNA, ADM 103/103.
3. TNA, ADM 2/123/338.
4. TNA, TS 21/81. For some time after the wars Row 135 was known as Old Prison Row.
5. *Norwich Mercury* 2 March 1793.
6. The Transport Board took over responsibility for prisoners of war in 1795.
7. TNA, ADM 105/144 19 August 1798.
8. When the Transport Board became responsible for prisoners of war the care of sick and wounded prisoners remained with the Sick and Hurt Board.
9. TNA, ADM 105/44 19 August 1798.
10. TNA, ADM 98/272 31 August 1798.
11. TNA, ADM 98/272 4 June 1798.
12. Duncan states this figure in TNA, ADM 1/526/328. Otway in TNA, ADM 105/44 19 August 1798 gives the capacity as 200, but events suggest Duncan was nearer the mark.
13. TNA, ADM 103/463.
14. ibid. There was always a problem with what to do with captured fishermen. As Chamberlain says, 'War was waged against nations, not local inhabitants who often supplied the Royal Navy with intelligence and fresh produce, although this limitation was ignored if the fishing vessel was found to have an armed solider on board. This prohibition did not apply to the fishing and whaling fleets that operated in the North Sea and around Greenland; these were national fleets supplying the nation at war and so were legitimate targets.' Chamberlain, *Hell Upon Water*, p.12.
15. TNA, ADM 103/463, *Norfolk Chronicle* 24 May 1794.
16. TNA, ADM 103/103. *Norwich Mercury* 2 January 1796. Palmer. *Perlustration*, Vol. II, pp.294-5.
17. Walker, *The Depot for Prisoners of War at Norman Cross*, pp. 10-12.
18. Chamberlain, *Hell Upon Water*, pp. 16-17.
19. TNA, ADM 98/272/61.
20. ibid 63.
21. ibid 87.
22. *Norwich Mercury* 17 June 1797.
23. Anderson, *Lynn during the Napoleonic Wars*, p. 2.
24. TNA, ADM 98/272 24 July 1797, ADM 103/103.
25. TNA, ADM 99/269/126, ADM 98/272 26 December 1797.
26. TNA, ADM 1/526/328, ADM 98/272/60-1, ADM 99/272 18 June 1799.
27. *Norwich Mercury* 5 May 1798.
28. TNA, ADM 99/269/110. Palmer, *Perlustration*, Vol. II, p.109.
29. The two prisoners were Bernard Gimbal, 2nd Lieutenant of the frigate *La Vengeance*, taken on 3 March and paroled on 24 March 1796, and Lieutenant-Colonel Jacques Blanchet, taken on board the American vessel *Ann & Mary* on 22 June and paroled on 2 July 1796.
30. In 1857 the then vicar of East Dereham and two friends erected a memorial to de Narde in the churchyard there, 'AS A TRIBUTE OF RESPECT TO THAT BRAVE AND GENEROUS NATION, ONCE OUR FOES BUT NOW OUR ALLIES AND BRETHREN'.
31. TNA, ADM 105/44 12 August 1801. Fielding had lost the confidence of the Transport Board and having been dismissed by the Sick and Hurt Board from his post of surgeon and agent at Yarmouth he never worked for the government again. His standing locally, however, was not diminished by the experience and in 1810 he became Mayor for the second time. He died in 1816, aged 84.
32. ibid.

33. TNA, ADM 98/273 18 September 1801.
34. TNA, ADM 98/273 23, 25 October 1801.
35. The first of these prizes was the *Jonge Willim Ling*, of and from Amsterdam, bound for Rouen. She was sent in on 22 May with a cargo of general merchandise *'among which were four swans consigned to Bonaparte,'* *Norfolk Chronicle* 28 May 1803.
36. TNA, ADM 99/149/12-13. On 12 July the Mayor sent the Transport Board a bill from William Worts for subsisting these men from 6 to 11 June.
37. TNA, ADM 104/8. Benjamin Fielding, the agent in the previous war, also wrote to the Transport Board in a similar vein, but his letter went unanswered.
38. TNA, ADM 1/1633 3 July 1803, ADM 99/149/99, ADM 99/150/41.
39. TNA, ADM 99/149/113-114.
40. ibid 142, 158, 174, 178, ADM 99/150/19.
41. TNA, ADM 99/149/178, ADM 99/150/19.
42. TNA, ADM 99/150/68, 169, 170, ADM 99/152/31.
43. TNA, ADM 99/152/31-32, 56-57, ADM 104/8.
44. ibid ADM 99/152/96, 113.
45. TNA, ADM 99/152/134-5, ADM 103/461. *Norfolk Chronicle* 17 December 1803.
46. For many years afterwards Row 110 was known as Prison Row or New Prison Row.
47. TNA, ADM 105/44 8 October 1805.
48. ibid 16 December 1808.
49. Palmer, *Perlustration*, Vol.II, p. 294.
50. TNA, ADM 99/152/154, 155, 157.
51. Palmer, *Perlustration*, Vol. II, p. 295.
52. TNA, ADM 98/235 19 September 1808, ADM 98/236 28 November, 15 December 1810.
53. TNA, ADM 98/235 9 June, 20 July 1808, ADM 98/236 12 November 1810.
54. TNA, ADM 104/8, ADM 98/235 7 December 1808, 27 April 1809, ADM 98/236 13 June 1812, 1 March 1813.
55. *Norfolk Chronicle* 3 March 1804.
56. ibid 12 January 1805.
57. TNA, ADM 1/1429/89 10 February 1811. The reason for the demise of the Batavian Republic is given succinctly by Jonathan I. Israel in his, *The Dutch Republic. Its Rise, Greatness, and Fall 1477-1806*, Clarendon Press, 1995, p. 1128, 'After Napoleon proclaimed himself Emperor of the French, in 1804, the regime in France no longer looked with favour on the persistence of republican forms and attitudes amongst the satellite states. As the dimensions, and cost, of, the war against the European monarchies ranged against France grew, so the temptation to reduce the allies to pliable auxiliaries, under tight French control, increased.' As a result in March 1806 Napoleon's brother Louis became King of Holland but he sided with the Dutch more often than his brother would have wished and in early 1810 he was deposed and Holland became part of France.
58. TNA, ADM 1/1425/379 30 July 1806.
59. TNA, ADM 1/1427 4 April 1808.
60. TNA, ADM 103/455, 456, 457, 459, 460, 461, 462.
61. TNA, ADM 103/461.
62. TNA, ADM 1/1428 20 August 1809.
63. ibid TNA, ADM 103/461.
64. ibid.
65. TNA, ADM 1/1432/671.
66. ibid 725,747.
67. ibid 748, ADM 1/1433/4.
68. TNA, ADM 1/1433/157. Walker, *The Depot for Prisoners of War at Norman Cross*, p.55.
69. As note 60.

12 Communication

1. Wilson, *The Old Telegraphs*, pp.11-14.
2. Fone, *Signalling from Norwich to the Coast in the Napoleonic Period*, p.58. TNA, ADM 1/4997/145 18 April 1801. Roebuck was to be paid travelling expenses of 1 guinea a day, 'when he returned the glass and compass to the office,' TNA, ADM 354/202/190.
3. Kitchin, *The Napoleonic War Coast Signal Stations*, pp.337-41.
4. TNA, ADM 2/134/505, 552-557.
5. ibid, TNA, ADM 1/1624/133.
6. NRO, Y/C 19/40/6, Y/C 19/15/211. TNA, ADM 1/1624/134.
7. ibid. *Norwich Mercury* 14 April 1798.
8. TNA, ADM 2/135/324-9, ADM 9/3/612.
9. TNA, ADM 2/135/325.
10. Kitchen, *The Napoleonic War Coast Signal Stations*, p. 340.
11. TNA, ADM 2/135/325, 328-9.
12. ibid 324-6.
13. TNA, ADM 1/531/497, TNA, ADM 1/533/166.
14. TNA, ADM 2/143/150.
15. NRO, Y/C 19/16/13.
16. TNA, ADM 1/533/161.
17. Palmer, *Perlustration*, Vol. II, p.174.
18. Benham, *Once Upon A Tide*, p.206.
19. *Norfolk Chronicle* 21 February 1795.
20. Lavery, *Nelson's Navy*, p. 277.
21. Sussex & Shelton, *Continental Mail Service*, pp. 2,16, 21.
22. Palmer, *Perlustration*, Vol. II, p 192.
23. Sussex & Shelton, *Continental Mail Service*, pp.11-13.
24. ibid pp. 13-14. Palmer, *Perlustration*, Vol. II, pp. 173-4. Row 102 was known as Packet Office Row.
25. ibid p.192.
26. Sussex & Shelton, *Continental Mail Service*, pp.14, 23, 40.
27. ibid p.13.
28. Benham, *Once Upon A Tide*, pp. 193-204.
29. Sussex & Shelton, *Continental Mail Service*, p.14 quoting PMG reports, 7 March 1795.
30. ibid pp.13-14 quoting PMG minutes 1 December 1795.
31. *Norfolk Chronicle* 21 February 1795.
32. *Norwich Mercury* 24 August 1799.
33. Palmer, *Perlustration*, Vol. II, p.192.
34. *Norwich Mercury* 29 April 1797.
35. ibid 12 August 1797.
36. ibid 21 July, 18 August, 15 September 1798.
37. Sussex & Shelton, *Continental Mail Service*, p.25.
38. Grocott, *Shipwreck of the Revolutionary & Napoleonic Eras*, p.79.
39. TNA, ADM 1/523/288.
40. Sussex & Shelton, *Continental Mail Service*, p.11. Benham, *One Upon A Tide*, p. 206.
41. Sussex & Shelton, *Continental Mail Service*, p.11. *Norwich Mercury* 19 July 1800. The relationship between the two *Dolphins* is unclear.
42. Benham, *Once Upon A Tide*, p.207.
43. ibid pp. 207-8. Sussex & Shelton, *Continental Mail Service*, p. 28.
44. ibid pp. 25-26 quoting PMG Reports 28 December and a letter of 31 December 1798.
45. *Norwich Mercury* 5 January 1799.
46. ibid 9 February 1799.
47. Sussex & Shelton, *Continental Mail Service*, p.27.
48. *Norwich Mercury* 9 March 1799.
49. Knight, *Britain Against Napoleon*, p.135.
50. Grocott, *Shipwrecks of the Revolutionary & Napoleonic Eras*, pp.70-2.

51. Knight, *Britain Against Napoleon*, p.136.
52. *Norwich Mercury* 21 November 1801. Sussex & Shelton, *Continental Mail Service*, p. 45 quoting PMG Reports 5 November 1801.
53. TNA, ADM 2/145/140-150.
54. TNA, ADM 9/6/1667 (Marsh).
55. TNA, ADM 49/112, No 21.
56. ibid No 16, 17, 18.
57. TNA, ADM 1/1634 25 July 1803.
58. ibid 30 July 1803.
59. TNA, ADM 2/146/221.
60. TNA, ADM 1/1634 30 November 1803.
61. ibid.
62. ibid 6 December 1803, ADM 2/146/354. Cobb pointed out that none of the village posts had people attached to them to receive the signals from Yarmouth Church.
63. TNA, ADM 49/109/89. Fone, *Signalling from Norwich to the Coast in the Napoleonic Period*, pp. 356-7.
64. TNA, ADM 49/109/85, 88.
65. ibid 96, 97, 99, 103.
66. TNA, ADM 2/166/100-105, 361-366. The Norfolk stations closed on 3 May 1814 and those from Yarmouth to Dungeness on 18 November 1814.
67. TNA, ADM 2/162/514.
68. TNA, ADM 11/16 19 February 1812, ADM 1/1432/292.
69. TNA, ADM 1/1643 26 April 1805. Cheap wrote to Cobb to say he was not able to join the ship and requested leave to go home on half pay.
70. ibid 26 April, 26 May 1805.
71. ibid 24 June 1805. *Norfolk Chronicle*, 11 January 1806.
72. TNA, ADM 1/1425/28.
73. TNA, ADM 106/1976 3, 4, November 1805.
74. ibid 9 January 1806.
75. TNA, ADM 1/1431/506, 562, 572.
76. Wilson, *The Old Telegraphs*, pp.10, 26-30.
77. On the 16 November 1807 the Corporation's Committee of Liberties recommended, that a lease be granted. This was approved by the Assembly on 22 March 1808, NRO Y/C 19/43/26, Y/C 19/16/135. The well-known print of the Yarmouth South Gate showing a shutter telegraph on the western tower has led most writers on the subject to conclude that this was the terminus of the Admiralty line. It is clearly too small for that purpose and probably relates to the short-lived commercial service established between Norwich and Yarmouth in 1805.
78. *Norfolk Chronicle* 28 November 1807.
79. TNA, ADM 1/4999/299. Wilson, *The Old Telegraphs*, p.30.
80. TNA, ADM 1/1427 25 August 1808.
81. Wilson, *The Old Telegraphs*, pp.14-16.
82. TNA, ADM 1/1427 29 June 1808.
83. TNA, ADM 1/1430/869.
84. ibid 897.
85. ibid.
86. ibid.
87. Munday, *The Yarmouth and London Telegraph*, pp. 512-3.

13. Defence

1. Kent, *Fortifications of East Anglia*, p.210. TNA, WO 30/67/101. The North Star Battery stood on the site of Blake Road/Collingwood Road, the Town Battery on the North Drive, just south of Euston Road, and the South Star Battery on the site of Harboard Crescent.
2. ibid p.100. TNA, WO 55/2357. The garrison was an anachronistic survival from an earlier age. At the start of the war it comprised a governor (Captain John Arbuthnot) and a master-gunner

(John Eaves). Until early in the previous year there had also been two gunners, but these were not replaced after Samuel Newman died and George Goldhawke was 'lost in the snow'. Arbuthnot was paid a salary of £172-17-6 for what was in effect a sinecure, for he was not expected to reside in Yarmouth and was always 'absent on King's leave'. In 1810/11 he was succeeded by Major-General W. M. Richardson. John Eaves died in 1797 and was replaced by Andrew James who was still in post at the end of the Napoleonic Wars. TNA, WO 12/11596, WO 55/1827.

3. NRO, Y/C 19/37/161.
4. ibid Y/C 19/15/109.
5. ibid. Page distinguished himself at the Battle of Bunker Hill in 1775 where he was severely wounded. Before visiting Yarmouth he was in command of the Royal Engineers in the Eastern Coastal District and supervised the refurbishment of the defences at Dover, Chatham, Tilbury, Gravesend, Sheerness and Landguard Fort.
6. TNA, MPHH 1/222/4. Page was known to Townshend through his work on the Bedford Level.
7. TNA, WO 30/67. Reynolds refers to the works carried out by Page as 'Alterations Additions & Repairs were making to these works in September last', which suggests he was writing in 1796, p. 101.
8. ibid p.101.
9. ibid p.104.
10. ibid p.108.
11. On occasion regular units were stationed in or near the town. A monthly return for 1 May 1795 records the presence of a detachment of Royal Artillery comprising 97 men and 21 horses, TNA, WO 17/834. Later, during November and December 1798, the 1st Battalion of the 9th Foot (East Norfolk Regiment) spent time there before, embarking for Guernsey, *Norwich Mercury* 1 December 1798, 5 January 1799.
12. Norfolk's Lord Lieutenant, Marquis Townshend, was instrumental in the passing of the Militia Act in 1757.
13. Beckett, *The Amateur Military Tradition 1558- 1945*, p.71.
14. TNA, WO 5/101/1/18-19.
15. ibid 283, 300, 311, 281.
16. *Norwich Mercury* 28 September 1793.
17. ibid 12 October 1793.
18. TNA, WO 5/101/460.
19. TNA, WO 5/102/28, 34, 37, 148, 154.
20. Townshend wrote to the Ordnance Board in November 1794 concerning a letter he had received from the Mayor of Yarmouth, 'stating how much the Innkeepers were distress'd from the Quartering such a number of Artillery Horses and Drivers upon them,' TNA, WO 47/2366.
21. Palmer, *Perlustration*, Vol. III, p. 79.
22. NRO, Y/C 19/15/151, 193, Y/D 92/2.
23. *Norwich Mercury* 19 March 1795.
24. TNA, WO 5/102/254, 257, 312, 322, 334, 347. *Norwich Mercury* 22 October 1795.
25. *Norwich Mercury* 9 May 1795.
26. TNA, WO 5/17/82.
27. ibid. Among the 20 Regiments was the 33rd Foot commanded by Lieutenant-Colonel Arthur Wesley. This unit lay in the Roads for two days before proceeding to Harwich so it seems likely that the future Duke of Wellington set foot in the town,
28. *Norwich Mercury* 6 June 1795.
29. TNA, WO 5/102/403. *Norwich Mercury* 17 October 1795.
30. TNA, HO 42/37 4 December 1795. The South Lincolnshires were not overly involved.
31. ibid.
32. ibid TNA, WO 5/103/53.
33. ibid 56, 58.
34. ibid 112, 125, 127, 136.
35. ibid 240.
36. *Norwich Mercury* 20 August, 3 September 1796.

37. *Norwich Mercury* 8 October 1796.
38. *Norwich Mercury* 27 May 1797.
39. TNA, WO 5/103/311.
40. *Norwich Mercury* 25 November 1797.
41. TNA, PC/2/150 14 March 1798.
42. TNA, ADM 2/135/139-154.
43. *Norfolk Chronicle* 14 April 1798.
44. TNA, ADM 28/21, 23.
45. NRO, Y/C 36/20/20.
46. *Norwich Mercury* 21 April 1798.
47. NRO, Ms 5361.
48. NRO, Ms 5364.
49. *Norwich Mercury* 4 August, 1 September 1798. NRO, Y/C 19/15/262.
50. NRO, Ms 5364.
51. *Norwich Mercury* 20 April 1799.
52. ibid 8 November 1800.
53. ibid 15 November 1800.
54. ibid 7 June 1800.
55. ibid 28 February 1801. TNA,WO 5/105/240.
56. ibid.
57. *Norwich Mercury* 20 March 1801. TNA, WO 5/105/308, 510, 511, WO 5/106/68. *Norwich Mercury* 1 May 1802.
58. TNA, WO 30/100/168.
59. ibid.
60. TNA, WO 55/2357.
61. Kent, *Fortifications of East Anglia*, p.212 quoting TNA, WO 55/733, WO 55/734.
62. TNA, WO 54/704. At the outset Manby lodged in the Rows. The house he subsequently occupied stood near the barracks. After the Napoleonic Wars it was enlarged for the managing partner of Grout and Co., whose silk factory stood on the barracks site. It was then called Bauleah House and still stands alongside Manby Road, Palmer, *Perlustration*, Vol. III, p. 78.
63. The source of this account of Manby's early life is Walthew. A slightly different version is to be found in Palmer's, *Perlustration*, Vol. III, pp. 208-9.
64. Thomas Manby went to sea in 1783 and towards the end of 1790 he joined the *Discovery* as a senior midshipman. At the time the vessel was fitting out for an expedition led by navigator George Vancouver. Though critical of his commander throughout, Manby was recognised as a brave and competent officer and was progressively promoted during the voyage. In early 1799 he was raised to the rank of captain and served with distinction in the early part of the Napoleonic Wars until he became stricken with yellow fever and was invalided in 1808. He became a rear-admiral in 1825 and died in 1835. John M. Naish in his, *The Interwoven Lives of George Vancouver, Archibald Menzies Joseph Whidley and Peter Puget*, (Edwin Mellon Press, 1996), describes him as a 'boastful daring and highly sexed member of the upper classes of England (p. 92). This echoes the fact that later in life he was to have notoriety thrust upon him as one of a number of dashing naval officers accused by the Prince of Wales of scandalous behaviour with his wife, Princess Caroline. This was to have unfortunate consequences for his brother, George, for the two became muddled up when honours for the latter were being considered and as a result the honours he craved were denied him.
65. The name of the barrack-sergeant has eluded me.
66. NRO, Y/C 19/43/85-88.
67. TNA, WO 68/123.
68. TNA, WO 5/106/179, 194, 200, 335. *Norfolk Chronicle* 9 July 1803.
69. ibid 7 January 1804.
70. ibid 18 February 1804.
71. ibid 7 July, 15 September 1804. Palmer, *Perlustration* Vol. III, p. 56.
72. *Norfolk Chronicle* 3 November 1804.

73. ibid 19 July 1806.
74. ibid 8 June, 29 June 1805.
75. ibid 1 August 1807.
76. ibid 2 April, 20 August 1808. TNA, WO 13/216.
77. Preston, *The Picture of Yarmouth*, p. 177.
78. *Norfolk Chronicle* 6 October 1810.
79. ibid 11 May, 25 May 1811, TNA, WO 13/1574.
80. *Norfolk Chronicle* 30 May 1812, 8 May, 10 July 1813.
81. ibid 12 February 1814.
82. TNA, WO 68/123.
83. TNA, WO 13/4477 (Yarmouth). *Norfolk Chronicle* 20 August 1803. According to Jenny Uglow Gould had been in the North Gloucestershire Militia and then the marines before his father-in-law bought him a half-share in a Yarmouth brewery, (*In These Times*, p. 100).
84. *Norfolk Chronicle* 12 November 1803.
85. NRO, Ms 67.
86. ibid.
87. ibid. This document lists 16 Troops of volunteer calvary and 10 companies of volunteer infantry who carried out garrison duty at Yarmouth in 1803. The newspapers in later years mention more.
88. TNA, ADM 1/1634 11 March, 22 March, 13 July 1803.
89. ibid 13, 25 July 1803, TNA, ADM 11/14.
90. TNA, ADM 28/147.
91. ibid.
92. TNA, ADM 1/1638 6 March 1804.
93. TNA, ADM 28/17, ADM 1/1643 31 July 1805.
94. TNA, ADM 28/147.
95. TNA, ADM 1/1634 12 December 1803.
95. TNA, ADM 1/1638 7 January 1804.
97. ibid 9 February 1804.
98. TNA, ADM 11/15.
99. TNA, ADM 1/1643 1 September 1805, ADM 11/16. Berry had commanded ships at the Battles of the Nile and Trafalgar.
100. TNA, ADM 1/1648 22 September 1807.
101. ibid 22 September to 9 November 1807. Knight, *Britain Against Napoleon*, p. 202. Davey p.156.

14 Peace and Closure

1. The source for this and subsequent paragraphs is, *A Narrative of the Grand Festival at Yarmouth on Tuesday, the 19th of April 1814.*
2. *Norfolk Chronicle* 9 July 1814.
3. ibid 28 May 1814.
4. *Norfolk Chronicle* 14, 28 May, 25 June, 2, 23, 30 July 1814. The *Utile* was sold at Deptford in June 1814. The *Solebay* (formerly the Iris) was fitted out in late 1814/early 1815 for use by the Marine Society, Winfield, *British Warships in the Age of Sail*, pp. 195.
5. TNA, ADM 98/238 26, 30 May 1814.
6. ibid 16 October 1815.
7. *An act for enabling the Trustee of certain Premises at Great Yarmouth in the County of Norfolk, held in Trust for His Majesty, to execute a Conveyance of the same to a Purchaser thereof,* 58 George III CAP XLII 28 May 1818.
8. TNA, ADM 2/166/246.
9. TNA, ADM 104/1. *Norfolk Chronicle* 10 September 1814. Generally referred to as captain or governor, Larke remained in the Yarmouth area after the hospital closed. His first wife, Mary, daughter of Joseph Haw of Yarmouth, died in 1807. He then married the widow of John Lucas Worship, who was the sister of the surgeon William Taylor. Dawson Turner refers to him as 'a man, si quis alius, of sound mind and kind heart, and universally held in the estimation he deserves.' He is buried at Stokesby, Turner, *Sepulchral Reminiscences*, p. 86, Palmer,

Perlustration, Vol. II, pp. 80-81, 144.

10. NRO. Y/C 19/16/259 6 October 1814, Y/C 19/17/1 30 November 1814.
11. TNA, ADM 2/166/100-105, 361-6.
12. TNA, ADM 49/116, NRO Y/C 19/17/1 30 November 1814.
13. NRO, Y/C 19/16/259 6 October 1814, 261 17 October 1814, Y/C 19/17/1 30 November 1814.
14. TNA, ADM 112/200-201.
15. TNA, ADM 111/212-215.
16. TNA, ADM 106/1976, 23 November 1814, 26, 27 April 1815.
17. ibid 24, 30 November 1814, 4, 28 January 1815.
18. ibid 30 March, 12 April 1815, 30 July, 8 August 1818.
19. TNA, WO 54/516, 520, 524, 528, WO 55/2704.
20. According to census records there were 3,159 houses in Yarmouth in 1801, 3,594 in 1811 and 4,158 in 1821, Given the post war slump following the departure of the navy it is likely that this increase of 1,000 houses had largely taken place by the end on 1814. This exceptional demand for housing created pressure to build on the Denes which the Corporation struggled to resist. In order to protect the interests of the existing townsfolk in March 1808 the Assembly ordered that buildings erected there should not be any higher than 20 feet and should not be either shops or public houses, NRO Y/C 19/16/142.
21. *Norwich Mercury* 24 July 1802.

Epilogue

1. *Norfolk Chronicle* 24 September 1814.
2. ibid 6, 13 May 1815.
3. ibid 3 June 1815.
4. ibid 13 May, 3 June 1815.
5. ibid 1 July 1815.
6. ibid 15 July 1815.
7. TNA, WO 12/13115. *Norfolk Chronicle* 15 July, 12 August 1815.
8. ibid 9 September 1815. The last men were not discharged until April 1816.
9. ibid 3 November 1814, 19 August, 11 November 1815. Tooke, *Great Yarmouth and Gorleston Front Line Towns*, p.2.
10. *Norfolk Chronicle* 9 September 1815.
11. *Norfolk Chronicle* 30 November 1805. Lewis, *Nelson*, pp. 128-32.
12. ibid. NRO, Y/C 19/16/262 17 October 1814.
13. Lewis, *Nelson*, pp. 129-130. NRO Y/C 19/17/73 14 January 1818.
14. Preston, *The Picture of Yarmouth*, pp. 165-173.
15. Tooke, *Great Yarmouth and the Nelson Connection,* p. 25. Preston, *The Picture of Yarmouth*, pp. 172-3.
16. ibid p. 172. Lewis, *Nelson,* pp. 141-2.
17. NRO, Y/S 10/1, *Names of Persons authorized to keep Common Inns, Alehouses or Victualling houses,* 1819.
18. Davies, *History of Medicine in Great Yarmouth*, p.236.

Sources

Manuscript

National Maritime Museum, Caird Library
ADM/A Navy Board: In-letters from the Admiralty 1689-1815.
ADM/B Admiralty: In-letters from the Navy Board 1738-1809.
ADM/BP Admiralty: In-letters from the Navy Board 1780-1832.
ADM/E Sick and Hurt Board: In-letters 1702-1806.
ADM/F Admiralty: In-letters from the Sick and Hurt Board 1742-1806.
AGC Letters.
DAR Dartmouth Papers.

Norfolk Record Office
FX 200 Copies of miscellaneous documents mainly relating to Great Yarmouth and the Nichols family.
MS 67 Norfolk Yeomanary & Volunteer Units. Inspection Returns 1803.
MS 5361-5364 Collection of Papers re Norfolk Militia, Volunteers, and Yeomanary 1760-1800.
PD 28 Great Yarmouth Parish Records.
Y/C 16 Great Yarmouth Borough Records: Admiralty Court 1698-1836.
Y/C 19/ 14-17 Great Yarmouth Borough Records: Assembly Books, Minutes and Files 1771-1828.
Y/C 32/2 Great Yarmouth Borough Records: Register of Leases 1795-1812.
Y/C 36, Great Yarmouth Borough Records: Miscellaneous Correspondence and Working Papers pre-1835.
Y/D 37 Diaries of William Youell 1765-1815.
Y/PH 1 Port and Haven Commissioners Minutes 1750-1823.
Y/S Great Yarmouth, Sessions of the Peace.

The National Archives
ADM 1 Admiralty: Correspondence and Papers.
ADM 2 Admiralty: Out-letters.
ADM 6 Admiralty: Service Records.
ADM 7 Admiralty: Miscellanea.
ADM 9 Admiralty: Returns of Officer's Service.
ADM 11 Admiralty: Officer's Service Records.
ADM 12 Admiralty: Digests and Indexes.
ADM 28 Navy Board: Sea Fencible Pay Lists.
ADM 30 Navy Board Pay Office, Various Registers.
ADM 42 Navy Board and Admiralty: Yard Pay Books.
ADM 49 Navy Board and Admiralty: Accountant General's Department, Miscellaneous Accounting Records.
ADM 50 Admiralty: Admiral's Journals.
ADM 51 Admiralty: Captain's Logs.
ADM 52 Admiralty: Master's Logs.
ADM 97 Sick and Hurt Board: In-letters.
ADM 98 Sick and Hurt Board: Out-letters.

ADM 99 Sick and Hurt Board: Minutes.
ADM 101 Sick and Hurt Board: Medical Journals.
ADM 102 Admiralty: Naval Hospitals and Hospital Ships Musters and Miscellaneous Journals.
ADM 103 Navy Board: Registers of Prisoners of War.
ADM 104 Admiralty: Service Registers.
ADM 105 Admiralty: Miscellanea (Reports of Visitations).
ADM 106 Navy Board: Records.
ADM 108 Transport Board: Records.
ADM 110 Victualling Board: Out-letters.
ADM 111 Victualling Board: Minutes.
ADM 112 Navy Board: Accounts and Contracts.
ADM 140 Maps and Plans.
ADM 352 Admiralty: Hydrographic Department, Original Surveys.
AO 1 Auditors of the Imprest and Commissioners of Audit, Declared Accounts.
HO 42 Home Office: Domestic Correspondence, George III.
MPHH 1 Maps and Plans.
MRQ 1 Maps and Plans.
PC 2 Privy Council Office: Registers.
SP 46 State Papers Domestic, Supplementary.
TS 21 Treasury Solicitor: Deeds, Evidences, and Miscellaneous Papers.
WO 5 War Office: Marching and Militia Orders.
WO 12 War Office: General Muster Books and Pay Lists.
WO 17 War Office: Monthly Returns.
WO 30 War Office: Miscellaneous Papers.
WO 47 Ordnance Board: Minutes.
WO 54 Ordnance Board: Entry Books and Registers.
WO 55 Ordnance Board: Miscellaneous Entry Books and Papers.
WO 68 Ordnance Board: Militia Records.

Printed

Anderson, G. H., *Lynn During the Napoleonic Wars*, (King's Lynn, 1919).
Barney, John, *The Defence of Norfolk 1793-1815*, (Mintaka Books, 2000).
   North Sea and Baltic Convoy 1793-1814: as experienced by Merchant Masters employed by Michael Henley & Son, (Mariners Mirror, Vol. 93, 2009).
Beckett, Ian F. W., *The Amateur Military Tradition 1558-1945* (Manchester University Press, 1991).
Bell, John, '*Memoir on the Present State of Naval and Military Surgery'*, (Yarmouth, 20 January 1798).
Benham, Hervey. *Once Upon A Tide*, (Harrop, 1955).
Brooks, F.W., *The Cinque Ports' Feud with Yarmouth in the Thirteenth Century*, (Mariners Mirror, Vol.19, 1933).
Camperdown, The Earl of, *Admiral Duncan*, (Longmans, Green, and Co, 1898).
Chamberlain, Paul, *Hell Upon Water. Prisoners of War in Britain, 1793-1815*, (The History Press, 2008).
Coad, Jonathan, *Support for the Fleet: Architecture and engineering of the Royal Navy's Bases 1700-1914*, (English Heritage, 2013).
Coats, Ann, and MacDougal, Philip, (eds), *The Naval Mutinies of 1797:Unity and Perseverance* (The Boydell Press, 2011).
Coleman, Terry, *Nelson: The Man and the Legend*, (Bloomsbury, 2001).
Dancy, J. Ross, *The Myth of the Press Gang*, (The Boydell Press, 2015).
Davey, James, *In Nelson's Wake: The Navy and the Napoleonic Wars*, (Yale University Press/National Maritime Museum, 2015).
Davies, J. D., *Pepys's Navy: Ships, Men & Warfare 1649-1689*, (Seaforth Publishing, 2008).
Davies, Dr Paul P., *History of Medicine in Great Yarmouth*, (privately published, 2003).

SOURCES

Dictionary of National Biography.

Dirks, J.J.B., *De Nederlandsche Zeemagt in Hare verschillende Tijdperken Geschetst*, (Rotterdam, 1871).

Douet, James, *British Barracks 1600-1914: Their Architecture and Role in Society*, (London, 1998).

Drower, George, *Heligoland*, (Sutton Publishing, 2002).

Druery, John Henry, *Historical and Topographical Notices of Great Yarmouth*, (London, 1826).

The Second Dutch War, (National Maritime Museum booklet, 1967).

Ecclestone, A. W. and J. L., *The Rise of Great Yarmouth. The Story of a Sandbank.*(Privately published, 1959).

Edler, F., *The Dutch Republic and The American Revolution*, (University Press of the Pacific, 2001).

Finch-Crisp, William,*Chronological Retrospect of the History of Yarmouth*, (1877).

Fone, J. F. *The Naval Yard at Yarmouth in the Napoleonic Wars,*(Norfolk Archaeology Vol. 41, 1992).
    Signalling from Norwich to the Coast in the Napoleonic Period, (Norfolk Archaeology Vol. 42, 1996).

Fortescue, J.W., *A History of the British Army*, 13 vols (Macmillan, 1899-1930).

Foynes, Julian, *East Anglia against the Tricolor 1789-1815*, (Poppyland Publishing, 2016).

Franks, R. D., *Admiral Sir Richard Onslow,*(Mariners Mirror, Vol. 67.1981).

Gardiner, Robert, ed., *Fleet Battle and Blockade. The French Revolutionary War 1793-1797,* (Chatham Publishing, 1996).
    Nelson against Napoleon. From the Nile to Copenhagen, 1798-1801, (Chatham Publishing, 1997).

Glover, G., *Two Battles of Copenhagen 1801 and 1807: Britain and Denmark in the Napoleonic Wars* (Pen & Sword, 2018).

Goodman, Nigel, Ed, *Dawson Turner. A Norfolk Antiquary and his Remarkable Family*, (Phillimore, 2007).

A Narrative of the Grand Festival at Yarmouth on Tuesday the 19th of April 1814, (Keymer, Yarmouth, 1814).

Grocott, Terence, *Shipwrecks of the Revolutionary & Napoleonic Eras*, (Chatham Publishing, 1997).

Hayes, Derek R., *His Majesty's Late Ship the Invincible: Third Rate 74 Guns 1765-1801*, (Dormers Associates, 1985).

Higgins David, *The Beachmen*, (Terence Dalton, 1987).

Hill, Richard, *The Prizes of War, The Naval Prize System in the Napoleonic Wars 1793-1815,* (Royal Naval Museum/Sutton Publishing, 1998).

Israel, Jonathan I., *The Dutch Republic. Its Rise, Greatness, and Fall* 1477-1806, (Clarendon Press, 1995).

James,W. M., *The Naval History of Great Britain*, 6 vols, (London 1837. Reprint by Conway Maritime Press, 2002).

Jonge, Johannes Cornelius de, *Geschiedenis van het Nederlandse zeewezen,* 3rd ed.(Zwolle: Hoogstraten & Gorter, 1869).

Kent, Peter, *Fortifications of East Anglia*, (Terence Dalton, 1988).

Kitchin, Frank, *The Napoleonic War Coast Signal Stations*, (Mariners Mirror, Vol. 76, 1990).

Knight, Roger, *The Pursuit of Victory. The Life and Achievement of Horatio Nelson*, (Allen Lane, 2005).
    Britain Against Napoleon. The Organisation of Victory 1793-1815 (Allen Lane, 2013).
    With Wilcox, Martin, *Sustaining the Fleet 1793-1815*, (The Boydell Press, 2010).

Lavery, Brian, *Nelson's Navy, The Ships, Men and Organisation 1793-1815,* (Conway Maritime Press, 1989).

Lewis, Charles, *Nelson "I am myself a Norfolk man,"* (Poppyland Publishing, 2005).

Macranie, K. D., *Admiral Lord Keith and the Naval War against Napoleon*, (Gainesville, Florida, 2006).

Mallinson, Howard, *Send it by Semaphore: The Old Telegraphs During the Wars With France,* (The Crowood Press,2005).

Malster, Robert, *Saved From The Sea*, (Terence Dalton, 1974).

Maritime Norfolk, Part Two, (Poppyland Publishing, 2013).

Munday, Rev. J. T., *The Yarmouth and London Telegraph*, (Norfolk Archaeology, Vol. XXXV, 1973).

Naish, John M., *The Interwoven Lives of George Vancouver, Archibald Menzies, Joseph Whidley and*

Peter Puget, (Edwin Mellon Press, 1996).

Norfolk Chronicle 1780-1816.

Norwich Mercury 1780-1816.

Paget, S., Ed, *Sir J. Paget, Memoirs and Letters*, (1901).

Palmer, Charles John, *Manship's History of Great Yarmouth,* (Meall, 1854).
 The History of Great Yarmouth designed as a continuation of Manship's History, (Meall, 1856).
 The Perlustration of Great Yarmouth, 3 vols. (George Nall, 1872-1875).

Pocock, Tom, *A Thirst For Glory, The Life of Admiral Sir Sidney Smith*, (Aurum Press, 1996).

Pope, Dudley, *The Great Gamble: Nelson at Copenhagen*, (Chatham Publishing edition, 2001).

Preston, John, *The Picture of Yarmouth,* (Yarmouth, 1819).

Ralfe, James, *The Naval Biography of Great Britain, 4 Vols.* (London, 1828).

Saul, A., *Great Yarmouth and the Hundred Years War in the Fourteenth Century*, (Bulletin of the Institute of Historical Research, Vol. L11 No 126, November 1979).

Smyth, James Carmichael, *The Effect of the Nitrous Vapour, in Preventing and Destroying Contagion*, (Philadelphia, 1799).

Steel's Original and Correct List of the Royal Navy, 1782-1816.

Sussex, Vivien & Shelton, Sidney, *Continental Mail Service 1793-1815*, (East Anglian Postal History Study Circle, 1978).

Swinden, Henry, *The History and Antiquities of the Ancient Burgh of Great Yarmouth,* (Norwich, 1772).

Syrett, David, and DiNardo, R. L., *The Commissioned Sea Officers of the Royal Navy 1660-1815*, (Scolar Press for the Navy Records Society, 1994).

Tooke, Colin,*Great Yarmouth and Gorleston Front Line Towns*, (privately published, 1999).
 Great Yarmouth and the Nelson Connection, (privately published, 2005).

Turner*, Dawson, Sepulchral Reminiscences,* (Charles Barker, 1848).

Turner, Eunice, *The Russian Squadron with Admiral Duncan's North Sea Fleet, 1795-1800,* (Mariners Mirror, Vol.49, 1963).

Uglow, Jenny, *In These Times*, (Faber & Faber, 2014).

Walker, Thomas James, *The Depot for Prisoners of War at Norman Cross, Huntingdonshire 1796-1816*, (London, 1913).

Walthew, Kenneth, *From Rock and Tempest*, (Geoffrey Bles, 1971).

Western, J. R., *The English Militia in the Eighteenth Century: The Story of a Political Issue 1660-1802,* (Routledge & Kegan Paul, 1965).

Wilson, Geoffrey, *The Old Telegraphs*, (Phillimore, 1976).

Winfield, Rif, *British Warships in the Age of Sail, 1793-1817*, (Chatham Publishing, 2005).

Woodman, Richard, *The Victory of Seapower*, (Chatham Publishing, 1998).

Index

General

Abercromby, Gen. Sir Ralph 33,34
Addington, Henry, P. M. 43,45
Admiralty ix, x, 3, 6, 9, 12, 16-18, 20-26, 28, 30, 32-37, 39, 41, 43-44, 47-48, 50, 52-53, 55, 60-61, 76, 79, 87, 89-94, 96, 101, 103, 105-106, 108, 110-111, 113-118, 120-126, 130-134, 136-139, 142-143, 147, 150, 153-158, 162-165, 167-170, 185, 190, 192-193, 204, 218
Alexander, Tsar 42, 51, **51**
Alkmaar, Convention of 35
Amiens, Treaty of 43, 45, 193
Anderson, Lieut. James 157-158
Anglo-Dutch Wars 3, 4, 214
Anholt 53, 169-170
Anson family 97, 99, 214
Arbuthnot, Capt. John 223

Bacon, Lady 178
Baird, Dr. Andrew 79, 132-135
Baker, Capt. Thomas 36
Balearres, Earl of 175
Baltic Sea vii, xi, 1, 9, 11, 14, 16, 36, 38, 40, 42-43, 51-52, 54-55, 79, 91, 99, 116, 130, 134, 138, 143, 153, 155, 168, 170, 193
Bamber, Lieut. William 150, 185
Banyard, Robert 63
Barbara 175
Barbara, Capt. 175
Barber, Mary 119, 215
Barker, Capt. Samuel 38, 178, 184
Barrack Office 124-126, 131-132, 190, 192, 216
Basilico, Mr. 160
Basset, Mr. 20
Batavian Republic (see Holland)
Beachy Head 43, 46
Beccles 148, 182
Beck, Mr. 120
Belcher, Andrew 81, 192
Bell, John 216
Bell, John Masters 150
Bennett, Lieut. Edward 185
Bentham, Samuel 137, 218
Bentinck, Count 160
Berlin Decree 51
Berry, Capt. Sir Edward 186, 225
Bickers, John 105
Bicknell, Charles 127
Blair, Dr. 120, 122-123, 125, 127
Blanchet, Lieut-Col. 219
Blane, Dr. 127
Blaquire, Lieut. Edward 118, 190, 215
Bligh, Capt. William 16, 23, 42-43, 130, 206
blockade ix, 4-5, 9, 20, 47, 51, 54-55, 193
Boorder, Capt. James 26
Borough, Lieut. William 115
Boulogne 43, 48, 50, 55, 172
Boult, Edward 105
Boult, James 105
Boult, Mr. 101
Bowater, Capt. Edward 111
Bowen, Capt. 138
Braam, Capt. Van 32
Bramham, Col. 6
Bremen 11, 13, 142, 159
Brest 9, 10

Bridge, Capt.163,
Briggs, Ann 119, 122, 215
Brodie, Lieut. 25, 28
Bromley, Surgeon 122
Brown, Capt. 184
Bryce, Major Alexander 99, 180
Buckner, Adm. Charles 23
Bullock, Mary 215
Burgess, Capt. Richard 29
Burgh, General de 175
Burke, Ann 122
Burke, J. D. 135
Burnham Thorpe 197
Burton, Major William 3
Butcher, John **Front Cover, 104**
Byles, Belcher 80-81

Caister 165-166, **165**, 173-175, 204
Calais, 2, 159, 190
Callantsoog 33, **33**
Campbell, Capt. Thomas 113-116, **114**, 149-151, 214-215
Camperdown, Battle of x, **27**, 28, 30-32, 34, 41, 46, 70, **71**, 84, 103, 120-121, 124, **121, 123-124**, 127, 131, 134, 147, 173, 177, 202, 204, 209, **Back Cover**
Cape St. Vincent, Battle of ix, 217
Capon, Mr. 74
cartel 152
Castricum 35
Cathcart, Lieut-Gen. 52
Catherine the Great 16, 26
Cawsand Bay ix
Channel Fleet, The British ix, 9, 21-23, 39
Channel Islands 35, 39, 129
Chatham 49-50, 59, 90, 96, 132, 142-143, **145**, 145, 149, 152-154, 217, 223
Cheap, Lieut. Andrew 167, 222
Chesterfield 152, 154
Christiansand, British Consul at 17
Cinque Ports 1
Civil War, English 3
Clements, Capt. John 156-157
Cobb, Capt. Charles 44, 96, 132, 164-166, 184-186, 222
Cockle Gat 29, 41, 105
Cockrill, David 81
Colby, Dover 145, 218
Collingwood, Cuthbert, Vice-Adm. 197
Colls Mr. 95
Columbine, Lieut. Edward 12
Continental System 51-52, 54
convoys 11-12, 14, 16, 48, 55, 74, 153, 193
Cook, George 117
Copenhagen 36, 52, 54, 75, 91, 130-131, 134, **135**, 142, 186, 193
Copenhagen, Battle of x, 41-42, **42**
Cornwallis, Marquis 177
Craig, Gen. 180
Crane and Holmes 49
Crockford, John 80-82, 192
Cromer 96, 164-167, 184-186
Cromwell, George Kimber 92-93
Curry, Capt. Richard 56, 117-118, 169-170
Curtis, Rear-Adm. Sir Roger 25

Custance and Stone 49
Cuxhaven 37, 50, 159-164

Daniels, Capt. 35
Davy, Mr. 91
Day, John 94, 192-193
Deal 15, 76, 93, 131, 135, 144, 155, 168, 217
Deane family 160-162, 205
Deans, Capt. Robert 103
Delanoe, Comm. George 158
Denmark 14, 36, 38, 42, 51, 55, 115, 159
Deptford x, 50, 59, 62-66, **62**, 68, 70, 72-77, 79, 86-88, 102, 190, 192, 225
Dickens, Capt. 182
Dickens, Charles 197
Dickson, Vice-Adm. Archibald 32, 35-38, 40, 43-44, 76, 87, 102-105, 113, 127, 130, 158-159, 197, 206
Dillon, John 108
Dirking, Capt. Von 203
Dogger Bank, Battle of 5, 39
Douglas, Rear-Adm. Billy 6, 48, 50, 56, 90, 92-93, 106-108, **107**, 117, 134, 136, 138, 140, 151, 153, 167, 169, 186, 197, 207
Dover 59, 63, 72, 96, 159-160, 223
Downs, The x, 5, 9, 11, 13, 15-17, 35-36, 41, 46, 55, 125
Drake, Vice-Adm.5, 195
Druery, John 141, 218
Drury, Lieut. Thomas 118
Duncan, Adm. Adam 2, 14-36, **15-16, 22, 24, 28**, 46, 64, 70, **71**, 73, 76, 101, 103, 108, 119-120, 122, 125, 128-129, 147, 156, 162, 197, 199, 203-205, 219, **Back Cover**
Duncan, Miss 31
Dundas, Henry 13-14, 177
Dunkirk 10, 20, 48, 145, 172
Dunstable Downs telegraph station **170**
Dutch
  East India Company 3
  merchants 4
  navy x, 5, 13, 16-17, 19, 21, 23, 25, 30, 32-34, 46-47, 70, 122, 125
  prisoners of war 121-122, **123**, 150, 152
  sick and wounded 30, 121-123
  surgeons 122, 147,
  volunteers 154

East Dereham 148, **148**, 219
East India Company 3, 113
Eastern Military District 96, 172, 178, 180
Eastmure, Benjamin 105
Easton Cliff (Ness) 164, 184
Eaves, John 223
Edge, Capt. William 157, 177
Egmont-op-Zee 35
Elbe 35, 45, 50, 52, 87, 142, 159, 162-163
Ellis, Lieut. John I 109, 113
Ellis, Lieut. John II 185
Elsinore Roads 36
Ems 50
Erlon, Gen. 128
Essington, Rear-Adm. Sir William 52, as captain 122
excise cutters 10

231

Eye 148

Fagee, James 154
Fagel, Gressier 160
Fenn, Robert Boult 100, 193
Ferrier, Rear-Adm. John 55
Fielding, Benjamin 4-5, 119-123, 132, 143-146, 148-149, 215, 219-220
Fisher, John 149
Fisher, Mr. 64, 87
Fisher, Thornton 91, 185, 192
Fisher, William 143, 149
Fletcher, Sir William 81, 193
Flushing 45, 47, 55, 142, 153, 160, 202
Flynn, Capt. Matt. 160, 162
Folds, Lieut. Thomas 116
Foley, Timothy 152
Fontainbleau, Treaty of 189
Forrest, Capt. Thomas 116-117
Fortune, Mr. 95
France ix, 2, 4, 6, 9, 11, 38, 43, 45, 51, 145, 149, 189, 196, 220
Fraser, Capt. 10
Freeling, Sir Francis 162-163
Frost, Mr. 97, 99

Gambier, Adm. James 52, 186
Gardner, Adm. Alan, Lord 21
Gardner, Rear-Adm. Alan Hyde 55-56, 168-169
George, Sir Rupert 150
Gibbons, Sir William 127
Gibson, Richard 3
Gibson, Thomas 100
Gilchrist, Lieut. William 117-118, 215
Giles, H. 81
Gillingham Reach 44
Gimbal, Bernard 219
Glasford, Capt. James 109-112, 214
Glasford, Jane 110
Glendenning, Adam 133
Glorious First of June, Battle of ix
Godsell, Thomas 144, 149
Gog Magog telegraph station 170
Goldhawke, George 223
Goodrich, Simon 137-138, 218
Goodwin Sands 36
Goree 43
Gorleston 6, 37, 66-67, 71, 106, 141, 172, 175, 177, 179, 182, 185, 195
Gosport 143
Gothenburg 134
Gould, Lieut-Col. William 184, 225
Gower, Lieut-Col. 175
Graham, Lieut. 167
Grant, John 60, 76-81, 149, 208
Graves, Rear-Adm. Sir Thomas 39-41, 43-44, 206
Green, Charles 192
Green, John 100, 166, 169
Greenland whale fishery 163, 211
Greenwich Hosp. 114, 217
Grenville, Tom 163-164
Griffiths, George 182
Grimsby Roads 29
Grout Bayliss and Co 192, 224
Gunfleet, Buoy of 23
Gunthorpe, Capt. Matt.11, 202
Gunton Common 164

Haisborough Sand 105, 160, 167
Halkett, Capt. Peter 27
Hamburg 12, 14, 159-160, 163
Hamilton, Lady Emma 37
Hamilton, Sir William 37
Hammond, Capt. 163
Hammond, Mr. 161
Hammond's Knoll 41
Hamood, Capt. Harry 84, **85**

Hanikoff, Vice-Adm. Peter 16, 55, 125
Happisburgh 105-106, 165-167, 174, 206, 213
Hardy, Cmdr. James 112
Hardy, Capt. Thomas 40
Hardy, Capt. William 183
Harford, Capt. Charles 107
Harford, Lieut. Henry 167
Hart, Capt. George 47
Harvey, Rear-Adm. Henry 202
Harwich ix, 3, 9, 13-14, 43, 48, 50, 56, 76, 129, 143, 159-160, 164, 174, 177
Haslar naval hospital 116, 119, 131
Haw, Joseph 225
Heddington, Capt. Thomas 117, 152-153, 215
Helder, The 13, 19, 33-35, 46, 104, 128, **129**, 142, 155, 161, 194
Hellevoetsluis 13, 32, 46, 50, 159
Helloet 21, 36, 205-206
Heligoland 52, **81**, 81, 163, 192
High Court of Admiralty 11
Hills, Surgeon 123
Hinton, Capt. Martin 185-186
Historic Building Rescue 199
Holland 3-4, 6, 9, 12-13, **12**, 33, 36, 45, 128, 150, 153-154, 159, **161**, 195-196, 202, 220,
Hollesley Bay 32, 55
Holstein 51
Home, Lieut. Alexander 185
Homfray, Rev. John 140
Hood, Vice-Adm. 9, 197
Hook, Capt 176
Hook of Holland 113
Hopton 6, 173, 175
Horatio Channel, The 54
Horrocks, Christopher 81
Horsford, Capt. 160
Hoste, Capt. George 100, 213
Hoste, Capt Sir William 213
Howe, Adm. Lord 9
Howe, Gen. Sir William 178
Howes and Hodskinson, Messrs 93, 115
Howes, Robert 115
Hubbard, Joseph 152
Hull ix, 9, 11, 48, 96, 143, 177
Humber, The 5, 10, 29, 46, 153
Hunt, Capt. Anthony 4
Hunt, Capt. William 153
Hunt, Mr. 69
Hunter, Capt. Laughlin 110-113, 120, 123, 131-132, 214
Hunter, Miss 214
Hurry, Ives 151
Hurry, Margaret 151
Hurry & Co. 88, 193

Idles, Scott & Co. 79
Infield, Lieut. Caleb 167
Inglis, Capt. John 30
Inspector Gen. of Naval Works 136-137
Ives, John 4
Ivie, Lieut. Daniel 133

James, Andrew 223
James, Capt. William 116
Jamieson, Dr. 134
Johnston, Dr. 127
Johnston, Lieut-Gen. James 144, 174-175
Jones, David 95, 99

Kartzoff, Vice-Adm. 32
Keats, Rear-Adm. Richard 52
Keith, Admiral George 46, 50
Kelly, George 119
Kemp, Richard 77, 192
Kent, John 182
Kerridge, John 59-61
Kessingland 105, 164
Kett, John 74, 81
Keymer, John 204

Keymer, Matthew **39**
Killwick, Capt. 177
King, Ann 120
King's Lynn 146-147, 215
Kinsale 90, 93
Knight, Capt. John 30, 84
Køge, Battle of 52
Krabbe, Capt. 36

Lacon, Sir Edmd. 64, 72, 132, **133**, 134, 160, 217
Lacon, Capt. Edward K. 184, 197
Lambert, Lieut. 22
Lancey, Col. Oliver de 175
Larcom, Capt. Joseph 63, 186
Larke, Lieut. William 133, 137, 152, 190, 225
Lawford, Capt. Sir John 35
League of Armed Neutrality 38, 41-42, 130
Learmouth family 134
Leeder, Robert 81
Leith ix, 5, 9, 11, 15, 17-18, 25, 48, 76, 91, 93, 156-157, 159, 190
Leland, Gen. 160
Letters of Marque 10
Lewes, Samuel 68-77, 209
Litchfield 153
Lloyds of London 162
Loftus, Major-Gen. 177-178
Lord Lieut. of Norfolk **166**, 178, 183
Lorient 9
Losack, Capt. 49
Louis XVIII, King 52, 189
Lovell, George 100
Lovewell, James 49, 140
Low Countries (see Holland)
Lowden, John 81
Lowden, John Jnr. 81
Lowden and Son 77
Lowestoft 23, 38, 96, 105, 118, 146, 156, 174, 179, 185-186
Lucas, Lieut. Mark Robinson 114-116, 214
Lynne, Lieut. Thomas 131-132, 217

Macbride, Vice-Adm. John 17-20, **18**, 32, 46, 62-64, **102**, 186, 203
Mackay, Capt. 154
Makaroff, Rear-Adm. 16, 25-26, 32
Manby, Capt. George 106, **126**, 180-181, **181**, 192, 224
Manby, Capt. Thomas 47, 181, 223
Mant, Surgeon Thomas 122
Margate 20, 29, 35, 186
Mars Diep 34
Marsden, William 137
Marsh, Lieut. William 109, 113, 164, 167
Martin, Kit 199
Martin, Nathaniel 81, 192
Martin, Thomas Jnr. 59-63, 68, 74, 210
Mash, John 4
Maurice, Governor 53,
M'Douall, Capt. Robert 31-32
Mediterranean Sea ix, 9, 37, 46
Medway 44, 130, 192
Mellish, Peter 74, 77, 210
Mellish, William 74, 77, 79, 81
Melville, Lord 48
Metzner, Lieut-Col. 184
Miles, John 140
Millison, Gabriel I 4
Millison, Gabriel II 4
Minty, Richard 99, 100
Mitchell, Vice-Adm. Andrew 33-35, **33-34**, 108
Moody, Robert Sadleir 76-77
Moore, Major-Gen. Sir John 33, 55
Morley, Thomas 185, 213
Morse, Lieut-Gen. 96-97, 99
Mosquito War, The 55
Mosse, Capt. James 37, 206
Murray, Lord George 155

Murray, Vice-Adm. Robert 56, 118, 154, 168, 190, 208

Napier, Sir Charles 199
Napoleon Bonaparte xi, 45, 50-51, **51**, 55, 154, 181, 189-190, 195-196, 220
Narde, Jean de 148, **148**
Nash, Thomas 148
Navy Board x, 48, 83-84, 86-94, 101-106, 111, 117, 131-132, 167, 192-193, 208
Naze of Norway 17
Nelson, Vice-Adm. Horatio vii, 28, 37, **37**, 39, **39**, 40-43, **40**, **42**, 46, 108, 131, 178, 180, 186, 196-197, 201, 205-206
Nepean, Evan 17, 20, 23, 103, 131, 155, 206
Netherlands (see Holland)
Neuwerk Island 164
Newcastle 9, 50, 56
Newman, Samuel 223
Nicholas, Henry 100
Nicholas, Mr. 53
Nichols, William 89, 93, 185
Nieuport 11
Nieuwe Diep 33, 35
Nile, Battle of ix, 37-38, 209, 225
Nore x, 4, 9, 11, 14-15, 17-18, 20-23, 25-26, 29-30, 32, 35, 41, 45, 47, 76-77, 87, 89, 109, 125, 150, 153, 156-157, 166, 192, 204
Nore Mutiny 23-25, 216
Norman Cross 133, 145-150, **146**, 152-154, 173, 183,
North Sea vii, ix, xi, 1, 4-6, 9-10, 12-15, **15**, 20, 32, 36, 38, 46-47, 50, 55, 76, 111, 116, 125, 143, 145, 147, 158, 160, 163, 170-171, 184, 193, 198, 203
  cruisers x, 4, 6, 10-11, 78, 119, 145
  Naval Squadron ix-x, 4, 6, 9, 14-18, 20-21, 23-27, 31-33, 35-36, 38-41, 43, 55, 60-61, 63, 68, 70-71, 73, 76, 79, 84, 105, 119, 125
  Naval Station ix, 12, 14, 31, 43, 190, 197, 132, 155, 193, 203, 206
North Shields ix, 143
Northampton 152, 154
Northern Convention (see League of Armed Neutrality)
Norway 13
Norwich 13, 33, 35, 47, 111, 114, 116, 122, 165, 168, 171-173, 175-177, 182, 190, 196, 204, 222
  Bishop of 30, 127, 139,
Nutt, William 81

O'Brian, Capt.178
O'Callaghan, Major 179
Ogden, Benjamin 80
Onslow, Vice-Adm. Sir Richard **18**, 20-21, 24-26, 28-32, 39, 66, 68, 78, 108, 119-120, 131, 197-198, 205, **Back Cover**
Ordnance Board x, 95-97, 99-100, 171, 209, 223
Orford Ness 10, 23, 29, 43, 159
Orkney Islands 14, 46
Ostend 11, 20, 45, 47, 172, 196
Otway, Capt. William 143-144

packet boats 159-161, 164
Page, Capt. Sir Thomas Hyde 171, **172**, 173, 176, 223
Paget, Sir James 60-61, 210
Paget, Samuel Jnr. 59-77, **60-61**, **69**, **71-73**, 79, 81, 95, 100, 102, 178, 184, 193. 197, 208, 210
Palgrave, Lieut. William 38, 178-179
Palmer, Charles John 4, 129, 131, 141, 145, 151, 160-161, 206, 214, 217-218
Palmer, Nathaniel 49
Pampus, The 26
Panhays, Colonel de 154
Parker, Vice-Adm. Christopher 43
Parker, Adm. Sir Hyde 38-42, **39-40**, 52, 75,

155, 206
Parker, Vice-Adm. Sir Hyde 4-5
Parker, Adm. Sir Peter 17
Parker, Richard 23, 25, 204
parole 148
Pater, Comm. Charles 55
Patterson, Col. 47
Patterson, George **28**, 103-105, 213
Paul, Tsar 26, 32, 38, 42
Perbroun, John 1
Perpencher, Baron 154
Peterborough 145, 148
Peto, Henry 140-141, 218,
Peto, Samuel Morton 218
Petten **33**
Petty, Capt. 48
Phillimore, John 105
Phillip, Rear-Adm. Arthur 113, 185, 214
Pickis, Robert 190
Pilkington, William 139-140, 166, 218
Pinkerton, Thomas 59-60
Pitt, Thomas, 62-68, 70-72, 76
Pitt, William P. M. 13, 33, 162
Plymouth ix, 13, 30, 59, 96, 119, 143, 154, 168, 181, 184
Pole, Vice-Adm. Charles 42
Popham, Comm. Sir Home 52
port-admiral x, 6, 20, 48, 52, 55, 106-108, 167-169
Portland, Duke of P. M. 51
Portsmouth ix, 13, 47, 59, 68, 96, 119, 143, 154-155, 157, 168, 175, 190
Portugal 51
Post Master General 160, 163-164
Poulden, Capt. Richard 186
Preliminaries of Peace 43
press gang 109, 113, 117
Preston, Jacob 189
Preston, John 49-50, 108, 141, 183, 189, 211, 218
Pringle, Rear-Adm. Thomas 14-18, **16**, 61, 101, 111, 202
prisoners of war x, 9
  American 6
  Dutch 6, 122, 147-148, 152
  French 6, 9, 143, 145, 147, 149-150, 153
privateers
  British 4, 10
  French ix, 2, 10-11, 143
prize agents 11
Prussia 12, 38, 51, 115, 159, 164
Purvis, Mr. 148

Quota Acts 111

Ramsgate 35
Reddy, Lieut. James 23, 204
Rennie, Capt. John 41
revenue cutters 10, 33, 116
Reynolds, Francis Riddle 81, 223
Reynolds, Major Thomas **xi**, 172-173
Richards, Capt. Francis 6
Richardson, Major-Gen. W. 223
Riches, Capt. Thomas 11, 202
Richmond, Duke of 175
Robinson, Mrs. 120, 122
Rochefort 9
Rodney, Mr. 69
Roebuck, George 155, 164, 168-170, 190, 221
Rogers, Capt. 47
Ross, Rear-Adm. Sir John 5
Rowlandson, Thomas 215
Rowley, Lieut.-Col. 99
Royal Dockyards 3, 30, 48, 83
Rummer, Thomas 107
Russell, James 93, 105
Russell, Rear-Adm. Thomas Macnamara 47-48, **47**, 50, 55-56, 78, 88-89, 93, 108, 115, 138, 207

Russia 33, 38, 42, 51, 125, 129, 218
Russian
  army 34-35, 129, **130**
  navy 16-19, **19**, 25-26, 32, 38, 42, 54-55, 66, 74, 83-84, 104, 125-126, 128-129, 178
  sick and wounded 125-128, 217
Rysvort, Capt. Gysbert Jan Van 127

St. Helens ix
St. Malo 148
St. Nicholas Gat 41, 54, 105, 141, 173
St. Nicholas Sand 160
St. Vincent, Earl of 38-39, 41, 197, 206
Salmon, Joseph 115
Saumarez, Vice-Adm. Sir James 54-55, **54**
Saverland, Mr. 159-160
Schelde 45, 51, 55, 208
Scheveningen 13, **14**
schuyts, fishing 12, **12**, 68, 147, 154, 195
Scotland 1, 5, 14, 32, 36, 46, 156
Scott, Capt. 22
Scott, Claude 64
Scott Mary 122
Scott, Dr. William 128
Scroby Sand 67
sea fencibles 177, 184
Sea Palling 105, 213
Seaman, Thomas 160, 164
Serle, Ambrose 148-149
Sharman, James 197
Sheerman, Mary 215
Sheerness x, 13, 17, **19**, 23, 25, 44, 46, 87, 91, 103, 125, 155, 159, 166, 168, 206, 215, 223
Shetland Isles 14, 46
Shoebury Ness 156, 164
Shorten, Mr. 183
Sibert, James 150, 152
Sibthorpe, Col. 176
Sick & Hurt Board x, 5, 30, 119-123, 125-128, 132-133, 136, 143-144, 146, 219
signal stations, East Coast 156-157, 164-167
Silvers, Samuel 152
Simpson, David 175
Simpson, Lombe 167
Skaw, The 41, 206
Slight, John 70
Sluys, Battle of 1-2, **2**
Smith, Simon 218
Smith, Comm. Sir Sydney 47-48, 153, 197
Snipe, John 124-128, 131, 216-217
Sole Bay, Battle of 3, 29
Solent 48
Sound, The 53-54
Southwold 146, 157, 177
Sparks, Capt. 35
Spencer, Lord 14, 20-21,23, 26
Spithead ix, 5, 13, 21, 23, 25, 30, 40, 128, 130, 147, 153
Stanford Gat 173
Stanhope, Vice-Adm. Sir Henry 52
Stannard, Joseph 136
Stephenson, Mr. 19
Steward, Messrs T. and A. H. 11
Stewart, Comm. Keith 5
Stewart, Lieut.-Col. 40
Stonehouse naval hospital 119, 131
Story, Vice-Adm. Samuel 34, **34**
Strachan, Rear-Adm. Sir Richard 55
Stralsund 52
Stratton, Harriet 133
Strumpshaw 165, 169
Stuart, Capt. 106
Suckling, Mrs. 206
Surridge, Capt. Thomas 186
Sutherland, Capt. 95, 171
Sweden 38, 42, 51, 54, 115, 134
Swinden, Henry 4

Tait, William 134, 136, 138

Talbot, Capt. John 55
Tate, Gen. 172
Tate, Rear-Adm. George 16-17, 19, 32
Taylor, William Jnr. 121-123, 132-133, 135-136, 217, 225
Taylor, William Snr. 160, 202,
telegraph system 155, 164
Texel x, 5, 13-14, 16-21, 23-27, 31-33, 47, 50, 53, 55, 70-71, 73-74, 77, 81, 89, 125, 153-154, 162, 193, 213
Thackray, Mr. 169
Thompson, Capt. Sir Thomas 130
Thornbrough, Rear-Adm. Edward 46-47, **46**, 88, 115, 207
Tilsit, Treaty of 51, **51**, 54
Tonningen 163
Tonyn, General 122
Torbay ix, 43
Totty, Rear-Adm. Thomas 39-41, 206
Townsend, Marquis 6, 171, 174, 177, 223
Towry, George Phillips 64, 76-77
Trafalgar, Battle of ix, 28, 48, 180, 196-197, 225
Transport Board x, 35, 62, 115, 134-139, 143-150, 152-153, 167, 190,192,215, 219-220
Tremlett, Capt. William 167, 184-186
Tresson, Francis 149
Trimingham 165-167
Trollope, Capt. 30, 121-122
Troubridge, Sir Thomas 41, 206
Tryon, Major-Gen. 6
Tupper, Martin 217
Turner, Dawson 61, **61**, 70, 72, **72**, 181, 208
Turner, Eunice 16
Turner, J. M. W. **65**
Turner, Rev. 37

United Provinces (see Holland)
Urquhart, David 4

Vancouver, Capt. George 117, 224
Vass, Nicholas 157, 166
Veere 142
Victualling Board x, 18, 59, 61-81, 192, 209
Vlie Passage 87, 161, **161**
Vlieter Channel 34

Walcheren Expedition 55, 142
Walcott, Mr. 159
Wallis, James 164
Walter, John 77, 79, 210
Warmington, Robert 4, 44, 59-60, 83-84, **84**, **85**, 86-91, **92**, 93-94, 101-103, 105-106, 110, 132, 159-161, 163-164, 167, 205, 208, 212, 217
Waterloo, Battle of 195-196, 199
Watson, Lieut. James 6
Watson, Mr. 37
Watson, Thomas 217
Webb, John 140
Weir, Dr. John 135-137, 141
Wellesley-Pole, William 92, 108
Wellington, Duke of 52, 197, 223

Weser 35, 45, 50, 142, 163
Whitmore, Capt. George 96-97, 99
Whitworth, Lord 36
Wilhelmina, Princess of Orange 13, **14**
Wilkins, William 197
Willem V, Prince of Orange 13, 34-35, 154
Williamson, Capt. John 30
Wilson, Isaac 133-134
Winchelsea 1
Winter, Gen. de Brigade Johann De 13, 27-28, **28**, 103, 202, 204, 216
Winterton 96, 105, 150, 165-166, 185, 213
Wismar 11
Woodger, Lieut. Charles 167, 190
Woodriff, Capt. Daniel 35, 147
Woolnough, Joseph 135
Worship, John Lucas 225
Worts, William 75, 149-150, 220,
Wyatt, James 97

Yarmouth, Great
  Admiralty Court 11, 101, 204
  Angel Inn 182
  arms of 2
  barracks 122-123, 126, 128, 175, **176**, 177 **182**, 182, 198
  bathhouse 199
  batteries
    Gorleston Cliff 171-172, 177
    Haven 171-173
    North Star 169, 171, 173, 222
    Town 171, 180, 222
    South Star 95, 100, 171, **180**, 222
  Bauleah House **126**, 216, 224
  beach companies 105
  Brush, The 64, **65**
  cooperage 65-66, **66**, 79
  Dean signal station 136, 157, 159, 164, 166-167, 192, 198
  Denes, The 66, 131, 136, 141, 169-171, 175, 182-183, 197, 208, 218
  Duke's Head Hotel **71**, 209
  Duncan's Pump 67, **67**
  Dutch Sunday 195, 202
  fishery protection 12, 112
  Fort, The 3, **96**, 171, 180
  Freedom of the Borough 4, 36-37, 205
  Grand Festival, The 190, **191**
  Great Yarmouth in Bloom 198, **198**
  Haven and Pier Commissioners 105, 108, 218
  Herring Fishery vii, 1, 3, 12, 112
  horse racing 183, **183**
  Jetty, The Front Cover, **3**, 11, 31, 101, 104-105, **104**, 107-108, 116, **123**, 131, 136, 145, 173, 196, **198**, 198, 207
  mackerel fishery 12
  Marine Hotel 198
  Market Place 115, 131, 178, **179**, 207
  master attendant 92-93, 103, 105
  master shipwright 92-93
  merchants 6, 64
  Military Gen. Hosp. 196
  naval burial ground 127-128

naval hospital vii-viii, 122-125, 128, 131-141, **137**, **139**, **140**, **141**, 166, 190, 194, 199
naval mutiny at 21-25, **22**, **24**, 68, 119, 124
naval store 90, **90**, **92**, 93, **94**, 212
naval storekeeper 83, 88
Naval Support Base vii, xii, 1-2, 4, 30, 44, 50, 52-53, 195, 197
naval vessels built at 48-50, **49**
Norfolk Pillar, The 196-197
North Gate 190
North Mill 169
North Yarmouth xii, 39, 76, 90, 135, 208
ordnance store 2, **69**, 100, 185, 193
Prison I 143, 145, 147, 149
Prison II 116, 150, 152, 190
Roads, The Front Cover, ix-x,3, **5**, 6, 10, 12-13, 17-21, 24-27, **24**, 29-43, 47-48, 52-55, 60-65, 67-70, 72-75, **78**, 79, 82-83, 87, 92, 101-102, **102**, 104-106, **104**, 108-110, 112-113, 115, 118, 121, 127-130, 134, 142, 145, 153, 156, 160-161, 163, 167, 171-172, 177, 189, 193-195, 201-203, 213, 215
Rows 198, 224
  22 207
  102 Packet Office Row 159, 221
  110 New Prison Row 150, 220
  113 150
  135 Old Prison Row 143, **144**, 219
  White Lion Row 120
Royal Arsenal vii **97**, **98**, 99, **99**, 193, 199, 212
Royal Naval Hospital (see naval hospital)
St. Nicholas Church 165, **166**, 222
sea fencible district 184-186
Ship Tavern 147
ship yards 49
signal station, port-admiral's 167, **168**, 190, 212
South Denes 140-141, **183**, 197, 218
South Gate 86, 95, 222,
South Quay 49, 77, 96, 99, 199, 209
Southtown 140, 214
telegraph 155, 170, 191, 198, 222
Trinity House store 91
victualling stores 63-65, 71, 75-77
Water Frolic 196
whale fishery buildings 86, **86**, 141
Wherry Quay 121, **121**
White Lion Steps 67, 199, 209
Wrestlers Inn 37, **37**, 40, 47, 157, 179, 197, 206, **Back Cover**
Yarmouth, Little xii
York, Duke of 13, 34-35, 146, 175, 205
Yorke, Charles 181, 183
Young, Robert 119, 121-125, **124**, 216
Young, Adm. William 55
Youell, William 24, **24**, 121

Zealand Point, Battle of 134
Zeske, Major Von 53
Zoutman, Adm. Johan 5
Zype Polder 35
Zyper Sluis 34

Military Units, Warships and Merchant Vessels
Regular Army, Royal Marines Militia and Volunteers

3rd Foot 175
5th Foot 142
8th Foot 142
9th Foot 223
10th Foot 6
17th Foot 33
28th Foot 142
30th Foot 172
32nd Foot 142
33rd Foot 223
42nd Foot 142

49th Foot 177
53rd Foot 175
54th Foot 184
55th Foot 196
60th Foot 148
63rd Foot 142, 175
71st Foot 142
77th Foot 142
80th Foot 175
84th Foot 142
85th Foot 142

Inniskilling Dragoons 146, 176
Royal Artillery 176, 223
Royal Engineers 180, 223

Royal Marines 118

Anglesea 180
Bedfordshire 175, 184
Berkshire 183, **183**
Cambridgeshire 6, 177, 180-181, 183, 196
Cheshire 182

Dorset 184
Durham 177, 179
Essex, East 6, 179
Fifeshire 183
Gloucestershire, North 225
Huntingdon 6, 175-176, 194
Kent, East 177
Kent, West 175
Leicestershire 13, 174
Lincolnshire,North 175
Lincolnshire, South 175-177, 184, 223
Mayo, North 184
Middlesex, West 174

Montgomeryshire 180
Norfolk, East 173, **174**, 180, 182, 184
Norfolk, West 183-184
Oxfordshire 127, 146, 177
Pembrokeshire 175
Ross-shire 183
Shropshire 49-50, 182-183
Somerset 177
Suffolk, East 143, 174-175
Westmoreland 180
Wexford 184, 189
Yorkshire, East Riding 174-175

Armed Association 6
Cromer Battery Volunteers 185
Norfolk Volunteers, Sixth Battalion 184
Norwich Volunteers 47
Third Eastern Regiment of Local Militia 184, 189
Yarmouth Company of Sharpshooters 184
Yarmouth Volunteer Cavalry 38, 43, 178-179, 184
Yarmouth Volunteer Infantry 6, 178-179, **179**, 184
Yarmouth Volunteer Infantry Apollonian 178-179

British Warships,* Excise and Revenue Cutters, Packets and By-boats

Active (cutter) 19, 26
Active (victualler) 63
Acton (victualler) 65
Acute (gun-brig) 153
Adamant (50) 21, **22**, 24-27, 29-30, 122
Africaine (frigate) 47, 52
Agamemnon (64) 24-25, 31
Agincourt (64) 27, 29-30, 153, 216
Albatross (sloop) 22, 31
Albemarle (frigate) 3, 201
Albion (armed ship)130
Alcmene (frigate) 217
Alderney (sloop) 4, 6, 214
Alexandria (frigate) 53
Ambuscade (frigate) 17, 203
America (64) 74
Ann (sloop) 158
Antelope (50) 47, 89, 107
Apollo (frigate) 101
Ardent (64) 24-27, 29-30, 32, 40, 119, 121-122, **124**, 206, 216-217
Argo (transport) 69
Ariadne (frigate) 44
Ariel (sloop) 207
Asia (74) 17, 61, 203
Astrea (frigate) 147
Aurora (frigate) 145

Badger (revenue cutter) 150
Beaulieu (frigate) 29, 31
Beaver (sloop) 48
Bedford (74) 27, 29-30, 216
Belette (sloop) 48
Bellerophon (74) 55
Belliqueux (64) 24,-25, 27, 29-30, 32, 122, 216
Bellona (74) 130, 217
Black Joke (cutter) 203
Blanche (frigate) 42
Boreas (frigate) 207
Bourdelois (frigate) 181
Brilliant (frigate) 84, 161
Bristol (prison hulk) 145
Britomart (sloop) 55, 153

Cadmus (sloop) 195
Caesar (victualler) 64, 73
Calypso (sloop) 153, 169
Camilla (frigate) 203
Carteret (packet) 159
Carysfort (frigate) 46
Censor (gun-brig) 48
Cephalus (sloop) 207
Champion (frigate) 163
Chanticleer (sloop) **80**, 107, 189
Charles (armed vessel) 153
Charlotte (victualler) 74
Chatham (survey brig) 117
Chilvers (sloop) 9
Christian (victualler) 63, 65
Circe (frigate) 26-27, 30, 102, 147
Cleopatra (frigate) 10, **10**
Clyde (frigate) 46

Comus (frigate) 207
Courier (packet) 159-160
Crane (schooner) 207
Cuckoo (schooner) 207
Curlew (sloop) 9, 115
Cygnet (sloop) 23, 49, 207
Cynthia (sloop) 132

Defiance (74) 16, 41, 43, 217
Delft (troopship) 129
Deptford lighter 86, 88, 192
Desiree (frigate) 55
Diana (packet) 159-161
Diligence (sloop) 153
Director (64) 19, 22, 27, 29-30, 67
Dolphin (packet) 159, 162, **162**
Driver (sloop) 44, 87
Druid (frigate) 132
Duke of York (by-boat) 160

Eagle (74) 47
Edgar (74) 217
Eleanor (victualler) 65
Elephant (74) **42**, 217
Eliza (victualler) 74
Elizabeth (ordnance lighter) 213
Endymion (frigate) 29
Espion (frigate) 145
Ethalion (frigate) 46
Exertion (gun-brig) 50, 53, 207
Explosion (bomb ketch) 53
Express (packet) 159

Fancy (gun-brig) 207
Fanny (victualler) 68
Fly (sloop) 6
Fortune (frigate) 46
Fox (cutter) 32
Frederickscoarn (hospital ship) 134

Galgo (sloop) 89
Ganges (74) 31, 125, 217
Garland (frigate) 11, 25
Gayette (frigate) 101
Gelykheid (64) 47
Glatton (56) 18, 24-25, 74, 84, 184, 203, 217
Glory (98) 133
Grace (cutter) 155
Greyhound (frigate) 9, 11
G. T. (transport) 190
Guernsey Lily (ordnance transport) 104

Havock (gun-brig) 207
Hawke (sloop) 161
Hearty (gun-brig) 55, 195
Hebe (frigate) 217
Hecla (bomb) 35
Helena (sloop) 49, 207
Hero (74) 78-79, 145
Hero (prison hulk) 145
Holstein (hospital ship) 42, 130, 217
Hope (lugger) 23

Hope (victualler) 63
Horatio (frigate) 54
Hunter (revenue cutter) 11, 106, 202
Hyacinth (sloop) 207
Hydra (frigate) 31

Inflexible (64) 61
Invincible (74) 41
Irresistible (74) 43
Isis (50) 24-25, 27, 29, 33, 42, 130, 206, 217

Jalouse (sloop) 147
Jamaica (frigate) 132
Jane (transport) 192
Juno (frigate) 35

Katherine (yacht) 4
Kent (74) 31-32, 103-104
King George (packet) 37, 159-160
Kite (sloop) 37, 42, 131
Kitty (tender) 6

Lancaster (64) 27, 29-30, 113, 216
Lapwing (frigate) 46
Leda (frigate)113
Leopard (50) 24-25, 119, 175
L'Espiegle (sloop) 9, 26, 102, 162
L'Imperieuse (frigate) 19
Lion (64) 19, 24, 203
Lively (excise cutter) 11, 202
Lizard (frigate) 9-10
London (98) 40-41
Lord Amhurst (powder vessel) 100
Lutine (frigate) 161, **161**
Lynx (sloop) 44, 53

Majestic (74) 53
Mallard (gun-brig) 89
Manchester (victualler) 63, 68, 72
Martin (sloop) 11, 13, 31, 145
Medway lighter 192
Minerva (frigate) 24
Minotaur (74) 52, 107, 203
Monarch (74) 26-29, 31-32, 36-37, 42, 44, 130, 206, 217
Monmouth (64) 24-25, 27, 29-30, 47, 103, 116, 122, 153, 216
Montagu (74) 24-25, 27, 30, 203
Musquito (sloop) 207

Nancy (cutter) 19
Nassau I (64) 20-22, 24, 68
Nassau II (64) 134, **135**
Nautilus (sloop) 19
Nemesis (frigate) 36

Oak (victualler 74
Orion (74) 54
Otter (sloop) 9, 112

Pandora (sloop) 207
Penelope (frigate) 46, 113, 115

INDEX

Phoenix (frigate) 18-19, 155, 203
Pigeon (schooner) 207
Polyphemus (64) 217
Port Roseway (victualler) 74
Portia (sloop) 189
Portsmouth 4
Powerful (74) 27, 29-30
Prince George (98) 217
Prince of Orange (packet) 159-163
Prince of Orange (victualler) 63
Prince of Wales (98) 52
Prince of Wales (packet) 159-160, 163-164
Prince of Wales (victualler) 68
Princess (victualler) 64, 68, 73
Princess Carolina (74) 55
Princess of Orange (74) 43-44, 47, 63, 184
Princess Royal (packet) 159, 162
Procis (sloop) 207
Prometheus (fireship) 117
Proserpine (frigate) 18, 163
Providence (2) (victualler) 74
Pylades (sloop) 159

Quail (schooner) 207
Quebec (frigate) 53, 55
Queen (victualler) 74

Raccoon (sloop) 207
Ramillies (74) 17
Ranger (sloop) 19
Redbreast (gun-brig) 50, 207
Repulse (64) 18, 24-25, 61, 203
Resolution (cutter) 12, 60, 137

Reunion (frigate)19
Robust (74) 17, 19, 46
Roebuck (44) 48, 50, 56, 134, 169
Romney (50) 35
Romulus (frigate) 153
Rose (cutter) 23, 25, 28
Ruby (64) 47
Russell (74) 17-19, 25, 27, 29-30, 63, 186, 206, 216

St. George (98) 40-41
Sandwich (98) 23, 25, 124, 204, 216
Sans Pareil (80) 25
Savage (sloop) 10
Scipio (64) 203
Scourge (sloop) 101, 145
Seagull (sloop) 17
Sensible (transport) 129
Sibyl (frigate) 203
Skylark (sloop) 106
Snipe (gun-brig) 48. 106
Solebay (frigate) 56, 154, 168, 189-190, 225
Spanker (hulk) 123
Sparkler (gun-brig) 53
Sparrow (sloop) 207
Speculator (lugger) 26-27
Squirrel (frigate) 203
Standard (64) 21, 24, 203
Stately (64) 89, 134
Stork (sloop) 25
Surprize (frigate) **3**
Sussex Oak (transport) 91
Swan (cutter) 116

Swan (transport) 69

Thomas and Sally (cartel) 145
Thorn (sloop) 9
Thunderer (74) 55
Tremendous (74) 17
Trent (frigate) 25, 111, 203
Trial (cutter) 159, 203
Triumph (74) 27, 29-30, 122, 216

Unicorn (frigate) 189
Union (packet) 159, 162
Utile (sloop) 93, 108, 117-118, 153-154, 190, 225

Venerable (74) 14, 18, 21, 25-27, **27**, **28**, 67, 103, **124**, 203
Vestal (frigate) 11, 23
Veteran (64) 27, 29-30, 32, 44, 74, 216
Victory (100) 54, **54**, 197
Vixen (gun-brig) 48, 150

Wagtail (schooner) 50, 207
Wanderer (troop ship) 53
Watchful (H.M.S.) 199
Weazle (sloop) 9
Woodcock (schooner) 50, 207
Wright (armed ship) 113, 130

Yarmouth lighter 36, 88, 92-93, 192

Zephyr (sloop) 102

* The figurers in parenthesis denote the
number of guns each ship deployed

Foreign Warships

Admiral de Vries (Dutch) 29, 216
Alkmaar (Dutch) 29-30, 216
Argo (Dutch) 18

Brutus (Dutch) 205

Delfi (Dutch) 29, 215-216
Dispatch (Russian) 19, 125
Dogger Bank (Dutch) 205

Endrought (Dutch) 205
Europa (Russian) 19

Fly (Dutch) 205
Freya (Danish) 36, 38
Freya (Swedish) 52

Gelykheid (Dutch) 29-30, 216
Gouda (Dutch) 35
Graf Orlov (Russian) 19
Guerviere (French) 153

Haarlem (Dutch) 29-30, 215-216
Hercules (Dutch) 29-30, 127, 205, 216
Holstein (Danish) **135**

Jean de Witt (Dutch) 205
Juno (Dutch) 205
Jupiter (Dutch) 29, 216

La Vengeance (French) 219

Neptunus (Dutch) 205

Nickanor (Russian) 66, 83
Phoenix (Dutch) 205
Prindts Christian Frederic (Danish) 134

Republican (French) 162
Retvizan (Russian) 19
Riga (Russian) 66, 128

Saint Peter (Russian) 103-104

Transport 90 153

Venus (Russian) 19
Vryheid (Dutch) 27, 29-30, 204, 216

Wassenaar (Dutch) 29-30, 216

British Merchant Vessels and Boats

Anson (brig) 70

Benjamin (yawl) 213

Dover hoys 67
Duncomb 48
Dutton 185

Elizabeth (brig) 70
Elizabeth (yawl) 213
Elizabeth & Ann (ketch) 67, 209

Fanny 12

Hazard 153

Industry 11

Lord Duncan (yawl) 213

Percis (yawl) 213

Triton 10

Foreign Merchant Vessels and Privateers

Anacreon (privateer) 148
Ann & Mary 219
Aurora 150
Buonaparte (privateer) 145

Dutch hoy 147

Eliza (brig) 25

Goede Verwagtig 11

Isabella (fishing boat) 11

Jonge Willim Ling 220

Le Custine (privateer) 10, 143
Le Fruit de la Mere 11
Le Sans Culotte (privateer) 10
Le Vigilant (privateer) 150
Le Voyageur (privateer) 149
L'Impressable (privateer) 149

L'Vaillant Custine 10
Lyonois (privateer) 150

Mary 11

Nareissa (cutter) 145

St Peter (fishing boat) 11
St Peter (hoy) 11
Stiver (privateer) 147